"The question of why good people make bad movies has never been answered more persuasively than in this book."

—*Entertainment Weekly*

"It's probably the best book yet on how a big studio can shape the content of a movie. This wasn't a case (like 'Heaven's Gate') of the executives losing control; this was a case of executives who were so controlling—so 'responsible'—that they gradually drained the satiric fun out of the material. Julie Salamon shows us the process, step by horrible step."

—Pauline Kael, film critic and author of *5001 Nights at the Movies*

"Julie Salamon has written, without wickedness, a devastating account of the multiplicity of wrong decisions, as well as brilliant portraits of the wrong decision makers, that led to the cinematic destruction of Tom Wolfe's remarkable novel."

—Dominick Dunne, author of *An Inconvenient Woman* and *People Like Us*

"Beautifully, beautifully done."   —*Los Angeles Times*

"*The Devil's Candy* is elegantly written and sharply observed, a masterful portrayal of the movie business hard at the business of making movies. It is reminiscent of Lillian Ross's brilliant reportage, *Picture*. Julie Salamon has given us an original and disturbing view of a Hollywood disaster with verve, intelligence, and a keen sense of the absurd."

—Marie Brenner, author of *The House of Dreams: The Bingham Family of Louisville*

"It reads like a textbook on cinematic self-delusion."   —*Variety*

"A great story has found its meticulous teller . . . Ms. Salamon conveys with energy and tenacity the characters and emotions that shape the progress of a forty-million-dollar film-production juggernaut, and gives us one of the few panoptic accounts we have of a demanding and dangerously collaborative art."   —*The New Yorker*

"In *The Devil's Candy*, Julie Salamon gives new intimacy to the phrases 'inside story' and 'fly on the wall.' When this book gets around (and I believe it will become a classic), its characters—Brian De Palma, Bruce Willis, Melanie Griffith, Tom Hanks, and a host of other potentates and hustlers of Hollywood—will be more famous for starring in the real-life *Devil's Candy*, in some cases unwittingly, than for appearing in the filmed *Bonfire of the Vanities*. This book is not only about the hilarity and brutality of the way movies are made. It is also about the way life is lived."   —David McClintick, author of
Indecent Exposure: A True Story of Hollywood and Wall Street

". . . a fine, cool-headed, fact-filled exposé. [Salamon] is a crackerjack reporter. . . ."   —*Chicago Sun-Times*

"Delightful. . . . *The Devil's Candy* is quite simply the most telling examination of movie making since Lillian Ross's memorable 1952 *New Yorker* report on the making of John Huston's *The Red Badge of Courage*. Salamon is the perfect reporter . . . she has the novelist's gift. . . ."   —*Vogue*

"Illuminating."   —*People*

"Exhilarating . . . A book that works as a novel, as a standard reference work and, most of all, as great entertainment. It explains, with authority, insight, and élan, the literature of our times: the movies—the who, what, when, where, and why. . . . An amazing re-creation of the 9,271 details and subdramas that go into making a movie."
—Richard Condon, author of
Prizzi's Honor and *The Manchurian Candidate*

The
Devil's Candy

The Bonfire of the Vanities
Goes to Hollywood

Julie Salamon

Delta

A Delta Book
Published by
Dell Publishing
a division of
Bantam Doubleday Dell Publishing Group, Inc.
666 Fifth Avenue
New York, New York 10103

The trademark Delta® is registered in the U.S. Patent and Trademark Office.

ISBN: 0-385-30824-8

Reprinted by arrangement with Houghton Mifflin Company

Manufactured in the United States of America

Published simultaneously in Canada

November 1992

10 9 8 7 6 5 4 3 2 1

RRH

To Bill and Roxie

CONTENTS

PART IV
Postproduction

THE PLAYERS

Randy Bowers   *Bruce Willis's Stand-in*
Eddie Iacobelli   *Transportation Coordinator*
Rob Harris   *Unit Publicist*

THE CAST

Tom Hanks   *Sherman McCoy*
Bruce Willis   *Peter Fallow*
Melanie Griffith   *Maria Ruskin*
Morgan Freeman   *Judge Leonard White*
Beth Broderick   *Caroline Heftshank*
Kim Cattrall   *Judy McCoy*
Alan King   *Arthur Ruskin*
Rita Wilson   *P.R. Lady*
Andre Gregory   *Aubrey Buffing*

THE STUDIO

Lucy Fisher   *Executive Vice President, Production*
Mark Canton   *Executive Vice President, Worldwide*
                                Motion Picture Production
Rob Friedman   *President, Worldwide Theatrical*
                                Advertising and Publicity
Terry Semel   *President and Chief Operating Officer,*
                                Warner Bros., Inc.
Robert A. Daly   *Chairman and Chief Executive Officer,*
                                Warner Bros., Inc.
Bill Young   *Vice President, Production*
Ron Smith   *"Bonfire" Production Executive*

THE EXTRAS

Peter Guber   *Executive Producer*
Tom Wolfe   *Author*
Judge Burton Roberts   *Model for Judge Kovitsky, the Model*
                                for Judge White
Michael Cristofer   *Screenwriter*
Marty Bauer   *Agent*
Steven Spielberg   *Brian De Palma's Best Friend*
Dawn Steel   *Former Head of Columbia Pictures*

PROLOGUE

A genteel murmur presided in the dining room of the Carlyle Hotel, at Seventy-sixth and Madison Avenue, on the Upper East Side of Manhattan. There was, naturally, a certain bustle at breakfast as the well-groomed patrons of this refined enclave made their way to the buffet table. But there was none of the purposeful table-hopping that was so noticeable at Park Avenue's Regency Hotel, known for the "power breakfasts" of its Wall Street and entertainment industry clientele. Discretion ruled the Carlyle, where the bellhops wore white gloves and the opulence was obvious yet understated, and the mood cheery yet subdued.

Dominating the center of the room was a huge Japanese iron vase filled with a luxurious spray of bright flowers. The walls were covered with subtle brown linen velvet and nineteenth-century English hunting prints. For more intimate conversation, one could move into one of the smaller offshoots of the main room — into the smoking room, with its fussy, fabric-lined walls and eighteenth-century French *redouté* floral prints, or into the "Chinese room," named for its decorative Oriental silk screens. Everything was just so. The china was Villeroy and Boch, the silver was Chambly. The Louis XV furniture completed the sensation that manners as well as money still mattered here.

This stronghold of luxe Victoriana was one of the few places in New York City circa 1990 where Tom Wolfe didn't look like an anachronism. Dressed, distinctively as always, in a three-piece gray-plaid suit, a cream-colored shirt with an old-fashioned high-necked cut, and shoes designed to look as though they sported spats, he spoke in a mild voice, touched slightly by a Virginia accent. With his soft, pale face and fine, graying hair, the author appeared delicate, slightly otherworldly.

It was difficult to connect this frail, courtly gentleman with the glinting satirical wit that had made him one of the most famous writers in America. Could this meticulous dandy really be the same man who composed the sixth spoken line in the best-selling novel *The Bonfire of the Vanities*: "*Heh-hegggggggggggggggggghhhhh-hhhhhhhhhh!*" That was it. The entire thought. "*Heh-heggggggg-ggggggggggghhhhhhhhhhhhhhhh!*" And *Bonfire* was only the latest example of Wolfe's singular style. For twenty-five years as a journalist he'd gleefully jabbed at the pretensions of the American middle and upper classes — especially the New York intelligentsia. He'd merrily debunked *The New Yorker*, the Bauhaus movement, liberal chic, and Freud with uniquely rambunctious prose and enthusiastic punctuation.

That morning the slender, contradictory man was eating grain cereal with stewed fruit and speaking in a thoughtful, slightly formal fashion about how the people from Hollywood were progressing with the movie version of *The Bonfire of the Vanities*. He mentioned diplomatically that they were being attentive to details.

"I must confess I get my shoes made at New & Lingwood," Wolfe said, dropping the name of the London fabricator of two-thousand-dollar-a-pair men's shoes with his cultivated mixture of snobbery and modesty. "And the salesman was here in New York, and he said that Tom Hanks had arrived and wanted two pairs of shoes for the movie — Tom Hanks or whoever was buying shoes for him — and asked the salesman what kind should we get? And the salesman says, 'Well, in the book it says half-brogues,' and the movie person says, 'Okay, give us those.' I was rather impressed by that because, unless they make a point of it in the script to have the camera focus on the shoes, who's going to know? You have to have a very picky eye like myself to sit around and figure out where the shoes are from. They seem to be concerned with accuracy — in certain respects."

He wasn't willing to criticize the moviemakers — just yet. "I think it's bad manners in the Southern sense to be sharp and critical of it," he said. "I did cash the check." However, with his good Southern manners the author had made it clear to the Hollywood people right after he accepted the $750,000 they paid him for the rights to his book that he didn't want to have anything to do with the making of their movie.

"To tell the truth, I've never wanted to write any script based on something I've done," he said. "From my standpoint it's too bad that movies don't run nine or ten hours. The way I constructed the book, almost every chapter was meant to be a vignette of something else in New York as well as something that might advance the story, and to me one was as important as the other."

The author paused briefly. "It's a fairly simple story. It's not a complicated story. But I wanted there to be all these slices, one after another. Not that I gave very much thought to how the movie could be made, but I never could see how you could do that."

Tom Wolfe found the title for his novel *The Bonfire of the Vanities* in the story of Girolamo Savonarola, the fifteenth-century Florentine monk whose crusade against secular temptation won him a huge cult following. The zealous Savonarola convinced his followers that, in return for the privilege of living in Florence, God's chosen city, they had a moral duty to cleanse themselves of earthly distractions. Conducting a house-to-house search, Savonarola's most devoted followers, mostly adolescent boys, would collect the earthly manifestations of spiritual decline — jewels, gold, pictures, sculptures, playing cards, musical instruments, perfumes, powders, wigs, and books — and then burn these forbidden items, known as the "vanities," in a bonfire in the town square.

Before long, though, this pious undertaking took on a carnival atmosphere. Savonarola's young minions, wearing white robes and olive wreaths and carrying red crosses, would lead the faithful through the streets toward the square, whipping their collective urge for purity to a feverish pitch. As the bonfire billowed, the crowd sang hymns and danced wildly. The Bonfire of the Vanities had become a form of entertainment.

For a time a great many people were caught up in this orgy of asceticism. Then, as monkish rivals began denouncing Savonarola as a heretic and a barbarian, the Florentines tired of the repetitive purification rites. Inevitably Savonarola's teachings fell out of favor and he himself was publicly burned.

* * *

The story of Savonarola had always intrigued Tom Wolfe, who had taken it upon himself at a relatively early age to become *the* mocker of vanity as practiced in America in the second half of the twentieth century. Wolfe didn't explain the roots of his provocative title anywhere in his book, however. He'd considered including an epilogue explaining the title's origins but finally decided against it. Even Tom Wolfe hesitated to identify himself with the man who was burned at the stake for his convictions.

But Wolfe was never immolated for his cautionary tale. On the contrary, his first novel, published when he was fifty-six years old, achieved legendary success. Pundits hailed Wolfe as a prophetic writer, and his satiric story of the fallen mighty was taken as an apocalyptic warning in the guise of amusing popular fiction. There were naysayers, to be sure, but their voices were buried by the avalanche of praise.

As it turned out, the wrath of public opinion was reserved for those who dared to tamper with Wolfe's novel. In the end it was the heretics from Hollywood who went up in flames.

PART I

Pre-
production

Chapter 1

THE DEVIL'S CANDY

On January 12, 1990, a cold Friday afternoon, Tom Hanks met with Brian De Palma in the comfortable old apartment on Lower Fifth Avenue the director used as an office. The room where they sat was small and sunny with a number of books and a curved Formica desk that held De Palma's computer and telephone.

Tom Hanks was seated next to a plaster Madonna that had been a prop in De Palma's film "Wise Guys." The actor was dressed in black jeans, a black shirt buttoned to the neck, and a black jacket. He had just met with the costume designer for "The Bonfire of the Vanities" and was reporting in. He touched his dark, wavy hair. "She talked about lightening my hair up a little bit, which I've done before," he said matter-of-factly. "I had lighter hair in 'Dragnet.' "

De Palma was also dressed in black — a black cashmere sweater and black slacks, with New Balance sneakers. He was a large, imposing man with a bald spot and a short, graying beard. He nodded slightly and waited. Though Hanks was the star of the film and his salary was twice as much as De Palma's, he seemed eager to please. "We talked about some process that won't alter my scalp permanently," Hanks continued, and then added earnestly, "I will do it if you think we must for the picture."

But De Palma hadn't called Hanks downtown to discuss his hair. Warner Bros. had plans to release "The Bonfire of the Vanities" by Christmas and as of January 12 the movie didn't have a starting date for production and many crucial parts hadn't been cast. Perhaps the most critical of these parts was that of Maria Ruskin, the mistress of bond trader Sherman McCoy, who would be played by Tom Hanks. Maria is the young Southern wife of a rich, elderly man and the catalyst to Sherman's downfall. Tom Wolfe had described her as "something from another galaxy," a seductive composite of clothes, shoes, a style of walking, all "calculated to provoke maximum envy and resentment." Tom Hanks would have to make a convincing show of making love to the actress chosen to play Maria.

Warner Bros. and De Palma had wanted Michelle Pfeiffer to play the part, but she'd turned it down. At De Palma's suggestion, the studio then began negotiating with Melanie Griffith. De Palma had directed Griffith before and thought she had the potential to make Maria a sparkly bad girl. The thirty-three-year-old actress had been a semianonymous starlet seven years earlier when De Palma cast her as a saucy porn star called Holly Body in his suspense picture "Body Double." De Palma liked the work she'd done on that film, but he didn't like what it took to get it out of her. Griffith had been a whine and a nag and she liked to get high. Since then she'd gotten off the drugs and alcohol and become an established star, which meant working with her could be easier — or more difficult. He told Warner Bros. not to close a deal with Griffith until he was sure she was the best Maria they could get.

So, while Warner Bros. stalled on Griffith's contract, Brian De Palma looked for Maria in New York. When he met Uma Thurman, the nineteen-year-old actress who had made her sensational debut in the film "Dangerous Liaisons," he thought he might have found her. He asked Tom Hanks what he thought. Hanks said Thurman was too young for the part, that the obvious choice was Griffith. But De Palma kept saying to him, "Uma's so beautiful. Like Veronica Lake." Hanks agreed to read at her audition.

The movie's original producer, Peter Guber, had his own vision of Maria. As he sat in his office and talked about her, Guber would smack his hands together and keep them clutched, as though he were holding the very idea of Maria between his palms.

"This woman, Maria, she's the devil's candy," he said. "This woman's the devil's candy. You know, the apple . . . in . . . in . . . 'Little Red Riding Hood'! When the guys see her in the audience, the guys have gotta go, 'Unnnnnnh!' " He made a gesture that approximated the yanking of a gear shift. " 'I think I might risk my career, my business *to get into that*!' "

As he considered who might play Maria, he said, "The girl, whoever she is, she's a good actress, that's all important, great, great, great. But if it's gotta be . . . just . . . it's just gotta operate on a visceral sexual level. This is the Eve's apple. If you don't see that, you don't see the picture."

Tom Wolfe had introduced Maria by showing her effect on Sherman McCoy: on the pretext of taking the family dachshund for a walk, Sherman leaves his Park Avenue apartment and ventures into a drenching rainstorm just so he can call his mistress from a pay phone. Trying to imagine what kind of woman could make a man like Sherman act in such an obviously irrational way set Guber off again. "The second he's out the door he's got an erection, just thinking about that girl! You know what I mean? We could have gone with an unknown girl if she had that quality. I wouldn't have gone with, for example, Meryl Streep. No way! She's attractive, she's attractive . . ." He didn't want to insult Meryl Streep by articulating exactly what it was he thought she lacked. "She's attractive, but would you want to —" He interrupted himself and then answered his own unspoken question. "No way! You wouldn't! You wouldn't want to! She doesn't have that Rita Hayworth thing —" He interrupted himself once more. "It's gotta be, she's gotta be the devil's candy!"

Monica Goldstein, De Palma's assistant, tapped on the door to the director's office and ushered in Uma Thurman. Thurman was very tall and very slender. She was wearing a tiny, snug brown skirt, black tights, and a short jacket, all of which only emphasized her endlessly long legs. Her face had the startling ageless beauty of a classical statue.

The nineteen-year-old actress tossed her long, straight brown hair self-consciously and avoided looking anyone in the eye, like an awkward teenager.

"Uma, Tom. Tom, Uma," said De Palma. They nodded at each other, and Hanks mumbled something glibly polite. De Palma then introduced the casting director, Lynn Stalmaster, who had joined them for the audition. Thurman smiled, still not looking at anyone directly. De Palma got up from his chair and led the actors into the living room, which served as the audition room. It was decorated with inexpensive utilitarian furniture and posters from De Palma movies, as well as photographs of the director with various luminaries: Orson Welles, George Lucas, Michael Caine. There was also a photograph of Alfred Hitchcock, one of De Palma's heroes. De Palma and Stalmaster took their seats on lightweight chairs.

"The jungle scene," said De Palma.

The jungle scene begins when Maria and Sherman, having driven into the Bronx by accident, are so terrified to find themselves in this dangerous "jungle" north of Manhattan that in their haste to get out they panic and Sherman's Mercedes-Benz fishtails and hits a young black man they think is trying to mug them. Maria, who is driving, doesn't stop to see if he is hurt or not, and she hotfoots it home. In the safety of the apartment she sublets for her rendezvous with Sherman, she calms her guilt-ridden lover by treating the incident as if it were an adventure — an *erotic* adventure.

Hanks and Thurman stood in the middle of the room and began the scene. Hanks, who is close to six feet tall, looked almost directly into Thurman's eyes — and she was wearing flats. He clutched yellow script pages in his hand.

Thurman's hands were empty; she already knew her lines. She peeled off her jacket, revealing a black leotard scooped low to expose the voluptuous swell of her breasts and clinging tightly to her reed-thin waist and concave tummy. None of the three men showed any sign of being affected.

As Thurman began to say her lines in a sultry Southern accent, all traces of awkwardness disappeared. She really seemed to have become somebody else: a sexy, self-assured woman called Maria.

"We were in the jungle . . . we were attacked . . . we fought our way out." Thurman exhaled her lines as she slithered over Hanks as though she'd been greased.

Hanks, his arms full of lissome young woman, was having a hard time finding his place in the script. He went through his responses to Maria not exactly by rote, but not exactly with great conviction either. The scene ended with Thurman stroking him and moaning Maria's final lines, "Don't think. Just fuck . . ."

Then it was over and they disentangled themselves and looked across the room at De Palma, who was already on his feet, moving toward them.

His commentary was terse. "Very good, but stand like this, Uma." The large, bearded man struck a comically slinky pose, which Thurman obediently mimicked. On her, it looked seductive.

As Hanks and Thurman went through the scene again, De Palma watched impassively from across the room. Though he focused his attention intently on the actors in front of him, his face registered no emotion. He controlled the room the way a psychiatrist might, absorbing information without divulging anything. His intense concentration conveyed the message that he was absolutely in command.

Directors are intimidating by the very nature of their job, though some assume the position of authority more gently than others. These approachable types openly welcome comments from their collaborators and make an effort to appear warm and friendly. Others, however, abuse their power, using it as an excuse for outbursts of sarcasm and hysteria, even cruelty.

De Palma was neither approachable nor abusive. He never ranted and he rarely socialized, which made him all the more forbidding. At work he was the remote patriarch, the leader whose very aloofness made his approval especially hard to discern and especially desirable. Few people could read him. Was he simply rude, or was he so absorbed in his own thoughts about the day's work that he couldn't be distracted by ordinary civility? When he remembered to be polite, the words sounded awkward, as though he were lip-synching phrases from a foreign language.

Forty minutes later, after watching Thurman and Hanks perform the jungle scene two more times, and another scene called the party scene three times, De Palma said stiffly to Thurman, "That was very good, Uma." She grabbed her bag, yanked on her coat, shook hands with Hanks and Stalmaster, and then quickly kissed De Palma on the cheek and left.

De Palma stared momentarily at the space where she had been a moment before, then stood and jerked his head in the direction of his office. By the time Stalmaster and Hanks realized they were to follow him, the director had already seated himself behind his desk.

The audition had convinced De Palma that he shouldn't rush to sign Melanie Griffith until he'd had a chance to see Thurman with Hanks on film. Before he decided, however, he wanted to hear from Hanks and Stalmaster.

"Well?" asked the director.

Hanks went first. "When she walked in here I was stunned," he said in the friendly yet guarded tone that was familiar from his movie roles. "She's quite attractive, almost erotic. She certainly has a sense of play."

De Palma countered, "With Melanie you have the natural co-medic talent. Uma is sexy and funny, but she doesn't have the natural comedic talent."

In his politely hesitant way, Stalmaster asked, "Melanie isn't that disciplined, is she?"

The question instigated a three-way analysis among these men of the relative merits of Griffith's funny, squeaky voice and likability as opposed to Thurman's freshness and beauty. They talked about the actresses much the way Frank Perdue, the mass marketer of poultry, described his chickens on television commercials: as crea-tures whose delectability is measured by standards both objective (weight, color) and subjective (desirability, likability). Hanks raised the delicate issue of Griffith's "shape"; she'd had a baby just three months earlier.

Suddenly Stalmaster broke the businesslike tone of the con-ference. "I'm overwhelmed by Uma," he said. "I didn't expect this. I can't get over it. She's really *listening*."

De Palma joined Stalmaster's excitement. "I worked with her three hours last night. She's very directable. Very directable."

They looked over at their star. Hanks nodded. "All the parts fit . . ." He seemed about to say something else, then left the thought unfinished.

It was agreed that the following week Thurman would fly out to Los Angeles to test on film with Hanks, who lived there and who would be looping — rerecording lines that didn't come out clearly — his most recent picture, "Joe Versus the Volcano." Meanwhile, De Palma would continue to audition other actresses in New York.

*　*.　*

Almost a year had passed since the producer, Peter Guber, had approached Tom Hanks at the Governor's Ball following the 1989 Academy Awards ceremony. Guber asked him if he would like to play the critical role of the bond salesman Sherman McCoy, the lead character in "The Bonfire of the Vanities," the man Tom Wolfe had described as the "Master of the Universe."

Hanks thought the producer was joking. "Me?" he asked.

Guber winked and said, "We're working on it, and I'd love you to consider it."

Peter Guber never had a doubt. Before he hired anyone else — his writer, his director — he knew who his star had to be. He had one choice, and he made it the instant he read the book: Tom Hanks. "With Sherman McCoy I saw a character I could empathize with," said the producer, who was best known in the business for his talent at sniffing out interesting projects and for his tendency to distance himself from them when they didn't work out. "I have been at the edge where just one little event could unravel me. And I realized there was part of me in Sherman McCoy. So I felt that even though this was a character who went downhill the whole way, the other characters are *worse* than him. So here's a character where you can root for him even though he's bad, because the other characters are worse!"

In choosing Hanks, Guber was taking head-on the central problem *The Bonfire of the Vanities* presented the studios. The book was populated by *unlikable* characters, whose sole purpose was to illustrate the greed and ambition that propelled New York through the go-go eighties. It was axiomatic in the film business that *unlikable* characters were box office poison. Guber saw Hanks as the perfect solution — and eventually he brought Warner Bros. and Brian De Palma around to his point of view.

De Palma wasn't sure about Hanks at first. He thought the actor might be too young. He'd been toying with the notion of using Steve Martin, an older comic actor who might bring maturity to the role as well as the humanity Guber was after. The studio's choice for a time was Tom Cruise, who was even younger than Hanks but a bigger star.

But Guber would hear of no one else. He would call the director and the executives and chant: "Tom Hanks, Tom Hanks, Tom Hanks, Tom Hanks, Tom Hanks." To Guber, the choice was obvious. "You look at this arrogant rich guy and you know that somewhere in his past he was a likable kid. Tom Hanks brings that to it. You're waiting for him to fulfill your *best* expectations, not your worst expectations. So as he loses everything, he loses the arrogance, and you begin to think, See, I was right!"

Guber had a talent for finding parallels in unlikely places, and he found one in the casting of Tab Hunter in "Damn Yankees," the story of a man who sells his soul to play center field for the Yankees. As Guber saw it, Sherman McCoy sold his soul to be Master of the Universe and he had to pay the price to the devil at the end. "The devil wanted a big price," said Guber. "I thought that was a great way to look at this film. And Tom Hanks was the vehicle."

Hanks had been surprised at Guber's offer, even though the actor was well aware that his status in the industry had grown immeasurably with the success of "Splash," in which he played a man who fell in love with a mermaid. By the time Guber sought him out at the Academy Awards, Hanks had become even more desirable. He had starred in the hit movie "Big," a comedy about a twelve-year-old boy trapped in the body of a thirty-five-year-old man. "Big" was one of the most successful pictures of 1988. It won Hanks an Oscar nomination and drove his asking price to $5 million.

The thirty-three-year-old actor had read Tom Wolfe's book and had imagined Sherman McCoy as someone older, a man in control, a man quite different from the light comic characters Hanks specialized in. But he was willing to suspend his doubts. He had made thirteen films before "Bonfire," and none of them held the promise of this one, the movie version of a book that had influenced the national consciousness. This role could establish Hanks as a serious dramatic actor. For once he wouldn't be playing Joe Regular, the ordinary guy in an extraordinary situation. Sherman McCoy was a man who grasped for the world and briefly had it in the palm of his hand before his fall from grace.

Hanks understood that with his pug nose and boyish demeanor, he wasn't the obvious choice for Sherman. Someone like William Hurt, whose refined features and fine blond hair implied a certain kind of Wasp lineage, was the obvious choice. From the beginning,

Hanks knew that taking the part was a risk. "The idea of me playing Sherman McCoy is a huge, massive crapshoot," he said. "Maybe I'm perfect, maybe I'm absolutely wrong." He figured it was always risky casting the film version of a best-selling literary work about which millions of people had strong feelings. The result could be a monument like "Gone With the Wind," or a dud like "The Fountainhead."

Hanks left De Palma's office that Friday right after he agreed to test with Thurman in L.A. As soon as the actor was out the door De Palma put in a call to Mark Canton, the head of production at Warner Bros. De Palma reported that the audition with Thurman had gone well and asked Canton if he could prolong the negotiations with Griffith another week, while they tested Thurman on film. Canton had only two questions, which De Palma answered.

"No, no, that's no problem. There's no age problem," said De Palma. "No, no, they're the same height. Tom is pretty tall."

Canton was satisfied that Thurman wasn't disqualified for reasons of age and height, and the subject seemed closed. They'd see how Thurman looked with Hanks on film. Two days later, on Sunday evening, De Palma took Hanks and his wife, the actress Rita Wilson, out to dinner, and Uma Thurman's name was never mentioned.

But Hanks hadn't told De Palma what he really thought of Thurman. During the rehearsal he kept waiting for that electric moment, for that crackling of dialogue that meant two actors had really connected. It never happened, in Hanks's opinion. He left the audition convinced that Thurman was wrong for the part. It was inconceivable to him that a man like Sherman McCoy could be so done in by a woman like Maria if Uma Thurman was that woman. Sherman might get a hard-on for her, but that would last maybe a day, he thought. Acting with Thurman had felt like being in a high school play. Griffith, at least, would bring the unexpected to the part, something serendipitous, something exciting.

He hadn't expressed his reservations to De Palma and Stalmaster because he knew it was tricky for an actor to interfere in these matters. He didn't know De Palma very well yet and didn't want to start off their relationship by contradicting him. On the other hand, if someone from the studio asked his opinion, he'd say what he thought. And he knew someone would ask his opinion because according to the terms of his contract the studio had to ask him. The studio executives might not have to listen to him, but Hanks also knew they would be unlikely to make a choice that would make their leading man cranky before filming even began.

On Tuesday morning, January 16, De Palma was back in his office auditioning actors for many roles. He watched five more actresses read for the part of Maria, even though the field had pretty much been narrowed to Griffith and Thurman. That meant he had heard the jungle scene eighteen times and the party scene twelve times (if the actress didn't have a chance, he didn't bother having her read the party scene a third time). Every time an actress left the room — a new one arrived every fifteen minutes — he leaned back in his chair and sighed.

At 11:45 A.M. he was leaning back in his chair and sighing when Monica Goldstein poked her head in the door to report that she'd gotten a call from California from Fred Caruso, De Palma's line producer: Hanks didn't want to test with Thurman and the studio was upset. It wasn't clear from the message whether the studio was upset with Hanks for refusing to test with Thurman, or upset with De Palma for inadvertently upsetting the star.

De Palma turned to stone. "If Tom had a problem with Uma, why didn't he talk to me," he said, staring at the plaster Madonna facing him from across the room.

He turned to Goldstein, a small, intense woman in her early thirties. "Get him on the phone and get Lucy Fisher on the phone."

Lucy Fisher was the Warner Bros. executive in charge of "Bonfire"; not surprisingly, she couldn't be reached right away. It wouldn't do to be immediately available.

De Palma frequently growled about the duplicity and gamesmanship that were part of the ordinary course of business in Hollywood. But he was a survivor and had survived by playing the game. So he went to lunch, knowing that sitting by the telephone waiting for Fisher to call back could be interpreted as a sign of weakness.

De Palma had lunch at Il Cantinori, a Greenwich Village restaurant that specialized in serving well-prepared food and making its customers feel as though they were dining at a friendly country inn rather than an expensive enclave for wealthy businesspeople and celebrities. A creature of habit, De Palma tended to eat within a few blocks of his home when he was in New York, at exclusive restaurants like Il Cantinori or the Gotham Bar and Grill, or at the far more casual Elephant and Castle. He didn't demand much: good food, good cappuccino, and a smoking section. He was dieting, so lunch consisted of a bowl of minestrone, a bottle of Pellegrino mineral water, and three cappuccinos, each sweetened with two packets of Sweet 'n Low.

When he returned to his office, Lucy Fisher returned his call. The executive spent twenty minutes doing what studio executives do. She tried to make De Palma happy without making Tom Hanks unhappy, and to arrange it so that their mutual happiness didn't detract from the bottom line of the movie. Fisher was under considerable pressure as it was becoming clearer every day how difficult it would be to make the scheduled Christmas release date.

De Palma spoke in the quiet, firm voice that parents use to let their children know they aren't kidding around, that they are in control and don't need to yell. "Number one. Tom should communicate with me directly. I had dinner with him on Sunday, and I didn't hear a word. I did not like hearing information about this via his managers, through you, back to me. I know how to deal with Tom Hanks, and it annoys me the way he's doing things.

"Number two. I don't want you to close any deal with Melanie until I've tested Uma." Now he shifted tactics by raising the specter of trouble. "The thing that disturbs me about Melanie is, she's fragile. Right? Always." These were words no studio executive wanted to hear. Studios didn't want to hire someone who could be an accident waiting to happen. Problems with stars mean delays. Delays cost money.

Griffith was on location for a John Schlesinger film, "Pacific Heights." If she were hired to play Maria, the start date of "Bonfire" would have to be delayed until April, and even then she would have to step out of one picture directly into another.

"This is going to put a lot of pressure on Melanie," said De Palma, sitting very still behind his desk. His green eyes were glowing ominously, like something out of an early De Palma film, when he was still making stylish horror movies. "This isn't like 'Body Double,' where I had her alone in a room and she didn't have a career yet and she was malleable. If anybody can handle her, I can handle her. I don't even know what she's going to look like. I don't have a clue."

He paused, deliberately. "You never know what's going to happen with Melanie."

De Palma had spent many years wheeling and dealing in the movie business, and just as he knew how to instill anxiety in an executive, he also knew he shouldn't push too hard. His voice lightened, took on the tone of a patient accountant.

"I know how Melanie will do it, it'll work," he said, now reassuring. "I'm more concerned about the time schedule she's going to be on. We've got to move our schedule all around to deal with it, which can only wind up being expensive."

Expensive. Bingo. He'd struck a nerve. With the movie's original $29 million budget already pushing $35 million, Thurman would be much cheaper than Griffith, whose fee had escalated to $1 million after the success of "Working Girl."

Fisher agreed to try to arrange the test with Thurman. "Thank you, Lucy," said De Palma in a sugary singsong voice. "I really think this is worth looking at. I wouldn't go to the trouble of doing it otherwise." He hung up the phone.

"Studios," he muttered.

Fifteen minutes later Goldstein announced that Fisher was on the phone again. Would De Palma test Lolita Davidovich? The bosomy actress had become hot that season for the way she played Gov. Earl Long's mistress in "Blaze."

"Sure," said De Palma. Lolita . . . and Uma.

Lucy Fisher, the Warner Bros. executive, and Peter Guber, the producer, had agreed that they weren't making an art movie when they took on "Bonfire of the Vanities." They were making an expensive picture, though Fisher preferred to refer to it as "a big entertainment." Fisher accepted the conventional wisdom that the studio would have to approach Wolfe's book cautiously in order to draw the broad audience the movie would need to be profitable.

Fascinating as Wolfe's "unsympathetic" protagonists might be on the page, they were decidedly unromantic, almost always choosing pragmatism over idealism, self-interest over morality. Studio executives thought such characters spelled box office death, no matter how good the film was. "Sweet Smell of Success," a barbed portrait of a power-hungry newspaper columnist and a venal press agent, may have been a brilliant movie but it was a commercial flop. "You have to figure out a way not to de-ball a great book, yet figure out a way to give yourself a line through it in which maybe people are slightly less complex," Fisher said.

That idea — making the characters "slightly less complex" — explained much about Hollywood casting. Tom Hanks may not have been aristocratic, but he was likable. The actress who would play Maria would have to be sexy, and funny enough to keep her from seeming too venal. As for the third main character, Peter Fallow, everyone agreed that he would have to be very much less complex.

In the book, Fallow is a dissipated British tabloid journalist whose career is revived when he turns Sherman McCoy's accident in the Bronx into a cause célèbre. Fallow's stories transform Sherman into a lightning rod for the class division and racial hatred that swept through New York in the eighties. The irony, of course, is that Sherman and his class distinguish themselves from the mob by their good taste, which is, of course, modeled on British good taste — and that it is a tasteless *British* sod who rises to glory on Sherman's downfall.

De Palma and the screenwriter Michael Cristofer had decided early on that the best way to capture the tone of Tom Wolfe's exuberant language would be to have a narrator tell the story. Fallow, the writer, was the likeliest candidate. But if they were going to use a narrator, De Palma wanted him to be American. Stanley Kubrick's adaptation of the Nabokov novel *Lolita* had been narrated by the British actor James Mason. De Palma had loved that movie — and it had flopped. De Palma worried that American audiences wouldn't accept an Englishman guiding them through an American story.

The executives weren't entirely convinced. They tried to hire John Cleese, the Monty Python actor who had had a big success with the offbeat comedy "A Fish Called Wanda." He wasn't available.

So they began thinking of Americans and asked Jack Nicholson if he'd like the part. He was busy. Bruce Willis heard about the role and sent word that he was interested. The thirty-five-year-old actor had become a superstar in an action picture called "Die Hard." He couldn't be ignored, even though every one of his forays into other kinds of movies — comedy, drama — had been unsuccessful.

Five years earlier, Willis hadn't had a career. He was living in New York's Hell's Kitchen, going to unsuccessful auditions, and earning a living tending bar. Then, in 1985, he tried out for the part of a private eye on a new, idiosyncratic television series called "Moonlighting." The show became an instant success, and Bruce Willis became a phenomenon. The working-class kid from New Jersey became completely identified with the character he played on TV, a fast-talking, charming detective.

Like Hanks, Willis said he wanted to go against type. He'd played a psychologically damaged Vietnam veteran in "In Country" and a romantic lead in "Blind Date." The movies failed. "Bonfire" would give him another chance to expand his range — in a prestigious film based on an *important* book.

No studio felt it could afford to turn its back on a major star, someone who, in the right vehicle, could almost certainly draw from the most desirable demographic group — the eighteen- to twenty-four-year-olds who spent more time in movie theaters than anyone else. Lucy Fisher said that she wouldn't have considered Willis for the part of Fallow if he hadn't been so outrageously popular. "We wanted a movie star," she said. That wasn't necessarily a compromise, she added. "Sometimes stars are the best people for the part, and that's why they're stars sometimes. People like to look at them."

Shortly after De Palma finished his conversation with Fisher about Uma Thurman's screen test, Monica Goldstein brought in Lena Olin, the gorgeous Swede who had played the mistress in "The Unbearable Lightness of Being" and the sexy Holocaust survivor in "Enemies: A Love Story." Two days earlier De Palma had told Olin's agent he could only see the actress if she had time to prepare for a formal audition. Olin was flying into New York from Santo Domingo, where she was filming Sidney Pollack's picture "Havana," to pick up an award from the New York Film Critics Society.

Olin walked into the room calmly, without any of the anxious flutter of the American actresses who had preceded her. Her hair had henna highlights and was hanging loose from a clip in the back; she was wearing a long, black high-necked dress and a faded jean jacket. She was the only actress auditioning for the part who hadn't dressed for seduction, at least not in any obvious way.

As Olin settled into her chair, she seemed wholly undisturbed by the awkwardness of the situation: she hadn't prepared, hadn't even seen the script, had only the vaguest notion of what "Bonfire of the Vanities" was.

"Santo Domingo is awful," she said in perfect English modified slightly by her Swedish accent. "I hate New York, but after Santo Domingo it's wonderful. You can eat the food." She laughed and told De Palma all about the journalists who had been interviewing her, how they seemed to think she was the Holocaust survivor she had played in "Enemies," how they treated her as though she were a fragile creature instead of the robust, self-assured actress she was.

"My agent told me I should come to talk to you because it would be a good thing to be in a movie with Tom Hanks." She leaned forward in her chair, toward the white Formica desk separating her and De Palma, and looked a little sheepish. "I don't know what Tom Hanks is exactly. I hear he's a big star in this country, but I don't know him. Do you have a photo?"

De Palma stared at her for a moment. There was nothing in Olin's round face and healthy complexion to signal duplicity. He laughed — no, cackled. He mentioned some Hanks pictures. "Dragnet"? "Nothing in Common"? "Splash"? "Turner and Hooch"?

No recognition.

"Big"?

"Ah, 'Big.' " She brightened. "When I was on the jury at the Venice Film Festival there were posters for that movie everywhere. I understood it was very popular, but I thought it was a children's movie."

De Palma's manner changed. He relaxed and chatted with Olin as though they were equals. Clearly she wasn't just another supplicant. He asked her if she'd done comedy, and she told him her experience in that area was mostly confined to the Italian classic comedies. In fact, she said, most of her work had been on stage — Strindberg and Ibsen.

The cackle erupted again. Strindberg! Ibsen! Tell that to Warner Bros.!

As planned, Uma Thurman flew to Los Angeles and tested with Tom Hanks on film. She was astounding. At least that's what some people said. She was marvelous, or maybe she just seemed to be because she was so very beautiful. But there were dissenters, and in this case the only dissenter who mattered was Hanks. The studio had indeed asked for his opinion, and he had given it. He'd said she was awful, high school material. "I just can't act with Uma," he said, and proceeded to prove his point in the test. He wasn't terrible, he wasn't good.

So it was settled. Maria would be played by Melanie Griffith, who didn't know she'd been competing with Thurman (and Davidovitch and Olin and a half-dozen others) throughout her negotiations with Warner Bros. De Palma conceded to Stalmaster afterward that Hanks may have been right.

"Even I, who was Uma's strongest supporter, had doubts after I saw the test. She's a great actress, but she isn't comedic. She didn't have the comic timing — you either have it or you don't. Tom's a natural comedian and he wasn't able to play off her."

As he talked about Griffith afterward, it was hard to believe he had ever considered anyone else for the part. "She's likable, she can get away with murder," he said. "Maria can't just come off as a sexy woman who's mind-fucking Sherman. You have to believe her manipulation isn't venal."

It was elusive, this business of casting. Griffith could be perfect, De Palma felt, if only she had the aristocratic carriage of Sigourney Weaver perhaps, or the sensuality of Uma Thurman. Perhaps there would never be a perfect Maria — outside the realm of Tom Wolfe's imagination.

Chapter 2

GREAT, GREAT, GREAT

Peter Guber could talk circles around anybody and would talk in circles even when there was nobody to talk around. A born embellisher, he was one of the few people left in Hollywood who would have fit in with the old-timers. He was crude and shrewd and never afraid to say exactly what he thought about something, and if you didn't get it, he'd say it again a slightly different way.

The tall, thin Bostonian with the hawkish face and a law degree was considered one of the most successful producers in the movie business. He saw himself as an artist; he liked to show up for meetings in moccasins and jeans, sometimes tying back his wild, wiry black hair in a ponytail. And he was an artist, in his way, a master of sizzle. Guber could take an idea and spin from it a metaphor that kept hatching new metaphors until his listeners were too exhausted to follow any longer. His words, spoken with a thick New England inflection, spilled out so fast they tripped up against one another. The strange thing was, no matter how convoluted it was, what he said always seemed to make sense. And even if it didn't, his enthusiasm compensated for any failings in logic.

His temptation, his devil's candy, was "Bonfire" itself, this book that everyone said could never be made into a movie. Guber's talent, his *genius*, was his ability to convince people that nothing was impossible.

"Here was a story where a tiny little event, the pea at the bottom of the mattress, so to speak, the bottom of twenty mattresses, the little pea, this tiny event, unrolled the whole carpet. The whole entire fabric created an event that would otherwise go unnoticed, an event for any other ordinary person that might not get pursued!

"When this person had lost his soul to buy this dream, what happened to him? It unraveled his entire world. And with it like a golf ball covered with . . . you unsheathe a golf ball and you find all those elastic things and you start taking them out and all of a sudden the thing is running around the room randomly. It has no course, you don't know which direction it's going to be. That's what happened.

"So," said Peter Guber, explaining why he wanted to produce "The Bonfire of the Vanities" and why he thought audiences could be made to feel sympathy for its hero Sherman McCoy, an adulterer who could leave a hit-and-run accident for which he thought he was responsible because he didn't want his wife to know he was cheating on her. "So."

"So we, my partner, Jon Peters, and I, we thought we could create an environment where we could come to root for the character and come to understand his pain, that his pain and punishment were greater than his crime. So what happened was we had an interesting morality play going on. The slobs tore down the snobs and we rooted for the snob at the end because he understood what it was like to be down there, to be the center of this carnival. He became the meat on the bone, he became the barbecue. One little act of redemption at the end, one recognition of it all, allowed him to become worthwhile in our eyes, so at the end we could root for him and understand him."

Even Peter Guber occasionally had to take a breath. And even Peter Guber had to admit, "That's a difficult film to execute."

Tom Wolfe wrote the first version of *The Bonfire of the Vanities* in serial form for *Rolling Stone* magazine in 1984 and 1985. Those pieces, which bore only a slight resemblance to the book they would become, were a nonevent. No one paid much attention to Wolfe's attempt to follow in the footsteps of Émile Zola and Charles Dickens, who wrote their novels on deadline for periodicals. No one in Hollywood proposed making a movie out of *Bonfire* then.

Wolfe completely revised the novel before submitting it to Farrar Straus Giroux for publication. In early 1987 the manuscript was sent around to the various studios. The reactions were various but all could be compressed into one thought: there was no "through line." The story and themes could not be adequately compressed into a sentence or even a paragraph.

But when the book was published and became an instant literary and sociological phenomenon, a great many people *wanted* to find a through line. Suddenly *Bonfire* seemed very desirable. Still, nothing happened. No one could completely overcome his or her doubts — not until Peter Guber read the book in late autumn of 1987 and put in a call to Jeff Berg, chairman of Wolfe's literary agency, International Creative Management. Before Berg could even begin the opening round of negotiations, Guber told him, "Here's what we're ready to do. We'll make the deal this afternoon. Now!"

Guber and his partner, Jon Peters, had an exclusive production contract with Warner Bros. at that time, a deal that allowed them to purchase the rights to anything they wanted within a certain range. The $750,000 they offered for the rights to *Bonfire* — $500,000 up front and $250,000 when shooting commenced — fell comfortably within that range. They met with Terry Semel, the president and chief operating officer of Warner Bros., who asked them, "How do you see the film?"

"Great," said Peter Guber. "Great, great, great. That's how we see it. Great. You know, we'll develop it and make it. How do you make 'Color Purple'? How do you make any of these pictures that are difficult? 'Witches of Eastwick'?" He answered his own question. "You make 'em. You make 'em."

Not long after he bought the rights to the book, Guber attended a movie première with Michael Cristofer, an actor, playwright, and screenwriter who had written the script for "The Witches of Eastwick," another Guber project. Cristofer told Guber he'd heard about the *Bonfire* acquisition and said he wanted to write the screenplay. Though Guber had already promised the project to another writer, the producer told Cristofer he could have the job if he could go to work immediately. The book had been number one on the best-seller list for several weeks and Guber wanted to capitalize on its success.

Cristofer began writing in early 1988. For the next several months, Guber set "Bonfire" aside while he waited for the script.

Lucy Fisher felt that Michael Cristofer seemed like a "very obvious choice" the minute Peter Guber mentioned his name. He had many things in his favor. High on the list was his Pulitzer Prize for *The Shadow Box*; the studio executives weren't all that familiar with his other plays.

Moreover, Cristofer had written only two screenplays that had been made into movies when he was hired for "Bonfire." "Falling in Love" was a contemporary variation on David Lean's "Brief Encounter," a story about two married people who fall in love but decide in the end to restrain their passion and remain with their spouses. Cristofer's script changed the ending. Instead of parting forever, the way Lean's lovers do, the couple in "Falling in Love" meet again a year after they decide to go their separate ways. In the interim, they've conveniently shed their former spouses and children and are free to marry.

It wasn't "Falling in Love" that inspired Lucy Fisher to say of Cristofer, "I think he's one of the most brilliant screenwriters I've ever known." The script that demonstrated Cristofer's brilliance, in Fisher's eyes, was his adaptation of John Updike's *The Witches of Eastwick,* also produced by Peter Guber and Jon Peters, and financed and distributed by Warner Bros. "Witches" was a money-maker, and Cristofer had been an uncomplaining workhorse. In a day and age when screenwriters who were paid hundreds of thousands of dollars for their services actually refused to rewrite their screenplays, simply doing his job qualified Cristofer as a hero.

"We had a million problems on 'Witches' and weathered them all and lived to love each other subsequently," said Fisher. "So he was an easy, good choice. On this one we thought we needed someone who we really knew because it was such a hard book. Michael's a really really really creative guy and he's a fantastic writer. I can't speak highly enough of him. I love him." Cristofer was hired for $600,000, plus $25,000 for "fringe benefits."

Tom Wolfe couldn't imagine how a screenwriter would be able to condense the vast sprawl of his 659-page novel into a movie that would run, the studio insisted, a maximum of two hours.

He had no illusions that the movie would be faithful to his novel. The first time he'd seen Philip Kaufmann's three-hour-and-thirteen-minute film version of his book *The Right Stuff* he was shocked. It was only on his third viewing of the movie that it dawned on him why: "What was on the screen was not my book. It was something else. It was something else pretty good. I realized it was a pretty good movie." He decided to spend no time whatsoever wringing his hands over the fate of *Bonfire* because he already knew the movie was bound to be something else — especially if it were only two hours long.

Still, even though he would always insist that the book was a thing apart from the movie, he wanted the movie to be good. It would, after all, bear the same name as his book, and many people would assume he had something to do with it.

Wolfe firmly believed that movies were only as good as their scripts. "A great movie is about 85 percent writing and 15 percent not ruining the writing with the pictures," he said. He wasn't all that familiar with De Palma's work, though he had seen and liked "The Untouchables." However, he was concerned that De Palma's visual finesse might be overwhelming. He remembered the scene in "The Untouchables" in which Al Capone descends the stairs while delivering a soliloquy about his philosophy of civic rule. "Visually it is so spectacular that it's a real test of your senses to get it all in at the same time."

Wolfe was most curious about the writer chosen by Peter Guber and Warner Bros. to adapt his book. He was completely unfamiliar with the work of Michael Cristofer, though he had heard of *The Shadow Box*, the play for which Cristofer had won the Pulitzer.

"I gather the play was downbeat and didn't last all that long," said Wolfe. "Wasn't the subject cancer?"

He said he really wouldn't have anything more to say about Michael Cristofer until the movie was made and he'd seen it.

No one liked Cristofer's first script, which he submitted to Warner Bros. on October 1, 1988. He deviated significantly from Wolfe's plot and his intent. Wolfe returned over and over to the theme of a city run amuck with rampant self-interest. He left Sherman McCoy stripped of money and position — and alone. His wife Judy deserts him, and his mistress Maria lays the blame on him for their hit-and-run accident, even though she was driving the car. In an effort to redeem the characters and make them more likable, Cristofer had the wife and mistress join forces to help save Sherman. The screenplay ended with a chastened but wiser and happier Sherman Mc-Coy living in an isolated cabin in the woods with his wife and daughter. For the final image, Cristofer had Sherman put his arm around his little girl as they watch "a blazing sunset." He described the setting as "fantastic . . . the mountains, the sky, the setting sun."

That script did little to overcome widespread doubts that Tom Wolfe's novel could be made into a movie. In February 1988, not long after taking on the project, Guber told the *New York Times* that he was "deluged with interest from the creative community to be involved with the project." A year after that optimistic blurb appeared, "Bonfire of the Vanities" still had no director.

No one was brave enough or foolhardy enough to put his reputation on the line for a project that was generally thought to be impossible. This was not the time to take risks. Movie costs had escalated wildly in the past decade, from an average cost of $8.9 million in 1979 to $23.5 million in 1989. And *Bonfire* was not only difficult to condense, it was inflammatory. Tom Wolfe had meticulously insulted almost everyone: the rich, the poor, blacks, Jews, Wasps, the British. Though the book had become the symbolic capstone to the eighties, the decade of greed, no one could predict how this material would appeal to the great unwashed, the moviegoing public. A movie that echoed the downfall of the financial wizards of the 1980s was unlikely to find much of an audience among the young people who bought most of the tickets.

The studio had tried to interest Mike Nichols and Norman Jewison, directors who specialized in topical comedy and drama. Nichols was just finishing "Working Girl," a comedy about a secretary who becomes a Wall Street whiz. But Guber didn't like Nichols's recommendation for Sherman McCoy, the comedian Steve Martin. "Steve Martin looks fifty-one years old," said Guber with disgust. "Sherman McCoy is thirty-eight years old, about to sit down at the table of life." Norman Jewison studied the material for several weeks and told the executives that the only way to manage the book's sprawl would be to do a television miniseries. Lucy Fisher was pushing for director James Brooks, who had an almost uncanny instinct for making movies of content that were both intelligent and widely appealing, films like "Terms of Endearment" and "Broadcast News." Peter Guber wanted Martin Scorsese, a great stylist and New York filmmaker.

The executives had also sent the script to Steven Spielberg, whose fantasy films had made him the most commercially successful director in Hollywood. Everyone, including Spielberg, thought he was the wrong choice. However, Warner Bros. sent every script to "Steven" first. In the Warner executive suite Spielberg was described as "our brother." Spielberg and Warner Bros. president Terry Semel vacationed together in Hawaii; Steven J. Ross, chairman of Time-Warner, the corporate parent, summered near Spielberg in their gargantuan "cottages" in the Hamptons.

No director would touch "Bonfire." One big bomb could set a career back years. True, the book had been on the hardcover best-seller list for more than a year, even after it climbed onto the paperback best-seller list. But what were 1 million readers, or even 2 million, or even 3? Enough to make for a supersonic literary phenomenon and barely enough to register a film's existence.

By February 1989 Peter Guber had grown impatient with this project, which had been sitting on the books for more than a year. He wanted to get moving and decided it was time to try something daring. "What about Brian De Palma?" he asked the Warner Bros. executives.

De Palma's name was received as it always was at the studios, with mixed emotions. He had made nineteen movies since 1963, and the Hollywood establishment still didn't know what to make of him. He was considered a gonzo provocateur, having dabbled for years in stylish horror movies that pushed the limit, visually and emotionally, sometimes at the expense of plot and frequently at the expense of what was considered good taste — though much of what had seemed scandalous in Hollywood a decade before had now become tame, as films became raunchier and bloodier. Opinions about him among critics and audiences were mixed: he was a genius, he was a monster. People were either enthralled or appalled by the underlying cackle, the wild note of hilarity and despair that gave De Palma's films their sometimes contradictory mix of romantic yearning and cruel absurdity.

De Palma had made his first full-length feature while he was a graduate student at Sarah Lawrence in 1963, a movie called "The Wedding Party," which starred two young actors, Jill Clayburgh and Robert De Niro. Already De Palma had an uncanny nose for talent; over the years he would give a catalytic boost to a great many actors, including John Lithgow, Michelle Pfeiffer, Kevin Costner, and Melanie Griffith.

He was an avid student of film and a diligent entrepreneur, a requirement for any starting movie director. His early films were low-budget ventures that reflected the spirit of the times. While his contemporaries were listening to the Doors and taking drugs and living the counterculture experience, De Palma was filming it. He made his mark with two loose-limbed pieces of street theater, "Greetings" and "Hi Mom."

"Greetings," which was released in 1968, tells the story of a group of pals coaching one of their buddies on the art of draft dodging. Episodic and raunchy, the picture was a sly bit of comedy with fashionable splashes of conspiracy theory and antiwar mockery. Pauline Kael of *The New Yorker* said the movie was a structural mess, but she was also encouraging — and this was at a time when encouragement from a leading critic meant something. Even then De Palma provoked conflicting reactions. The *New York Times* dismissed "Greetings" as "tired, tawdry and tattered."

But "Greetings" and "Hi Mom" were successful enough to land De Palma a deal with a major studio. In 1970, at the age of thirty, he left New York for Hollywood to make a picture for Warner Bros., a comedy called "Get to Know Your Rabbit," starring Orson Welles and Tommy Smothers.

Instead of bringing the New York filmmaker the acceptance he was seeking and the chance to expand his skills into bigger, more complicated movies, "Get to Know Your Rabbit" was a crushing experience. Tommy Smothers didn't like De Palma's ideas. The Smothers Brothers were at the height of their popularity. Tommy

Smothers was a star; De Palma was an unknown. His credentials —
some encouragement from Pauline Kael and five completed features — meant nothing in Hollywood. He was fired from his first
studio picture. To De Palma his conflict with the studios seemed
clear. They were Los Angeles; he was New York. They were money;
he was art.

   Terribly shaken, De Palma returned to New York and independent filmmaking.

After that devastating experience in Hollywood, De Palma's films
changed. Now he began to make the shocking suspense pictures
with which he would most frequently be identified. They were
emotional, operatic films, repeatedly invoking the idea that terror
was the only possible response to the cruel and irrational forces
that governed the universe. An admirer of Alfred Hitchcock's cinematic technique, De Palma gravitated to the suspense genre as a
way to tell violent stories of obsessive love, sexual anxiety, death,
and betrayal. His movies were filled with disturbed families and
confused identities. They were filmed with such technical precision
that they called attention to the presence of the man behind the
camera, whose invisibility protected him from the intense emotions
he aroused as he moved his characters through the treacherous,
sometimes sadistic world he created on film. His movies were
bloody yet oddly poetic, feverish yet carefully planned, full of
passion yet distant.

   Critics were impressed by the intelligence behind these movies
that toyed with the trashy sensibilities of the horror genre, and they
admired De Palma's familiarity with film history. His movies could
be seen as both entertainments and as treatises on other films.
Psychologists were intrigued by De Palma's fascination with pa-
thology, by the aberrant behavior aroused in characters who find
themselves manipulated by others.

   A great many people simply thought De Palma was a fraud.
They argued that he had simply dressed up his woman-hating
wickedness so artfully that the intelligentsia didn't see him for what
he was: a perverse misogynist.

   At first De Palma was startled by the attacks, and then in-
vigorated by them. He willingly, sometimes gleefully, went head to

head with journalists eager to denounce him for the violence and violent sexuality in his movies. People were almost always thrown off guard when they met the well-spoken graduate of a Quaker school in Philadelphia, Columbia University, and Sarah Lawrence. Articulate and convincing, De Palma could defend himself very well indeed.

The filmmaker was governed by conflicting impulses. He wanted to be recognized as an artist by the critical establishment, and he wanted to achieve box office success. Yet his most personal films could never have the mass appeal of more conventional movies. When he followed his own instincts, he made movies that were almost guaranteed to offend. Certainly there was an audience for Brian De Palma movies. "Carrie" and "Dressed to Kill" were hits, but they weren't huge hits. They weren't comparable to successes like Steven Spielberg's "Close Encounters of the Third Kind," George Lucas's "Star Wars," and Francis Coppola's "The God-father."

De Palma complained about the treachery and money worship of Hollywood. He said sardonically that whenever he walked down Rodeo Drive he had the feeling that the box office score from his last picture was flashing in neon on his back. But he wasn't satisfied to stay in New York and make low-budget pictures that were entirely his, even though he knew that the bigger the movie, the bigger the pressure to compromise. As he grew more experienced, he wanted to expand his range to bigger canvases, and to be recognized for his ability to fill them.

He gathered a cult following with "Sisters" and "Phantom of the Paradise." Then, his successful adaptation of the Stephen King novel "Carrie" in 1976 legitimized him in the industry's eyes. The movie did very well at the box office. De Palma may have been New York, but he was becoming Hollywood too. He began to live on both coasts and was riding high. "Dressed to Kill," released in 1980, was a certifiable hit.

But De Palma was tired of being compared to Hitchcock, and he was tired of having to justify what he did to people who didn't want to understand. By 1981, after his thriller "Blow Out" failed at the box office, he wanted to change his image. He was hired to direct "Prince of the City," the story of a corrupt policeman who betrays his fellow officers. For eighteen months he helped develop a script, then was replaced by another director. That experience confirmed his feeling that his position in Hollywood was tenuous, and that it always would be.

His next film was "Scarface," a remake of the classic gangster film with a contemporary Cuban mobster replacing the original Italian. By then, De Palma was wearing the image of bad boy provocateur like protective armor. Yet he was hoping this sizable film, financed by Universal Pictures and starring Al Pacino, would make him respectable in Hollywood — even though he claimed he had no respect whatsoever for the people who ran Hollywood.

His ambivalence about that desire for respectability was reflected in an *Esquire* magazine article written by a reporter who visited the set of "Scarface."

"I want to be *infamous*," De Palma said. "I want to be *controversial*. It's much more colorful." He went on to say, "As soon as I get this dignity from 'Scarface' I'm going to go out and make an X-rated suspense porn picture . . . I'm sick of being censored . . . So if they want an X they'll get a *real* X. They wanna see suspense, they wanna see terror, they wanna see SEX — I'm the person for the job."

Later De Palma would claim he said those things because he was angry that the ratings board of the Motion Picture Association of America thought the violence in "Scarface" warranted an X, a designation that would keep anyone under eighteen out of the theaters and would prevent many newspapers from advertising the movie. "Scarface" eventually received an R rating, but the *Esquire* piece wasn't forgotten. Those words, "If they want an X, they'll get a real X," would come back to haunt De Palma again and again.

"Scarface" did make De Palma infamous. He became the man to call on when journalists needed an articulate expert to talk about violence. And "Body Double," his next movie, only enhanced his notoriety. Now he was the expert on violence *and* pornography. By then, he'd had enough. He didn't want to fight anymore.

De Palma followed "Body Double" with "Wise Guys," a modest farce about a couple of low-level Mafiosi. The picture didn't attract much attention, but for De Palma it was a transition, a move away from infamy toward respectability. Producer Art Linson and Paramount Pictures offered him "The Untouchables," a remake of the television series about the Chicago G-men who captured Al Capone. He accepted the job without great expectations, and then was pleasantly surprised. The movie turned out to be his broadest success, critically and commercially. He'd taken everything he'd learned about filmmaking up to then and modulated it. His operatic style lent depth and weight to the essentially simple story of Good versus Evil, and he never let the film get bogged down in the stiff biblical language that sometimes encumbered David Mamet's script. The film lacked the psychological complexity and sneaky humor of his earlier films, omissions his fans noticed with regret, but these omissions opened his work to a much wider spectrum of viewers. Sean Connery won the Academy Award for his portrayal of the cynical beat cop who becomes one of the Untouchables, and suddenly De Palma found himself embraced by the Hollywood establishment.

The success of "The Untouchables" gave the director the confidence and the clout to find studio backing for the movie he had wanted to make for a decade. "Casualties of War" was the true story of a squad of American soldiers in Vietnam who kidnapped and raped a Vietnamese girl, then murdered her to erase the evidence. One of the soldiers protested but didn't help the girl escape. Later, tormented by a guilty conscience, he convinced the army to prosecute his fellow soldiers. De Palma had read about the episode in *The New Yorker* almost twenty years earlier; the incident was also the basis of the 1972 Elia Kazan film "The Visitors."

This story didn't allow for the satiric distance De Palma usually put between himself and his emotions on film, and it certainly didn't allow for the pop playfulness that made "The Untouchables" so safe and so popular. He saw "Casualties" as a chance to confront directly his recurring theme: the serious moral consequences of a failure to act, or of acting too late. There would be no hiding behind the conventions of suspense or action genre films this time. He would be openly admitting that he longed to make a big, important film that was visually splendid but also had serious thematic concerns. "Casualties" would be his chance to pay homage to the movie he admired perhaps more than any other, David Lean's epic antiwar film "The Bridge on the River Kwai." He knew there was no chance that a dark picture like "Casualties" could match "The Untouchables" at the box office, but he told himself over and over not to get caught up in the Hollywood value system, that he should be grateful to be making a film that meant something. But he knew the success of "The Untouchables" had enabled him to make "Casualties." He'd been on the other side too many times. He knew all too well how fast the doors closed after a failure. When he considered the possibility that "Casualties" would not be a commercial hit, he felt physically ill.

De Palma spent the better part of 1988 filming "Casualties" on location in Thailand. By the beginning of 1989 "Casualties" was edited, but Columbia Pictures didn't plan to release it for several months. To ward off the inevitable panic that set in when one of his movies was about to open, De Palma began planning his next project. He had four different writers working on scripts, though none was near completion. When his agent mentioned that a script of *Bonfire of the Vanities* was making the rounds, he wanted to see it. He'd found reading the book a wonderful escape back in Thailand and was curious to see how it could be turned into a movie.

Michael Cristofer's script was discouraging. The bite of the novel was gone. Still, De Palma decided to meet with the Warner Bros. executives. This was the first time he'd even considered returning to Warner Bros. since 1970, when he was fired from "Get to Know Your Rabbit." He couldn't imagine what it would be like to return to the scene of his first Hollywood humiliation.

He was calm as he walked up the stairs of the Warner Bros. executive building, built by the founding moguls in the style of a low-rise villa. As he entered Lucy Fisher's large office to meet with her, Peter Guber, and Mark Canton about "The Bonfire of the Vanities," he knew he had the advantage. He didn't really want the job.

The executives were apprehensive. They didn't know what to make of this solemn fat man wearing a safari suit and sneakers. De

Palma had returned from filming "Casualties" looking like a bearded Buddha. Never thin, he'd gone beyond husky, beyond chubby during his marriage to actress Nancy Allen, who had starred in several of his movies, and had become even rounder after their divorce. As he'd grown larger his wardrobe had gotten smaller. He started wearing safari suits all the time because the loose jackets didn't have to be tucked in. His size was intimidating. Though his appearance would have marked him as an eccentric in any day and age, De Palma was particularly out of place in the New Hollywood, run on Perrier and aerobics and "family values."

After cursory greetings, the executives asked De Palma to tell them how he thought the movie should be done. They were pleasantly surprised by the intellectual analysis that came naturally to him. He explained that he wanted to present the story as a broad satire, a dark farce on the order of Stanley Kubrick's "Dr. Strangelove," a comedy about nuclear warfare. He told them he thought the way to convey the spirit of Tom Wolfe's exaggerated, energetic prose would be through exaggerated, energetic imagery.

Lucy Fisher saw in De Palma a man who had no fear. He was a man who said, "I know exactly how to do this. I know exactly the tone I want. I don't think it's a problem to shrink it down. I know how to do it. I don't think it's racist and I don't care if some people think I am."

When the executives reported their favorable impression to Terry Semel, Warner Bros. president, he put in a call to Steven Spielberg, whose best friend in the world was De Palma. The two filmmakers had known each other for fifteen years and had remained friends even as De Palma's career had gone up and down and Spielberg's had shot into the stratosphere. De Palma was godfather to Max, Spielberg's son with Amy Irving. Spielberg assured Semel that he wouldn't be sorry.

On March 3, 1989, Warner Bros. agreed to pay Brian De Palma $250,000 not to accept any other directing projects while he worked on a revision of "Bonfire" with Michael Cristofer, the screenwriter. De Palma and Cristofer met, and they agreed that Cristofer would reinstate the book's plot and add a narrator who would use as much of Tom Wolfe's language as possible. Then there was nothing for De Palma to do but wait for the revised script and for "Casualties of War" to open.

That spring De Palma concentrated on his relationship with Kathy Lingg, a studio executive at Tri-Star Pictures. After his divorce from Nancy Allen in 1983, he had embarked on a series of one- and two-year relationships with women who were almost always surprised to discover what a tender and amusing man the aloof director could be. They were equally surprised by the abrupt way he'd drop them when he found someone else or when they indicated they'd like some deeper level of commitment.

Lingg was strong willed, attractive, and astute about the business in which De Palma operated — and just as wary of marriage as he was, having only recently been divorced herself. Lingg had an additional asset, a little girl De Palma adored. Much as he was a solitary man, he enjoyed their family outings and recorded many of them on videotape. His life seemed to have reached a point of equilibrium.

That sense of equilibrium was thrown completely off when "Casualties of War" was screened before a Boston preview audience in April 1989. The reaction was dismal. People found the film too stark, too full of sorrow. Though he'd told himself all along that "Casualties" might not be a big hit, he'd never really believed it. This was his finest film, and now a preview audience was telling him they wouldn't recommend it to their friends.

For the next several months he re-edited the film, cutting out significant sections near the end to make it more palatable for the public. But he worried that the cuts wouldn't make any difference for audiences and that he would have compromised his material for no reason.

A couple of weeks before "Casualties of War" opened, De Palma received an advance copy of Pauline Kael's review. He nearly wept. Ms. Kael, who had been a generally enthusiastic supporter of De Palma throughout his career, interrupted her summer leave from *The New Yorker* to put her imprimatur on "Casualties." She began her emotional review of the film with the kind of sweeping appreciation De Palma had been waiting for his entire career:

Some movies — "Grand Illusion" and "Shoeshine" come to mind, and the two "Godfather"s and "The Chant of Jimmie Blacksmith" and "The Night of the Shooting Stars" — can affect us in more direct, emotional ways than simple entertainment movies. They have more imagination, more poetry, more intensity than the usual fare; they have large themes, and a vision. They can leave us feeling simultaneously elated and wiped out. Overwhelmed, we may experience a helpless anger if we hear people mock them or poke holes in them in order to dismiss them. The new "Casualties of War" has this kind of purity.

On opening night, August 18, De Palma went to check out the crowd at an Upper East Side theater in Manhattan. It was sold out. Kathy Lingg flew in from Toronto, where she was trying to moderate the tension between Marlon Brando and the director of "The Freshman," the picture she was overseeing. Lingg had seemed a little distant to De Palma the previous week, but that evening seemed perfect. They celebrated at the Broadway steakhouse Frankie & Johnny's, and were still in good spirits the next morning when De Palma got "the call" from the Coast. The call always came the day after a movie opened to report, swiftly and with deadly accuracy, whether it had failed or succeeded: the call brought with it the numbers, the first day's grosses.

The call this time came directly from Dawn Steel, who was then studio chief of Columbia. Steel had been the studio executive in charge of "The Untouchables" at Paramount and had gone on to run Columbia not long after that movie opened. Many people in the business didn't like her. One of the very few women in the upper echelons of Hollywood, she was tough and crude — attributes common enough among her male peers but less acceptable in a woman. She would typically start a telephone call with "Hey, motherfucker, how are you doing?" Brian De Palma was not offended. After all, Steel had taken on "Casualties" with its obvious attendant risks.

He knew he was in trouble when Steel simply said, "Hello, Brian." Without embroidery she reported, "It doesn't look very promising," and proceeded to give him the numbers. That sold-out theater on the Upper East Side had been a fluke. "Casualties of War," playing on 1,486 screens around the country, had taken in $2 million Friday night. It was dismal.

De Palma's habitual response to bad news was to retreat to the nearest cave, generally in his bedroom. He stayed under the covers until afternoon, rousing himself only to take Lingg to the airport to catch a four o'clock flight back to Los Angeles and "The Freshman."

The last thing in the world he wanted to think about was "Casualties," but he was scheduled to talk about the movie at a press conference at the annual film festival in Montreal. He flew to the festival with plans to spend several days, going to movies and seeing old acquaintances, before flying on to Deauville, France, where the film was opening the film festival there the week before Labor Day. Lingg was scheduled to travel with De Palma to France, though she'd warned him as she left New York that she wasn't sure she'd be able to make it. Miserable and lonely, he called her from Montreal to beg her to come along.

She put him on hold. When she got back to him it was only to tell him she had to get off the line, that Marlon Brando was calling a press conference to denounce "The Freshman." When Lingg finally returned his call, nine hours later, her message was short and to the point: "I can't deal with you now. I'm all jammed up."

On the Thursday before Labor Day weekend De Palma flew off alone to Deauville. At the black tie opening Friday night, he and his film were the center of attention. The crowd sobbed, then applauded — and none of it meant anything. Sunday morning De Palma wandered out of his hotel to buy a newspaper and collapsed on the street. Two French journalists rushed over to help him get to his feet, but he couldn't stand. His right ankle was badly sprained.

The next morning, one week before his forty-ninth birthday, he flew back to New York, feeling defeated in every way possible: by the woman he loved, by his body, and by his art.

When De Palma returned home he found the "revised first draft" of "Bonfire" that Michael Cristofer had delivered on August 23. Though the script would eventually undergo at least a dozen more revisions, De Palma was satisfied that they now had a blueprint.

De Palma's feelings about the script were confirmed by the studio. On September 22, Warner's "creative" department — where readers are assigned scripts to critique — released a six-page memo to "file," analyzing Cristofer's new rendition of "Bonfire."

"This latest draft of *Bonfire of the Vanities* has been vastly improved," said the anonymous person in creative. "The addition of Fallow's narrative voice and new business in our ending help give this draft a reality and edge that is more faithful to Wolfe's book."

The person from creative then elaborated in great detail how the script might be improved, point by point, character by character. Creative observed, "We'd like to find a way to retain the strength and controversy of the book but make us feel at the end that somehow Sherman is a better and cleaner man for all his troubles."

But despite the progress with the script, De Palma didn't have the heart for it. As the movie moved closer to becoming a reality, he began to complain almost daily to his agent, Marty Bauer, "This movie's going to be an endless talkfest. I'm having real second thoughts about this."

Bauer had reached the bottom of the great reservoir of patience and sympathy he had for the man he would always refer to as his favorite client. "You should go back to work," he said. "This is the best thing that's around. Get back to work."

And indeed, work seemed to do the trick. De Palma began a liquid diet, and over the next three months he lost sixty pounds and began wearing tweed jackets he'd had in the closet for ten years. He went shopping at Armani. Acquaintances who hadn't seen him for a while would ask him what his secret was, and he would say with a cackle, "Grief."

By the time Michael Cristofer submitted his "second revised first draft" on October 12, 1989, the movie's producer, Peter Guber, had left the project.

In September, a Japanese electronics company, Sony Corporation, had bought Columbia Pictures Entertainment for $3.4 billion. Sony wanted to replace Dawn Steel; her loyalty to filmmakers like De Palma meant nothing to a company looking for a studio chief who had a proven roster of hits. That summer the Japanese had offered the job to Michael Ovitz, the head of Hollywood's powerful talent agency, Creative Artists Agency. After he turned it down, they turned to the hottest producers in town in the summer of

1989, the producers of "Batman," Peter Guber and Jon Peters. "Batman," which Guber and Peters had produced for Warner Bros., opened bigger than any picture in the studio's history. It would go on to gross $450 million worldwide.

Warner Bros. wasn't willing to relinquish Guber and Peters easily. The studio had signed an exclusive five-year contract with the producing team six months earlier. Steven J. Ross, chairman of Time-Warner, the movie company's corporate parent, retaliated with a $1 billion theft-of-services lawsuit against Sony. As part of the settlement, Sony paid Warner $600 million for the producers, and agreed to abandon Columbia's stake in the Burbank lot that had been jointly owned by the two studios for twenty years. In addition, Warner Bros. kept all fifty of the Guber-Peters projects then in development, including "The Bonfire of the Vanities." From that moment on, Guber's only imprint on "Bonfire" would be his name on the credits, under the title executive producer.

After Guber left, Warner Bros. tried briefly to hire another producer to act as a liaison between the filmmakers and the studio. But there wasn't much time. After all the stalling, the studio was determined to get "Bonfire" out by Christmas of 1990. Art Linson, who had produced "The Untouchables" and "Casualties of War" for De Palma, was busy. Spielberg was reluctant to mix business and friendship on this particular project, which promised to be a difficult one.

That left "Bonfire" without a producer. But the studio quickly convinced itself that it didn't need one after all. It had been a heady year for Warner Bros. The merger of the company's parent, Warner Communications, with Time Inc. had made the top Warner executives into very rich men. The success of "Batman" gave the studio executives a feeling of invincibility. They asked themselves if the movie owed its success to Guber and Peters after all, or if it had really been the star, Jack Nicholson, who'd made it work, or Mark Canton, the chief production executive of Warner Bros.

Morale was so high at Warner Bros. when De Palma went to work there in the post-"Batman" period that the director laughingly referred to the executives as the Medici princes, because they seemed to think of themselves as the bravest, the most intellectual, the most invincible. So "Bonfire" would move forward without a producer, leaving De Palma and the Medici princes at each other's mercy.

When the studio system was operating at full strength in the thirties and forties, the studios themselves kept producers on staff to oversee individual pictures. The producers helped influence the script, the direction, the budget, and the schedule, as well as the editing. There were independent producers even then, men like Samuel Goldwyn and David Selznick, who dominated every aspect of the films they produced, the artistic side as well as the financial, then distributed their product through the studios.

After the studio system was dismantled, producers became independent contractors like everyone else working in the business. Most often, producers acted as packagers. They found artistic properties, found financing and distribution outlets, hired the people needed to make the film, and followed the film through to completion. These hands-on producers not only chose the director and the screenwriter, they helped assemble the stars, the director of photography, the art director — all the elements. In an ideal situation, the producer acted as the director's partner, offering advice on artistic matters while handling questions from the financiers and the problems that arise in the course of production.

Lucy Fisher always said that Peter Guber had "the best nose, a fantastic nose." He knew how to pick material, she said. "He's the bee with the pollen."

By October, Guber had put together a book, a screenwriter, a director, a leading man, and a promise to Warner Bros. that "Bonfire of the Vanities" would be ready for release in just over a year, by Christmas 1990. His departure left Brian De Palma, who became the film's de facto producer, fourteen months to make script revisions, to cast one hundred speaking parts — including all but one of the leads — to hire a crew, to find locations, to build sets, to shoot and edit the film, and to oversee its marketing. De Palma had never felt that kind of pressure, and that kind of power. He had never felt so alone.

Chapter 3

HEAD BANGERS

Perhaps it was inevitable that De Palma would end up in a high-profile, nastily competitive business like filmmaking, where one's accomplishments were judged publicly and often harshly — and a regular cycle of rejection and acceptance was an immutable fact of life. To his family, his films would seem like a running metaphoric autobiography. The ineffectual, manipulative psychologist married to one of the twins in "Sisters" has a large birthmark on his forehead, much like the birthmark over the eye of De Palma's brother Bruce. The townhouse office of the transsexual psychiatrist in "Dressed to Kill" was decorated almost exactly like the De Palma home. "Home Movies," a picture De Palma produced and directed when he taught a film class at Sarah Lawrence College, is the story of a teenage boy obsessed with catching his father in an adulterous act, just as De Palma was when he was in high school.

De Palma's family liked to tell an anecdote from the director's childhood that seemed to speak volumes about the personality of the man he would grow into. When De Palma was a toddler, he'd wake in the night, lift himself to his hands and knees, and start beating his head against the headboard of his crib. The force of the baby's banging head moved the crib across the room, right up against the wall that separated him from his parents. His two older brothers, sharing a room on the other side, were frightened by the noise — *boom, boom, boom*. It would stop only when their father would go into Brian's room.

Even then, Brian saw life as a perpetual contest for attention. The son of a depressed, overbearing mother and an aloof, physician father, De Palma spent his childhood in Philadelphia competing with his older brothers, Bruce — his parents' favorite — and Bart, who later claimed that Brian needed the struggle so badly that when it didn't exist, he created it.

Perhaps the battle started before he was born. Their mother Vivienne married Dip — the family nickname for Dr. Anthony De Palma — just after she graduated from high school. He was eleven years older than she and trying to establish himself as an orthopedic surgeon in the middle of the Depression. Her father was a lawyer; his was an immigrant hatter. The couple spent the early years of their marriage in Newark, New Jersey.

The eighteen-year-old Vivienne soon realized her husband's only passion was his work, and she decided to fill the empty hours with children. The oldest De Palma son, Bruce, was born a year after Dip and Vivienne married.

"I had Bruce and Bruce was *mine*," recalled Vivienne, who, even as a senior citizen, showed strong traces of the pretty girl she had been. "I had Bart because one of the girls I would push carriages with had had a child who'd inhaled a piece of carrot and died. Right then I decided I had to have another child. Bruce meant too much to me. So that's why I had Bart."

Having had one child for love and another for insurance, Vivienne didn't want to add another heir to her loveless marriage. But on September 11, 1940, Brian De Palma was born in Newark. "Brian was a mistake," she said. "Brian was a surprise. I didn't really want to have another child. He was a premature baby. He weighed four pounds when he was born. I was in labor for three days, too. He just didn't want to be born. He would scream and scream. When he couldn't talk, he would scream. I think he had to do it. It was his way of asking for attention."

Months before Brian turned two, his father went off to war and was away from home for four years. He spent more than half his time in the service on a hospital boat in the Pacific, following combat troops and collecting the casualties, a horrifying assortment of mangled bodies. By the time he returned he was a stranger in his own home. Dip — a man who could be coldly analytical yet also charming and emotional — didn't dwell on the distance between himself and his children. He was too busy. Not long after the war, his alma mater, Jefferson Medical College, asked him to move to Philadelphia from New Jersey and head the department of orthopedic surgery.

He excelled in the Machiavellian world of academic medicine. His sons, who occasionally visited him at work, remembered him as a general, marching through the hospital followed by a trail of functionaries — nurses, residents, medical students — all there to do his bidding. He'd leave the house at 7:30 in the morning and stay away until 10:30 or 11:00 at night. He'd come home, have a bite to eat, and then spend a few hours writing textbooks. That drive continued into old age: in 1989, when he was well into his eighties, he wrote a novel, a thriller called *The Anatomist*, the story of a brilliant doctor who becomes a murderer to satisfy his necrophiliac sexual urges.

The De Palma boys received no religious training apart from the Quaker philosophy taught at Friends Central in Philadelphia, the school each of them attended for twelve years. Friends Central was more than a school for the boys and for their mother. Vivienne spent nearly every day at Friends Central, and became so closely identified with its athletic program that one year she was even invited to the school's father-and-son dinner. The president of the boys' athletic association presented her — the only woman there that night — with a charm bracelet inscribed FROM THE BOYS. A little gold basketball, football, baseball, and tennis ball dangled from the gold links.

Vivienne's competitive spirit permeated the atmosphere at home. Meals were especially tense, bristling with psychological and verbal one-upmanship between the boys — but no yelling. Voices were never raised at the De Palmas'.

None of the children rebelled, not then, anyway. Like his brothers, Brian was a good boy of the fifties. They were privileged children who weren't permitted to take their privilege for granted. They worked all kinds of odd jobs; for example, Brian sold newspapers on the street, and he worked as a dockhand cleaning out toilets when the family summered at the Jersey shore. He didn't drink and he didn't smoke and he tried hard to please his parents. There was no overt sign of rebelliousness in the long record of accomplishments listed in his senior yearbook: he was president of the Service Committee and the Science Club; he worked on the yearbook, the chess team, the prom; he acted in the *Wizard of Oz* and *The Crucible;* he played varsity football and varsity tennis; he won first prize in the Delaware Valley Science Fair and second prize in the National Science Fair.

But none of these outstanding accomplishments proved sufficient to win him the attention and affection reserved for his brother Bruce. The science fair epitomized the impossibility of Brian's position at home. Bruce had been dubbed the family genius, and his genius manifested itself in science. When he took third place in the Philadelphia Science Fair, he was celebrated as a hero at school and, especially, at home.

Bart concentrated on excelling at things Bruce didn't seem to care about, art and athletics. Brian, however, couldn't resist the challenge. It was as though he were *compelled* to take Bruce on. He too had inherited his father's remarkable ability to concentrate and his doggedness, and he applied it all to his science fair project. Brian entered the Science Fair and won — more resoundingly than Bruce had won. As the yearbook correctly noted, he took first prize in the local competition and went to the national finals twice.

Yet his parents diminished his success. His father attributed Bruce's achievements to his "brilliant mind," to the fact that "Bruce had always been a very intellectual youngster right from the start." Brian, however, succeeded, in Dip's mind, because he was "a contending individual." This was one of the few matters Dip and Vivienne agreed on. "Brian was trying real hard to be Bruce," said his mother. "And he succeeded because he is a showman and Bruce is not. Brian has a natural gift, this ability to arrange things beautifully." Almost thirty-five years later, she was proud to remember the name of Brian's project: "The Application of Cybernetics to the Solution of Differential Equations."

The message to Brian was clear: He was style over substance and he would never be as good as Bruce in either his father's or his mother's eyes, especially his mother's. It would take him a very long time to stop trying.

After his brothers had already left for college, Brian was able to "prove" himself to the person who mattered most, his mother. Her long history of depression culminated in a suicide attempt a week after her husband moved out of the house, during the spring break of Brian's senior year in high school.

His mother turned to Brian, her only child left at home, as her confidant. She repeatedly told him that his father, who had returned home, was having an affair. Brian consulted with a friend's father, a divorce lawyer, and decided he had to catch his father *in the act* in order for his mother to obtain a divorce.

The summer after he graduated from high school, Brian worked as an assistant to an engineer doing computer research at the Burroughs Corporation in Philadelphia. He spent the weekdays at home with his father, and weekends with his mother at the family's vacation home on the Jersey shore. Before he left home on Fridays, Brian hooked the large reel-to-reel tape recorder his mother had gotten him for Christmas to the telephone system. He set the recorder on slow speed so he could tape the first three or four hours of telephone calls that were made after he left. All summer long he recorded his father's telephone calls.

Brian became obsessed with "helping" his mother. The seventeen-year-old had always had a vivid imagination, and his dramatic instincts had been developed further by the theatrical group he'd joined at school. On more than one occasion he climbed up a tree outside his father's office and snapped pictures of him and his nurse, with whom, De Palma's mother was sure, the doctor was having an affair. But his attempt to catch his father in flagrante delicto failed, and his mother still had no proof of his infidelity.

One night, fevered by his mission, Brian dressed himself all in black, and bought a .22-caliber rifle and a long knife. He imagined himself on the witness stand, testifying: "I couldn't help myself." Before he went to his father's office he reversed all the locks in the family's home to keep his father out.

He left the gun behind, having decided it was too big to carry. When he got to his father's office, he couldn't get the keys to work so he pounded at the double-paned glass doors until he broke through. With blood dripping from one hand and a knife in the other, he ran upstairs shouting, "Where is she? Where is she?"

"She" wasn't there, and Dip looked at his son as though he were insane. "You're crazy," he said. Brian went from floor to floor, rattling all the doors. Finally he found the suture nurse on the fourth floor. He remembered her cowering in a slip. She was terrified, as well she might have been at the sight of this teenage commando with his blood-covered hand. Uncertain of what to do next, Brian left, after telling his father, "I'll see you in court." From there he drove to the shore. By the time Brian arrived, Dip had already called his wife and told her what had happened.

Shortly afterward they separated, and would never live together again, though it would be years until they officially divorced. Dip married his suture nurse, and Vivienne married another doctor, and they all eventually retired to Florida, settling on opposite sides of the state.

A few months after the raid on his father's office, De Palma left Philadelphia for New York and Columbia University, and discovered film, women, and rebellion. A few years passed before his mother became aware of how much her son had changed, when she got a call one night from the New York City police, informing her that Brian had been arrested. Distraught because a girlfriend had left him, he got drunk, stole a motorcycle, and went for a joy ride. When he ignored a policeman's order to stop, the policeman shot him in the leg.

Brian spent the night in the hospital. His mother and his brother Bruce came to New York and bailed him out, and then found a lawyer who knew whom to pay off. The film student was sprung the next day. The few hours he spent in jail with other accused criminals waiting for arraignment scared him so much he was teary-eyed when he assured the judge he'd learned his lesson.

Thirty years later, on February 23, 1990, De Palma was going to face another judge, under entirely different circumstances. After lunch, Judge Burton Bennett Roberts, chief administrative judge of the Bronx, was going to take a break from the eleven thousand criminal and eighteen thousand civil cases currently pending in his jurisdiction, and the fifty-one judges who reported to him. That afternoon, Judge Roberts was going to drive downtown to audition for a part in "The Bonfire of the Vanities."

At sixty-seven years old, Judge Roberts was still robust and hungry for glory. He always gave the impression that no matter how much he succeeded, no matter how great his accumulation of power, it wasn't quite what he'd hoped for. Yes, he was the chief judge of one of the busiest courts in the country. But it was in the Bronx, no man's land in the eyes of many New Yorkers.

Today might be the day that Roberts could show at long last what he was born to be. Everyone who met him recognized immediately that whatever else he was, he was a great character, an astute showman with a natural instinct for what played and what didn't. He had already rehearsed in front of his friend Judge Lawrence Bernstein, and Bernstein told him he was terrific.

The judge had the feeling that today was going to be the day that he, Burton Bennett Roberts, was going to prove that he wasn't merely the toughest judge in New York and the most rambunctious — and, he felt, the most compassionate, and, he had to admit it, the most interesting. On that day he felt ready to demonstrate, once and for all, that he was ready for immortality. That he was nothing less than . . . the Jewish Spencer Tracy.

Roberts was auditioning for the part of Judge Myron Kovitsky. There would be a kind of justice in having Roberts play the part. It was Roberts, after all, who had inspired Tom Wolfe to write the book, and there were obvious parallels between Roberts and the fictional Kovitsky (as well as the devious district attorney, Abe Weiss). No one could accuse Roberts of grandstanding. There it was right up front, in the author's dedication: "And he wishes to express his deep appreciation to Burt Roberts, who first showed the way." On the flyleaf of Roberts's own personal copy, Wolfe had inscribed, "No words ever written are the equal of the gospel according to Burt."

Roberts had met Wolfe through a mutual friend, Herbert A. Allen, an investment banker who had controlled the board of Columbia Pictures. The judge had met Allen years before, back in the sixties, when Roberts was still working as a prosecutor in the Manhattan district attorney's office and meeting everyone who counted and wanted to be counted in New York Democratic politics. The red-haired, barrel-chested dynamo naturally gravitated to the rich and powerful, and he and Allen became friends. Fifteen years later, after Allen had become a force in the movie business, he invited Roberts, now a judge, to his Hamptons beach house to meet Tom Wolfe.

Wolfe had become a major celebrity with the success of his best-selling book about the astronauts, *The Right Stuff*, and he was casting around for ideas for his next book. He knew he wanted to write a work of fiction about New York, high and low, and the courts seemed like a good place for him to do research. He was taken with Roberts, and they arranged for Wolfe to watch the courts in session.

Wolfe started observing Roberts in action down at Centre Street, in Manhattan, sitting at his elbow as Roberts sat with lawyers and worked out pleas. When Roberts was transferred to the Bronx, the writer went with him.

Almost a decade after he first met Roberts, Wolfe published *The Bonfire of the Vanities* in 1987. The book wasn't exactly what Roberts had been expecting. He thought the novel was brilliant but heartless, an overly cynical vision of New York as a place overrun by greed and duplicity at every level, with no redemption in sight, anywhere. Roberts was put off by the book's unrelenting pessimism and a little annoyed by the portrayal of Kovitsky.

Wolfe had depicted the judge who roared with Old Testament wrath as a little old bald man who drove a decrepit car. Though he was the only character in the book who retained a shred of decency, Kovitsky was a bit of a pig as well, a man who responded to prisoners taunting him with, as Wolfe put it, "a prodigious gob of spit."

The judge didn't see how anyone could read Wolfe's description of that gruesome little judge and believe that he was inspired by Roberts. Judge Roberts wasn't a tiny little man. He had a powerful physique, dressed in dignified pinstripes, and drove a dark gray, late-model Audi. And he didn't spit in public.

Not that Burton Roberts was averse to playing the wild man. As a prosecutor in Manhattan, then in the Bronx, he had lunged at organized crime and police corruption like a hungry dog, and then made sure photographers were there to watch him devour the spoils. The press adored him and happily recorded the legend he was building around himself. "The Golden Cockerel of the Courts," they called him. "See him whirl around, stomp, march, curse, threaten, croon, cajole, charm," swooned a *New York* magazine caption writer in 1969, three years after Burton Roberts had been elected district attorney of the Bronx.

He was a great character, a journalist's dream, a great D.A., and even better copy. Who could forget the story of his prosecuting a bunch of gypsies in the early sixties for swindling. In the courtroom the gypsies tried to scare him by spitting at him and screaming, "We curse you to die! We curse you never to marry! We curse your children if you ever have any!" Roberts responded by cursing them right back. He stuck his index finger and little finger into the air in an ancient hex sign and screamed, "I'll give you the oldest curse in the world! It's two thousand years old! It's the Jewish curse!" Then he hissed at them, with the force of an exploded steam pipe. The gypsies ducked behind the benches.

But many people had forgotten. The Bronx County Building, which housed his courthouse, had once been the pinnacle of the Grand Concourse, the Jewish Park Avenue of the Bronx. A vast limestone building decorated with sculpture and bas-relief figures celebrating Religion, Justice, Commerce, Industry, Agriculture, and the Rights of Man, it was a gleaming 1930s monument to the promise of big government. But inside, the marbled lobby was dingy, and the maze of hallways was dark and smelled of ammonia. Now it seemed very much the way Tom Wolfe described it, a fortress of the white criminal justice system that was vainly trying to process unmanageable numbers of criminals, most of them black and Hispanic. Except for a few holdouts, the Jews were long gone; the Grand Concourse had become a war zone. Crack was the number one industry. Judge Roberts's car had been broken into twice, right outside the courthouse, in broad daylight.

Roberts wanted recognition — beyond the plaques shining proudly on the wood-paneled wall of his office — for all he'd done, dealing day after day, year after year, with the dregs and their victims. He wanted people to remember his glory days, and "Bonfire" seemed like the perfect vehicle.

His friend Judge Bernstein agreed to go along with him to the audition, scheduled for 1:30 that chilly February 23. As he left his office that afternoon, he glanced at a framed copy of the November 23, 1969, edition of the *New York Sunday News*. The twenty-year-old clipping was dry and crinkly, but the sentiment expressed in it remained fresh for Roberts, particularly on this day. An infatuated writer named May Okun began her "Personalities in the News" piece about Roberts like this: "If you were typecasting a tough but diamond-in-the-rough D.A. for a movie or a TV series, after no more than a glance and an exchange of greeting you'd be sure you had your man in Bronx County D.A. Burton Bennett Roberts."

Roberts pretended that the "Bonfire" audition was a lark, that he was just going downtown to give the director some guidance, as a courtesy. But in his heart of hearts he knew no one could play Kovitsky better than he could.

Judge Roberts's destination that day was twelve and a half miles south of the Bronx County Building, the Tribeca section of Manhattan, a designation that hadn't existed twenty years before. In some ways the city of New York has always resembled a giant movie set: neighborhoods are constantly being dismantled and reassembled as something else entirely. Tribeca had been dreamed up in the 1970s by a clever real estate man who recognized the potential for residential development in this warehouse and manufacturing district. The area had already been invaded by artists and young professionals who wanted to feel somewhat bohemian but in a comfortable way, and who could no longer afford Soho.

All the area needed was a name to define it the way Soho — South of Houston Street — had been imprinted onto the blocks that lay between the southern part of Greenwich Village and Little Italy. So too was Tribeca — the Triangle Below Canal Street — differentiated from the rest of Lower Manhattan by its acronym. The old commodities trading houses in the district offered architectural challenges to yuppies with a spirit of adventure and a desire for vast interiors to live in.

By 1990 Tribeca had become very chic. The director Martin Scorsese lived in the area for a time, and his friend the actor Robert De Niro still did. When the Martinson Coffee factory stopped processing beans in the red-brick, eight-story building at 375 Greenwich Street in De Niro's neighborhood, the actor decided to go into the movie business the way the old moguls had, by way of real estate. With a group of partners, De Niro bought this building at 375 Greenwich Street and established the Tribeca Film Center. De Niro's own production company occupied three floors, Miramax, a production and distribution company, bought one floor, and the rest was rented out to independent producers. The ground floor of this Hollywood-on-the-Hudson was being converted into a restaurant owned by De Niro and many other celebrities, including the actors Bill Murray, Sean Penn, and Christopher Walken, and the ballet star Mikhail Baryshnikov.

One of the first tenants to occupy the Tribeca Film Center was the production company for "Bonfire of the Vanities," which would spread over three floors in the building for six months. As the "Bonfire" crew moved in, workmen were still laying carpet in the atrium lobby on the seventh floor of the building. The restaurant downstairs, Tribeca Grill, wasn't yet completed, and the Polish-language posters from De Niro's movies which would eventually decorate the lobby still hadn't been hung.

Monica Goldstein, De Palma's assistant, wearing jeans and a sweater and tortoiseshell glasses, was unpacking boxes when her work was interrupted by the production office coordinator, a thin, harried woman named Liz Nevin. "Dave Grusin won some Grammys and Fred wants to send a congratulations note," said Nevin. Nodding toward the empty director's chair sitting in the middle of the mess, Nevin said, "Maybe *he* wants to, too."

Dave Grusin would be composing the music for "Bonfire." Fred Caruso was the line producer. His duties covered everything from specific demands, like figuring out how many teamsters were required to transport people and equipment, to more intangible matters, like making sure that the movie's principals were made to feel that they mattered.

Goldstein's lips tightened a bit as she made a note. She had so much to do, and now, once again, she had to make De Palma look good. She was still an assistant and like assistants all over corporate America, but especially in Hollywood, orderly women like Nevin and Goldstein were quite accustomed to invisibly supplying the warm, personal touch on behalf of their bosses. Thousands of gifts and notes were passed back and forth by powerful people who didn't have a clue that they were being so very thoughtful.

Goldstein was thirty-two years old and had been De Palma's assistant for five years. The entertainment industry was bottom-heavy with bright, efficient women who might have excelled in businesses like insurance or retailing, which placed value on essential organizational skills. But those more pedestrian businesses didn't hold out hope, the way the entertainment business did, that a lowly assistant might discover the next hot rock group, or the perfect script that would lead her to the center of things. Who could tell? An assistant might even become a producer.

After graduating from high school Goldstein had worked here and there and eventually landed a job as assistant to an agent at the William Morris Agency. Assistants who wanted to move up the ladder felt compelled to be up-to-date on the theater and movies, so Goldstein spent most of her salary on tickets and her days feeling exhausted from all the shows and club hopping.

Goldstein left William Morris to work as a production assistant on the movie "Wise Guys," where she met De Palma. Since then, she kept telling herself, she was learning what she needed to know about the film business as she wrote De Palma's checks, screened his phone calls, made sure his refrigerator was stocked when he flew in from the Coast, and typed the scripts and notes he wrote by hand. She followed the director to Chicago to film "The Untouchables," and to Thailand for "Casualties of War." She relayed messages to and from some of the most important people in the business. She earned a good salary. For her work on "Bonfire" alone she would be paid almost $50,000.

But she wasn't happy. After all this time her relationship with De Palma remained unchanged. He didn't confide in her or ask her opinion. He barely said hello most days. He had never promised her anything more, but she kept hoping he would see her as more than a secretary, and that unfulfilled hope often felt like resentment. She was determined that by the time "Bonfire of the Vanities" was over she wouldn't be just an assistant anymore.

Goldstein was distracted from her filing when Lynn Stalmaster, the casting director, walked into the Tribeca office looking the way he had looked for the past several days — worried. Only six weeks remained until shooting was scheduled to begin, and a great many of the one hundred speaking parts for this mammoth production were as yet unfilled. He needed to talk to De Palma.

Goldstein was distracted again when a call came from Bruce

Willis. He was in New York until Tuesday and wanted to meet Tom Wolfe and to hang around reporters at the *New York Post*, to help him prepare for the part of Peter Fallow, the journalist. He too wanted the director.

As Goldstein was talking to Willis, De Palma arrived, wearing a tweed jacket with suede patches at the elbow. Goldstein mouthed "Bruce," and Brian De Palma took the phone. After the most perfunctory "how are you," he asked his star to meet him for dinner that evening at Il Cantinori, at six, in the Village.

De Palma huddled outside the office with Stalmaster for a few minutes, then returned just in time for a phone call from Lucy Fisher, the Warner Bros. executive in charge of the film. De Palma listened for a minute and then said, "Hey! All we can do is call the writer 73,000 times." He hung up and took a call from Mary Selway, the London casting agent. Stalmaster, who crept in quietly behind De Palma, asked Goldstein if he could monitor the call. Goldstein had been fighting the complicated new phone system all morning. "I have absolutely no idea," she said.

De Palma was explaining to Mary Selway in London what type of actress he wanted for the part of Judy McCoy, the socialite wife of Sherman McCoy. They had brought in Selway because in all of the United States the filmmakers hadn't been able to find an actress, so far, who suited their notion of a moneyed aristocrat. "They are the social X-rays," De Palma said in a flat voice, referring to Wolfe's sarcastic phrase. "They should be in their mid to late thirties. They should be tall. They should be thin, and they have to be able to play comedy. This can't come off as heavy handed, bitchy wife stuff." He told Selway that he would be flying to London Friday on the Concorde and staying two nights at the Savoy, and that he'd be able to look at seven or eight Judys on Saturday, at half-hour auditions.

Next, De Palma described what he was looking for in an actor to play Sir Gerry, the newspaper publisher modeled on Rupert Murdoch, the Australian empire builder. "He has to have a kind of power to him that's chilling. He has to have a physicality because I'm shooting these people as caricatures, grotesques. So I don't want someone normal looking, even if he's a great actor," said De Palma. "You can schedule them every fifteen minutes. It isn't so much the acting we're looking at but how they look. They have to carry a certain amount of weight." Then, in a dutiful voice, he said, as an afterthought, "Nice talking to you."

He asked Goldstein to get Tom Wolfe on the phone for Bruce Willis, and at 1:45, just as she was dialing, a young woman stuck her head in the office and said, "Judge Roberts is here for his 1:30 audition."

De Palma had been avoiding this day for weeks. The judge had nudged and nudged to get this audition, and when he got tired of nudging he had his friends nudge for him. Finally De Palma could no longer ignore the messages faithfully relayed by Goldstein. Messages like: "Judge Roberts called to tell you he and Tom Wolfe had lunch the other day and wanted to tell you they'd heard you tried out Joel Grey for the part of Kovitsky and did they laugh."

De Palma's response to that particular message had been curt. "Good, they laughed." At other times, he told Goldstein to send a message back. "Tell him I'm out of town." At last he succumbed because he had no other choice. He would have to test the judge for the part of Kovitsky because the judge had remained a good friend of Tom Wolfe. Even though the author had relinquished creative control when he sold his book to the movies, the studio executives and De Palma wanted the approval of the celebrated writer. The judge had other powerful friends it wouldn't do to offend as well — like Herbert Allen and Ray Stark, a producer who still retained an aura of power even though he was no longer a major force in the business.

De Palma walked out into the lobby, a two-story atrium that looked as if it belonged in a Hyatt Hotel. Judge Roberts and Judge Bernstein were waiting, with a group of slender black women wearing skimpy dresses, a few large black men, and a couple of little white girls. Only the judges, who weren't auditioning to play pimps or prostitutes or Park Avenue children, weren't studying scripts. De Palma shook hands with them and started walking very fast, as he always did, across the lobby toward the large, bare room he and Stalmaster were using for auditions. Judge Roberts, wearing a smart gray suit, white shirt, and lavender and blue tie, propelled himself forward to catch up. "Did you fly in from California for this?" he asked. De Palma laughed and kept walking.

The walls of the audition room had recently been painted a hard white; the functional wall-to-wall carpet was an equally impersonal blue. There was a video camera and a monitor, a few folding chairs scattered around the room, and a large square table covered by piles of eight-by-ten glossies of actors, résumés, and handwritten notes from actors begging for minor parts; one actor's face was obscured by a half-eaten sandwich, another's by a Styrofoam container of Thousand Island dressing congealing into a murky paste.

Judge Bernstein, a slender man with delicate fingers, sat at the table across from Stalmaster. Roberts stood at a small table set up in the front of the room, a few feet away from the video monitor. De Palma stood next to the young man operating the video camera.

"Should I wear my glasses?" Roberts spoke in the voice of someone accustomed to having large groups of people stand up when he entered a room. De Palma, deferentially, told him to do whatever felt comfortable.

The judge put on his glasses and then said in a mildly scolding tone, "Can I say one thing, Mr. De Palma, if I may? Now, I'm not being critical . . ."

De Palma, who was now sitting backward on a folding chair, his arms folded over the back, remained silent, though there was the slightest tensing in his back.

The judge continued, "This third scene is very unrealistic, if I may. No judge is going to . . . I understand poetic license in a movie, but no one is going to grab a gun . . ."

De Palma nodded politely.

Judge Roberts glanced at the video camera. "We're not filming yet?"

De Palma said, "No, this is a rehearsal." His voice sounded strained.

Judge Bernstein leaned back in his chair, looking amused. Clearly no one was expecting much.

Then the judge launched into his opening speech. He boomed with the intimidating bellow of a native New Yorker well versed in the art of intimidation.

"Let me explain something to you," growled the judge at the imaginary assistant district attorney who's just brought an improperly documented case before him. "This case is what we call a piece of shit. Which means, loosely translated, that you have no evidence."

Judge Bernstein smiled a little as he looked at the video monitor, then at his watch. It was 1:56. He'd heard this speech before, at one of Judge Roberts's spontaneous rehearsals. De Palma sat impassively.

Lynn Stalmaster, however, had leaned forward in his chair and his eyes had narrowed. He had the look of a pleasant lapdog who had suddenly been transformed into a hunter. His nostrils weren't quivering, exactly, but he looked as if he had caught the scent of something exciting.

Stalmaster had been in the business more than thirty years and was one of the most highly regarded casting directors in Hollywood, with credits that included "West Side Story," "The Graduate," and "Harold and Maude," as well as "The Untouchables." Stalmaster viewed his job as a giant metaphysical puzzle. At every audition he tried to imagine how the nervous men and women reading lines in a bare room would fit together on location, in costume and make-up, surrounded by other actors. A failed actor himself, this small, gentle man with the moon face and the honeyed voice had great sympathy for the endless parade of souls willing to court rejection over and over, sometimes just for the chance to appear on-screen for a few seconds in the part of a pimp. He took copious notes on everyone he saw and saved the notes in files, knowing that one day a part might come along for the actor he'd liked in New Orleans or Seattle or St. Louis, but who wasn't quite right at the time.

Now, watching Judge Roberts audition, Stalmaster felt the tingle that came along once in a great while, the sensation that he was seeing something he'd never seen before.

Stalmaster had come to this audition with no expectations whatsoever, and all of a sudden he felt quite emotional. He had never witnessed anything like Roberts, who stood before the casting director in a well-tailored suit, delivering his oration with a rich, roaring nasality. *That* could send a shock wave into the soul of the toughest criminal. He was terrific! He was Moses!

De Palma's reaction was more muted. He nodded and asked

Judge Roberts to move on to the Great White Defendant speech. Wolfe created the conceit of the speech to explain a fact of life: most of the prosecutors, judges, and defense attorneys holding the power in the Bronx were white, and most of the defendants they processed through the court system were not. In order to curry political favor with a mostly black and Hispanic constituency, Wolfe's fictional Bronx District Attorney Abe Weiss needed to convict a white defendant. The district attorney has made it clear to all his assistants that they will be rewarded for the successful prosecution of a white man, which is why it becomes so important to exploit Sherman McCoy's arrest. But the case before Judge Kovitsky has no merit; in the harshest language, Kovitsky lets the assistant district attorney know that he won't be party to this blatantly political attempt to throw a white man to the mob, not without sufficient evidence.

Judge Roberts played the scene with loud indignation. His howl of disdain shook his jowls and lit his eyes until they sparked like blue steel. Just as his righteous ferocity was amplifying to a magnificent explosion, De Palma held up his hand.

The judge looked confused, as though he couldn't believe what was happening. Had someone dared to interrupt *him*? His mouth remained open even though his oration had sputtered to an astonished silence.

"Do it again," De Palma muttered. No longer the respectful younger man, the director said testily, "This is a rehearsal. This is what movies are, Judge Roberts. Repetition. That was too much like a speech, pontifi—"

"Pontification." Judge Roberts had regained his composure. "Yeah, I got it."

He ran through the speech again, and this time he was even better, more authentic.

He had been performing for fifteen minutes, five minutes longer than the ten minutes De Palma had allotted for this courtesy call. When he finished, the director asked the judge to do the speech again. "Don't look up so much this time," he said.

Judge Roberts nodded enthusiastically, without offering any suggestions of his own. The dynamic in the room had perceptibly shifted. The judge no longer tried to outguess the director. He had become the supplicant, eager to please the man in charge. Without complaint or advice, he repeated the Great White Defendant speech.

Meanwhile, Judge Bernstein had pulled out his driver's license from his wallet and was studying it very closely. He pulled out another identification card and began comparing the two pictures as studiously as if he were going to be tested on them. He'd figured out quickly that a primary ingredient in the moviemaking process was tedium.

De Palma explained to Judge Roberts that at a certain point in the speech he had to shift gears: his tone had to indicate that the point of his lecture was to intimidate the assistant district attorney to whom he was speaking. The judge looked pixilated, enthralled with this game. "Go into second, yeah, uh, all right."

He began the "piece of shit" segment of the speech in a modulated tone. Then, as he moved into the Great White Defendant portion, he turned up the volume, and De Palma said, "Now!"

"Shift?" asked the judge.

"Yeah," said De Palma, who had started to smile. The judge shifted again, into overdrive. For a moment, the spare, sterile room seemed crowded, as though the sheer power of the judge's voice had created a mob for him to shout down.

De Palma smiled broadly. "That was very good." He laughed. "Very good."

The judge looked pleased with himself. "That good?"

Stalmaster nodded. "Good," he said.

Next came Judge Kovitsky's "I want some fucking order" speech, which Roberts managed quite effectively, even though he objected briefly to the word *fucking*, which he said no self-respecting judge would use. Judge Bernstein smiled, then laughed out loud when his friend roared, "I want some fucking order," as naturally as if he said such a thing every day.

At the end of the speech, Roberts said with some surprise in his voice, "You're a good director."

De Palma's only response was to laugh.

Stalmaster said, "You should have been an actor."

"I should've been an actor," agreed a jovial Roberts. "Spencer Tracy."

Stalmaster started to tell the judge about working on "Judgment at Nuremberg," and the judge interrupted to tell a story about his grandmother.

De Palma thanked the judge, and they stood a bit uncomfortably, like a couple returning from a first date uncertain whether the evening's events warranted a kiss or an awkward "This was pleasant."

The judge coyly asked De Palma who he was going to cast for the part.

"I don't know," said De Palma.

The judge brightened. "Really? How do I match up?"

De Palma, who had spent years perfecting the nonanswer, laughed and ushered the judges out the door. Forty-five minutes had gone by.

When the director stepped back into the audition room and met Stalmaster's eyes, they both howled.

"It's very tempting," said Stalmaster. "I *was* thinking Spencer Tracy all the time. He's an ethnic Spencer Tracy. He's got that power."

The video operator had cued up Judge Roberts's tape. Stalmaster and De Palma stared at the screen, and burst out laughing again when Roberts yelled "woiked up!"

"It's an honest reaction," said Stalmaster, with unusual enthusiasm for a man who had learned to keep his reactions muted. "The sound is *incredible*!"

De Palma was staring very quietly at the monitor and stroking his short, graying beard. Stalmaster, who specialized in reading faces, saw the troubled expression on the director's face and grasped immediately what he was thinking: How would Judge Roberts handle the conditions on the set, having to reproduce a scene over and over again on command? How many retakes would he endure before he lost enthusiasm for the game and started lecturing? De Palma didn't say a word. Stalmaster spoke for him, scolding himself in a mocking tone: "But Lynn! You don't have to be on the set with Judge Roberts . . ."

The jovial note was lost on De Palma, still intently watching the video monitor where Judge Roberts was lecturing: "Justice is what your grandmother taught you. It's in your bones."

De Palma suddenly snorted. "This doesn't work," he said. "This is the most important speech in the whole thing. The judge is authentic, but is he *likable*. You've got to bring out the *compassion*. That's why I wanted Walter Matthau."

But Walter Matthau had asked $1 million for the eight days or so it would take to film Judge Kovitsky's scenes, and that was more than the studio was willing to pay. Alan Arkin, who had auditioned by videotape, was not only likable but was willing to play the part for $120,000.

Stalmaster, now businesslike, asked, "Is Alan the final word?"

De Palma stared at the blank video screen. "Yeah, I think so."

With dramatic emphasis Stalmaster tapped on somebody's eight-by-ten glossy and said, "Alan Arkin is Judge Kovitsky."

Fred Caruso was delighted to hear that De Palma had opted for the less expensive star in his choice for Judge Kovitsky. It was Caruso's job to work out a budget for "Bonfire" and then keep the film within it.

When Peter Guber left Warner Bros., De Palma had taken on the title of producer to compensate for his additional responsibilities, and he had hired Fred Caruso as coproducer. Caruso managed the film day to day, making sure locations were secured, crews were hired, stars were kept satisfied. Though Caruso had to be familiar with all the artistic decisions and technical considerations to do his job, he wasn't directly responsible to the studio for the consequences of those decisions. He wasn't the *producer*. That was De Palma's job.

Still, Caruso knew that for the sixty-seven days currently scheduled for the shoot, he'd be getting sixty-seven phone calls a day from the studio. In reality, when there was a problem, the director was the call of last resort. When the budget ran over, and it inevitably would, it wouldn't be the star director who would be called on the carpet. No one could afford that because the star director could just decide to sulk a day or two, while the $130,000-a-day clock was ticking, or he could decide he really needed that extra take that pushed the production into overtime and sent the budget up a million dollars within a week. No, it was better not to disturb the director, even when he was the producer, unless it was absolutely necessary. That's why there had to be an underling who took it on the chin. There had to be a fall guy, and Caruso was fully aware, right from the start, that being the fall guy was his job.

It had been clear to Caruso that nothing would be simple with this movie since the day he had started looking for locations in New York in the fall of 1989. Many of the people Tom Wolfe parodied in his roman à clef took the work of fiction quite seriously, and quite personally, as an insult. It was always tricky convincing the managers of large public places that film crews wouldn't destroy their property; now Caruso had to deal with wounded feelings as well.

The American Museum of Natural History, a proposed film site, turned him down because, he was told, the people who were mocked by Wolfe donated money to the museum and they might not feel so generous next year if the board implicitly approved *Bonfire* by allowing the movie version to be filmed there. Period. End of conversation.

Caruso was thrown out of Temple Emanu-El, the Fifth Avenue synagogue that served the "Our Crowd" crowd, the old-line German Jewish aristocracy. He and his location manager thought Emanu-El, with its lovely rose stained-glass windows, would be perfect for the funeral scene.

When Caruso sent his request to the temple, he did not specifically name the movie to be filmed. The rabbi had invited him down to discuss the project.

"Come in," said the rabbi. "What's the name of the movie?"

"It's a Warner Bros. picture, gonna star Tom Hanks . . ." Caruso was hoping maybe he wouldn't actually have to reveal the name.

"What's the name of the movie?"

"And Bruce Willis . . ."

"Yes, but the name of the movie?"

"Bonfire of the Vanities."

"*Out!* You can't be here. Out! We don't want you here. Out!"

The rabbi said, or at least Caruso remembered him saying, "All of them Jews that are in this book are in this synagogue. They know who they are and Tom Wolfe wrote about them. They're all here. The X-rays and so on. Out!"

Fred Caruso was unfazed. Insults and evictions had become commonplace to him in the twenty-three years he had worked in the movie industry.

And he enjoyed every minute of it. The son of immigrant parents, Caruso grew up in Newark, New Jersey, and was married and had three kids by the time he reached the age of twenty-seven. He'd spent seven years as band director and orchestra leader for the Monmouth, New Jersey, Regional High School and had enjoyed every minute of that too — especially conducting the majorettes in those cute little skirts. He had four hundred kids in his program and then the budget was cut. He decided to get out.

He sent a hundred letters to producers, directors, studio executives, television stations, and record producers. "Exposure is the secret to success," the letters began. "Let me tell you about myself." For weeks no one responded. Then Otto Preminger's secretary in New York called and told Caruso to come for an interview. Caruso bought new socks, a new tie, new shoes, and new underwear. Feeling so starched he could barely move, he drove into Manhattan to meet Preminger. The director was blunt. "You're too old, you're married with a family, you don't have any skills, no connections, and you're not Jewish," he said. "There's nothing I can do for you." The only other thing Caruso remembered about the meeting was that Preminger's office wasn't decorated with posters of his movies but with Picassos and Mirós.

But Preminger did do something for Caruso. He told the music teacher he could travel to Baton Rouge, Louisiana, and work as an unpaid observer on the set of "Hurry Sundown," a lurid melodrama about race relations in the South starring Michael Caine and Jane Fonda. Caruso borrowed two hundred dollars from his brother-in-law and took a thirty-six-hour train ride to Baton Rouge from Newark and introduced himself to the film's music composer. After several days of hanging around with the composer, spending his own money, Caruso offered to write a song about catfish and tadpoles for the picture. Preminger liked it and paid Caruso two hundred dollars for the song, and then hired him as a production assistant for fifty dollars a week.

Caruso stayed close to the production office, the movie's nerve center. He learned to read upside down and how to make himself indispensable for whatever needed doing. He became friends with the first assistant director, Burtt Harris, who went on to produce for the director Sidney Lumet, and Harris got him his next job. Caruso was out of Monmouth High forever.

Over the next few years, he worked all kinds of jobs on various films — location scout, associate producer — and was hired as production manager for Francis Coppola's "The Godfather." That put him directly in charge of the day-to-day business of filming. After that he wasn't afraid of anything or anybody. He'd handled some rough people and worked the streets of New York, and he treated everybody with the same easy charm, no matter how high their position or how low. He had a good reputation in the business, but he made the studios nervous. In a business where hysteria was considered a show of interest, Caruso's unflappable style was considered suspect.

This dark-eyed ameliorator wore his black hair slicked back to a little duck tail, and he had a tendency to hug people he liked. He'd made himself a success in the movie business even though he'd avoided Hollywood as much as possible, even keeping his family in New Jersey. Caruso was part psychologist, part manager, and part con artist, and he'd worked on some of the biggest pictures ever made and some of the toughest. He had an impressive list of credits, including "Once Upon a Time in America" and "Blue Velvet," in addition to "The Godfather," and he'd worked with De Palma on three previous films: "Dressed to Kill," "Blow Out," and "Casualties of War." He admired De Palma's work and liked to be part of it, even though the director was demanding and rarely openly appreciative. They never socialized.

As coproducer on "Bonfire," Caruso spent day after day in the office he shared with Monica Goldstein at the Tribeca Film Center working out the schedule so he could plan a realistic budget. There had been so many schedules already. De Palma and Michael Cristofer kept revising the script, and every new version altered the schedule.

The major stars added more complications. Melanie Griffith wouldn't be available until May because she was finishing "Pacific

Heights." Bruce Willis had to be off the picture by July 9 so he could move on to "Hudson Hawk," which would be filmed in Europe.

The "start date" had already been postponed twice, as everything took longer than expected. Now, Friday, April 13, was set for the first day of shooting, and there could be no more delay if they hoped to make a Christmas release. They would have only seventeen weeks from the time shooting was completed in July until it was time to put the picture in theaters. And that was if everything went according to schedule, a big if, as the studio had already shaved two weeks off the time De Palma said he needed.

It wasn't impossible, Caruso thought. It would just seem that way. He predicted that everything would have to be double-teamed: the editors, the sound people, all the assistants, and all their equipment. The crew would have to work six days a week for most of the sixty-six shooting days the studio said the shoot should be limited to (and which Caruso and De Palma had already increased to sixty-seven days).

The tension in the air was palpable at the Tribeca Film Center, where the steady drone of work had started to crackle with flashes of panic as the first day of principal photography approached. After sitting in limbo at Warner Bros. for a year, and in development for another year, "Bonfire" had suddenly become an urgent project, with the urgency becoming more pronounced with every million added to the budget. The movie had become expensive inventory, and the studio wanted to get it off the books as quickly as possible. They wanted that Christmas release. The clock was ticking, more insistently by the minute.

But with only six weeks left before production began, everything was still in flux: the script, the cast, the schedule, the locations, and the budget. The only thing that was certain was the feeling that this wasn't going to be an ordinary movie. "Bonfire" was already bigger than life. There was no escaping the fact that this literary phenomenon had itself become, to use Tom Wolfe's phrase, "something else." This *something else* was no longer merely a good book, a huge best seller. This *something else* had been transmogrified into everything that was perverse and destructive and . . . silly about modern-day life. It had become the perfect shorthand for decadence, greed, manipulation, and ambition. Even the much-publicized marital problems of billionaire Donald Trump and his wife, Ivana, were heralded in the tabloids as "Bonfire of the Inanities."

Already, everyone working on the film, from the lowliest production assistant up to De Palma himself, had the sense that they were working on something monumental. They couldn't articulate exactly what this particular *something else* was, but down at the production office in lower Manhattan, it was repeated again and again, a declarative sentence spoken with great emphasis, and exasperation: "This . . . is . . . 'The . . . Bonfire . . . of . . . the . . . Vanities.' "

Chapter 4

THE MAGIC HOUR

To a driver approaching the southernmost tip of Manhattan, a strange Oz appears to rise out of the Hudson River less than a mile north of the Staten Island Ferry landing and a few blocks west of Wall Street. A corporate Disneyland stands there on the landfill that serves as the foundation of New York's newest neighborhood, Battery Park City. The four towers of the World Financial Center, architect Cesar Pelli's glass and marble monuments to capitalism, serve as the commercial hub for this feat of urban planning, entirely removed from the grime and noise and crowds of New York. The make-believe atmosphere of Battery Park City seems more akin in spirit to the backlots of Burbank, twenty-five hundred miles away, than to Brooklyn or the Bronx, or even the rest of Manhattan.

The towers serve as corporate headquarters to three symbols of the American free enterprise system: American Express, Dow Jones & Company (publishers of the *Wall Street Journal*), and Merrill Lynch. The centerpiece is the Winter Garden, the enormous glass-domed public space where sixteen desert palms rise up forty-five feet out of the marble floor. The palms were brought in at great cost all the way from Borrego Springs in the southern California desert. The Winter Garden forms a central courtyard for an expansive network of offices and elegant shops — Tahari, Barneys, Rizzoli. The businesspeople who work in this hothouse universe can dine al fresco, in facsimile, all year round, in "outdoor" cafés built under glass. Here they are protected from the weather and from the fear of being bothered by pigeons or panhandlers.

On February 27, 1990, well before shooting was to begin, Tom

Hanks entered this pristine enclave through the revolving doors of the north tower. The purpose of the actor's excursion downtown was "research." He wanted to visit the bond trading room at Merrill Lynch, which would be a location for shooting, so that he could experience the world of the bond salesman Sherman McCoy. He'd already visited Yale University, McCoy's alma mater.

Though Hanks, a pragmatic man, actually believed that actors could simply *pretend* to be somebody else, it was no longer acceptable to embark on a role without doing research, not since Robert De Niro made it a point of honor to try actually to live in somebody else's skin. De Niro had become a fat blob to play Jake La Motta in "Raging Bull," and learned to play the saxophone for "New York, New York" (though not for the soundtrack). At least "Bonfire" wasn't a war movie: Hanks wouldn't have to enlist in boot camp for a couple of weeks. He had, however, had his teeth capped, to make them appear more "aristocratic," and he'd toyed with the idea of cosmetic enhancements meant to give his nose a more regal slope. That experiment was abandoned.

Hanks rarely complained openly about these requirements of his profession, which he felt were somewhat extraneous, but as he headed downtown to watch the bond traders work he felt a little silly. He was fully dedicated to the appearance of unpretentiousness at all times. He'd even refused the stretch limousine the studio offered and traveled in a plain black sedan — exactly like the cars that stood at the ready outside the brokerage firms, waiting to take the stock brokers and traders uptown at the end of the day.

Two Merrill Lynch executives with portentous titles greeted Hanks upstairs in the executive offices. Fred Yager, a tall hulking man, was Vice President of Corporate Staff, Manager of Consumer Markets and Media Relations; Daniel T. Napoli, a little man with large expressive eyes, was Senior Vice President, Director of Global Risk Management. One of Yager's assistants, a tall blonde woman, gaped at Hanks until she saw one of the location scouts laughing at her expression. The blonde shrugged. "Dan Napoli's considered the best-looking guy here. You see what we're dealing with."

Napoli and Yager, both dressed in pinstriped suits, led Hanks toward a bank of elevators and past a giant cafeteria where lunches were being placed into little cardboard boxes decorated with a cutout of the World Financial Center. Napoli explained that lunches are served to the bond traders so they don't have to leave their desks. Hanks didn't seem to register the importance of this. Napoli handed Hanks a box lunch.

As Yager was explaining that Merrill Lynch's trading room had been the world's largest until the Japanese built a bigger one, he opened the doors onto a cavernous blur of white. Hanks blinked at the white walls and the white fluorescent lights, and at the hundreds of young men in suit pants and white shirts scurrying around in a purposeful frenzy. There were a few women in suits as well; they tended to keep their jackets on. The women seemed to fall into two groups: the ones wearing suits with a Brooks Brothers cut and knee-length skirts tended to have neatly trimmed hair; the others, wearing cheaper suits with very short skirts, tended to wear their hair long and wild. The women wearing the knee-length skirts were traders; the women with the short skirts and big hair were clerks.

The room vibrated with a giant hum, the muted chorus produced by six hundred voices murmuring into telephones and thousands of fingers typing on computer terminals. Up on the wall one set of digital lights carried stock quotes, and another the news of the minute. Napoli explained that $22 billion of securities were traded on this floor every day, and that the twenty-two people working with Pat Rothstein, the trader Hanks was there to see, accounted for about 50 percent of the volume. Most of them were M.B.A.'s, Ivy Leaguers; their average age was twenty-eight.

Rothstein, however, was thirty-eight, the same age as Sherman McCoy. Unlike Sherman, though, he was a trader, not a salesman. Actually, said Napoli, thirty-eight was old for a trader. "Burnout," he explained. What Napoli was really saying to Hanks was this: "You're spending the afternoon hanging out with the wrong person."

Pat Rothstein was a tall, thin man with small features and little, sleepy eyes; his left arm was injured and rested in a sling. His desk sat in the middle of one of the endless rows of terminals and traders. As Yager and Napoli guided Hanks toward Rothstein's place, the room's comfortable hum contorted, as though an impudent drumroll had interrupted a minuet. Suddenly the aisle in front of Hanks was filled with women in short skirts and big hair, all crowding toward Pat Rothstein's desk.

Without a whisper of warning, the celebrity had been sniffed out within minutes of his arrival, as though the digital monitor blinking out the stock quotes had suddenly started flashing: MOVIE STAR! MOVIE STAR!

Napoli and Yager stood by helplessly. They didn't know what to do. But Hanks did. He started asking for names and signing the pieces of paper thrust in front of him.

The Merrill Lynch men recovered and placed themselves on either side of Rothstein and Hanks, to allow the two men to exchange information as casually as they could as the aisles all around them filled with gawkers. Napoli stared at the cluster of women at the end of the aisle and recognized a few of them. "Jeez, they're coming from the sixteenth floor. A different elevator bank. They're switching *elevators* to come here."

Nearby, a young Indian trader bent intently into the mouthpiece of his phone, looking as though he were in possession of the year's most lucrative trading tip. "Yeah, Tom Hanks is here today and all hell has broken loose," he was whispering. "I walked in and thought . . . I don't know what."

Yager, the media relations man, looked incredulously at Napoli, as the two men held back the mob. "This is what it was like when Walter Cronkite came by," he said.

"No, it isn't," said Napoli. "Cronkite was nothing like this! We've had a Soviet delegation come through here, we've had the entire team of the New York Giants! No one picked up their heads! This is amazing!"

Pat Rothstein ignored the commotion and explained what he did for a living to Hanks, who kept a mild, indecipherable expression on his face. The trader spoke in a philosophical way. "The fabric of this business is ephemeral," said Rothstein. "There is no fabric. It isn't just get rich quick. It's get everything quick. There is no building of anything."

Rothstein talked to Hanks about the markets in Chicago and Hong Kong and explained how when the price of gold goes down, the fixed securities go up. Hanks stared contemplatively at the screen. After a pause, he asked, "Is there a dress code here? Or does everyone gravitate . . ."

Rothstein grinned. "I take a lot of shit for my blue shirts. The one thing you don't want to look like is a yuppie."

Hanks nodded.

At 1:45 Hanks opened the box lunch Merrill Lynch had supplied for him. He pulled the plastic wrap off the little plastic plate of celery and carrot sticks and chewed on a celery stick. He sipped the Diet Coke and nibbled the turkey sandwich, but gave the small bag of Fritos to the plump trader sitting on the other side of Rothstein.

Suddenly the steady hum in the room amplified into a noisy rumble. Had another celebrity walked in? In a way, yes. The digital ticker tape had just relayed the news that Drexel Burnham Lambert had gone belly up. The investment banking firm that symbolized the excess of the eighties, the corporate counterpart of Sherman McCoy, was filing for bankruptcy protection.

Hanks seemed impatient for the noise to die down. He had a question. Napoli smiled sympathetically as he waited for the buzz to settle, his eyebrows raised to indicate that he was ready to explain the fine points of junk bonds, to analyze the significance of Drexel Burnham's financial troubles. Within a minute or two the traders had shifted their collective attention to the next thing, and Hanks could be heard.

"Is there a shoeshine man on the floor?" he asked.

Now it was Napoli's turn to put on the uncomprehending look. Hanks explained: Sherman has his shoes shined while he's working the phones.

Napoli nodded enthusiastically. "Yeah, we've got 'em, just like in the book." He surveyed the vast room, but no shoeshine man seemed to be in evidence. "It's like a cab in the rain — never there when you need 'em. Usually the place is *crawling* with shoeshine guys."

He yelled across the room: "*Any shoeshine guys around?*" When no one responded, he grinned and shrugged his shoulders. "The women won't let them in."

Finally a shoeshine man was located and dragged over to shine Hanks's shoes. While the thin, nervous little man worked with his polish and rags, Hanks asked Rothstein how often he got his shoes shined.

"A couple times a week . . . Where'd you get your shoes?" Rothstein looked at Hanks's black leather running shoes, then glanced up at his black jeans, black shirt, and black blazer.

"I stole them from Costume. Let's see. The jacket's from 'Dragnet,' the pants are from 'Turner and Hooch'. . ."

Hanks was interrupted by the young man next to Rothstein who hadn't made a trade since the movie star arrived. "You were great in 'Dragnet,' " he said.

"That was a hideous movie," said Hanks in his friendly way, his left shoe now up on the shoeshine rack. "If it had been good it would've made $100 million."

Hanks wasn't aware that three months of negotiations had preceded his visit and the agreement to use the Merrill Lynch office in the film. De Palma wanted everything big, outsized, and the "Bonfire" location scouts had determined, after months of looking, that Merrill's was the most impressive trading room in the city. None of the brokerage firms were keen to be associated with Wolfe's book, not even Merrill Lynch, which had earned millions as one of the principal financers of the Time-Warner merger.

The location scouts had met several times with Yager and other Merrill Lynch officials, and so had their bosses, the production manager, Peter Runfolo, and his boss, Fred Caruso. In addition to $135,000 to cover Merrill's expenses, Yager required several things before he and his superiors would break Merrill's prohibition against allowing movie crews to film on the brokerage firm's premises. He wanted a personal letter from Time-Warner chairman Steven J. Ross to the chairman of Merrill Lynch, script approval, and a guarantee of secrecy. Merrill Lynch's name was not to be mentioned.

Ross's letter was dispatched to William A. Schreyer, chairman and C.E.O. of Merrill Lynch, on February 22, five days before Hanks's visit. The letter, which began "Dear Bill" and ended "With best regards, Steve," was an impersonal request for permission to film, with assurances that "all insurance, legal and financial arrangements will be mutually agreed upon."

Napoli told Yager he figured 70 percent of the people in the room had read *Bonfire of the Vanities.* Yager said that Merrill Lynch had turned down many movie companies in the past. "But I read the script on this one and it seemed okay. I'd been worried about the racist stuff, but most of that's been toned down."

Hanks nodded as he glanced at the numbers on Rothstein's computer terminal, without comprehension.

Rothstein said, "I told my wife about this and she said, 'Keep a million miles away from it. The last thing you need is to be associated with that fucking book.' She hates this business."

A broker walked up to Hanks and said, "I have a trader here on the phone from the Bank of Dallas who said she'll do $100 million if you tell her to. Just say, 'Do $100 million at one.' "

Hanks took the phone and put his hand over the mouthpiece. "What's her name?"

"Hello, Betty," he said cheerily. "Yes, yes, it's me. Betty, do $100 million at one . . . Yes, yes. All right, Betty." He handed back the phone.

By 3:15 Hanks had had enough. He'd gone there to learn something and ended up talking to somebody's friend on the phone. Once again he had confirmation of the value of just pretending. As he left he shook hands with Rothstein. "Hey, hope that flipper's better soon," he said, nodding at the trader's injured arm. "Catch you at the game sometime!"

He waved at the gaggle of young women pressed up against the glass at the visitors' gallery overlooking the trading floor and headed down to the lobby with a location scout. They passed a group of firemen who had been called in to answer one of the numerous false alarms that had plagued the tenants of this new building ever since they'd moved in a year before. One of the fireman spotted Hanks and yelled, "Hey, Tom!"

Soon all the firemen turned around and started waving. "Hey, Tom! Hey, Tom!"

Hanks waved back. "Shouldn't you see about that fire, guys?" he asked, and disappeared out the revolving doors.

As preparations for the actual shoot accelerated, things seemed to be falling into place. On March 5, the Warner Bros. people in "creative" sent De Palma an updated copy of the most recent script evaluation sent to "file."

"The script is great," declared creative, with a caveat: "It is still

too long and has some moments that lag or are repetitious."
Creative's three pages of suggestions included cutting a scene showing District Attorney Abe Weiss sitting on the toilet and getting rid
of a scene that implicates Annie Lamb, the mother of the hit-and-
run victim, Henry Lamb, as yet another of the opportunists trying
to gain from Henry's tragedy.

On March 7, a cold evening, De Palma set out to do some research
of his own. For months his location scouts had been covering the
Bronx to find the streets they'd designated Prostitute Street and
Desolation Street. These would be the sites of two critical sequences: Sherman and Maria's initial foray into the unknown
territory of the Bronx and the hit-and-run accident. The studio had
impressed upon De Palma the importance of making the Bronx
seem threatening, a war zone populated by terrifying people, alien
beings. The executives wanted the audience to understand that
Sherman McCoy had good reason to think Henry Lamb and his
friend were trying to mug him — though Tom Wolfe had deliberately left the question of whether or not the boys were potential
muggers unclear in the scene. The writer's point was that to someone like Sherman McCoy every young black man was a potential
mugger.

The studio saw it differently. Lucy Fisher said, "I wanted to
make sure that Sherman was threatened, that he had a very good
reason for dashing his car out of there. To panic. I didn't want him
to be so — pardon the word — *racist*, that when he sees a black
person he immediately has to gun his car. I wanted it to be so scary
that were most people in his shoes they would also be nervous
because it was just so alien, that these people looked like they were
going to hurt him."

De Palma and his top lieutenants were going to visit the sites for
Desolation Street and Prostitute Street which had been approved
by Richard Sylbert, his production designer. Before the director met
the others in front of the Regency Hotel, where the out-of-town
crew would be staying during the shoot, he stopped at the Costume
Depot on Twenty-second Street, for a brief conference with Ann
Roth, the costume designer.

The loft where Roth worked was crowded with racks and racks

of dresses and suits, as well as a washer and dryer. On a table were an electric burner, grapes, a box of saltines, and several empty takeout Chinese food containers.

Ann Roth greeted De Palma affectionately as he stepped off the creaky elevator.

"Did you just get your hair cut?"

"No," he said, as she reached up to straighten the fur collar on his Eddie Bauer parka. She was always straightening somebody's collar.

Roth, a small, brisk woman in late middle age with short blonde hair, was wearing loose gray pants and a comfortable sweater. Always in motion, she resembled an elegant pheasant on amphetamines. The costume designer prided herself on her powers of observation. She knew something was different about De Palma, whom she'd last worked with on "Blow Out," a decade earlier. She couldn't be faulted for failing to recognize immediately the weight loss hidden beneath the director's bulky parka.

De Palma had stopped by to discuss the evening gowns for one of the film's big set pieces, a society ball.

Roth led De Palma past the clothing racks to a desk where she propped a large board to which she'd stuck swatches of glittery fabric and pictures cut from the pages of fashion magazines and the *New York Times* society section.

"Vilmos is going to light this like it's sunset at the Sphinx," said De Palma, referring to his cinematographer, Vilmos Zsigmond. "Gold."

Roth pulled a spangled dress off the rack.

De Palma glanced at the dress. "I was watching an old Rita Hayworth movie," he said. "She was wearing a forties jacket with lots of sparkle on it so every time she turns, she sparkles. I thought Melanie could wear something like that at the ball. She's supposed to sparkle."

Roth nodded thoughtfully, then showed De Palma some of her other costume ideas. She pulled out the "little black number" she thought Maria should wear to her husband's funeral, and then pulled out a pair of very red Yves St. Laurent shoes with dangerously high heels.

"Aren't these positively wicked?" Roth looked delighted. De

Palma gave a polite smile that indicated that, while he understood the importance of wicked shoes, this wasn't a subject that lit his passion.

Roth asked De Palma whether she should come to the location scout in the Bronx that night. He told her the van would be leaving the Regency at 7:15 P.M., in forty-five minutes.

"Is it going to be a bloodbath up there?" Roth asked.

Ann Roth, who had a flair for the dramatic, had grown up on a farm in Pennsylvania and decided to become a costume designer at the age of sixteen. After graduating from Carnegie Tech in 1953, she headed for Hollywood and a job with the Western Costume Company, which then made costumes for big-budget movies. She was the intermediary between the clothes manufacturer and the costume designers for "Oklahoma!," "Around the World in 80 Days," and "Guys and Dolls."

The work was exciting and the pay was good — good enough for her to splurge on a white MG sports car. But when she got an offer to work for the legendary Broadway costume designer Irene Sharaf, she sold the MG and headed back East. After that she alternated between film and theater work and never lost her intensity or seriousness of purpose. "I don't dress movie stars," she insisted, "but actors portraying characters." Her certainty of opinion could intimidate the toughest actor or the most daunting director.

Her work had obsessed her. She didn't marry until she was thirty-three, at a time when twenty-five-year-old single women were considered old maids. She took her young daughter, Hannah, to movie sets in remote places all over the country, and left her in the care of her husband and housekeepers when Hannah was older.

Roth's credits went on forever. She'd worked on almost everything director Mike Nichols had ever done, on stage and screen. She'd made Dustin Hoffman into a lowlife for "Midnight Cowboy," and had dressed Jane Fonda every which way in "Klute," "Coming Home," "Nine to Five," and "Rollover." She'd figured out how to make Michael Caine a convincing transvestite in

"Dressed to Kill," and how to make John Lithgow's transsexual football player in "The World According to Garp" seem *lovely*.

Roth was worried that *Bonfire of the Vanities* might already be dated. The fun of the book had been in gloating at the awful things that happened to the kind of powerful people who were still on top when the book was published. In the real world, however, the rich were having their comeuppance, just as Wolfe had predicted. Billionaire Donald Trump was under siege at home and in his business empire. Michael Milken, Drexel Burnham's junk bond king, was facing criminal charges, and his firm had filed for Chapter 11. David Dinkins had just taken office as New York City's first black mayor.

"The problem with *Bonfire* is that it was an emblem of the eighties," she mused. "Maybe there's no more need for it."

Still, she couldn't resist the challenge of conveying the book's nasty sparkle through the costumes required for the film's set pieces encompassing high society and low. After nearly forty years in the business, Roth still looked revitalized when she was struck by inspiration. She worked hard to make each costume perfect. She wasn't so much interested in beauty as in "integrity." Integrity meant a great deal to her, and she had definite ideas about what constituted it. She believed that the right clothes would never save a bad actor, but a good actor in the right clothes could be magic.

During the filming of "Bonfire," De Palma was chauffeured by an affable teamster in the teamster's Grand Marquis station wagon. (The drivers, along with many other crew members, from make-up people to camera operators, earned substantial additional income by renting their equipment to film companies.) De Palma's next stop after the Costume Depot was Park and Sixty-first, where a van and bus were parked on the side street by the Regency Hotel, waiting to take De Palma and his crew to the Bronx site. The van was reserved for De Palma and his top lieutenants: Vilmos Zsigmond, the cinematographer; Richard Sylbert, the production designer; Fred Caruso, the line producer; and Eric Schwab, De Palma's second unit director and "visual consultant." Each of the five men needed to see the site for different reasons. Sylbert had to figure out what props were needed to enhance reality. Caruso had to get a sense of how long shooting would take there and how it would affect the schedule and the budget. Schwab would be filming scenes that would connect to Desolation Street and Prostitute Street. Zsigmond had to anticipate the lighting problems of this night shoot, which was why they were making the trip at night.

The bus was reserved for the technicians who would have to fulfill the vision of the men at the top. Colin Campbell, the "gaffer," or chief lighting technician, rode on the bus with the electricians and the "grips," the stagehands responsible for moving props and scenery, laying dolly tracks for the camera to move on, and pushing the dolly — the platform on wheels that carries the camera and the cameraman on tracks for smooth, moving shots in a small space. Ann Roth, who showed up at the last minute, after the van was filled, also rode on the bus, with her associate Gary Jones. So did Peter Runfolo, the film's production manager, a giant bear of a man with a fondness for egg sandwiches, who made sure the cast and crew had everything they needed: cars, food, locations, drivers, plane tickets. Monica Goldstein, De Palma's assistant, rode in the bus carrying a Thermos of decaffeinated cappuccino for her boss, as well as his gum and Players cigarettes.

The bus, the van, and the Grand Marquis formed a caravan heading north to the Bronx; the station wagon came along just in case De Palma wanted to leave early.

The combined salaries of the five men crammed into the van that evening came to almost $3.5 million (weighted heavily by De Palma's $2.5 million). Money proved no comfort against the damp, bone-chilling night, however. There was misery and tension in the cold air as the van pulled out, followed by the bus, followed by the station wagon.

Richard Sylbert, sitting in the back, accepted a red licorice Twizzler from Fred Caruso and broke the silence by entertaining the group with a typically caustic commentary on his ex-wives and the ex-wives of his twin brother Paul Sylbert, who was also a production designer.

"My brother is living in Pennsylvania with his fourth wife. He finally did something sensible. He got out of this town." It wasn't clear whether "this town" was New York or Los Angeles, and it didn't matter.

Sylbert, a tall, thin man in his early sixties, curled his long legs up toward his chest. His steely gray hair was combed back from his forehead. He wore a tan safari suit covered by a parka, and Topsiders. He gnawed at his Twizzler. "He's working on the Streisand picture, God help him. Thank God he doesn't have to photograph her." He swallowed some licorice. "I love her, Barbra Streisand. You know what, though, she's made a lot of mistakes. I admire her. But she thinks of herself as an actress. She's not an Egyptian beauty anymore. She's an old Jew. You have to put a box over her head. Barbra!"

He sighed and stuck the Twizzler back in his mouth. "We're all out of Brooklyn, you know."

Sylbert never minced his words because he didn't care what anybody thought, a character trait that had made him a favorite source for the Hollywood press. Sylbert was the best production designer in the business and had been for a very long time. Also called the art director, the production designer was responsible for a film's overall physical appearance. Like most aspects of filmmaking, production design combined artistic and practical skills. Sylbert was in charge of all the set decorations and construction, and of making sure all locations outside the studio were appropriate to the mood and style of the film.

Nothing could faze him. He'd run Paramount Pictures for a couple of years in the seventies, and he'd won an Oscar and four Academy Award nominations. His credits included a remarkable number of great films: "Chinatown," "The Manchurian Candidate," "The Pawnbroker," "Catch-22." He'd come to "Bonfire" after he completed his work on "Dick Tracy" for Warren Beatty; that picture was scheduled for release in June.

For a time, back in the sixties, when making movies was one big party, Sylbert's closets were filled with beautiful suits, all hand tailored on Savile Row. But things had changed from the days when Sylbert and his Hollywood friends lived like princes, when every night there was another dinner party, another evening at La Scala. His pals were Beatty and Jack Nicholson and Roman Polanski.

Sylbert was with Polanski in London when the call came that Polanski's wife, Sharon Tate, had been murdered by the Charles Manson gang.

The parties were over for him, but Sylbert said he didn't care about that either. His life was work; he told his history according to what movie took him where. He did "Carnal Knowledge" in Vancouver, then was off to New York to do a Broadway play with Mike Nichols, then traveled with Nichols again to the Bahamas for "Day of the Dolphin." When he took a break from filmmaking it was to run a studio. He just rolled from film to film, from continent to continent. Wives and children came and went between films.

He picked his projects by the director, not the script. He'd wanted to work with De Palma before, on "The Untouchables," but Paramount Pictures wouldn't pay his price. He was hired for $194,000 for "Bonfire."

Sylbert didn't shop at Savile Row anymore, he shopped by catalogue. For the past twenty-five years he'd worn safari suits, as John Huston did, and he admitted he was attracted to De Palma in part because he wore a safari suit too. Sylbert, whose life was devoted to the proposition that any story could be enhanced by the right props, saw his wardrobe in metaphoric terms. "This safari suit is a uniform. I wear a uniform because to me a movie is a war. And if you don't know it's a war you're missing something," he said. "The war is between the problems, the people with the ideas, and the people with the money. The crazies versus the bean counters. And it's the only war there ever is. It never changes. But you better know that it's there."

No one enjoyed Sylbert's monologues as much as he did. He cocked his head toward the front of the van where Schwab and Zsigmond were discussing how to block out a shot. Sylbert whispered, loudly, "All cameramen have a tendency to make trouble. They don't think their job is difficult enough, so they try to intellectualize it."

A natural tension exists between production designers and directors of photography. Each of them is given an idea of the movie's look by the director, frequently with magazines and art books as guides. (De Palma's favorite dictum on the subject of locations was

"If there's a great location, somebody's taken a photograph of it.")
When De Palma had met with Sylbert and Zsigmond back in Los
Angeles, he explained he wanted the audience to see how the fall of
Sherman McCoy caused the collision of two entirely different New
Yorks.

The difference had to be immediately palpable. One world belonged to Sherman McCoy, the cloistered elegance of Park Avenue,
where rich, thin ladies and their pampered husbands and dogs trod
gently on Aubusson carpets — and knew what Aubusson carpets
were. The other world belonged to the streetwise citizens of the
Bronx, where the toughened ethnic masses battled it out, every day,
in the courts and on the streets. De Palma told Zsigmond and
Sylbert he wanted a satiric tone, not a heavy dramatic statement.
His specific instructions to his visual architects were terse and
vague.

"Acrylic!" he said. "It should be acrylic."

In the simplest terms, Sylbert's job was to choose the settings, the
materials, the colors, and Zsigmond's job was to photograph it all.
But as anyone who's been photographed badly knows, nice light
can make the cheapest make-up glow, and cruel light can turn a
beauty into a hag.

At first Zsigmond, a Hungarian with strong views of his own,
resented the director and the production designer hitting him with
this abstract idea. "Acrylic!" As far as Zsigmond was concerned,
acrylic lighting didn't exist. He figured out how to light what he
saw when he walked onto a set.

De Palma had worked with Vilmos Zsigmond on two previous
films, "Obsession" and "Blow Out," and felt that Zsigmond was
the only cameraman he'd ever worked with who could come up
with a better idea than he could.

Zsigmond, a gnomish man with a beard and narrow, twinkly
eyes, remembered his last experience with De Palma as a series of
impossibilities. "In 'Blow Out,' there we were in the middle of the
winter and there was this huge canyon and we were shooting a frog
in the foreground and the river beyond and the trees and bridge
above, and he just walked up to it and said, 'Light it. I don't care

how long it's going to take. Light it.' " Zsigmond laughed. "He's just that kind of guy. 'Light it!' "

The Hungarian cameraman had almost refused to work on "Bonfire." The issue wasn't De Palma. He thought De Palma had developed into one of the best visual stylists in the business. The issue was billing. Zsigmond insisted on being listed in all newspaper ads, no matter how small. The matter of credit had become a major sticking point between the industry's top cinematographers and the studios, who didn't want to clutter their ads with non-celebrity names. Warner Bros.' refusal to list Zsigmond in ads smaller than a half page led to an impasse during contract negotiations. When the studio started to look for another cameraman, Zsigmond backed down.

But it irked him. "When you see what's happening on the set, the director is really the guy who directs actors and is holding the reins, so to speak," said Zsigmond. "But after that it's the cameraman who really talks to everybody. It's a very important job and it has to be respected and it has to be rewarded by having his name in the advertisement no matter how big it is!"

Zsigmond's search for recognition had been going on for a long time. Born and educated in Hungary, he'd left after the 1956 revolution. For ten years he worked at the bottom: first as a lab technician, then as a camera operator for educational movies and commercials. Finally he made his way to Hollywood, where he developed a reputation for "poetic" lighting with a Robert Altman picture, "McCabe and Mrs. Miller." In 1977 he won the Academy Award for his work on Steven Spielberg's "Close Encounters of the Third Kind." The door chimes at Zsigmond's villa in the Hollywood Hills still played the movie's theme.

He'd worked on big films and small, on successes and failures. In fact, he was the cameraman on Hollywood's most notorious financial flop, "Heaven's Gate."

But he'd accomplished a lot. He had his Oscar, he earned a great deal of money from the television commercials he directed. However, he wanted more — and he still had abundant energy though he turned sixty the year "Bonfire" was filmed. He hopped around the set, peeking over everyone's shoulder and offering advice even to those who hadn't asked for it. He wasn't satisfied just doing his job. He wanted to direct — and that's what he planned to do when "Bonfire" was over. "I've reached as far as I can go as cinematographer," he said. "The director is the captain of the ship. He's the general and you have to go along. Otherwise you go to endless discussions and what will happen to the movie? It has to be one man's vision. It cannot be two men's vision."

"We've crossed the border, boys," said Sylbert. The van left the Third Avenue Bridge, which links Manhattan to the Bronx, and eased onto the Grand Concourse, the wide boulevard that was once the Park Avenue of the Bronx. That former grandeur was still evident in the sweeping scale of the street, especially at night, when the rundown condition of the buildings was hidden by shadows. When the van turned onto a side street, the landscape began to resemble Dresden after World War II. The windowless buildings with their torched facades were more forlorn than frightening.

Eric Schwab, who had worked with De Palma on three previous films and become his most trusted adviser on locations, had been on these desolate streets many times over the course of the past few weeks with the scouts. At thirty-two, Schwab was by far the youngest of the group in the van and the only person not wearing a parka. Apparently oblivious to the fact that it was thirty-one degrees outside, he was wearing a short, worn brown leather jacket, jeans, and sneakers. He moved and talked with the enthusiasm and directness of a smart kid — Sylbert called him "The Kid" — but there were noticeable patches of gray in his mop of fine dark hair.

He was telling Caruso about seeing drug deals taking place openly. "We were scared, young white guys driving around in circles, people thinking we were cops. We thought someone might take a shot at us," he said, excited by the prospect.

The van stopped at the site chosen for Desolation Street, where Maria and Sherman first miss the turnoff back to Manhattan, and De Palma stepped out and started pacing up and down the street, oblivious to everything but the shot he was trying to establish in his mind's eye. No one was on the street except a stumbling drunk holding a wine bottle in a bag. "Hi, I'm Stewie," he said.

De Palma ignored him as he ignored everyone else. Meanwhile, the van and bus emptied, and two dozen people tried to follow De

Palma in an oddly choreographed dance to which only he knew the steps. He moved two steps forward, the group followed. He turned, they turned. He looked, they looked. He hadn't said anything yet that might illuminate what they were looking at. Somebody shrieked, "A rat!"

Without a word, De Palma got back into the van and everyone followed. The domino effect was becoming apparent. The director waved his hand and the legions beneath him fell into place, trying to interpret what the gesture meant. He reached his hand out in a certain way and Goldstein automatically handed him a cup of steaming coffee, flavored with chocolate mint.

The van drove up 167th Street past a corner where a few young black men milled around wearing parkas much like the parkas the film people were wearing. They were shivering in the cold and didn't look particularly threatening, though Sylbert assured De Palma that this was a bad neighborhood and the men were drug dealers.

At 9:00 P.M. the van and the bus and the station wagon pulled up at the corner of 167th Street and Sherman Avenue, the location picked for Prostitute Street. The filmmakers had decided to populate this street, part of Sherman and Maria's orientation to the Bronx, with an exaggerated assortment of pimps, prostitutes, and derelicts, to accentuate the terror the characters feel. Zsigmond walked up the street, past Pop's Fried Chicken and a video store, snapping photographs. De Palma walked briskly up and down the street with two dozen people following him. Goldstein took notes as she walked.

Sylbert returned to the van clutching a rolled-up slice of pizza. Orange grease dripped onto his khaki pants. De Palma got back into the van and turned to Zsigmond, who was sitting in the middle. "Light it with neon," he said. "It should be as garish as possible."

"Green and red," said Zsigmond, as he looked at this street that looked much like streets all over New York. There were men and women heading for dinner at the pizza parlor and the Chinese restaurant at the corner, and young boys were riding along on bicycles.

"It should be ridiculously bright," said Sylbert. "No one's going to walk out of the theater because it's too bright."

The caravan continued on to a dark, deserted spot under the Third Avenue Bridge, the site of the hit-and-run scene. De Palma sat in the van and studied his storyboards — the scene-by-scene picture outline of the entire movie — with a flashlight. He stretched his arms and the flashlight tilted toward the window, flashing onto the bit of graffiti scrawled on a girder holding up the highway. JEW, it said. This grim terrain would appear to be terrifying enough, but now there were two dozen people tramping around in the mud, discussing how to make the place even scarier. All of a sudden, Zsigmond ran away from the group and disappeared into a shadow.

Sylbert laughed. "I took a leak on the tire pile back on Desolation Street."

All that was left to do that night was to drive across the Triborough Bridge, so De Palma could see how Schwab planned to film the second unit shot of Maria and Sherman driving into the city from the airport. Most large productions had a second unit, a small group of technicians with its own director, to film scenes that didn't require the stars to be on camera. Schwab, who had first worked for De Palma as a location scout on "Body Double," had shot the second unit for "Casualties of War." For "Bonfire," he was scheduled to direct, among other things, a Mercedes-Benz driving through the Bronx, an airplane landing, a tape recorder rolling, an opera program being read, the scenery moving past subway and automobile windows, and close-ups of license plates.

Staring at the view of Manhattan from the bridge, Zsigmond asked dubiously, "Is this the Magic Hour shot?"

The Magic Hour was that brief period at dusk and dawn, the two times of day when the light had a perfect ambiguity. It was the sweetest time to film, during those fleeting moments of implied beginnings and endings.

Everyone agreed the angle was no good, and Sylbert suggested substituting the view from the Fifty-ninth Street Bridge.

"No, no," said Schwab. "That's a nice shot, but it isn't authentic. That isn't what you'd see if you were driving toward the Bronx."

Zsigmond stared out the window at the city lights. "This is not a pretty shot," he said with disgust. "What's the shot Richard suggested?"

Sylbert answered. "The ramp at the Fifty-ninth Street Bridge. But Eric's right. That's really cheating."

From the front came De Palma's voice in the dark. "I think we should just have a Manhattan sign you point to."

Schwab piped up. "I thought you said you *hated* signs."

De Palma threw up his hands. "I'm not going to shoot this silly skyline. It's going to be another cheesy Manhattan shot. We'll shoot it and then we won't use it."

The van drove all the way to Queens and all the way back, with the bus and the station wagon dutifully in tow. "This is the second unit," said De Palma with an exaggerated sigh. "I shouldn't even be here."

Sylbert laughed. "You should be napping."

"Why is this taking so long, Eric?" De Palma asked. "I'm getting a sense of what it's like to get lost in the Bronx without a clue." The van crossed the bridge for the last time that night, back into Manhattan, and headed south for the Regency.

De Palma's voice had lightened perceptibly when he was teasing Schwab. The younger man had become the closest thing to a protégé De Palma had ever had. His mood altered noticeably when he was alone with Schwab, as though an invisible shield protecting him from the world had been lifted. With Schwab he could joke around and sometimes even say more than what was absolutely necessary to the job at hand.

They were an unlikely pairing, this master and protégé. De Palma was like a large cat, capable of sitting in one place for a very long time without giving a clue about what lay behind those light eyes. When he moved, he moved fast. Schwab was compact, clean-cut, and open. He looked like a California preppie, which he was. When he was enthusiastic, he blurted out his ideas in a rapid-fire patter. When he was disappointed, he sulked. On those occasions De Palma called him "the dark one." Their conversations were cryptic, encoded by a way of looking at the world. They understood their stories would be told through the all-encompassing yet limited frame of a camera. They tried to convince themselves that what didn't fit in the frame didn't matter.

Schwab hadn't really wanted to work on "Bonfire." He'd been a precocious assistant at twenty when he got his first job in film. He had worked his way through the ranks to second unit director, but he was still spending his energies on somebody else's movie. He knew it was time for the long apprenticeship of Eric Schwab to end.

He had devoted his twenties to the adventure of learning how to make movies, and to adventure itself. The film business had taken him around the world, and, as he would say in Encino parlance, he "had a blast." He'd found himself in the middle of a student revolution in Ecuador during "Vibes." He prowled the dangerous South Side of Chicago and dated Miss Great Falls, the runner-up for Miss Montana, during "The Untouchables." He spent nine months traveling throughout Thailand, Mexico, and Australia during "Casualties of War." "Casualties" also introduced him to Puntip Limrungroj, the spunky, spiritual receptionist at the elegant Oriental Hotel in Bangkok. Like half the Thai population, male and female, she was nicknamed Lek, or "Little One." For almost two years he'd been seeing this young woman whose father was a monk who wandered through the forest and whose mother supported the family selling smuggled goods near the Cambodian border. There was an undeniably old-fashioned movie romanticism to their relationship, an innocence that had long disappeared from the flakes and the sharpies he met in Los Angeles. Their first half-dozen dates were chaperoned by one of Schwab's Thai friends. Lek was a universe away from women he met in show business, women like the TV producer who, half an hour into their first date, looked at him and said, "Let's take our pants off." Schwab had been back to Thailand nine times since "Casualties" to see Lek, sometimes just for a weekend.

It was a great life, well removed from the conventional comforts of Encino, the Los Angeles suburb, where Schwab had a privileged life as the son of a successful fashion industry executive. (To his chagrin, though, his parents had followed him from *schmatta* into the film world, to dabble in the movie business as producers.)

Schwab had always been a combination of athlete and film nerd; in his North Hollywood prep school, then known as the Harvard

School for Boys, he skied competitively but would spend his nights and weekends going to movies and reading about movies. The Harvard School encouraged experimentation; Schwab never wrote a paper. He fulfilled his requirements with movies. For English Lit, he made a film about Shakespeare's Globe Theater burning down. For biology, he made a film that explained anatomy by having his classmate Jon Lovitz portray a toy fussball player who described the difference between him and humans. (Lovitz would go on to join the cast of "Saturday Night Live" for a few seasons.) Schwab enrolled at Berkeley, then transferred out after two years to go to film school at U.C.L.A.

He took his first movie job at twenty, between semesters, and continued to alternate between school and work until he got his degree. Having the advantages of youth and affluence, Schwab took a princely view of his film work: he never accepted a job for money but for what he could learn. Besides, the money was exceptionally good no matter what job he took. (He would earn more than $100,000 on "Bonfire.") He never wanted to hear himself repeat the salesman's cliché he heard from his father on occasion: "Sell the sizzle, not the steak." Schwab didn't want to sizzle. He wanted to make films. However, the American film business, rigidly controlled by an almost impenetrable network of unions and nepotism, didn't endorse the Japanese apprenticeship system that Schwab greatly admired. So he created his own.

On "Golden Girl" he tagged after the production manager, who adopted the eager student as a surrogate son. The younger man learned the nitty-gritty of film production: how to get people to give you what you needed, and how to take it when they wouldn't give it to you. On "True Confessions" Schwab attached himself to the director, Ulu Grosbard, and to the late Steven Grimes, the art director, the man who'd designed all of John Huston's films. He also met Ida Random, Grimes's assistant, who would go on to become Brian De Palma's production designer on "Body Double," and who would hire Schwab to scout locations for the film.

Schwab didn't wear outward signs of the neuroses that many young directors carry as proudly as their Directors' Guild of America union cards. This made him very appealing to the people he followed around because the people who succeeded were the ones who got things done, not the self-styled Doomed Uncompromisers.

Hollywood was full of them, the bright and the not-so-bright people who never actually did anything but hang around the Farmer's Market or Hugo's, drinking cappuccino while they analyzed the failure of this script and that development deal and complained about the idiocy of the business.

The experienced professionals were happy to teach this eager kid what they knew. It was flattering to have somebody pay attention. Schwab had the added advantage of having acquired an enormous body of knowledge without actually making a nonstudent film. He was unencumbered by bitterness; no matter how bad the movie he was working on, he did a good job and would always be recommended for another film. He wasn't the director. He didn't get the glory, and he didn't get the blame.

De Palma, who typically kept a distance from his crew, didn't pay much attention to Schwab at first. In fact, he was so brusque to the lowly location scout — as he was to everyone — that Schwab almost quit a week after he was hired. One day, as the director was telling a small group about his new idea for the film's opening, he mentioned an obscure British film called "Peeping Tom." Schwab got the director's attention when he described in detail the scene De Palma was referring to. He began to speak up more frequently, revealing an extensive, obsessive knowledge of film history — and a sense of humor with a mean bite. De Palma liked Schwab's mind and his pugnaciousness. Soon he began to rely on Schwab's evaluation of locations and his ability to fulfill De Palma's most difficult demands. Though De Palma didn't encourage frivolity on his sets, he was amused when his production manager on "The Untouchables" put Schwab in costume and included him among the extras, in the part of a Prussian prince.

By the time he signed on for "Casualties," Schwab had come to the realization that he didn't want his legacy to be simply that he could be De Palma's best advance man. He was a little embarrassed at the significance he sometimes saw in the fact that his middle name was Bryan. He told De Palma he would work on "Casualties" only if he could direct the second unit. De Palma, who sponsored Schwab's application to the Directors' Guild, gave him the go-ahead to shoot anything he wanted, with his own crew. In Thailand Schwab put together a local crew who would be much cheaper than the unionized Americans, allowing him the freedom to experiment. He recreated shots from "Rashomon," tried all kinds of lenses, even had the Thais construct a village for him to burn down. During the long weeks and months on location in Phucket, he interrogated cameraman Steven Burum on the difference between a thirty-five millimeter and a forty-millimeter lens, and about the principles of composition. Burum, who had been injured during the shoot, would scratch out the framing for a scene with his cane in the dirt.

After that, De Palma had no doubts about Schwab's abilities. But he wasn't at all convinced his protégé was going to pick up the mantle. During his twenty-five years in the business, he'd seen a lot of astute, intelligent boys like Schwab come and go. They knew everything there was to know about film but were too proud to sell themselves. So many of them never got it, that in the movie industry art was a product and the only way to succeed was to figure out how to move the merchandise. He was afraid that Schwab was too arrogant to sell himself, too much the Prussian prince.

By the time Schwab returned to Los Angeles in the summer of 1988, he was determined to get his own film going — because it was time and because he wanted to prove himself to De Palma. Schwab and his friend Lynn Kuwahara had been writing scripts together off and on for five years, which had brought them a stack of rejection letters from all the studios. They spent months working on "Golden Triangle" (later called "Chasing the Dragon"), a screenplay about an American drug enforcement agent living in Thailand who had become corrupted by power.

The script was promising enough to link Schwab with an agent at William Morris; the agent was so enthusiastic he encouraged Schwab to hire an entertainment lawyer to handle his contract. The agent's excitement lasted about a week, long enough for the negative "readers' reports" to come in from the studio. The agent, who had been calling almost hourly — even on Sunday — when he thought the script was a sure thing, was suddenly hard to reach.

It was during this period that what was left of Schwab's prolonged boyhood began ebbing at a rapid rate. His father was dying of prostate cancer. Schwab spent most of the late summer and early autumn in his father's hospital room, reading for hours while his father slept, and arguing with his brothers about whether he'd been a good father.

As Schwab's father lay dying, De Palma was telling Fred Caruso, "Get Eric," as the search for locations in New York and Los Angeles had started to intensify. Three weeks after his father's death in early November, 1989, Schwab decided to battle his grief with work.

The joy he usually felt when he boarded a plane was absent on that trip to New York. There was much to think about, and he didn't want to think about any of it. A week before his father died he'd flown to Thailand for a couple of days, to spend his thirty-second birthday with his girlfriend, Lek. She'd taken him to a party where he'd met a fortuneteller. This was no casual prognosticator: he had a considerable reputation in Bangkok. The fortuneteller took a lengthy history from Schwab and spent almost two hours analyzing the data. When he was finished, he told Schwab that certain years would be troublesome for him. His forty-second year would be dangerous unless he fought the evil spirit with a certain mixture of dried herbs. When he was forty-eight the only way he could ward off horrible disaster would be to gather twelve eels and a special coin and throw them into a river. The fortuneteller gave Schwab the coin before he left for the evening.

But the number that lingered in Schwab's mind was thirty-two. It could be the Magic Hour for him — that's what the fortuneteller was saying. This year he could strike out on his own. He could accomplish anything — and if he didn't, he'd have wasted the most propitious moment of his entire life.

In January Schwab and De Palma had gone through the script deciding which shots could go to the second unit. Schwab paused at the page where the screenwriter's stage direction appears for the image that heralds Maria's entrance to the movie:

> EXT — KENNEDY AIRPORT — NIGHT
> The sky is a labyrinth of planes taking off and landing.

He asked De Palma if he could have that shot. De Palma, who hadn't paid much attention to Cristofer's stage directions, replied that the day he included the cliché of a plane landing in one of his movies would be the day he retired. Schwab took him up on the challenge. De Palma bet him a hundred dollars that he couldn't do it, that the shot would never make the final cut.

Schwab became obsessed with proving De Palma wrong. Maybe he could make something as mundane as a plane landing a technical tour de force.

Tom Wolfe hadn't specified what kind of plane brought Maria back to New York from Europe to create havoc in Sherman McCoy's life. Schwab and De Palma agreed that a climber like her would travel only on the Concorde, the transportation totem for the jet set.

Schwab thought he'd figured out a way to make the sight of the Concorde landing something spectacular, something De Palma would be forced to admire. He wanted to film the Concorde's descent into Kennedy Airport at precisely the moment the plane, the setting sun, and the Empire State Building would meet within the camera frame. The Empire State Building was a stationary element, and the Concorde's pilot might be able to land at the specific angle required for the shot's composition. The trick would be pinpointing a moment when the sun's relation to the Empire State Building would make the shot conceivable at all. Schwab knew at the outset that there would be very few such moments in the entire year, and he wasn't quite sure how to figure out when, exactly, they were.

He explained his dilemma to the cinematographer, Vilmos Zsigmond, who introduced him to a specially designed little Casio computer that could help Schwab calculate the exact locus of the sun anywhere in the world, at any time of day, at any time of year. Schwab got in touch with the man who designed the computer and spent hours talking to him, trying to solve the mystery: When would the sun's proximity to the Empire State Building be at an angle that would line up with the appropriate landing strip at Kennedy Airport, and with the plane dropping down from the sky? Finally he settled on June 12, 1990, as the date when all the pieces would fit together. Yet even though he planned to use five cameras rolling simultaneously, as insurance, there was only a tiny chance that he could pull it off.

Schwab's Concorde shot became a standing joke around the

production office. Fred Caruso, who had gotten to know and like the young man on "Casualties of War," was encouraging as well as amused by Schwab's obsessive pursuit. The coproducer had gotten in touch with Air France officials about the project. They were enthusiastic, but not so enthusiastic that they would waive the $40,000 charge to pay for the crew and fuel. Perhaps, Caruso asked, Schwab could film a British Airways plane and call it Air France? Or shoot sunset in Paris and sunset in New York and merge the two?

"It's hard to do so it doesn't look fake," said Schwab, the purist.

Caruso sighed. "When Eric is shooting second unit you'll know where he is," he smirked. "The sky will be lit up. In fact, we're making two movies and they'll play at the same time in double theaters: 'Bonfire of the Vanities' in one theater, and 'Eric Schwab and the Second Unit' in the other."

Chapter 5

ON MEDICIS, X-RAYS,
AND BLOODY FRUIT FLIES

On March 8, the day following his trip to the Bronx to check out the locations, De Palma flew to Los Angeles to attend the American Film Institute's annual tribute dinner. The AFI, a publicly and privately funded organization, was founded in 1967 to promote the preservation and cataloguing of films and the training of young filmmakers. The annual tribute was, like so many Hollywood gatherings, yet another occasion for the community to dress in formal wear and engage in an evening of self-congratulation. The AFI banquet was sometimes deliciously hypocritical. Occasionally the bold experimenters honored there were in the odd position of accepting applause from the very people who had ruined their careers, the studio executives who pretended to admire daring films but didn't want to finance them.

One of De Palma's favorite episodes in show business lore was the 1975 AFI banquet celebrating Orson Welles. Welles had been pronounced a cinematic genius when he made "Citizen Kane" at the age of twenty-five. However, his films didn't make money; he hadn't been able to get a picture financed in town since he'd made "Touch of Evil" in 1957. Welles, who figured he had nothing more to lose, decided to treat the occasion with the bad taste he felt it deserved. That night, after being praised by Ingrid Bergman and sung to by Frank Sinatra, Welles gave a thank-you speech that ended with a pitch for money.

De Palma had two reasons to attend the banquet. David Lean

was that year's honoree, and De Palma had been one of many filmmakers asked to say something, if they wished, about the eighty-two-year-old director, the legendary craftsman and artist. Lean had built his early career making small gems like "Brief Encounter," building toward the epics that had won him almost universal admiration, as well as a reputation for being impossibly perfectionist and fiscally imprudent. For days De Palma had been thinking about what to say, though he wasn't certain he'd be able to give a speech in front of the Hollywood crowd. He didn't want to compete in that arena with people like his friend Steven Spielberg, who had developed into an able raconteur.

De Palma decided that if he did say anything, he would talk about what he considered to be the greatest entrance in cinema history, Omar Sharif's first appearance in "Lawrence of Arabia." The scene begins with a vast, empty desert. In the far distance, a tiny blur materializes in the middle of the screen, then a speck appears inside the blur, then the speck starts to move and it's a mirage — no, it's not a mirage, it's a man on a camel. Lean, in De Palma's view, knew exactly how long the build-up to a scene should be, how far to push the risk of boring the audience in order to thrill them.

De Palma had another mission to accomplish at the AFI dinner. He'd checked the guest list beforehand and knew Kathy Lingg would be there — and that as a middle-level studio executive she wouldn't be entitled to one of the better tables. He, on the other hand, was grouped with the "A" crowd, right next to the head table, and seated next to Ed Zwick, who was riding high on the success of his television series, "thirtysomething," and his Civil War movie, "Glory." Spielberg was at the table just across from his, on the other side of the head table.

De Palma knew his feelings were irrational, but it was very important to him at that moment for Kathy Lingg to see their respective positions in the room. He might disparage the Hollywood power game, but he was quite conscious of status and what it meant. He wanted her to know what she'd missed by rejecting him. After "Casualties" opened and Lingg had declined to join him in Deauville, she'd told him she couldn't take their relationship further.

That autumn, as "Bonfire" was about to go into preproduction, he set about finding a replacement for her with the obsessiveness he usually reserved for his work. There was the British novelist, the Israeli film director, the New York computer specialist. All of them were intelligent, passionate women, but none of them provided as compelling a challenge as Lingg's rejection did. When he wasn't thinking about why "Casualties" had done so poorly at the box office, he speculated on how he might win Lingg back.

De Palma decided he had to try, and he approached the project — his deliberate strategizing gave the courtship the feel of a project as much as a romance — with the force and logic he would apply to a movie he wanted to get going. For a time Lingg succumbed to the director's onslaught of attention and gifts, which culminated with a trip to Europe and an expensive engagement ring. But in the end she left. By the evening of the AFI dinner, their affair was irrevocably over, and De Palma knew it.

He didn't give his speech about David Lean that night. He later told his friends he couldn't extricate it from his laptop computer, an unlikely bout of computer illiteracy that closely resembled stage fright. He always felt as though he were being judged by "those people." He decided he didn't need to parade before them when it wasn't absolutely necessary.

When Lean, the guest of honor, got up to speak, De Palma tried to concentrate on the director's thrilling bravado as he took the occasion of this dinner celebrating him to chastise the Hollywood community for making drivel, and sequels to drivel. De Palma glanced around the room and thought about what a well-staged scene this was. Here were the most powerful people in the business — agents, producers, directors, and studio heads — all dutifully listening to this elegant gentleman tell them that they had lost all sense of daring and imagination, that they were going into one hole and coming out the same hole. As the group applauded Lean's indictment of them, De Palma imagined that they must really be thinking, This man is *insane!* And by their standard, they were correct. That eighty-two-year-old man was, at that very moment, making a movie out of Joseph Conrad's *Nostromo* (a book, De Palma would guarantee, that no one in the room had read and few had heard of). De Palma knew that to many people in Hollywood,

Lean would forever be thought of as the man who spent fourteen years sulking after "Ryan's Daughter" flopped.

Usually De Palma's private commentary helped him endure, and even enjoy, these Hollywood events. But he was distracted that night. As Lean talked and the power elite pretended to listen, De Palma couldn't stop thinking of Lingg, wondering where, exactly, she was sitting, and wondering, How do I get her to see me? How do I get her to know I'm here?

After the speeches were finished, clips of Lean's movies were projected onto a large screen. De Palma was transfixed, once again, by the climax of "The Bridge on the River Kwai," where the bridge that is the film's symbol of the brutal absurdity of war gets blown up. This was De Palma's favorite moment in film, one of the reasons he'd wanted to become a director. He was still searching for his bridge.

Yet he wasn't able to concentrate on the images in front of him. The evening was almost over and he still hadn't figured a way to make Lingg notice him — and he'd avoided the easiest route, giving the speech. Just as the bridge was about to explode, inspiration hit him. He poised himself warily, waiting for the clip to end. As soon as the lights went on in the room, De Palma jumped to his feet. For an instant he felt certain that, standing alone in the front of the room the way he was, he'd be visible even at the back tables where he assumed an *insignificant* executive like Lingg would be sitting. He yanked Ed Zwick to his feet and nodded at Spielberg to get up. As the entire room rose to a standing ovation, De Palma felt that *he* had done it, he had brought them all to their feet. He'd done it for David Lean, to be sure. But the gesture served an additional purpose. It allowed him to feel, for a moment, that he'd exacted some token of revenge against Lingg, and, possibly, for the failure of "Casualties of War" as well. He never would know whether Lingg saw him that night.

De Palma spent the next two weeks in Los Angeles, working on his blueprint for "Bonfire," his storyboards, which translated the script into pictures, drawn scene by scene in cartoon frames. He also reintroduced himself to the routine duplicity of Hollywood.

A couple of days after the AFI banquet, the director received a call from Bruce Berman, the production executive ranked above Lucy Fisher and below Mark Canton. Berman told De Palma the studio had an exciting script for him to read, the adaptation of Stephen King's *The Stand.* Though De Palma was absorbed by "Bonfire," he told Berman to send the script over — as a matter both of courtesy and of insurance. De Palma had learned over the years to seek his next project before his current film was released, one of his many self-preservation tactics.

Eight days passed and the script hadn't yet arrived. De Palma sensed that something was wrong and called Berman up. There were hems and haws, and then Berman said the script needed revisions. "But," said De Palma, "last week you said it was great." A few minutes later Berman's secretary called and said she wanted to send the script by messenger.

De Palma couldn't believe it. He was making a *prestigious, important, expensive* movie for these people, and they were playing games with him. He called Marty Bauer to find out what was going on — whether, as De Palma suspected, they'd sent the script to Spielberg first. Bauer confirmed De Palma's suspicions. When De Palma confronted Berman, the executive admitted there had been a mix-up. Spielberg had been sent the script by another Warner executive, and Berman hadn't been told until after he'd called De Palma. But Spielberg had passed. Wouldn't De Palma like to see the script now?

De Palma couldn't believe it. How could they be so dumb? Why did they want to insult him? He didn't think Berman was malicious, he just wasn't being smart.

He'd already had it with the Medici princes, and he hadn't even started filming yet.

De Palma wasn't really fed up with all the Warner Bros. executives. He wasn't fed up with Lucy Fisher. She did seem to understand what he was trying to achieve with "Bonfire," the crystalline tone he was seeking. They agreed the movie's humor had to be sharp, fast. Fisher had been encouraging all along, even as the budget kept growing, and even though she knew how tricky it would be to pull it off. Because De Palma had no producer, his relationship with her was the closest he'd ever had with a studio executive. She was, in effect, his fellow producer. That was fine as long as everything was going well. But there was one part of the producing role that Lucy Fisher couldn't possibly play. She couldn't protect De Palma from the studio executives. She was, after all, a Medici too.

The first thing everyone always seemed to know about Lucy Fisher was that she graduated cum laude from Harvard. When *Los Angeles* magazine ranked her among the "HOTSHOTS: 25 Hottest Young Comers in Hollywood" in 1984 the caption under the thirty-four-year-old Fisher's picture said, "Park the Rolls in Harvard Yard." At Warner Bros., this private school–educated daughter of a New Jersey steel merchant was the resident intellectual, the aristocrat, the perfect Medici princess.

The second thing people said about Fisher, a slight woman with large blue eyes and long brown hair, was that she was pretty. The third thing they said was that, even though she had become the highest-ranking woman in Hollywood, she was no Dawn Steel. This was meant as a compliment. No "Hey, motherfuckers" from Fisher.

The subtext to all of this? Fisher was a lady, and that in itself made her the subject of curiosity in a business where manners were trotted out only if they could help close a deal.

In the nine years she'd been a production executive at Warner Bros., Fisher had become the handler of "prestige" pictures. Her boss, Mark Canton, liked to joke that Fisher read books, whereas he read treatments. Canton, a tiny man who seemed to disappear inside his fashionably baggy suits, was the son of Arthur Canton, Alfred Hitchcock's publicist. He had come out of the music business and worked his way up the ranks producing goofy comedies. Now he occupied the large, dark-paneled office that had been part of Jack Warner's suite. Following the tradition of the old moguls, Canton kept the original scripts of the movies he produced bound in heavy maroon leather casings, each identified in gold lettering. Those elegant bindings preserved for posterity the scripts for "National Lampoon's Vacation," "Pee-Wee's Big Adventure," and "Police Academy."

The serious projects were channeled to the Harvard graduate. Fisher was responsible for "The Color Purple," "The Witches of

Eastwick," and "Gorillas in the Mist," all pictures that were never expected to compete with the $100 million action pictures, the slam-crashers starring hulks like Sylvester Stallone and Arnold Schwarzenegger. Fisher's pictures were the Oscar contenders, the pictures the studio hoped would attract enough adult theatergoers to provide a base for a successful afterlife overseas and on video.

At the time she was working on "Bonfire," Fisher's other projects included the story of Brazilian environmentalist Chico Mendes and a movie about photographer Robert Capa. She was bright, resilient, and highly opinionated, and she had developed a talent for transforming tough fictional works into mass entertainments. Greatly sought by the press, who were intrigued by this exotic creature — a high-ranking female movie executive — Fisher was, like all Warner Bros. executives, kept under wraps, allowed out for interviews on only the most special occasions.

She herself didn't seem to object to publicity. Before she joined Warner Bros. in 1981, she was featured in an odd photo spread in the June 1981 issue of *Town and Country*. Then the head of production at Francis Coppola's Zoetrope studios, the thirty-year-year-old Fisher posed in a slinky, shimmering dress by Adolfo, a glam-girl vision of ice blue lace and silver beads in the style of a 1930s vamp. (The dress was available at Saks Fifth Avenue, the caption noted.)

Warner Bros. may have limited her exposure to the press because she wasn't afraid to speak her mind. "Excuse me, John Updike, it wasn't a very good book at all," she said, referring to *The Witches of Eastwick*. "Anyway, the hell with him," she said, referring to its author. "It was a better movie than it was a book."

Fisher had moved up the ranks with the speed and efficiency of a determined careerist. She was quickly promoted from script reader at United Artists, and then she bounced around from Zoetrope to MGM to 20th Century–Fox, gathering experience and better titles. She landed at Warner Bros. in 1981 and had been there ever since.

Fisher was no stranger to dealing with artistic temperaments, either at work or at home. Like many bright, good girls, Fisher had had a rebellious side when she was younger. For eleven years she had lived with Peter Ivers, a Harvard classics major who went on to earn his measure of fame as an experimental New Wave musician who specialized in outrage: he once opened a Fleetwood Mac concert in the seventies wearing only a diaper. Fisher had followed Ivers to Los Angeles. While he recreated himself over and over in the underground music world, Fisher was moving on the corporate fast track.

When she turned thirty, the young executive was ready to settle down. She wanted children and a home; in 1980 she and Ivers split up, though they continued to be friends. Three years later, Peter Ivers was murdered in his loft in a commercial building in downtown L.A.

By the age of forty Fisher appeared to have what she said she wanted. She was married to a successful movie producer, Douglas Wick, whose most recent picture was "Working Girl" and whose father, Charles, was director of the U.S. Information Agency during the Reagan administration. She drove the regulation BMW, and had two small children and two nannies, and, as "Bonfire" was about to start filming, was two months pregnant with a third child.

"Bonfire" was the biggest movie of her career, and its importance wasn't lost on her. Whatever Mark Canton's real contribution to "Batman" had been, the fact was, he'd been the executive in charge of production of the studio's grandest hit and that would carry him a long way. It could happen to her.

De Palma wasn't concerned about his relationship with Lucy Fisher. They got along as well as necessary. It was another story with Robert G. Friedman, worldwide president for advertising and publicity. Friedman was crucial to the progress of "Bonfire," but the two men took an almost instant dislike to one another. De Palma thought the publicity man was condescending and arrogant. Friedman seemed to regard filmmakers as erratic children who had to be endured until they delivered the goods to the grown-ups, the rational studio executives who would know what to do with them. De Palma was especially irritated by Friedman's habit of interrupting a meeting to take calls and making a point of the fact that it was "Marty" (Scorsese) or "Steven" (Spielberg) on the phone.

The source of Friedman's mild antipathy toward the director was simple. He didn't like De Palma because De Palma didn't seem to like him.

Friedman, who wore impeccably stylish suits, bright ties, and crisp white shirts, never made a move that didn't seem calculated. He'd developed the habit from years of mastering public relations tactics, mostly fending off reporters with half truths and stonewalling.

He was a company man. Known by everyone in the industry as Rob or Robbie, Friedman had moved to Los Angeles from North Carolina when he was ten. He studied marine biology at college until he quit to go to work in the mailroom of the Warner Bros. publicity department. Except for a one-year experiment with jobs outside the company, Friedman had never worked anywhere else. The marketing and advertising people operated out of a sleek glass building just across the street from the Warner Bros. lot; perhaps appropriately, people who tried to peek in the windows from the outside saw their own reflection. Friedman's office was done in the earth tones of New Mexico and furnished like a comfortable living room. There was a private bathroom and a bar tucked into a closet, stocked with mineral water and Nutri-Grain cereal. This office said, "I belong here. This is my home." Filmmakers came to Warner Bros. and they left. Friedman was always there. He felt this gave him a perspective the filmmakers simply didn't have.

No one from production had asked his opinion, but Friedman couldn't understand why the studio was making "The Bonfire of the Vanities." He didn't like the book one bit. "I read so much for my work that when I read I want to have a good time," he said. "I didn't have a good time reading that book. I didn't find it very redeeming. Maybe I didn't get it. I'm not a New Yorker. I've never been to New York except as a traveler or a business person. So I probably didn't get it — or the way Tom Wolfe was writing it. I didn't care what happened to Sherman McCoy. He was such a putz."

He paused for a minute. "But that's because I probably didn't get it."

De Palma and Rob Friedman agreed on very little, but they both thought it was a good idea to keep the production of "Bonfire" under wraps. Quite often publicists encourage journalists to visit movie sets during the making of a film to collect anecdotes and enough "behind the scenes" material to generate advance stories and a sense of excitement. The director and the marketing man both felt that because *Bonfire* had already received so much publicity in book form, the danger would be overkill, not lack of coverage.

Endless essays had already been written about what Wolfe's book was and what it wasn't. Was it racist or merely satiric? Was it the final word on the eighties? What did it really say about the polarization of class and race in New York, and how had Tom Wolfe been able to forecast the rise of Al Sharpton, the black minister and media manipulator who came to prominence after Wolfe created the character of Reverend Bacon? Did *Bonfire* add to or detract from the development of the novel in the twentieth century? How could Wolfe dress the way he did and still manage to be taken seriously?

Before production began, it became clear that it would be impossible to keep the press away from "Bonfire." The media campaign didn't start in Friedman's Burbank office; the media campaign started all by itself. Journalists jumped on the movie as though they'd been hungry for a story to tell for months and months, and once the publicity started it just kept on going. One article generated another, and by the end Friedman would find himself looking at the biggest pile of production stories in the history of Warner Bros. and he hadn't had a thing to do with it.

The drum rolls started on March 27, 1990, with New York *Daily News* gossip columnist William Norwich. He had a big scoop:

> Social civilians rarely sneeze when Hollywood calls. To wit, a parade of posh types, or a reasonable facsimile, who are showing themselves before Brian De Palma this week.
>
> The opportunity? To play social locals in the film version of Tom Wolfe's "The Bonfire of the Vanities" . . . Casting directors Lynn Stalmaster and Jeff Passaro and film publicist Peggy Siegal had the idea to contact such uptown denizens as Kitty Hawks, David and Shelly Mortimer, Francesca Stanfill Tufo, Richard Feigen, Jenny Jay Lane, Jean Harvey Vanderbilt . . . and yes, yours truly . . .

By mocking the New York aristocracy and the gossip columnists who leech off it, Tom Wolfe had given new significance to a dying breed. Though the very point of *Bonfire* was that the Park Avenue way of life had become an anachronism, the publicity generated by the book had reinvigorated the people who inspired it. It had gotten to the point where exclusion from the book felt like a snub. Being insulted by Wolfe had become something of an honor.

So it really shouldn't have surprised anyone that when De Palma's personal public relations representative, Peggy Siegal, mailed letters to the right people offering them the chance to play themselves in the movie version of *Bonfire*, the right people were thrilled to say yes.

On March 26, a dozen of the regulars in the *New York Times* "Evening Hours" section and in Billy Norwich's column — and Norwich himself — had trooped downtown to the Tribeca Film Center to audition.

Norwich's report on the events the next day pointedly failed to mention one of the debutante ingénues who showed up for the auditions. The ingénue, a young woman with a round face, was named Alicia Hoge. Ms. Hoge, an aspiring actress, had brought along an eight-by-ten glossy, her brother Robert, an aspiring actor, and her father, James, the publisher of the *Daily News* and Norwich's boss.

The Hoge family arrived at 375 Greenwich Street at 3:45, forty-five minutes after the society people audition was scheduled to begin. Lynn Stalmaster and De Palma had been in the casting room since 9:30 that morning, watching little girls of seven who spoke with the authority of dowagers try out for the part of Sherman's daughter. They'd tested old men for the part of the shoeshine man, and groups of mixed race and gender for the reporters who had to yell "fuckface" at Sherman. They'd tested the ice skater John Curry for the part of the Russian ballet dancer serving champagne at one of the parties in the film.

Now they were looking for people who ran in the same social circles as Judy and Sherman McCoy, specifically for a scene at the party Sherman attends just after he's been publicly accused as a hit-and-run driver. Instead of damning Sherman, the society people applaud his new notoriety and at the same time disparage the press for hounding him. After all the difficulty they'd been having finding the right actress to play Judy, Stalmaster and De Palma thought the best place to find society people was in the real world.

James Hoge, a short, trim man with the blandly even features of a daytime soap opera star, was put in a group with his daughter Alicia, along with Jerome Zipkin, the gnomish escort of society women and confidant of Nancy Reagan, and with Marina Galesi, wife of the prominent real estate developer Francesco Galesi. Mr. Hoge had replaced Mr. Galesi in the audition after he flubbed his lines.

Hoge was remarkably composed, considering that as he was auditioning for this bit part in "Bonfire of the Vanities" his newspaper was being threatened by a labor strike and possible extinction.

Hoge read his lines through perfectly clenched teeth.

"Bloody fruit flies. That's what I call the press," said the publisher of the *Daily News*, reading the lines of "Man" at the party, without irony. "They like to think of themselves as bloodthirsty animals. But they are insects, really. Fruit flies."

De Palma asked the group to repeat their lines several times into a video monitor. After an hour, it was thank you, handshake, and they were gone.

"We could do something with the good-looking one," said Stalmaster. "Doesn't he own the *Daily News* or something?"

When Norwich's account of the auditions appeared in the *News* the next day, Warner Bros.' publicity man was furious. Friedman did not want to see anything about the movie in the press that wasn't planted there by him. He was convinced that the person responsible was Peggy Siegal, the public relations woman who had worked on seven De Palma films but who had not been hired for "Bonfire." From the beginning Friedman had told De Palma he didn't want Peggy Siegal involved with the movie. "She's a loose cannon," he said. De Palma agreed to keep Siegal away but did accept her help for the society people auditions. After that, unable to face telling her she wasn't working on the picture, he simply didn't respond to her calls.

People were either amused by Siegal's breathless patter and

relentless persistence or were so irritated by it that they wouldn't speak to her. She had a tendency to flatter journalists she considered important and to brush off those she didn't — forgetting that cubs may grow into importance and they might have long memories. She'd worked hard for De Palma and gotten him drawerfuls of coverage over the years. She didn't understand why she hadn't been brought onto "Bonfire," and kept trying to insinuate herself into the production, even though she was hurt that De Palma had iced her.

By the time Friedman called to complain about the *Daily News* article, Monica Goldstein had already heard from Siegal, who telephoned from an airplane en route to Los Angeles. As usual, she was frantic. She told Goldstein to tell De Palma that she, Siegal, had told Norwich he could come to the audition but that he — a gossip columnist — couldn't write anything about it. It apparently didn't occur to Siegal that she wasn't working on the film and she didn't have the authority to tell anybody anything.

"Has Brian seen it?" she screamed into the airplane's phone, as though being at an altitude of thirty thousand feet required extra amplification. Siegal began to read the article on the phone to Goldstein, occasionally interrupting herself to scream, "Can you hear me?"

Goldstein cut short the conversation by telling Siegal she could buy the *News* across the street. Siegal screamed, "I'll be at the Bel Air hotel by noon if you need me."

No sooner had Goldstein gotten the P.R. woman off the line when Jeff Passaro, Lynn Stalmaster's casting associate in New York, walked into the office.

"That article by Billy Norwich has caused us no end of trouble," said the usually mild-mannered young man. "The Connie Chung show has called twice about doing a segment on the socialites. I told the guy I'm the wrong person to call, don't even mention my name. Warner Bros. is furious. They're blaming it on Peggy."

Just then De Palma brushed by Goldstein and Passaro without a word, and listened silently as Goldstein told him about the Norwich piece. De Palma had come to the office for another round of society people auditions. Some were new, some were callbacks. He picked up a schedule in the casting room and saw that Jerry Zipkin, the society ladies' companion, had declined an invitation to return for a second audition.

Nan Kempner, however, was right on time. She was generally thought to be the woman who inspired Tom Wolfe's vision of women who didn't believe it was possible to be too thin or too rich — the original "X-ray." ("They keep themselves so thin they look like X-ray pictures," he described them.) Kempner was not only thin — her prominent hipbones poked at her long, belted sweater — she was prompt.

Nina Griscom, the Revlon spokeswoman, model, and charity fund raiser, had been called back for a second audition. Griscom was of indeterminate age, but she had the blonde blunt cut, the even, small features, and the perpetually girlish self-confidence of a debutante-cheerleader. Her bright grin seemed pasted into place, as though it had been set in perpetuity at one party too many.

De Palma met the new batch of society people in the audition room. The director played Sherman. During the fruit fly speech, Griscom's eyebrows arched precipitously as she smiled very wide. "Nina," De Palma told her, "you're doing too much with your face."

Dutifully she shrank the smile to a smirk. De Palma, watching the video monitor, flubbed his line, and Griscom giggled. "You certainly won't get the part," she said, with the flirtatious self-confidence of a woman accustomed to having her way. De Palma, matching her jovial tone — he'd gone to dancing school with women like Griscom — told her to try to read her lines without raising her eyebrows. She did, and he thanked her and told her to go.

"You stay," he said to Kempner.

"My hands are like ice," said the professional socialite. "I'm so nervous. I haven't slept for three nights."

De Palma smiled, kindly. During these auditions he alternated between playing sympathetic coach and cool appraiser. "Didn't you do any acting in school?"

Kempner shook her head. "I was Joseph in the Christmas pageant for three years." She paused and looked at him a little sadly. "You know, my dear, I got married and *zing*. There was no thought for a career."

Passaro took Kempner's photograph with a Polaroid, because the socialites, except for the Hoge children, didn't carry the standard eight-by-ten glossies that actors always had with them. Kempner said, "You know, Ron Alexander from the *Times* called to see if this was still going on, so I'm afraid to tell you, there may be more on this . . ."

At that moment fashion designer Mary McFadden walked in to audition. McFadden seemed sculpted all around: everything about her seemed squared off. Her shiny black hair, her short, short black skirt, even her fur coat. She was lean and lithe and youthful everywhere but her face, the only part of her that actually looked her fifty-one years. Kempner and McFadden hugged.

The two women auditioned together in the society people scene. Neither seemed to open her mouth when talking. McFadden's speech pattern, like her appearance, was blunt and ungiving. When they finished, De Palma said, "Thank you," and left the room.

McFadden squealed, without opening her mouth very wide, "You were wonderful!"

"I hope Mr. De Palma thought I was wonderful," muttered Kempner as she pulled on her fur jacket and left the room. A minute later she returned, saying, "I'm so nervous I forgot my bag."

Tom Wolfe was surprised and perhaps a little disappointed that the people he'd written about with such nasty precision were lining up to be associated with the movie version of his book. What was the point of insulting people if they didn't get the insult?

"I was surprised that they wanted to be in the movie," the author mused as he ate his cereal one morning at the Carlyle Hotel. "But I guess I underestimate the ongoing attraction of the movies. They're so glamorous. I found in writing fiction for the first time that people love their worlds to be written about, whatever way you want to write about them, as long as the finger isn't pointed squarely at them. I've never gotten as many invitations to speak before Wall Street in my life as I did after this book. They loved the fact that someone paid attention."

Wolfe spoke very carefully and slowly. "A lot of these people obviously love to be written about. Remember *Seven Days* magazine? The best headline of the eighties said, YOU WENT OUT LAST NIGHT. NOBODY WROTE ABOUT IT. DO YOU EXIST?"

* * *

The Sunday *Times* followed up on the "Lifestyle" page with a tongue-in-cheek account of the tryouts. "Clearly the place to have been this week was the Tribeca Film Center," the article began, and then mentioned the names of all the socialites who showed up for the event. Kempner told the *Times* she could always use a free trip to California and that Warner Bros. had promised to pay for airfare, hotels, and expenses.

Five days after the *Times* article appeared, Mark Canton received a handwritten note from Joan Tisch, wife of Preston Robert Tisch, former postmaster general of the United States and president and co–chief executive officer of the Loews Corporation. Their son Steven, a movie producer, was a close friend of Canton's. The note was written in the friendly tone that mothers tend to take with their children's pals.

Joan Tisch wrote Canton that she'd read about the auditions "with great interest" and thought she could play one of the small parts. To bolster her case, she assured Canton that Warner Bros. wouldn't have to provide hotel accommodations "as I have my own" (the Regency), or air transportation "as I have my own." Tisch added that the movie company wouldn't even have to give her space at the Metropolitan Museum of Art, "as I have my own wing." She added a P.S.: "Should Nan Kempner need an understudy, I am prepared to lose 50 pounds."

Warner Bros.' attitude toward the outbreak in the press wasn't nearly as good-humored as Joan Tisch's note. On March 29, the entire cast and crew of "Bonfire" received a memo. Subject: CONFIDENTIALITY. The notice warned "Bonfire" employees that their work was strictly hush-hush and that they shouldn't discuss the production with anyone outside Warner Bros. The forbidden list included members of the press and others working in media, friends, family, and acquaintances. Anyone who talked would be fired.

Chapter 6

THE WAR ZONE

Two weeks before principal photography on "Bonfire" was to begin, Lucy Fisher told Brian De Palma she was worried about something. As Michael Cristofer had revised the script, Sherman McCoy had become more and more likable, and Peter Fallow had become less despicable. That wasn't the problem; Fisher was happy with the progress of these characters. "We redeemed Sherman McCoy more, and gradually we redeemed Peter Fallow more. We wanted people to have consciences, we wanted them to come to some terms with the issues they were dealing with instead of just blindly going through their day and never learning anything." The problem, as Fisher saw it, was not with the way the two white male leads were depicted. Now, instead of mimicking the book's modus operandi, which was to insult everyone equally, the script painted an unfriendly portrait of blacks, Jews, and rich women, but begged sympathy for the white Wasp men in the lead roles. The women weren't a problem; the studio didn't anticipate a howl of protest from Nan Kempner's crowd. And, to balance District Attorney Abe Weiss, the cunning Jew to be played by F. Murray Abraham, there was the good Jew, Judge Myron Kovitsky, played by Alan Arkin. There wasn't, however, a sympathetic black character. That was the problem.

Fisher couldn't see an obvious solution. The only black character with a sizable presence in the story was the Reverend Bacon, the manipulative preacher who used the hit-and-run accident for his own political purposes. It wouldn't do to redeem the Reverend Bacon. Fisher wasn't sure what to do, but she found herself wishing that when she and De Palma were first discussing the movie's cast they hadn't dismissed her suggestion that maybe Judge Kovitsky should be played, as Fisher put it, "by a minority-type person," by somebody like Eddie Olmos or Morgan Freeman.

Lucy Fisher's concerns were pressing on De Palma as he was watching the Academy Awards on March 26 on TV. Morgan Freeman had been nominated for best actor for his role in "Driving Miss Daisy," and as Freeman's face flashed on the screen, De Palma wondered if he had compromised by rejecting Judge Roberts for the role of Judge Kovitsky. Roberts had undeniably given a great performance at his audition, but this wasn't a documentary. This was an expensive Hollywood movie, already much more expensive than the $29 million originally anticipated by the studio. Fred Caruso had notified him that the addition of Bruce Willis's $5 million star's salary had helped push the budget to the $35–$40 million range, and that was probably a conservative estimate. De Palma was well aware that in this arena he had to function as a businessman as well as a director. He felt he had a duty to consider the audience's reaction, whether he wanted to or not. An abrasive Jew like Judge Roberts might play on the coasts, but what about everywhere else?

Ten years earlier he wouldn't have worried about it for a minute, and maybe he wouldn't be thinking about it now if "Casualties" had been a hit. Ten years earlier he had just completed "Blow Out." Now, its $15 million budget looked paltry, just enough to cover the $11 million paid to "Bonfire"'s three top stars, De Palma's $2.5 million, and the $750,000 paid for the book and the $600,000 for the screenplay. But in 1980 a $15 million film was considered substantial. And De Palma had refused to compromise on that picture, which was released by Columbia Pictures. Against the advice of everyone he'd cast John Travolta, who had become popular as the disco dancer in "Saturday Night Fever," to play the leading role of the sound specialist who uncovers a political conspiracy. He denied his hero redemption, even though everyone told him not to do it. He killed the girl.

The film had integrity. It was true to De Palma's vision — and it bombed financially. So later, when he made "Casualties of War," he made the cuts the studio suggested after the depressing preview in Boston. When the film failed to succeed at the box office, De Palma was left feeling that he'd made a mistake. He'd made changes he hadn't wanted to make — changes he felt hurt the movie — for nothing.

He wasn't sure where integrity stopped and compromise began, and where irresponsibility fit into the mix. The bigger the movies got, the more they felt like an enterprise and the less they felt like artistic expression. This movie had become very big, and because he was in charge he found himself seriously considering these ideas the studio executives kept harping on, ideas that seemed to him entirely irrelevant to the production of a work of art: *Likability. Empathy. Racial balance.* Racial balance! What was he, the ACLU?

At first, De Palma had rejected the notion of creating racial balance in the movie because it seemed cowardly. The very idea undercut the satiric intent of the material. The book was about greed and self-interest across the board, and that included self-promoters like Reverend Bacon, the fictional black minister. It was about the jackals hovering over the carcass.

On De Palma's television set, the Academy Awards ceremony had just named "Driving Miss Daisy" best picture, and the sound of the cheers from the audience triggered the thought of Kovitsky's justice speech. De Palma began wondering if it would be easier to get an audience to cheer for Morgan Freeman or James Earl Jones — majestic black actors who seemed above considerations of ethnicity or race — than for an edgy persona like Alan Arkin. Maybe it would be easier for a noble black judge to confront the duplicitous Reverend Bacon than for a white judge.

By the time the Academy Awards were over, De Palma had convinced himself that it didn't really matter whether Kovitsky was black or Jewish. What mattered was whether the audience would be behind this voice of righteousness 100 percent. He went to sleep that night thinking that Morgan Freeman was looking interesting indeed.

When De Palma called Fisher with the idea the next day she was thrilled. Freeman was in excellent standing at the studio. He had starred in a film Warner Bros. had distributed called "Lean on

Me," the unabashedly uplifting "true story" of a tough black New Jersey principal who instills a sense of worth in his students. The picture was an unexpected hit, and it had elevated Freeman from the wilderness of good New York stage actors to the ranks of the box office draws. Warner Bros. also distributed "Driving Miss Daisy." The modest film would go on to gross over $100 million at the box office. As it turned out, Freeman was scheduled to start rehearsals for *Taming of the Shrew*, as part of Joseph Papp's free Shakespeare in the Park series in Central Park, and wouldn't mind the chance to do a movie in New York that required two weeks' work at most.

By April 3 it looked as though the actor was practically signed on. Alan Arkin had already been contracted for the part, and he would be entitled to full payment of the $120,000 he'd agreed to, but De Palma had fully brought himself around to the idea that the only place to instill any emotion into this movie driven by wit and satire and plot was in the person of Judge Kovitsky. Kovitsky would give the picture "heart" and "decency," and now Judge Kovitsky was going to be black.

Two days later the negotiations with Freeman had broken down. The actor was asking $750,000 to play Kovitsky, far more than the $120,000 Arkin had asked for. The studio had countered Freeman with $500,000. De Palma was outraged that Freeman hadn't accepted immediately. He was offended by the actor's greediness: a half-million dollars for two weeks of work! He started telling himself a Jewish judge wouldn't be so bad after all.

By the end of the week, however, it was settled. Freeman lowered his price to $650,000. The following week the casting change was made official in *Variety*, the show business paper of record. Fred Caruso was quoted saying:

> "We were thrilled when Alan was going to do it but sometimes you have a change of thought. We expressed our apologies to Alan — and we'll have to negotiate something. This is not the first time this sort of thing has happened — nor will it be the last, but we are concerned about his feelings." Asked about the reason given for the switch in players Caruso said, "The studio has requested us not to discuss it. . . . I'm not at liberty to say."

*   *   *

Until the decision to cast Morgan Freeman in the role of Judge Kovitsky was made, Tom Wolfe had maintained an attitude of polite, if distant, encouragement toward the movie. He had, as he himself pointed out, cashed the check. He'd met with Peter Guber, had tea with Lucy Fisher, chatted with Mark Canton, and had dinner with Brian De Palma. Nothing he'd heard from the film-makers had given him cause for alarm. However, the transformation of Judge Kovitsky distressed him. At that moment he started to think that this movie was indeed going to be *something else*, a something else he might not like very much.

Wolfe had made Kovitsky Jewish for a specific reason. Kovitsky and Weiss, the district attorney, belonged to the old guard of the Bronx, the Jews and Italians who had run the borough for years. They were still in power, though their constituency had changed. Both men — white and Jewish — faced the same situation and responded entirely differently. Weiss behaved opportunistically, like a political animal, hounding Sherman McCoy to impress voters. Kovitsky, on the other hand, at great cost to himself in the end, hewed to the line of justice.

"With Morgan Freeman, with all his presence, that's gone," said Wolfe sadly. "I don't know for a fact why they did it, but I think they lost heart. You know, there is an etiquette, particularly on television — and in the movies too, I guess — which says it's okay to raise the question of racial hostility only if somewhere toward the close of the action you produce an enlightened figure, prefera-bly from the streets, who creates a higher synthesis and teaches everyone the error of their ways. As the drama ends, everyone heads off into a warmer sunset. Sadder perhaps, but wiser."

The slightest edge crept into his gentle tone. "I was criticized for not doing that. But life is not like that. To me reality is extremely important in fiction as well as in nonfiction. I don't think you can understand the human heart if you move from reality." He touched his fine, graying hair. "That's the minority viewpoint."

Just before Freeman was signed, Fred Caruso had finally put to-gether a shooting schedule from which he could plan a realistic budget. He had broken the script down, scene by scene. Together with Chris Soldo, the first assistant director, he had planned each of the sixty-seven days, starting April 13 in New York and ending July 13 on the Warner Bros. lot in Burbank. The schedule detailed where each scene would be filmed — on location or on a set — how much time should be allotted for the scene, how many extras would be required, how many vehicles, how many props, what kind of lighting and electrical equipment, and how many meals. Would they need cranes to elevate the camera, or dolly tracks to glide it along the ground? There were a million details, and each one of them required payment. Without the schedule, there could be no realistic budget because the schedule determined not only what was needed, but how much time was needed, and time was the great consumer of money.

With Freeman on board, Caruso's careful budget, laid out scene by scene, day by day, with its detailed analysis of daily expenditures, had become obsolete. Judge Kovitsky's scenes could no longer be filmed in Burbank in June, in the courtroom that was being built at a cost of $100,000 on the Warner back lot. Morgan Freeman was committed to start rehearsals for *Taming of the Shrew* on May 17 and had to be finished with "Bonfire" by then.

Caruso couldn't yet estimate what the financial ramifications of the schedule change were going to be, but he knew they were going to be big. Already, Lynn Stalmaster had told him it would require him to renegotiate the deals of twenty actors, and nearly every deal revision was going to cost. If the courtroom scenes weren't filmed on the studio lot, the $100,000 already spent on the construction in Los Angeles would be lost money, as would the $30,000 that Sylbert, the production designer, had spent to have beautiful murals painted for the courtroom walls.

The decision to cast Morgan Freeman, coming so late in the game, put Caruso in the position of the foreman of a very large automobile factory who'd been given a brand-new design for the cars he was manufacturing one week before the plant was scheduled to go into production. Suddenly months of planning were nullified just as this $40 million enterprise was supposed to roll.

Caruso had a choice. He could have the courthouse construction in Los Angeles speeded up so the Kovitsky scenes could be filmed earlier. But the film crew was already in New York, and so were the actors required for the scenes scheduled to be shot there. They'd have to begin filming in New York, uproot the entire film crew and move to Los Angeles for two weeks, return to New York, and then fly everyone back out to Los Angeles.

His alternative was to gamble on finding a real courthouse in New York and film the Kovitsky scenes there. This would be a big gamble because judges were loath to allow film crews into their courtrooms, especially for a lengthy period like the two weeks the Kovitsky scenes would require.

But Caruso would still have been teaching at Monmouth High if he hadn't been a gambler, so he decided to gamble. He had able location scouts, and if they couldn't find a courtroom in the metropolitan area, he'd enlist Eric Schwab. And if they still couldn't find a courtroom, he'd hire additional scouts.

He had no idea how his decision to find a courtroom in New York would turn out. Still, he felt, his gamble was minuscule compared with the chance the studio and De Palma were taking by so drastically altering Judge Kovitsky. He wasn't sure if they'd made the right move from a dramatic point of view, but it certainly was gutsy. Caruso had to admit the uncertainty of it all gave him both a stomachache and a thrill.

Despite the apparent casualness of the troops — the shagginess and the sneakers — the film world was as rigidly hierarchical as the military. Richard Sylbert had been right when he'd said that moviemaking was like war. The perfect war, in fact. There were uniforms and regiments and communications on walkie-talkies in code, middle-of-the-night maneuvers under grim conditions, and an overwhelming sense of mission. But all that got shot was film.

Approaching the field, it was useful to understand the chain of command. At the very top was the director, commander-in-chief but also the pinnacle of the first unit. He was in charge of the main event, drawing together all the elements — script, cast, cinematography, production design, costumes. The first unit was not to be confused with the first team, the actors with speaking parts. The second team, the stand-ins who did the tedious job of filling in for the actors while the lights and cameras were set up, wasn't to be confused with the second unit. The second unit operated entirely independently of everyone else — but, of course, reported to the director.

There was a first assistant director, whose job was to orchestrate crowd scenes, help schedule shooting, rehearse the performers, and generally keep order on the set. The second assistant director made sure everyone got to where the first assistant director wanted them to be, and the second to the second did what the second assistant did when the second assistant couldn't.

Every lieutenant had an assistant, and every assistant had assistants. A complex assortment of union rules guaranteed that film sets would be schizophrenic. There would be squadrons of people who never stopped moving from the first call to the final wrap every day. And there would be squadrons of people who never moved at all. The latter group had one job only: simply to be there. For example, because Vilmos Zsigmond belonged to the Los Angeles cinematographers' union, a New York cameraman also showed up every day because the New York union rules demanded it. The New York "director of photography" was paid $3,850 a week to sit and watch Zsigmond work.

Almost every decision required aesthetic and technical judgments, and then manual labor to make things happen, always operating under the constraints of time and money. The usual conditions of a workplace existed but in a compressed form. There was competition, jealousy, and romance, just as there would be in any office or factory anywhere. But all of it had to be acted out in haste and on constantly changing terrain. The factory kept moving.

The social stratification was the only certainty on a film set. The players were always different, but status was constant. And almost everyone was angling for better status. The camera operator wanted to be cinematographer; the cinematographer wanted to direct. The secretaries wanted to be associate producers; the p.a.'s, the production assistants, wanted to be anything that wasn't the lowest rung on the ladder. The stand-ins wanted to act. Everyone was working on a script.

The class distinctions started at the top and ended at the bottom, sometimes they were obvious and sometimes they were subtle, and everyone knew they existed and joked about them. "What's the difference between an electrician and a grip?" the location scouts would ask. The answer: "The electricians take the dishes out of the sink before they pee in it."

* * *

On April 5, Brian De Palma upset the hierarchy by taking over the supervision of one of Eric Schwab's second unit shots, the view of the Bronx that presents itself to Sherman and Maria when they make a wrong turn off the Triborough Bridge. The director had decided to take the first unit crew to Prostitute Street, the place he'd visited with his top lieutenants a few weeks earlier. De Palma needed to see for himself whether the street, as reconstructed by his lieutenants, would convey the terror Sherman, the Master of the Universe, would feel when he found himself in an altogether different galaxy.

De Palma and Schwab had discussed what the street should look like shortly after the location scout. Schwab had brought photographs of the street to show De Palma in between auditions of the society people.

"We'll see drug deals, stripping cars, probably about three, don't you think?" Schwab had said. "Vilmos wants burning cars for interest. Probably about three, don't you think?"

De Palma had stared at the photograph and said, "I want to see drug deals, cars being bashed — bash, bash, bash. And burning cars."

As De Palma's station wagon headed north up the FDR Drive toward the recreation of the scene he and Schwab had imagined, he felt an overwhelming urge to turn around and go home. He felt claustrophobic, and he was just entering the tunnel. The tunnel was only one of the ways he described the experience of making a movie. He also called it the nightmare and the horror show. It wasn't the grueling pace he dreaded so much, though the Christmas release date would require a six-day-a-week schedule for many weeks. He was far more worried about responding to the ceaseless flow of decisions that would have to be made instantly, and by him. And worst of all, he now had to face the fact that for the next four months his blissful isolation would be obliterated. He would be surrounded by dozens of people every day, all of them looking to him, waiting for him to tell them what to do, watching for him to make a mistake.

As the car entered the Bronx, De Palma pulled out the looseleaf notebook that contained his storyboards and the script. Flipping to the page containing the shot being filmed that night, he wondered what it would feel like up there on the set. It had been almost two years since he'd finished shooting "Casualties of War." The directives had gone out to his lieutenants and now he'd see what they'd done. He glanced down at his notebook and saw the words Maria says to Sherman when their Mercedes turns onto Prostitute Street — words Melanie Griffith would record on a sound stage in Los Angeles with the footage they'd shoot tonight projected on a screen behind her. He read the line out loud: "Christ, we're in the middle of a war zone."

A huge caravan had preceded De Palma to the Bronx by several hours. By the time he reached River Avenue in the Bronx at 10:00 that night, the street the movie people called Prostitute Street was lit up like a carnival — and was just as crowded and noisy. There weren't any rides but there were vehicles galore. A backhoe, a bulldozer, a dump truck, and two regular trucks pulled trailers hauling the equipment needed for sound and for rigging the lights. There were the vans and station wagons that transported the crew and the fifteen additional cars hired to provide background traffic — plus the cars that were to be bashed and the cars that were to be burned. There was a sizable crew: almost sixty people. And even though no actors would speak that night, fifty-five extras — uncredited actors hired day-to-day for crowd scenes — were on hand to populate the street with drug dealers, prostitutes, vandals, and loiterers.

The intersection of 167th Street and River Avenue wasn't technically part of the South Bronx, but it had been designated an economic disaster area during the Jimmy Carter presidency. Though the movie people filled the street only with assorted lowlifes, the neighborhood's residents were in fact an ethnically and sociologically diverse mix of Chinese, Puerto Ricans, Nicaraguans, Salvadorans, Senegalese, Vietnamese, and other Southeast Asians. There was an abundance of pizza parlors and Chinese-Spanish restaurants, as well as check-cashing stores.

By the time De Palma arrived, the scene was part block party and part incipient riot as the real residents of the area gathered near the ropes marking the boundary of the "movie set" to watch this caricature of their lives being played out in front of them. The people from the neighborhood dressed like the movie crew: they wore jeans, sneakers, and parkas or bomber jackets. The fake locals, the actors, were wearing Ann Roth's interpretation of "neon": large, colorful hats and garish pants for the men; clingy, revealing dresses for the women.

"Director's coming to the corner," a man with a megaphone yelled as the station wagon pulled up to the curb at 167th Street. The director seemed to spill out, he moved so fast. Schwab joined De Palma, and the two men strode briskly up the street, not stopping until they reached a small sign that said, ALTERNATE ROUTE MANHATTAN.

"That's terrible" were the first words out of De Palma's mouth. "It's not big enough. What were they thinking about with that sign."

Within seconds a chain of men and women carrying walkie-talkies passed along a command: Get a new sign.

The street smelled of the propane used to create fires in the wrecked cars strewn along the edge of the road. Schwab and De Palma were joined by Chris Soldo, the first assistant director, and an assortment of technicians. All of them stood examining the alternate route sign. De Palma wore a mournful expression that said exactly what he was silently thinking: Why are they doing this to me?

The p.a.'s, the production assistants, started clearing the street for rehearsal. "Clearing the street" meant walking very fast up and down screaming, "Clear the street for rehearsal. Standby." The words echoed from walkie-talkies: "Clear the street, standby." There was a buzz in the air; the bustle and noise made this street in the Bronx feel a little like a college campus before a big football game. The crew would complain about the 4:00 P.M. to 4:00 A.M. schedule, and recapitulate the misery over and over again. But it was partly this rush, this middle-of-the-night lunacy, that drew them there.

De Palma would protest that he hated every minute of it. He'd posted himself on the corner of River and 167th, standing with the flaps of his cap pulled over his ears and his parka buttoned all the way up to protect himself from the cold and damp. "I could have been an electrical engineer," he muttered. "I could have been a doctor." He watched the progress of the rehearsal, which consisted of fifteen drivers guiding their beat-up cars through a maze of extras dressed like prostitutes and pimps and jive drug dealers. "And here I am moving cars up and down the block, looking at a *sign* you can't read."

Monica Goldstein, De Palma's assistant, had driven up to the Bronx with Fred Caruso and Ron Smith, the Warner Bros. location executive assigned to the film. Smith, a native of Texas who'd lived in Los Angeles the past seventeen years, was cold. A tall man with shaggy gray hair, he hunched over with his hands thrust deep into the pockets of his navy blue wool coat, stomping his sneakers to warm his feet. Smith's job was to keep tabs on the film's progress for the studio. He was intimidated by the director and kept out of his way. De Palma didn't know he was there.

Goldstein caught up with De Palma at the corner of 167th and River Avenue and told him she'd equipped his trailer with two television sets and two computers. For a moment he was distracted from his anger about *that sign*. Trailers! he thought. Yet another symbol of accomplishment. The more important you were, the nicer the trailer. He'd come a long way from "Carrie," when he had had to spend time between setups in a little changing room. It had taken him ten pictures to get his first trailer, on "The Fury" in 1978. The trailers had gotten nicer and nicer over the years. The irony wasn't lost on him as he considered the luxurious trailer Goldstein had set up for him for "Bonfire." What difference did it make? So what if his trailer had two television sets and two computers? Here he was, back in the tunnel again, and the sign was still too small.

He waited for forty-five minutes while the carpenters tried to build a bigger sign. De Palma was fuming. Where was Sylbert? Why wasn't that prima donna on the set? Tomorrow he'd have a little talk with him and Schwab. Maybe he'd fire someone, just to get across the message: Screw-ups weren't in the budget.

While the carpenters worked on the sign, De Palma climbed into a silver Mercedes and rode up and down Prostitute Street with the camera crew. The front passenger seat where Maria would be sitting had been ripped out and replaced by the camera, in order to film the street from Maria's point of view. They filmed the street scene from the inside of the car, over and over. Just after midnight De Palma inspected the sign the carpenters had built. It was better than the original sign but not good enough. He'd dispatched someone to a construction site somewhere in the Bronx to get another one. He returned to the Mercedes for take four.

By 1:30 A.M. the Mercedes had been rerigged so the camera sat on the driver's side, to record Sherman's point of view. By 2:00 A.M. De Palma climbed back into his station wagon, leaving Schwab to spend the rest of the night directing the view out the back window. As he drove off, he was muttering, "That stupid sign. What stupidity."

The crowd thinned as the night wore on, and the Mercedes trundled up and down River Avenue over and over again. A few dispirited protesters shouted from the sidelines, "No more stereotypes. No more stereotypes." One of the policemen guarding the set was called away when, one block from where the cameras were rolling, a taxi driver was shot dead.

De Palma spent the week beginning April 9 at the Tribeca Film Center rehearsing the actors. The rehearsals with F. Murray Abraham, who was playing Abe Weiss, were a pleasure. De Palma had worked with Abraham before, on "Scarface." The actor might be an egotist, but he was easy to work with. De Palma didn't have to explain anything more than once.

The rehearsals with Bruce Willis were much more difficult. Willis didn't have the skill or the self-confidence of someone like Abraham, or Tom Hanks, whom De Palma had come to feel warmly toward after their disagreement about Uma Thurman. Hanks was diligent and uncomplaining — and he had talent. Willis wasn't without talent, it just fell within a narrow range. When De Palma and Michael Cristofer watched Willis in rehearsal, it became clear to them that they would have to rethink the part of Peter Fallow. The journalist had been written as a despicable sellout. Willis, however, couldn't shake his persona. He wasn't an actor who could easily slip into somebody else's skin. He was a movie star more than anything else. The characters he played tended to become the same likable rogue.

De Palma had less than a week to work with Willis before the official first day of shooting. He had no time for distractions. But Mark Canton and Lucy Fisher did not think of themselves as distractions when they decided to fly East to check in on "Bonfire" as Friday the thirteenth — the first official day of production — drew near. With their movie's budget climbing toward $40 million without a schedule and without a courtroom in which to film Morgan Freeman, they were tense. Still, both executives had been pleasantly surprised with De Palma, and Fisher had spent more time with him than she normally would with a director, as Peter Guber had left the picture. In this instance, Fisher felt that she wasn't merely the studio executive overseeing the picture. She felt that she and De Palma were coproducers, that this was *their* baby.

De Palma had turned out to be quite different from what she'd expected from his shocking, aggressive movies. He was not combative, and he was never dismissive. He was always willing to listen to her ideas. It wasn't her imagination. Hadn't he come around to the studio's way of thinking on the question of racial imbalance?

Yet when she and Canton arrived in New York that Monday, and asked to come to the Bruce Willis rehearsal, a routine request in their minds, De Palma froze them out.

They were shocked. No director had ever pulled a stunt like this. De Palma wouldn't even take their calls. So they called Fred Caruso. They told him to tell De Palma they just wanted to come down to the production office and say hello to the actors and watch for a while. Their intent wasn't to judge; they simply wanted to make an appearance, to let De Palma and the actors know that they were all part of a team.

Caruso relayed the message to De Palma, who kept relaying the same message back: No.

De Palma never let executives into rehearsal. The moment was too delicate, a time of tentative intimacy, as the actors — most of whom barely knew the director — revealed their interpretation of the material for the first time. His job was to protect these vulnerable creatures.

De Palma knew that as producer he had to be diplomatic, but he couldn't concentrate on all his roles at once. He couldn't put the pieces of the puzzle together and coddle the executives at the same time. He didn't call anyone when he was feeling like this. His job at that moment was to deal with Willis, to see what the actor had to offer, and then to help Cristofer figure out what to do with the script. What appeared to be a simple gesture to the executives was out of the question. He would not talk to them.

Canton and Fisher, wheedlers by nature and profession, couldn't take the silence. As with most Hollywood executives, their weapon of first and last resort was the telephone. When the calls to Caruso didn't work, they put in a call to De Palma's agent, Marty Bauer. He was in Tahiti, so his partner, Peter Benedek, bore the brunt of Canton's frustration, then Fisher's. "This man is Dr. Jekyll and Mr. Hyde," she yelled. "He's a schizophrenic. What if he does to Tom Hanks what he does to me?"

Benedek urged De Palma to talk to Fisher. Finally De Palma agreed to accept her telephone call. She asked him directly if she and Canton could drop by for a visit. No, he said. His tone wasn't simply cold: he was positively glacial.

Fisher couldn't believe it. He was snubbing *her*? It was a personal insult. "What's your mother's phone number?" she snapped at him. "I want to tell her what a terrible job she did with you."

"She already knows," he said tersely.

Of course, Fisher couldn't guess from what she knew of this impenetrable man how nervous De Palma always got before shooting began. In this case, his anxiety couldn't have been more intense. The film — the real thing, the first unit — was going to be under way that Friday, and he and Cristofer still hadn't gotten a handle on the narration. Even after numerous revisions the script wasn't nearly complete. They didn't have a major location — the courthouse — lined up, and time was flying. With these technical and aesthetic problems pressing on him — these *real* problems — it was hard for him to take frantic executives seriously. Executives were always frantic. One week before shooting started on "The Untouchables" the production office in Chicago was crawling with

Paramount executives threatening to shut the picture down.

Finally he spoke to both Fisher and Canton on the telephone, reiterating his position. No, no, and no. On Wednesday, April 11, Fisher and Canton decided to assert themselves by visiting the Tribeca Film Center anyway, hoping that their physical presence would change De Palma's mind. They sat in Caruso's office for an hour or so, had lunch, then waited some more. Neither De Palma nor the actors emerged from the audition room, where the director and Cristofer were listening to a full run-through of the script. De Palma decided the only way to deal with the executives was to ignore them.

The executives were bewildered and insulted. There were rules to the game and De Palma wasn't playing by them. They decided to have it out with him at the dinner already planned with De Palma, Fred Caruso, and Michael Cristofer for the next evening, the night before filming began. Over dinner they discussed the budget, the cast, the script. The tone was amicable if not warm. Finally Canton and Fisher aired their grievance. They told De Palma how upset they were at being kept out of rehearsal, and that they were put off by his failure to greet them or to allow them to say hello to the actors.

De Palma's survival instinct kicked in. With the most sincere expression, he apologized to the executives and told them he hadn't been aware that they were in the office during rehearsals.

Caruso listened incredulously, gulped another glass of wine, and hoped no one would notice the shock on his face. The executives couldn't possibly believe that he hadn't told De Palma that they were there — or could they?

Caruso and Cristofer watched quietly as Canton and Fisher concentrated on their director. They told De Palma that all they wanted from him was his assurance that he would be available to them. He told them they had nothing to worry about. Everything was under control. Fisher and Canton walked away from dinner relieved by De Palma's apology, satisfied that he was a rational man and that they hadn't made a mistake after all.

PART II

The New York Shoot

Chapter 7

FORTY MILLION DOLLARS
OF TRANSFORMATION

The production of "The Bonfire of the Vanities" officially began on April 13. De Palma noted with fleeting apprehension that it was also Friday the thirteenth. It was obvious to him and everyone else associated with the movie that the chaos and uncertainty that accompanied the making of any film were going to be magnified on this one. The pressure came from all directions. The budget of the film alone guaranteed a certain amount of heat; nothing bigger had ever been shot on the streets of New York. No courtroom had been found for the Kovitsky scenes, so the shooting schedule was in limbo. With the schedule in limbo, so was the budget. The early barrage of publicity surrounding the auditions guaranteed that the press would be evaluating the film's progress every step of the way.

Yet the cast and crew entered De Palma's tunnel with an adrenalin rush, caught up in the excitement of setting out into the unknown. Even those who didn't like the director's films recognized the skill that went into them. De Palma's stature was enhanced by the very fact that he had been chosen to direct "Bonfire." Everyone working on the film had read the book, or pretended to have read it. The idea took hold that this particular movie could be the definitive vehicle of dreams, big enough and flashy enough to carry along a great many people — the stretch limo of hope and ambition. Everyone wanted to hop on, lured by the promise of fame or money or something else, some element of magic. "Bonfire" had already proved to be irresistible to everyone who came into contact with it. Why else had James Hoge, the *Daily News* publisher, traipsed down to Tribeca to audition for a bit part? And Judge Roberts? And Nan Kempner's crowd?

For the movie professionals, "Bonfire" came to symbolize the potential for success only Hollywood could offer. The temptation to risk everything in order to win a delectable prize was overpowering — it was the devil's candy. A grandly conceived movie like this, a film that hoped to combine intelligence and spectacle, came along once in a great while. If it worked, everyone associated with "Bonfire" would be lifted by the updraft. There would be Oscars and a new breadth of opportunity for those at the top, and a better shot at upward mobility for those farther down.

But no one was oblivious to the corollary possibility: a movie like "Bonfire" wouldn't fail quietly. Too many people were already paying attention. As the final preparations were made for production to begin, there was a feeling of nervous excitement in the air, and a sense of possibility, the sense that anything could happen.

After all the anticipation, however, the first day of shooting was anticlimactic, little more than a warm-up. The day's filming consisted entirely of shooting one small bit of action: Peter Fallow, the British reporter, staggering across a plaza toward his office. At 7:04 A.M. on April 13, Bruce Willis, wearing a disheveled suit and raincoat, took his place on a park bench in Liberty Plaza, two blocks north of Wall Street. It was clear and cold, thirty-four degrees. He made his way across the plaza, past a couple of actors playing vagrants, put on his hat and sunglasses, and shuffled toward the street. Willis staggered across the park a total of nine times. De Palma barely paid attention. He'd mapped out the shot with the camera crew beforehand, and there wasn't any dialogue to confuse things. At 8:00 A.M., the director was satisfied. They'd gotten what they'd come for — to establish the fact that Peter Fallow was a drunken bum. The crew was dismissed fifty-six minutes after principal photography had begun.

At 10:30 A.M. the next day, Saturday, April 14, De Palma was scheduled to meet Morgan Freeman for the first time. This would be the only chance Freeman would have to rehearse his scenes as Judge Kovitsky before they would be filmed. De Palma had asked the actors who would be playing opposite Freeman in those scenes to join them down at the Tribeca Film Center.

The actors were prompt. Monica Goldstein greeted them and directed them to the audition room, where they seated themselves around the table. In addition to Freeman and Tom Hanks, De Palma had summoned the actors playing Kramer, the assistant district attorney; Killian, Sherman's lawyer; and Roland, the friend of the hit-and-run victim. Melanie Griffith wasn't in town yet, so De Palma had enlisted Beth Broderick, who was playing the trashy society woman Caroline Heftshank, to read the female parts. Screenwriter Michael Cristofer also sat at the table, both to listen to how the lines sounded and to read any dialogue that didn't have an actor attached to it. The writer was a balding man with dark eyes, a sensitive mouth, and delicate, hairy wrists. A trim woman with short gray hair sat in the corner, apart from the group, her hands resting on the large notebook propped on her lap. She was Nancy Hopton, the script supervisor.

The actors were dressed in jeans and rugby shirts and T-shirts and sneakers, except for the tall and elegant Freeman, who was wearing a light blue silk suit, patterned socks (also light blue), and expensive loafers. With his grand Afro, large eyes, and goatee, Freeman was leonine.

The actors didn't say much while they waited for their director. De Palma arrived at 10:45 and seated himself at the head of the table.

He greeted the group by turning to Freeman. "We're trying to cut down on the racial imbalance in this movie," he said with a small smile.

Freeman responded in kind. "Spread the ethnicity around," he said. He too was smiling, though his eyes were quite serious.

The small talk dispensed with, De Palma introduced Freeman to the other actors, briefly identified their characters, and told Freeman to begin. Freeman peered at the script pages on the table in front of him and launched into the justice speech, the same speech Judge Roberts had delivered in this room two months earlier. Freeman spoke the words with oratorical fervor, and pounded on the table for emphasis.

"Be decent!" he concluded. Then he improvised. "Goddammit."

It was the kind of exclamatory finish that demanded applause, but this was a rehearsal so there was only silence.

De Palma kept his gaze on Freeman while the other actors concentrated on not staring at anything in particular. Finally, the director spoke.

"Okay," he said. "Let's go back to the beginning."

Freeman flipped through the script pages and began again. Before he'd gotten very far into the speech the second time, De Palma interrupted him and gave him roughly the same terse instructions he'd given Judge Roberts. "I want you to wait a little before you blast it out."

Freeman didn't argue with him but looked at De Palma quite directly. "Okay," he said, without enthusiasm.

Freeman began again, this time softly at first, as instructed. De Palma interrupted again.

"No, Morgan," he said. "I think you were doing it better the way you initially did it."

Freeman pressed his lips together. "Now you're confusing me." His voice was dangerously quiet.

De Palma shook his head. "No, now I'm saying I think you were right, go after him."

Across the table from Freeman, Tom Hanks began to eye the bowl of raisins and nuts in front of him. His presence wasn't really necessary for this rehearsal; he was just there to feed Freeman a few lines. Yet Hanks always went out of his way to distinguish himself from other movie stars. He believed, and he wanted everyone else to believe, that he was just a guy doing a job. So he always showed up for rehearsals and endured the boredom without complaint.

But not without a craving for a taste of those nuts and raisins. As Freeman's voice rose and fell, scolded and roared, Hanks stared at the bowl before him and then tentatively helped himself. First he tried one raisin, followed by one nut. Then he tried a raisin and nut squashed together. Then he took a bunch between his thumb and finger, and then an entire handful. Occasionally he'd have to throw Freeman a cue, though it began to seem as though the few lines he was required to speak were interrupting his snack. Soon Beth Broderick noticed Hanks's diligent consumption. For a while she simply watched, but she couldn't resist. Her fingers reached over to the bowl.

Suddenly De Palma stood up and told the actors to take a ten-minute break. He nodded at Freeman, indicating that the actor should follow him out of the room.

Michael Cristofer stood up and stretched. While the other actors walked around the room, Cristofer chatted with Hanks and Broderick. He told them he hadn't met Tom Wolfe and that he didn't want to. "It would be too distracting and serve no purpose," said Cristofer. "He's in a no-lose situation. If the movie's good, fine. If it isn't, nice, we screwed it up."

Cristofer said he was worried about the length of the film. "You don't usually do long comedy," he said.

Hanks grinned. " 'It's a Mad Mad Mad Mad World' was a long comedy."

Cristofer smiled weakly.

Twenty minutes later De Palma and Freeman returned. They had passed the time watching Judge Roberts deliver his speech on videotape. After everyone returned to the table, Freeman began the scene again. He roared, he preached, he whispered.

"Terrific," said De Palma, at the end.

Then the dignified Freeman stared solemnly around the table and started to whoop. "See that! I tol' ya, I tol' ya. I tol' ya!" He laughed and shook his head.

The other actors joined his laughter as if they'd been cued. De Palma smiled and told the group to go, shaking hands as they left.

Cristofer stayed behind to discuss the latest script revisions.

"It's going to be great," said the writer.

"Yeah," grunted De Palma.

Goldstein tiptoed in and laid a copy of *Vanity Fair* magazine on the table in front of De Palma, opened to the page with a photograph of Don Simpson, the producer. Simpson had sent the magazine and a note to De Palma, volunteering to play the part of a producer who asks Sherman McCoy for the rights to his story and says, "Listen, babe, I'll suck your dick for these rights."

De Palma stared at the photograph of Simpson, who had given himself a part in the last movie he'd produced, a movie about race car drivers starring Tom Cruise. After a few seconds De Palma closed the magazine and rolled his eyes. "Where does it end?"

Cristofer and De Palma turned back to the script. They were looking for scenes that could be condensed or eliminated; the studio was pressuring them to limit the movie to two hours. They spent a few minutes flipping through the script. Cristofer looked weary, as though he couldn't bear to think about this story he'd been thinking about for two years for another minute. De Palma glanced at the screenwriter's face and suggested they talk later. As Cristofer started to get up out of his chair, De Palma asked, "What do you think of our Kovitsky?"

"I think it's great," said Cristofer. "Of course, I don't know what we would have had."

"I guess we have to change his name," said De Palma.

"White?" said Cristofer. "Something White? Goodman? Judge Leroy Goodman." He shrugged. "You never hear the name in the movie. Why not call him Roberts? Judge Roberts."

De Palma laughed. "So are we done?"

"I'm done," said Cristofer, who knew that he might be done for the day but still had work ahead. "We say this every day. I'm out of here."

As he walked out the door De Palma said, "I have another wild idea . . ."

Cristofer kept walking.

The following week a "normal" dawn-to-dusk and dusk-to-dawn filming schedule would begin. Most of the action would take place on Park Avenue, the physical representation of the world of Sherman McCoy. Even the most imaginative set designer wouldn't have been able to construct a more perfect visual metaphor for the dwelling place of the Master of the Universe. Almost every other section of Manhattan left out-of-towners gasping for air, feeling claustrophobic. But the elegant buildings lining Park Avenue were separated by a wide boulevard divided by a spacious median covered with plantings that were seasonally rotated by the neighborhood's residents' association. The best place to spot the arrival of spring in midtown Manhattan was on Park Avenue, where, for blocks and blocks, tulips bloomed in the middle of traffic.

Like most of the physical locations scheduled to be filmed in New York, Park Avenue itself was the star of the scenes shot there.

As a writer, Tom Wolfe operated on the premise that atmosphere was character, that you knew almost all you needed to know about someone by the way he dressed, how he decorated his apartment. The filmmakers had to telegraph that information at a glance: This was Park Avenue, not the Bronx.

De Palma, who prided himself on his visual inventiveness, spent hours and days thinking about how to present the *idea* of Park Avenue without making the film look like a relic from the 1950s. Everyone had advice. Cristofer wanted the camera to point at a street sign that said Park Avenue. Ann Roth, the costume designer, wanted the camera to pan up the street and offer a glimpse of various symbols of Park Avenue: A bride on her way to a traditionally elegant wedding, an equestrian in formal gear on horseback, uniformed doormen. Vilmos Zsigmond, the cinematographer, wanted to linger on the tulips surrounded by pavement.

For one day and three nights the filmmakers would station themselves on Park Avenue to film Tom Hanks emerging from 800 Park Avenue. Some of these scenes would show Sherman McCoy looking the way he appeared before his fall, as a self-confident bond salesman. Others would show him as he appeared near the end, as a beaten man being booked for murder. The film crew would add six hundred tulips to the beds that ran down the middle of Park Avenue so that extras playing demonstrators could flatten the flowers when they lined up outside Sherman's home to harass him. For the shot of Sherman walking his dog during a thunderstorm so he can call his mistress from a pay phone, a rainmaker would create rain on a clear spring night.

All of this would cost a lot of money and not just for equipment, actors, and crew. New York had once again become a movie town — 110 film permits had been issued in 1989, compared with 26 in 1977 — and no one gave anything away. Every apartment co-op board on Park Avenue knew the going rate for location fees, and the rate moved up every time anyone decided to play hardball. Warner Bros. would pay $50,000 for the privilege of shooting in front of 800 Park Avenue: $35,000 to the co-op board and $15,000 for "out-of-pocket" expenses. Among the items in this indefinite category were payments for extra security people, for the doormen, for the superintendent.

* * *

On Monday, April 16, Ann Roth and her assistants were still preparing for the Park Avenue scenes that would start filming the next day. All of Tom Hanks's suits were ready. But they still needed fifty school uniforms for the classmates of Sherman McCoy's daughter, who would be riding on a bus; shorts for the women joggers Sherman eyes outside his building; and clothes for a woman playing a rich lady with a cane entering the building. Roth had also asked the casting person in charge of extras to send over a young woman to dress up in a bridal gown. De Palma had agreed to let Roth create this bit of background. "This bride," sighed Roth, "could be another potential Judy McCoy," Sherman's wife.

But before Roth met at the Costume Depot with the extra playing the bride, she had much to accomplish. She still hadn't found the design for what she hoped would be the movie's sartorial centerpiece: the dress Maria wears at the Opera Ball. The ball wouldn't be filmed until July, but Roth had to get started on the gown now. Judy and Maria would appear together at the ball, and the difference between Sherman's two women had to be immediately, spectacularly evident. Judy would wear something very tasteful. Maria, however, had to glitter, dangerously.

Roth took her associate Gary Jones with her to the garment district, to visit the dressmaker she'd hired to fulfill her vision for Maria. The designer worked in a loft crammed with torsos and sewing machines and bookshelves containing a worn copy of Proust and a few volumes on fashion design.

"Let's talk beading," Roth said to the designer.

They talked beading and they talked bugles, little glittering spangles in the shape of tiny trumpets.

The designer, a striking man dressed all in black, who spoke with a slight Germanic staccato, draped sheer nude fabric over a mannequin and then draped sheer gold fabric over that. Roth joined him. They draped in unison, enthusiastically, then began pressing little bits of gold sparkle to the fabric.

To the unpracticed eye the concoction looked like a pile of stockings tossed on a chair. "I'm thrilled with this," Roth said. "Thrilled."

The dressmaker laughed. "But I warn you," he said, "this clingy fabric will make this dress very difficult to pull off and on."

Roth waved her hand dismissively. "The scene is scheduled for a four-day shoot. Melanie has Mrs. Whatsername who can help her get it on and off. It just has to last four days."

The dressmaker seemed delighted at the idea of making a dress for several thousand dollars that had to last only four days. "Four days," he repeated. "And drop it in the garbage!"

Roth was relieved. That dress had been nagging at her. "There's no big philosophical point there," she said as she left the dressmaker's loft. "I just wanted sort of a glitz dress, kind of vulgar, yet original. You know, some element of . . . having been purchased in Milan."

A tall young woman who introduced herself as Marena was waiting for Roth at the Costume Depot. She said that she was the Park Avenue bride. "Marena is part of the scenery," said Roth to one of her assistants. "Marena . . . one of my favorite names."

Roth and her assistant draped a long-sleeved wedding dress with a massive hoop skirt over Marena. The actress was tall enough not to be dwarfed by the mountain of material. Roth shook her head and pulled the dress off.

"Try this one on," she said. Marena obediently squeezed her majestic frame into a slinky white dress meant for a smaller woman. To close the six-inch gap between the two sides of the dress, Roth stood on tiptoe and forced the dress together. The seams appeared ready to burst apart. "You are a tall girl," she said to Marena.

Roth stood back from Marena and shook her head. Quickly she unzipped the second dress and went back to the original. "Three strands of pearls at the neck?" she asked her assistant. Roth took three aspirin.

After Marena left, Roth received a call from the production office, the film's headquarters at the Tribeca Film Center. Someone wanted to know whether anyone had ordered a costume for Geraldo Rivera, the "tabloid television" celebrity. Did Roth know if Rivera had in fact been hired to play a tabloid television celebrity in the film?

"What is this, Teenage Mutant Ninja Turtles?" asked Roth. She said she didn't know anything about the casting of Rivera. "This is embarrassing," she said. "What do they think? In case the script is lousy, let's put famous people in and no one will notice?"

On Tuesday, April 17, a sunny day, traffic on the Upper East Side was paralyzed by massive gridlock. Between people celebrating Earth Week and people gawking at the cast and crew of "The Bonfire of the Vanities," the streets were jammed. The paparazzi were out in full force, eager to catch a glimpse of Tom Hanks or of the young women playing the sexy joggers who would run past Sherman's building in the scene being shot that day. In this scene, Sherman walks out of his building holding his little girl's hand; his wife is angry at him. When the joggers run by, Sherman contemplates their firm bottoms and wonders why he wasn't entitled to them as well as to everything else he has. De Palma had told Vilmos Zsigmond to film the joggers' backsides to play in slow motion, to create a dreamy feeling.

Despite the traffic and the gawkers, there weren't any glitches. They filmed the Park Avenue sign, and the tulips, and the equestrian and Marena in the bridal gown Roth had fitted the day before. At 5:15 the day's shooting was completed. It was a wrap.

At 7:00 P.M. on April 18, seventeen people gathered in the Technicolor screening room on West Forty-fourth Street to watch dailies, or "rushes," the footage printed from the previous day's filming. During filming, De Palma indicated to Nancy Hopton, the script supervisor, which takes should be printed. At dailies, he surveyed his selection and picked the best takes, which the editors would then patch together into a scene. The lieutenants watched dailies to look for mistakes and guidance for future scenes.

De Palma was silent as they looked at the close-ups of the tulips on Park Avenue and Sherman putting Campbell, his little girl, on a school bus.

These were followed by the Park Avenue sign. This elicited the first comment of the evening from De Palma.

"Oy," he said.

Next was the sweeping view of Park Avenue: There was a woman on a horse. There were doormen. And there, in the very back of the frame, barely visible, was the bride.

The next comment came from the front of the screening room. "It's beautiful!" said Zsigmond. "The sign! The horse! The bride!"

Next came five takes of the joggers trotting past Hanks, followed by the camera zooming in on their jiggling bottoms, and then returning to Hanks's face. Five times in a row the group watched the jog, the jiggle, the leer.

"No," grunted De Palma. "Lights on."

He called down to Roth who was sitting near the front. "The girls, Ann?"

"Their legs were . . . okay. Not wonderful." Roth hesitated and looked around. "The guys liked them. Right, guys?"

Fred Caruso stood up and stretched. "No, their asses weren't great," said the budget man.

"Stumpy legs," said Eric Schwab, the second unit director.

"Scandinavian shot-putters," said Dick Sylbert, the production designer.

"Monica should've played it," said cameraman Vilmos Zsigmond, smiling at Goldstein.

"We need long legs and heinies that are up in the air," said Roth, looking at Caruso.

De Palma nodded. "These should be classy-looking girls."

"Lemon tarts," said Sylbert. "We need lemon tarts."

"And then Kim Cattrall has to lose five pounds," said Roth. Cattrall was the actress playing Judy McCoy, Sherman's wife.

"I don't care if her ass is a little lumpy," said De Palma impatiently. "These girls have to look better than her. That's why Sherman is looking at them. I'm assigning this to Eric and to Ann. I want knockout backsides. When can we shoot this?"

As De Palma and his top lieutenants were watching backsides jiggle at dailies, the crew was up on Park Avenue completing preparations for that night's shoot: Sherman dragging the dachshund out into the rain, turning right, and heading to the corner telephone booth. Work had begun at 8:00 A.M. when the "parking coordinators" arrived at Park Avenue between Seventy-fourth and Seventy-fifth streets and began placing fluorescent orange cones every few feet on the pavement. The parking coordinators always preceded the rest of the crew by several hours, to reserve the parking spaces cleared by the city bureaucracy the day before. The need for abundant parking would become evident throughout the day as dozens of vehicles began showing up: trucks, vans, motor homes, campers, and cars, plus six cranes of varying sizes and two large generators.

The set dressers had constructed a fake telephone booth on the corner. The "crafts services" department — the food suppliers — had set up the snack table and were starting to prepare the 51 lunches and 119 dinners that would be served over the course of the day and night ($219,000 was budgeted for food for the New York shoot alone). Two giant cranes — one 100 feet tall and one 150 feet tall — were ready to drop rain; the generators stood by to create lightning and wind.

By the time the director arrived from dailies, the street and sidewalk in front of 800 Park Avenue had been transformed into a movie set. The three shots scheduled for that night weren't particularly complex in conception, but they were quite cumbersome in terms of groundwork and equipment. Each setup required two or three hours of preparation, as the cameraman and the gaffer — the chief lighting technician — calculated where the lights had to be placed for each new angle. Even with all the advance planning, De Palma couldn't visualize exactly what would be in the frame until he stood on the set. He and Vilmos Zsigmond paced around the building entrance, planning the dynamics of their shot. They were closely followed by Doug Ryan, the man who actually operated the camera, and Colin Campbell, the gaffer.

Karl Slovin, a twenty-five-year-old graduate of the theater program at Wesleyan University and an aspiring filmmaker, had only one chore of consequence while De Palma mapped out the shot. Slovin had to make sure that when De Palma returned to his trailer his popcorn was popped and his Dutch Chocolate Medifast was ready to be frapped in the blender. De Palma was determined not to regain the weight he'd lost after "Casualties."

Slovin had been De Palma's personal assistant on the set for five days, an assignment that directly resulted from Monica Goldstein's ambition to be more than a gofer for De Palma. She had assumed an assortment of jobs at the production office that she hoped would demonstrate her creativity. For example, she'd been keeping track of the script changes as they came in so wardrobe wouldn't prepare costumes for scenes that had been cut. Lately she'd sensed signs of respect from De Palma. She'd noticed that in meetings he occasionally glanced at her when he was looking around the room instead of ignoring her until he needed something. Goldstein had decided that she should be the film's associate producer, though she wasn't certain exactly what an associate producer did. However, she knew it had to be more fulfilling than being the person who kept the director's Thermos filled. Fred Caruso had agreed to let her take on additional tasks at the production office, but warned her that only De Palma could give her the associate producer credit. Goldstein worked up enough courage to ask her employer to let her work with Caruso more and he agreed. She didn't mention her desire to be credited as associate producer, however. She decided to wait for just the right moment.

But somebody needed to take care of De Palma on the set, so on the first day of shooting Goldstein had handed Karl Slovin what he needed to be De Palma's production assistant: a Thermos, ciga-rettes, chewing gum, and a lighter. She instructed him to keep the trailer stocked with the director's liquid diet drink, green apples, Pellegrino mineral water, popcorn, and mint chocolate decaffein-ated coffee. Other than that, she told him, his task was to stay close enough to De Palma to respond to his wishes, and far enough away to keep from crowding him.

Slovin was thrilled at the opportunity. How else would a lowly production assistant have a chance to watch the director work up close? And it was possible that over the course of the next few weeks, De Palma might take an interest in Slovin's career, offer him advice. Slovin's hopes were high, tempered only by the fact that after four days together De Palma didn't seem to know his name.

The production assistant wore his black hair pulled back in a short ponytail and dressed in black jeans and a heavy army jacket. Though he carefully tended to his menial duties with diligence and without complaint, he observed De Palma with a certain detach-ment and a certain snobbery. Park Avenue was quite familiar to Slovin, whose mother ran the American Museum of the Moving Image and whose father was a top adviser to financier Ron Perelman. Slovin, at that moment, was dating the granddaughter of Roger Straus, whose firm, Farrar Straus Giroux, published *The Bonfire of the Vanities*. Tom Wolfe was an old family friend of the Strauses.

At 9:30 P.M., De Palma entered the trailer and Slovin exited without either saying a word to the other. Slovin stood outside in the cold night next to the curb; the air was damp from the fake rain that had fallen from the cranes.

He was joined at his post by Doug Rushkoff, a wispy man with dark, dreamy eyes, whose shoulder-length, curly black hair was also pulled back in a ponytail. Rushkoff, an intern from the American Film Institute, sometimes wore a beret and gave the impression of wearing a beret even when he wasn't. He was twenty-nine years old and had plans to start shooting his own movie in August, budgeted at $250,000. De Palma had agreed to accept an AFI observer on "Bonfire" and had picked Rushkoff out of the four candidates he was offered. Rushkoff told Slovin he thought De Palma had chosen him because he told the best jokes.

"Jokes?" Slovin was incredulous.

"He was completely different in the interview from how he is here," said Rushkoff, enjoying his edge over Slovin. The two men had naturally gravitated to one another, pulled by bonds of class and aspiration. They were the only two people on the set who openly and routinely criticized the approach De Palma was taking to Wolfe's book.

"I'm kind of awed by the size of this film," said Rushkoff, staring up the street at the profusion of lights and people and equipment, his eyes lingering on the rain-making crane. "I'm a theater director. If pillars are there, you figure out how to use them. What happens with this $40 million film is this: if there's something they don't like, they tear it down."

Rushkoff had been cultivating an air of delicate amusement since he left Westchester to study English and theater as an undergraduate at Princeton University, and film as a graduate student at the California Institute of Arts and at the American Film Institute.

"The first day I thought I'd love to have all these trailers and stuff," he said, leaning against De Palma's trailer. "Then I decided there's almost more peripheral energy than directed energy. Brian has to be very focused because the possible distractions are endless."

He was interrupted by Monica Goldstein, who had walked up to the two young men. She jerked her head toward De Palma's trailer and put her finger to her lips. "He might be trying to sleep," she said tensely.

Rushkoff and Slovin moved a few steps away from the trailer, and Rushkoff continued his analysis of Hollywood moviemaking, at a whisper: "They don't like the street sign, they put up their own. They don't like the phone booth, they put up their own. I know it gives a storybook feeling, but it's different from how I've been taught. I'm from a European background where you use what's there."

He touched his beret and, even though he'd grown up in the New York suburbs, looked very much the part of the tormented European filmmaker. "Personally I think it's a sin to spend $40 million on a movie. I know movies transform people, but $40 million of transformation is a lot."

By 11:20 P.M. rain was pouring from sprinklers attached to the scissor-lift crane. Tom Hanks was dragging the reluctant dachshund out of the building. Inside, the animal's handler called out encouragement. De Palma sat in the middle of the downtown lanes of Park Avenue under a giant umbrella. Nancy Hopton, the script supervisor, and the video camera operator sat under another umbrella a few feet away. De Palma watched the monitor, analyzing the composition of the fake rain and the fake lightning and the fake wind. When he felt it worked, he nodded at Chris Soldo, the first assistant director. Soldo yelled, "Save the rain."

Karl Slovin and Doug Rushkoff had stationed themselves behind De Palma's chair, next to Eric Schwab. Schwab was talking to a friend who had dropped by the set. Pete Runfolo, the production manager, wandered around like a big grouchy bear muttering about how there were too many extra setups; the two nights originally scheduled for Park Avenue had been extended to three — an extra night of double-time that would have to be accounted for.

For the next hour and a half Hanks kept taking the dog inside and dragging him out again. Nancy Hopton recorded it all: on the first take there was a false start; the second take was flubbed entirely; on the third take Hanks's collar didn't stand up; the fourth take was okay; and the fifth take was entirely wrong. It was after take five that De Palma finally spoke.

"Could this be any sillier?" he asked.

The sixth and the eighth takes were good, according to Hopton, and the tenth and last take was the best. At 1:00 A.M. De Palma disappeared into his trailer while the crew set up the next shot. At 1:30 A.M. the crew broke for dinner. De Palma re-emerged at 4:00 A.M., and the camera wrapped at 6:06 A.M. It would all begin again twelve hours later.

Chapter 8

SILLY SEASON IN THE BRONX

New York had never fully recovered from its brush with bankruptcy in 1976. Though the eighties were a boom time for Wall Street and real estate entrepreneurs, crime was running rampant and subway stations had become home to large numbers of displaced, often psychotic people (even though a massive renovation had made the subways themselves nicer than they'd been in decades). By 1990 it was impossible to walk more than a block or two anywhere in the city, even on Fifth Avenue, without being accosted by beggars. But Park Avenue retained its magic. Park Avenue still conjured up images of Fred Astaire and Ginger Rogers and a world where elegant men and women wearing tuxedos and evening gowns sauntered around vast apartments, telling the servants what to prepare for dinner.

The Bronx, however, was something else. The Bronx had a serious image problem. Its wretched acreage of abandoned buildings had become familiar to people around the world, a propagandist's dream, the perfect symbol for the destructiveness of capitalism. American tourists in Moscow, no matter whether they were from Cincinnati or Connecticut, would be asked about the Bronx. The Bronx had become infamous. Every so often some filmmaker or writer would come along to remind the nation and the world that the Bronx equaled blight. In 1981 there was "Fort Apache: The Bronx," the Paul Newman picture that depicted the borough as a war zone. And in 1987 there was *The Bonfire of the Vanities*, with Tom Wolfe describing what had become of "the poor sad Jewish Bronx. . . . The Grand Hotel of the Jewish dream was now a welfare hotel and the Bronx, the Promised Land, was 70 percent black and Puerto Rican." The Bronx, wrote Wolfe, was the place where "every year forty thousand people, forty thousand incompetents, dimwits, alcoholics, psychopaths, knockabouts, good souls driven to some terrible terminal anger, and people who could only be described as stone evil, were arrested."

The Bronx had an image problem because the Bronx had a reality problem. Though borough officials wanted to highlight what was *good* there — the botanical garden, the zoo, the Hunt's Point market — the fact was that parts of the Bronx were as dangerous as Beirut. The *New York Times* reported that while crime in New York City generally had stabilized or declined in 1989, killings were up 16 percent in the Bronx.

On Monday, April 23, 1990, the day the crew from "Bonfire of the Vanities" arrived at the Bronx County Building, a woman and two men were bound and executed elsewhere in the borough. The woman's eighteen-month-old baby was found unharmed near his mother, who had been shot in the back of the head. And Judge Burton Roberts was getting ready to preside over a hearing on an equally gruesome case, which had become notorious all over the world: A young man, upset with his girlfriend, was accused of torching the nightclub — called The Happy Land — where he knew she'd be partying. The unlicensed club was a firetrap. The man's girlfriend survived the flames, but eighty-seven other people were killed.

No wonder Judge Roberts wanted a diversion from his routine. No wonder, three months after his audition for the role of Judge Kovitsky, he was still dreaming of the Oscar he'd never win and feeling a little sad about the fantasy that would never come true. He'd left the Tribeca Film Center fired up with excitement. He had the feeling that he'd been *sensational*. He thought he might really have been the Jewish Spencer Tracy. The casting director, Lynn Stalmaster, seemed to think so, Roberts was almost certain. He was just as certain that it was De Palma who didn't want him. De Palma seemed to have some fixation on Alan Arkin for the part.

Maybe Judge Roberts would have let the whole thing rest if he hadn't gotten another call from the movie people. They'd asked him if he wanted to come back to the Tribeca center again, to audition for the part of Arthur Ruskin, the husband of Sherman McCoy's mistress, Maria. He couldn't believe it! He wondered what they could have been thinking. It was one thing for someone in his position to play the judge, who was, after all, modeled on him. It was one thing to play a noble jurist, an Old Testament prophet who doesn't believe in the flexibility of right and wrong. It was quite another to play something less than that, some *minor* part. Did they think he was some desperate actor wannabe, waiting for his big break? "I'm no goddam waiter at Schrafft's," he said, by way of declining the offer.

Still, Judge Roberts helped clear the way for filming in front of the Bronx County Building when he could have stopped it. He simply could have said the trailers and commotion would disturb the function of justice, and the deal would have been off. But he didn't do that. He met with the location scouts and made certain — after some yelling and screaming — that the film crew would keep parking spaces open for the judges who worked in the building. In return, he would receive a photograph of himself standing in front of the Bronx County Building with Brian De Palma, and assurances from a Warner Bros. public relations man that he'd get his audition tape after the movie was released.

Two scenes were scheduled to be filmed that Monday: Sherman McCoy arriving for his arraignment with two detectives in a black sedan, and Sherman McCoy leaving the courthouse after the arraignment via a side door, where he bumps into the reporter Peter Fallow. The intervening action — scenes showing Sherman being fingerprinted and thrown into a jail cell — would be filmed later, on a sound stage in California.

The main point of the scene showing Sherman's arrival was to introduce the press pack, the "bloody fruit flies." The district attorney, Abe Weiss, had alerted the media to his conquest: the Great White Defendant would be arriving in the Bronx that day to be booked for murder. A mob of reporters would be waiting to humiliate the bond salesman as he began his ascent of the sweeping mass of stairs leading to the vast granite structure Tom Wolfe had described as the "fortress."

The subject of media hype lay at the core of *Bonfire*, just as it did in almost every one of Tom Wolfe's books. Both student and master of the art of media manipulation, Wolfe poked fun at the phenomenon of instant celebrity again and again, all the while adroitly packaging himself for mass consumption.

De Palma too was fascinated by the machinations of the media. *Bonfire*'s treatment of the subject was one of the reasons he'd liked the book so much. Moviemaking was a business that had always lived and died by publicity — and De Palma had never shied from the press. Yet he was repeatedly surprised by the public's apparently insatiable appetite for gossip, and the new seriousness with which entertainment was treated by the media. Over the last decade Hollywood had become the biggest story going. Movie stars were as likely as politicians to grace the covers of news magazines. Every day it seemed another publication had sprung up devoted in whole or in part to "serious" coverage of the entertainment business: *Premiere, Fame*, the new *Vanity Fair, Movieline, Entertainment Weekly*. Reporters were hungrier than ever.

On April 23, De Palma was to film a scene that had become standard fare in depicting the media's unrelenting rapaciousness: a mob of reporters crowding microphones and tape recorders toward its prey. The challenge was to reinvigorate this tired image. Cristofer's stage directions simply indicated that the crowd of reporters standing near the entrance to the court should "come alive" when they see the sedan carrying Sherman drive up, and begin "moving, walking, running, racing toward the car."

De Palma decided to transform Sherman's descent into terror into something beautiful by taking a cue from a scene in Alfred Hitchcock's "Foreign Correspondent." He would shoot the scene in the rain and have the reporters carry big black umbrellas as they ran down the stairs toward the car carrying Sherman. As the reporters swooped down, the camera would swoop up, giving the audience a bird's-eye view of this flock of black umbrellas forming a menacing mass around the car.

Vilmos Zsigmond was dubious about the shot. Sunny weather was in the forecast and he didn't want to deal with the problems created by making rain fall through bright sunlight. De Palma, fixated on the balletic movement of the black umbrellas descending, told the cameraman to figure it out.

That image would add about $65,000 to the day's budget of approximately $130,000. The additional money covered the cost of the two 150-foot rainmaker cranes and the 135 extras required for the huge mob of reporters. As the crew gathered alongside the Bronx County Building at 6:00 A.M., there were, as forecast, only a few fluffy clouds floating in an otherwise perfectly bright spring sky.

By 7:15 the street in front of the courthouse steps was crowded with reporter extras wearing raincoats. Assistants ran around shouting on their walkie-talkies; that day's shoot would require fifty-five walkie-talkies in all. Everyone was waiting for rehearsal to begin. Tom Hanks sat on the tall canvas chair with his name inscribed on the back which had been set up at the foot of the stairs. Nancy Hopton, the script supervisor, squatted on her portable canvas stool in the tent protecting the director's chair and video monitor from the rain that would be manufactured later. Bruce Willis stood on the courthouse steps, where his character, Peter Fallow, would be run over by his fellow reporters.

Chris Soldo, the first assistant director, walked by the tent speaking into his walkie-talkie: "I need to know if Geraldo is here," he was saying. The television journalist would be playing a character very much like himself in this scene, and Soldo wanted to be sure that things were running smoothly when he arrived.

Nancy Hopton glanced up at the courthouse steps and wondered how they'd manage to make this sunlit scene look like a rainy day. Her question was answered when one of the actors came by and reported that the shot probably wouldn't be put on film until later in the day. "Vilmos said it'll be 2:30 before the sun goes behind the building and shades everything." The actor pointed at his watch. It was 8:00 A.M.

Hopton peered up at the blue sky and sighed. Then she snapped Polaroids of the actors playing the detectives who deliver Sherman to the district attorney, to record precisely what they were wearing. She would also take photos just before the director called "cut," to record how the actors were positioned at that moment. The Polaroids were back-up in the unlikely event she missed recording a continuity detail in her ever present notebook.

Script supervisors used to be called script girls; this task, which required obsessive meticulousness, was one of the few crew positions that had always been reserved for women. Hopton was responsible for maintaining perfect continuity from shot to shot by keeping a record of individual takes and their details. These notes were crucial during the editing process, to make sure, for example, that an actor's shirt collar wasn't buttoned as he reached for a doorknob, then unbuttoned as he opened the door.

Hopton had been in the business thirty-three years, and much about the nature of her job was explained by the items she'd asked the production office to buy before she arrived in New York:

1. One case of 107 black and white Polaroid film (not 107C)
2. One box of Bic Auditors Fine Point black pens
3. One box (1,000) ring-hole reinforcements
4. Two boxes narrow correction tape
5. One box white pen and ink correction fluid

Geraldo Rivera strutted onto the courthouse steps wearing a very crisp raincoat. He tugged the already snug belt on the coat as though it were controlling his ramrod posture. Rivera spotted Willis on the steps, and they hugged. Nearby a walkie-talkie crackled, "We need Brian."

De Palma walked to the set from his trailer and showed Soldo how he wanted the "reporters" to move up and down the steps. As the extras rehearsed, Hanks joined De Palma under the tent, where they watched the dance of the black umbrellas. "They look like bats coming down," Hanks said. De Palma smiled, and the actor took his place inside the black sedan that brings Sherman McCoy to the courthouse.

The actor-detectives joined Hanks and waited for the rehearsal to begin. Vilmos Zsigmond was sitting on the hand-operated Titan crane, peering into the camera, setting up the shot for his operator. Two grips were in place, ready to tilt the crane's arm to lift Zsigmond into the air when De Palma gave the signal. Chris Soldo gave a last-minute pep talk to the extras playing reporters, whose rehearsal dash down the steps had looked a little sluggish to him. "This is not some Mafia wedding," he yelled through a megaphone. "This is the story of the year! Move!"

A beat later De Palma yelled, "Rise, Vilmos, rise!"

It didn't work. The crane went up too late.

At the rehearsal the rest of the cast and crew had nothing to do but kibitz, and that's what they did. De Palma's personal claque consisted of Doug Rushkoff, the AFI intern; Monica Goldstein, the assistant who was determined to be something else; and Eric Schwab, the second unit director who always made a point of stopping by the set to study De Palma's technique before he went off to scout locations for his own shots.

Rushkoff was animated. "Brian spoke to me and to Karl Friday night! We talked about dolly shots and crane shots." Rushkoff's earlier skepticism about Hollywood filmmaking had been eradicated — temporarily at least — by De Palma's acknowledgment of his existence. Now Rushkoff spoke of De Palma's work not with disdain but with admiration. "Even if I had the chance to do it and the understanding I wouldn't be able to do it," he told Schwab. "I've nowhere near the directing ability to do this." He waved grandly at the crane, at the reporters protecting themselves from the early morning sun with their big black umbrellas.

Karl Slovin joined the group, clutching De Palma's Thermos. He flashed a big smile at Monica Goldstein. "Brian called me by name Friday night," he said proudly. "We had a nice talk, too."

He saw Schwab grinning at him and shrugged his shoulders. Covering his embarrassment at the obvious pleasure he'd taken from that simple recognition, he asked Schwab why the umbrellas were all black.

" 'Foreign Correspondent,' " said Schwab absently. "Hitchcock. The high shot."

By 9:30 A.M. the filmmakers were satisfied that the actors knew their marks well enough to try a rehearsal with rain. The reporters ran down the steps as Zsigmond popped up in the air, and the rainmakers rained. They rehearsed again and again.

After the third rehearsal with rain, a thin man with wild gray hair and frantic dark eyes flew by De Palma's tent at the bottom of the stairs. This frail man was wearing clunky boots that looked too heavy for his thin legs to lift, and he was holding a pair of socks in one hand and a pink hair dryer under his arm. This was Charles Mercuri, Bruce Willis's personal wardrobe man. Mercuri, who'd been with Willis since "Moonlighting," specialized in "distressing" the star's clothes — making fresh shirts look worn, or worse. He'd perfected this skill during the filming of "Die Hard," the movie in which Willis's character single-handedly brought about the destruction of a band of terrorists and a glass skyscraper.

As the rainmaker released spray after spray, Mercuri, clutching the socks and the hair dryer, paced at the bottom of the steps, gazing up at Willis like a nervous mother.

"If I'd known about this I'd have gotten him rubbers," hissed Mercuri at Willis's make-up man, who had joined him. "Bruce is *wet*!"

Monica Goldstein watched Mercuri racing by, then glanced over at Clare Leavenworth, Willis's assistant, a woman with very short brown hair and orange-tinted sunglasses. "She keeps dropping Bruce bombshells on me," said Goldstein. "Today she wanted to know if he could have a cop *and* a bodyguard in front of his trailer. The fans won't listen to the bodyguard."

The bodyguard — one of two Willis brought with him to New York at the studio's expense — was one of the reasons Willis was generally disliked by the "Bonfire" crew and the rest of the cast. Unlike Hanks, who liked to shmooze with the crew between takes, Willis socialized only with the private entourage of assistants who accompanied him everywhere. Between takes, he disappeared immediately into the safety of his luxe trailer, the doorway of which was always blocked by his hulking guard, who'd trained in the Israeli Army.

After a half hour of rehearsal with rain, De Palma and Zsigmond agreed the light was too bright to film the scene right then and they'd have to wait for the sun to move behind the building. The reporters dispersed while the men in charge decided what to do next, and Bruce Willis disappeared into his trailer. Just a minute later he seemed to have reappeared on the steps. On closer inspection, it became obvious that the raincoat this man was wearing was a cheap version of the raincoat Bruce Willis had been wearing. The man on the steps had the same short brown hair and pale complexion as the movie star did, but he was several inches shorter.

The man was Randy Bowers, the thirty-four-year-old actor who for the past five years had been Willis's stand-in, the person who substituted for the actor during the tedious process of setting up the shot, standing in the position the actor would be in during the actual filming. Though stand-ins — the second team — were generally the same size as their first team counterparts and Bowers was noticeably smaller than Willis, he had worked on all the star's movies since they met on "Moonlighting," the television show.

Bowers always looked lonely, hanging around the set waiting for Willis to reappear. But he'd decided a couple of years back to keep a distance from movie crews after he discovered over and over that his main interest to people he'd thought were friends was his proximity to Willis. Because he was always dressed like Willis, and had the same pale coloring, narrow eyes, and short brown hair, he would frequently find himself mobbed by fans screaming, "Bruce! Bruce!" When they'd get close enough to discern that he wasn't Bruce, he could see the disappointment in their eyes. He'd feel so tiny, like an insect. Sometimes, if the barricades kept the fans at enough of a distance, he'd give them a little wave and let them leave happy, thinking they'd gotten a nod from the star himself.

Still, it was hard for this man from the little town of Deep Creek, Virginia, to complain. It was in many ways a grand life, spending holidays with *Bruce Willis*, bowling with Bruce Willis, living in New York at the Regency Hotel. Not to mention the money: On this film he was paid $2,000 a week in New York, $1,250 in Los Angeles (where he wasn't eligible for per diem expenses because he lived there). And Willis was kind to him. The actor felt more comfortable with the people who worked for him than with anyone else outside his family.

Bowers had worked for ten years as an actor when he'd applied to "Moonlighting" for an acting job and was asked if he'd like to stand in for Willis a couple of days a week. He'd gotten bit parts in almost every movie Willis had been in and was hoping something would come up for him in "Bonfire" as well.

But Bowers's primary part was to be Willis's double. The irony of it all was that Bowers had an identical twin brother, who worked as a supervisor in the Norfolk shipyard where their father worked. Their mother had made a great effort when the boys were young to give each a sense of individuality, always taking pains to dress them differently and to encourage separate paths. She had succeeded. Bowers and his brother might as well be on different planets, their lives were so different. But Randy Bowers hadn't escaped his fate. Every day of his working life he was reminded that he was someone's "twin," and that someone was a very powerful twin indeed.

De Palma and Zsigmond decided to film the second scene scheduled for that day while they waited for shadows to fall on the courthouse steps. This scene, a departure from the book, represented one of the major ways the script had been reconfigured to fit Bruce Willis's limited interpretation of Fallow. It opened with the reporter sitting at the bottom of the courthouse steps, drinking out of a pint bottle, after Sherman has gone inside to be arraigned. The downpour has stopped, the press pack is waiting at the top of the steps for Sherman to re-emerge. Unlike the character in the novel, the revisionist Fallow is a drunk with a conscience. Disgusted by his colleagues, he staggers around the side of the courthouse, where by coincidence he bumps into Sherman, who is making a quiet exit out a side door. Fallow helps the man his stories have ruined to escape from the mob. They flee into the subway together, where they ride the train downtown. It is on the subway that Sherman McCoy tells Fallow that he hadn't been driving the hit-and-run car, and Fallow resolves to help Sherman out of his predicament. The latter part of this warm-hearted scene — the subway ride — had been fabricated in part to satisfy the studio's desire to have the audience see its two stars together on the screen. It would be filmed later on a sound stage.

De Palma had decided to film Fallow's accidental meeting with Sherman in one unbroken stretch. The shot would start with Willis stumbling to his feet at the bottom of the steps, then follow him walking a quarter block around the edge of the building to a door from which Sherman would emerge. The mob at the top of the steps spots them, and they escape into the fake subway entrance the set dressers had built, along with a fake extension to the courthouse wall, at a cost of $30,000.

For this long, difficult shot, De Palma called in Larry McConkey, one of the top Steadicam operators in the business. McConkey would strap on sixty-five pounds of equipment and move alongside Willis as he walked up the street. The Steadicam itself was a steel harness that gripped the camera and gave an operator the flexibility of a hand-held camera without the jerkiness. Using the Steadicam required not only great strength, but also tremendous coordination to make the movement fluid. McConkey had perfected a flat-footed, splay-legged step that roughly approximated the waddle of a pregnant duck.

With his high forehead, wire-rimmed glasses, and whimsical mustache, the forty-year-old cameraman had the pleasant, scholarly look of a friendly academic (and indeed was the son of an English professor at Cornell University). McConkey had been introduced to the man who invented the Steadicam in the mid-1970s, after he'd moved to Philadelphia to study fine arts in graduate school at Temple University and had become a cameraman working for the local network affiliates. McConkey saw that the apparatus would allow him to glide around corners for complex shots that simply couldn't be done with dolly tracks. It had taken him years to perfect the strange gait that allowed him to lug the heavy camera and harness smoothly. Now that McConkey had established his reputation as a top Steadicam operator, he could take advantage of the freedom it gave him. Because he wasn't tied to one picture for an entire shoot, he could just parachute in for the few days his services were needed. He liked to fly himself to distant locations in his own plane.

His job today was to film the shot outside the courthouse, and for the rest of the morning Bruce Willis staggered up the block and around the building, while McConkey waddled backward in front of him with the Steadicam, and De Palma ran alongside yelling instructions: "Keep goin', keep goin', good, good, round the corner." At 1:30 the crew broke for lunch, and at 2:20 the sun finally moved far enough west to cover the south side of the courthouse in shadow. Up on the steps Geraldo Rivera posed willingly for paparazzi while Willis hid behind his bodyguard. By the time the artificial rain was ready to fall that afternoon, everyone's cheeks were pink from the sun.

The crowds had started to gather early that morning. Geraldo Rivera had rewarded them with a big thumbs-up sign from the top of the courthouse steps. Enthusiasm swelled when Bruce Willis and Tom Hanks showed up. "Oh, my heart," said a middle-aged black woman with long hair. "Bruce, baby, Bruce, baby, all the way." "Oh, he's got his famous coat on," said another woman. "Oh," said another, "there goes Tom Hanks."

Right up in front, just behind the blue police barricades blocking off the set, were the paparazzi and the print reporters, identified by their pink press badges.

The current edition of *Time* magazine had run a picture of the "Bonfire" shoot in its "People" section, a signal to the professional paparazzi that there was a market for "Bonfire" pictures. By afternoon the man from the *Daily News*, the stringer from *Newsweek*, and the free-lance writer for Gannett were joined by a dozen reporters and photographers.

None of them were impressed by Warner Bros.' closed-set policy. The street was open to anyone. This put the movie's unit publicist, Rob Harris, a storklike man with a little potbelly and a perpetually rueful expression, in a difficult position. Because of the closed-set policy, he wasn't allowed to accommodate reporters by arranging interviews for them, the way he normally would during production. But he couldn't ignore the "drop-by" press. It was obvious that nothing was going to keep them away, and he knew the more he tried to discourage them, the hotter the story would seem.

FILMING PUTS BRONX VANITIES OUT OF JOINT was the headline on the *New York Times* story the next day, prominently positioned on the front page of the "Metropolitan News" section.

The reporter had rounded up the usual suspects for his breezy piece on the Hollywood invasion of the Bronx. He quoted spectators on the street who acknowledged they hadn't read the book but who figured that, whatever it was, it wasn't good for the Bronx. He chided Warner Bros. for trying to keep the movie under wraps, and quoted publicist Rob Harris saying, "In practical terms, we are hiding an elephant in Times Square." He interviewed Judge Roberts being blandly noncommittal ("It's a good book and I hope it'll be a good movie"), and he quoted lawyers disparaging the casting. In good *Times* style he ended on a droll note, with a comment from a maintenance man who said he was disappointed with the scenes he'd watched being filmed in front of the Bronx County Building — but not because of what they said about the Bronx. The maintenance man didn't like what he'd seen of the movie, according to the *Times*, because he "expected more action."

The Bronx borough president, Fernando Ferrer, was not happy. Ferrer was a progressive young politician who had spent a great deal of energy during his three years in office trying to alter the Bronx's image as the sinkhole of the city. *The Bonfire of the Vanities* irritated him. It had irritated him when it was a book, and it was irritating him again as it was being made into a movie. Crime and racial tension were a problem in other boroughs too, but they hadn't been memorialized in a best-selling novel by an author who was a magnet for the media.

Not long after the book was published in 1987, just after Ferrer had taken office, the borough president had publicly suggested that Tom Wolfe was a superficial reporter and a fop. The *New York Times* ran an encyclopedic story on the Bronx's reaction to *Bonfire*.

It had all ended up just being another piece of publicity for the clever Wolfe. His photograph — not Ferrer's — accompanied the article. There he was, the monochromatic peacock in his double-breasted houndstooth suit, his cream silk necktie, his gold cuff-links, and his spats. The caption under the large photograph of Wolfe quoted him saying, "I have the eerie feeling that I'm one of the few real democrats in the world of letters."

Now, three years later, it was the Bronx versus *Bonfire* all over again. Even before the *Times* article appeared, Ferrer had decided that this time he'd do something about it. He had been urging Warner Bros. to put a disclaimer at the end of the movie, and had assured Fred Caruso in person that such a disclaimer would satisfy his concerns about the negative light cast on his borough. That was fine with Caruso. Most movies carried a disclaimer telling audiences that what they'd just seen was fiction, not fact. But Ferrer wanted more than the traditional boilerplate disclaimer. On the evening of April 23, as the crew was wrapping its first day of shooting in the Bronx outside the building that housed the borough president's office as well as the courts, Ferrer faxed his proposed draft to the "Bonfire" production offices. He wanted the movie to end with film clips showing housing under construction, the Bronx Zoo, and the Hunt's Point food market, all accompanied by the following words:

> The real story of the people of The Bronx can be found in their struggles and accomplishments as demonstrated in the last three years by the renovation of thousand of units of housing, new jobs and the pride that its neighborhoods are home to cultural institutions attracting more than two million visitors a year.

Fred Caruso was amused, then alarmed by the borough president's request. Several more days and nights of shooting were scheduled in the Bronx, and he couldn't afford to lose any more locations. Caruso immediately sent the fax to the Warner Bros. lawyer on the West Coast who'd been assigned to the film. By the next morning, the lawyer had made it clear to officials at New York City's office of film, theater, and broadcasting that Warner Bros. wanted Ferrer squelched.

Jaynne Keyes, who ran the city's film office, didn't need any prompting. She had taken the job just a couple of months earlier, as part of David Dinkins's new administration. Even though film production in New York City had been booming, the mayor's office was aware that its third-largest industry was in trouble. New York's tough unions had made the city prohibitively expensive; they were unwilling to make any of the concessions their West Coast counterparts had on the matters of double and triple time and other work rules. Keyes couldn't afford to antagonize any major players in the business of making television shows, movies, and commercials, a $4-billion-a-year industry for New York.

By Tuesday afternoon, while the crew was filming outside the Bronx County Building for a second day, Keyes had sent David Dinkins a letter asking the mayor to intercede on behalf of the filmmakers. She pointed out that "Bonfire" would bring more money to New York than almost any other single movie and would encourage other Hollywood studios to return to the city. Keyes warned Dinkins that allowing Ferrer to force "our film clients" to "run free commercials in their stories for our disgruntled constituencies" would set "a dangerous precedent." She told the mayor that, as a token of good faith, Warner Bros. had agreed to put in the usual "this is a work of fiction" disclaimer and to donate ten thousand dollars to any cause "the Borough President deems fit."

Keyes enclosed for the mayor a four-paragraph précis of Tom Wolfe's 659-page book, and observed in the last paragraph that the film script "takes a more gentle tack and attempts to universalize the story. Director Brian De Palma is a New Yorker and will undoubtedly reveal the multi-faced character of life in New York City."

While the faxes were flying, the story in the *Times* drew even more reporters to the set the second day. Notwithstanding the crowds and paparazzi, filming went smoothly, and the three-day shoot was completed in two days. The shortened schedule meant De Palma could avoid the issue of whether or not to lunch with Roberts during break on Wednesday, as the judge had requested.

Wednesday, April 25, was cloudy and rainy, but for once the weather didn't matter because scenes 259B and 260 — the scenes in the hospital room of the comatose Henry Lamb, the boy hit by Sherman McCoy's car — would be filmed indoors, on a set built in the middle of Studio A of the Veritas studio on West Forty-fifth Street between Tenth and Eleventh avenues. In these scenes the two self-promoters — the civil rights lawyer and the Reverend Bacon — chastise Peter Fallow for writing a story saying that Sherman wasn't the driver of the hit-and-run car. In these scenes too, Annie Lamb, Henry's mother, reveals that she is an opportunist like the rest — a departure from the book. The studio's creative department had objected to the change in Annie Lamb's character, but Cristofer and De Palma had decided to leave it in.

Bruce Willis was squeezed into this cramped set — the size of a small hospital room — with four other actors. During a break he cocked his head at the actor playing Henry Lamb, who was lying motionless on the bed. "How are we going to know he's alive?"

"His eyes'll flicker," said De Palma. "Your eyes can flicker in a coma."

Willis smiled. "My eyes don't flicker when I'm in a coma."

No one on the hospital room set was aware that, out in the dank little front office where the snack table had been set up, Fred Caruso was once again battling pandemonium. Fernando Ferrer, the Bronx borough president, had retaliated against the mayor's film office by calling a press conference to urge a boycott of the movie and to accuse the filmmakers of "Bronx bashing." Ferrer also accused Warner Bros. of trying to bribe away criticism with the ten-thousand-dollar cash payment the movie company had offered the Bronx. Ferrer insisted that the only way for Warner Bros. to atone for its sins was to put the disclaimer he suggested at the end of the movie.

It was Fred Caruso's job to field the barrage of phone calls from reporters with questions about Ferrer's impromptu press conference. Talking on two phone lines, with five more blinking on hold, he was soon caught up in the rhythm of the game. The expression on his face said: What could be better than this? "A ten-thousand-dollar donation was not given to the borough president," Caruso was saying in a deliberate voice that made each word sound like a proclamation. "It was not generated by this movie company or by me . . . Call Jaynne Keyes at the mayor's office . . . We are not making a movie that characterizes blacks or Hispanics in a dark light . . . Our budget is in excess of twenty million dollars, and we will be leaving in excess of seven or eight million dollars in salaries and services . . ."

Punching onto another line he held the phone up in the air like a cocky teenager, playing Mr. Big for the benefit of his pals, Pete Runfolo, the production manager, and the teamster captain Eddie Iacobelli, who had been hanging around the office when the phones started going wild.

"What's your name?" Caruso said into the phone, then paused while the reporter on the other end of the line answered. "Okay, Ken, I don't know what that means. The filmmaker, Warner Bros., or myself did not make an offer to the mayor, did N-O-T. Do you know Jaynne Keyes? If you call her and specifically ask about the ten thousand dollars, she will answer the question . . . Can you hold?"

He picked up line one. "I don't know what he means not spending money in the Bronx. Between lunch and dinner and hardware stores and flower shops we would have spent in the Bronx in the five- or six-block radius several hundred thousand dollars . . . The caterers may have come from Manhattan, but when that caterer runs out of oranges he buys it locally."

He raised his eyebrows at Runfolo, who was sitting on a folding chair behind a desk, his blue and green tweed cap pulled down to his glasses. "Where did the caterer come from?"

Runfolo shrugged. "We spent twelve hundred dollars at a Chinese restaurant in the Bronx yesterday."

Caruso hung up.

"No one knew this press conference was coming," he said to Runfolo. "We met with Ferrer Monday morning and everything was fine. Now this! CBS called, CNN called — first. Lucy Fisher called. Mark Canton called."

Rob Harris, the publicity man, ambled in looking defeated. Caruso, on the phone again, put his hand on the mouthpiece and told Harris he'd spoken to CBS, CNN, the AP, the *Daily News*, the *Post*. "This is *Newsday*," he said, holding up the telephone.

"I don't have anything left to say," said Harris, when Runfolo told him the BBC had called for him.

"Go cover the White House," Caruso was saying to *Newsday*. "I'm sure there are people stoned in front of the president's house." Then he hung up.

Caruso stood up and pulled on his black leather jacket. The fun was over. "We don't have anyplace to shoot tomorrow, and now all this publicity bullshit."

Jaynne Keyes of the mayor's office decided to mediate between "Bonfire" and the Bronx. She arranged a meeting between Ferrer and his people and Caruso and his people on Thursday, April 26, at the Bronx County Building.

By then, if one were to measure an event's importance by column inches, the making of "The Bonfire of the Vanities" had become a news event of worldwide significance. The story couldn't be avoided. Ferrer's press conference was everywhere: on radio, on television, and in newspapers all over the world, from the *Daily Mail* in London to the *Indianapolis News* to *The Oregonian* in Portland. Readers of New York City's main tabloids were led to believe that the biggest thing happening in the world on April 26, 1990, was the making of a movie.

BRONX CHEER FOR BONFIRE was the *New York Post*'s front-page headline. Inside, the newspaper printed a portion of the movie's script. The front page of the *Daily News* put it slightly differently: BRONX BURNS OVER "BONFIRE." The paper did acknowledge that there was other news in the Bronx. Across the top of the front page was a much smaller secondary headline: "Cop Wounded in Gun Battle." *Newsday* took the story seriously, but played it inside. The *New York Times* took a stance of amused aloofness and kissed the whole thing off in fourteen paragraphs, under the headline A BONFIRE OF IMAGE WORRIES: THE SILLY SEASON IN THE BRONX.

On their way to the meeting with Ferrer at the Bronx County Building, Fred Caruso and Ron Smith, the Warner Bros. production man, stopped for coffee at The Court Deli, which was crowded with policemen and lawyers having breakfast while they waited for the courthouse to open. Caruso and Smith spread the newspapers out in front of them.

"They have half the script in here," groaned Smith, reading the *Post*. The waitress, a small woman with black hair and a red-and-white-checked dress, came to take their orders.

Caruso winked at her. "It's a lot quieter now that those movie people are out, isn't it?" he asked.

"Yeah," she said.

"Don't you miss them?"

"Nah," she said with disgust. "I spent my whole lunch break there trying to see Bruce Willis. Nothin'!"

At 9:00 A.M. the doors to the Bronx County Building were opened, and Caruso and Smith took the elevator to the executive offices of the borough president on the third floor. Harsh fluorescent lights cast an unfriendly glare on the drab wall-to-wall carpet; a few sad potted plants looked like last gasps of life in this dreary compound of Formica and beigeness.

The receptionist asked Caruso the purpose of his visit. "It's on the front page of the newspaper," he said.

Rob Harris arrived, having exchanged his jeans for a proper dark blue suit and a tie and handkerchief. Ron Smith had put on a sport coat and tie as well; Caruso wore a jacket, no tie, and cowboy boots ("To keep me above the bullshit," he explained to Harris, who admired the boots).

The three men were ushered into a conference room in the back, where they were joined by Jaynne Keyes, the director of the mayor's film office. Her opening words were delivered to Fred Caruso, with a snarl. "I didn't expect you to hang me out to dry with that ten thousand dollars," she said. Caruso had directed reporters to Keyes if they had questions about the ten-thousand-dollar payment Ferrer had called a bribe.

Keyes had long blonde hair and glacial blue eyes, and she wore brown lipstick. Caruso looked admiringly at her short, rumpled, linen suit and her brown and black pumps.

"We just referred the calls to you," said Caruso lightly.

Keyes softened and nodded her head toward Ferrer's office. "*He* tried to hang me out to dry by saying it was my fault about the ten thousand dollars."

At that moment Ferrer's associates walked in: a stubby woman, a square young man, and a slightly older man with thickly greased black hair. The man with the black hair was Ferrer's publicity man; he said gravely, "No one in this office knows about this meeting, and that's how it will be kept."

A few minutes later Ferrer himself made his entrance. He was small and very crisp, like a paper-doll cutout. Even his mustache was crisp. To anyone who had spent much time on a movie set, there was something familiar about the glassy look in his large dark eyes. They had the blank intensity of a movie star's eyes. Ferrer shifted his gaze around the table like a weapon, aiming it at each person as he asked for a name and said, "Morning."

Keyes started things off. "I'm just worried about the mayor's office for future projects. I've already busted a lot of balls in the two months I've been there. I need some coverage on the ten thousand dollars."

From the head of the table Ferrer projected the manner of an impatient monarch having to listen to peasants gossip while his country was at war. "I have a hospital walkout, a cop shot full of holes," he said. There was a silence, broken by the entrance of Pete Runfolo, the movie's production manager, who had also been invited to the meeting.

The sight of his old pal seemed to give Caruso a lift. "Thanks for the publicity," he said to Ferrer.

The borough president managed a cold smile. "I didn't think you'd mind."

Caruso tried to ingratiate himself with Ferrer by telling him about how the film crew had hired an ex-convict Judge Roberts had recommended, and how the young black man had turned out to be the best production assistant on the film.

"I appreciate all these things happening, the judge's recommendation, all that stuff," said Ferrer impatiently. "We're talking about apples and oranges here. I have a proposal on the table. It's the same proposal that's been on the table since Monday."

Caruso knew when it was time to play hardball. "There's nothing to talk about. I will present this to my management."

Runfolo tried to steer the conversation back to the production company's good deeds in the Bronx, but Ferrer interrupted him. "I can tell you a lot of stories too. They are beside the point." He picked up the proposal. "I need you to do this. I don't need you to tell stories. This movie makes specific references to the Bronx. This is not General Hospital Anywheresville."

Caruso spoke again. "My question is, will there be more media hype and press before our next meeting. This didn't come out of *our* office."

Ferrer ignored the dig. "When will I hear from you?"

"Today or tomorrow," said Caruso. "There's a three-hour time difference in Los Angeles."

Keyes, who had been watching nervously, said, "I think you should let the borough president know what's going on so he doesn't feel he's being dangled."

Ferrer stood up. "You have our statement. See what you can do." He shook hands and left the room.

As the "Bonfire" group walked with Keyes to the elevator, the mayor's representative sneered at the disclaimer Ferrer was making such a fuss over. "Who reads the credits besides film people anyway," she said. "When I stick around at the end of a movie back home in Texas, they look at me like I'm stark raving mad."

As they walked out of the building she said to Caruso in a confiding tone, "Just between us, the mayor's office came down on him for this. He's an elected official using this for his own political gain."

Caruso gave her a little hug and got into his car with Ron Smith. On the way downtown Smith asked why Keyes had seemed so edgy. "Ah, she was a little pissed this morning because her name wasn't in the papers enough." Caruso laughed.

Caruso dropped Smith off at the Parker Meridien Hotel and headed down to Forty-fifth Street, where De Palma was still filming the hospital scene on a set built inside the Veritas studio. He liked Ron Smith well enough but thought he was like all the executives he'd ever known. Their job was to feed the negatives back to the home office so they could be part of the solution. He drove downtown singing "On the Sunny Side of the Street."

Doug Rushkoff, the AFI intern, and Karl Slovin, De Palma's production assistant, were waiting outside De Palma's trailer when Caruso arrived at the Veritas studio at 10:30 that Thursday morning. Slovin was saying to Rushkoff, "This is all bullshit. No one in the Bronx would say none of this stuff doesn't happen."

Rushkoff's reply was teasing. "And you're the one who was saying yesterday that it's a racist script."

Slovin ignored him. "Can you imagine people, like, boycotting this film? No way." He paused. "I still think it has racist elements, but that doesn't mean none of it never happens."

Inside the trailer, De Palma was trying unsuccessfully to rest between setups, eating his air-popped low-calorie popcorn and drinking Pellegrino mineral water. He'd expected the press coverage, but it still bothered him enough to disturb his nap. "What's Hollywood about this film except it's paid for by Warner Bros.? This is a complete New York unit," he muttered. "There's nothing Hollywood about Fred or me or Michael or Tom Wolfe. It's like outsiders have come to our town. Well, is Tom Wolfe an outsider?"

He'd been through it all before. On "Scarface" he'd been thrown out of Miami by the Cuban council. He and his crew were besieged with assassination threats; they were assigned bodyguards and lived in armed compounds. Instead of filming the whole movie in Florida as planned, after two weeks they moved the production to Los Angeles.

Now it was happening all over. Why did his life feel like a chapter out of *Bonfire of the Vanities*? Truth was beside the point. Now *he'd* become the butt of all those catch phrases. Hollywood! Mercenary! Exploitative!

The rest of the day was uneventful except for the excitement generated among the troops when news spread of the awful thing that had happened in De Palma's trailer at noontime. One of the production assistants had done the unforgivable. She'd wakened De Palma when he'd finally been able to take a nap.

De Palma's naps were legendary. The demons that always woke him before dawn every morning also arrived in the middle of the night whenever he was making a movie. He needed the naps for both physical and mental stamina. Almost everyone who had worked with him before had heard about the production manager on "Scarface" who had made the mistake of interrupting the director's nap. De Palma's face had been crimson when he came to the door. He didn't have to yell; the look in his glinting green eyes said it all. "That'll be the last time you ever wake a sleeping giant," the director said, and the production manager knew from his tone that he wasn't kidding.

This time the assistant who dared to interfere with De Palma's nap was Aimee Morris, a twenty-two-year-old graduate of the film program at Emerson College in Boston. She'd already established herself as one of the comers on the set. She was in charge of getting the first team out of their trailers on time, and she had become a favorite because she had the good sense not to call for them before it was absolutely necessary. Under normal circumstances she wouldn't have an occasion to be knocking on De Palma's door. But an actress De Palma was supposed to interview for a minor role had arrived for her audition, and Karl Slovin, De Palma's p.a., was at lunch. Morris knew about the strict prohibition against disturbing De Palma, but she also knew there wasn't much time left before he'd be called back to the set, and he might miss the audition.

So she took a chance. She knocked on the trailer door, then knocked louder when there was no immediate answer. The instant the young woman saw De Palma's stony fury she knew she was in trouble. She apologized profusely and left the actress to her audition.

Later that day, still shaken by her encounter with the director, Morris told Chris Soldo — the first assistant director who had brought her onto the film — what had happened. Soldo felt some sympathy for the young woman, who was hard-working — and long-legged, and cute. But he was harsh. He told her she had one chance to screw up and she'd used it. By the end of the day, everyone on the set knew that Morris was in purgatory, and they couldn't wait to see what would happen next.

By the next day Ferrer's attack on "Bonfire" was turned against him by the same journalists who had dutifully reported it to begin with. The *Daily News* ran a full-page spread: a news article reported the meeting with Caruso, and the columnist Mike McAlary chided Ferrer for being silly. His column ran under the headline FERRER'S BONFIRE OF THE INANITIES. There was a subhead as well: "Take a good look at your boro, Fernando." The next day the *New York Post* invoked the First Amendment and denounced "special interest groups" who tried to censor works of art. The headline read LET THE CAMERAS ROLL.

The movie people couldn't gloat over the fact that Fernando Ferrer's publicity storm backfired on him because it hurt them as well. The film's production people had already found securing locations for this film a maddening enterprise. The usual difficulties were compounded by De Palma's perfectionism. Nothing ever seemed good enough. Now, on account of the negative publicity, the location scouts had to contend with people's fears that demonstrations might materialize outside their buildings. Suddenly there didn't seem to be an apartment co-op on Park Avenue that would allow a film crew to use its lobby — to shoot the indoor sequence of the scene in which Sherman drags his reluctant dachshund out into the rain. It also looked as though officials at the Metropolitan

Museum of Art were starting to reconsider the museum's commitment to allow the opening party scene to be filmed in the Temple of Dendur. Worst of all, no courtroom had been found for Judge Kovitsky (who had been renamed Judge White). There was only a month left until Morgan Freeman would have to move on to his next obligation, rehearsals for Joseph Papp's Shakespeare in the Park.

No one knew exactly what to do — especially the studio executives sitting back in Burbank on the Warner Bros. lot. The studio dispatched Bill Young — Ron Smith's boss and the man in charge of the physical production — to New York with orders to shut down the film if necessary. Caruso and De Palma greeted the alarmist gesture calmly. They didn't believe the studio really intended to shut the film down. The publicity would be too damaging. Besides, suspending production would save money only if the studio didn't intend to release the picture and was cutting its losses — and the executives, Canton and Fisher, had expressed nothing but satisfaction with the footage De Palma had been sending back. Not surprisingly, after Young arrived in New York and met with Caruso, he advised the studio to keep the picture going. But his presence served as a symbolic warning to the filmmakers. Warner Bros. was not neglecting its fiscal responsibility; Young would stay in New York until De Palma found a courtroom.

Chapter 9

DEMENTED OPTIMISM

By Monday, April 30, the movie production offices down at the Tribeca Film Center appeared to be operating at an efficient clip. Only on closer inspection did it become apparent that the people responsible for the physical plant of this portable factory were feeling a great kinship with Sisyphus, the mythical Corinthian king doomed to spend eternity rolling the same heavy stone up a steep hill in Hades, over and over again. The stone they were pushing up the hill was Morgan Freeman, and the top of the hill was a courtroom where they could deposit him. But every time they thought they'd reached that courtroom, it vanished, and they found themselves back at the bottom of the hill again.

Now the location scouts and their bosses had only three weeks before Morgan Freeman would be gone — three weeks and no courtroom, no Park Avenue lobby, and, possibly, no museum. It was impossible to plan ahead. As a result, the other actors were sitting around the Regency Hotel in New York at two hundred dollars a day waiting for their scenes to be scheduled, and the actors in Los Angeles had been warned they might be needed on a moment's notice, once somebody knew what was going to be shot when.

The point man for the courtroom search was Brett Botula, the twenty-nine-year-old "location manager." Nothing in Botula's previous experience — most of which he'd gotten on a television series called "The Equalizer" — had prepared him for "Bonfire" or for Brian De Palma's perfectionism. The director said no to location after location. For weeks Botula and his crew had been scrambling to find a courthouse within reasonable traveling distance from New York. He'd even added a fourth scout, just for the courtroom. They'd already checked out at least fifty courtrooms, or official-looking rooms that could double as courtrooms, in Boston, Pittsburgh, Ohio, Philadelphia, Baltimore, Washington, D.C., Delaware, New Jersey, and New York. Over and over they met with rejection, either from officials in charge of the courts, or from De Palma, who wasn't satisfied with any of the available candidates.

Botula's group was headquartered in the office next to Fred Caruso's. The walls were covered with little Post-it notes with the names of states and telephone numbers. The floor and desks were littered with photographs and contacts for courtrooms as far away as Upper Sandusky, Ohio, and as nearby as Staten Island.

On April 30 Brett Botula looked around the office and started to laugh, a little wildly. Nothing was normal about this movie, he thought. Locations for a normal movie took up about two feet of folder space in a drawer. For this picture he had already jammed drawer after drawer with folders holding pictures of courtrooms that were either unavailable or unacceptable. Botula had stopped measuring this film by folders and started measuring it by the amount of aspirin he'd taken. He estimated he'd taken so much aspirin that if it were stacked up it would reach the top of the World Trade Center. He figured "Bonfire" had already given him 110 stories worth of headaches.

There was a good reason that movie companies often decided to build courtrooms for courtroom scenes. Real courtrooms tend to be occupied by real lawyers and judges, plaintiffs and defendants during prime filming hours. Even sympathetic judges couldn't, on such short notice, turn their courtrooms over to a movie production company. Botula's best hope — and everyone else's — was the Newark Federal Courthouse, where a judge with an actress daughter was eager to lend his courtroom to the film crew. But the matter was under consideration by his superior at the district court level, and no one knew whether that judge had any interest in show business or not.

Everyone was on edge, even Fred Caruso. He listened impatiently to Monica Goldstein when she asked him what to say to Peggy

Siegal, the public relations woman who kept offering her services to the film long after everyone had told her no one wanted them. "Tell her Brian De Palma doesn't want her on the set," said Caruso with an uncharacteristic edge in his voice.

Rob Harris, the unit publicist, was in the office at the time, and he perked up when he heard this. "Tell me too," he said. "Peggy called me again too."

Caruso sighed. "I'll talk to her," he said. Talking to Siegal would be the easiest thing Caruso had to do that day. The executives were going wild, and he didn't blame them. Why wasn't there a courtroom? Why was there no schedule?

De Palma tried to leave the location mess to the underlings. His tunnel had room only for the movie itself, for the dozens of technical and artistic questions that only he could solve. He couldn't pay attention to the problems he couldn't solve.

He knew Caruso and the studio executives thought he was being intransigent, rejecting location after location. He couldn't hope to make them understand the subtext he saw in the locations, how they influenced the rhythm of the movie. His challenge was to make this talkfest fly. Otherwise he'd be stuck with pictures of lots of people walking down corridors and talking. It would be like television: walk and talk. The pictures would merely illustrate what the people were saying.

He had an additional, practical problem with the courtroom. He and Cristofer had constructed the courtroom scenes to contain much of the critical, final action. First Sherman McCoy exonerates himself by throwing his mistress to the wolves. The judge dismisses the case, and demonstrators hoot down his decision. The hooting is followed by the lengthy justice speech. The speech is followed by an action sequence. Sherman grabs the judge to lead him away from the mob. A statue of blind justice falls. Sherman grabs the sword that breaks away from the statue and fights back the mob. De Palma needed a room that was interesting enough to sustain such a long sequence of events, and big enough to contain the action.

As he waited for his lieutenants to find a courtroom, he felt the pressure building. He worried whether he could make all the pieces fit together, and he was well aware of the public nature of his undertaking. He felt as though the world were waiting for him to fail. That week, the Conventional Wisdom Watch in *Newsweek* magazine had declared that "Tom Hanks is not right as Sherman McCoy and 'Bonfire of the Vanities' will bomb."

De Palma was certain that if he relinquished one iota of control he'd be seen as weak. He felt that if he dropped his facade of all-knowingness he would be overwhelmed by the 101 people who had an opinion on what he was doing and how it could be done better. That's why he tried as hard as he could to hold the line with the executives on matters he felt were important. They could give their advice about this actor or that sequence, and he would seriously consider what they had to say. But their emotional investment in the film ended when they'd passed their suggestions on to the director. De Palma, on the other hand, would be thinking about this movie for the rest of his life.

He knew that in the end he was the one who was completely responsible for "Bonfire." If the movie wasn't successful, he'd carry the blame. De Palma didn't care if the executives liked him or if they were angered by his attitude. He knew that if he stood firm they would fall away. They always fell away because they weren't in it the way he was in it. It wasn't their life. He knew he could be fired or replaced, and he was willing to take that risk.

Dick Sylbert, the production designer, and Eric Schwab were enlisted to help find a courtroom that suited De Palma. Finally they came up with a candidate: the courthouse in Washington, Pennsylvania, forty-five minutes outside of Pittsburgh. De Palma knew that courthouse very well. He'd wanted to use it before when he and a writer had been developing a script about union organizer Frank Yablonski. He liked that courthouse; moreover, the Washington county commissioner had already extended a "warmest welcome" to the movie crew.

Washington, Pennsylvania, was perfect except for one detail: it was located in Washington, Pennsylvania. De Palma had Caruso make a rough estimate of the costs of moving the cast and crew to Pennsylvania for ten days, the minimum they'd need to shoot all those scenes. The estimate wasn't encouraging. With airfares, hotels, per diem expenses — and overtime on Saturday and Sunday — it could easily total $900,000. Every day the $1 million Walter

Matthau had wanted to play Judge Kovitsky was looking more and more like a bargain.

The crew had been filming at night in the Bronx, and "turn-around" gave them a day off to make the adjustment from night to day. Caruso had scheduled Friday's filming out on the Hamptons on Long Island, a two-hour drive east of New York City. The film crew had rented a house to use as the summer residence of Sherman McCoy's parents. It was here that Sherman's wife, Judy, would deliver the "golden crumbs" speech, in which she retaliates against her husband by explaining Sherman's profession in demeaning terms to their daughter. Kim Cattrall, the actress chosen to play Judy, had flown in from Los Angeles for the scene. Tom Hanks was already on call in New York, as were the actors playing his parents and daughter.

De Palma spent his turnaround day hoping that the federal appeals court judge would give them a break and let them film in Newark. A decision had to be made by the next day. They were dangerously close to Morgan Freeman's deadline, and the studio was adamantly opposed to moving the film to Pennsylvania. The day before, Mark Canton and Lucy Fisher had notified Bill Young and Fred Caruso by fax that the executives were demanding immediate action on a courthouse. "If we need to dress a soundstage, or another large room, so be it," the executives wrote. "We are not going out of town to find a courthouse."

De Palma was feeling besieged. The Metropolitan Museum had finally confirmed that its board was canceling the party scene. The elaborately choreographed opening De Palma had been planning for months was history. By afternoon De Palma was praying for Newark to come through, because he knew there would be a showdown with the executives if it didn't. He'd already told Caruso to start preparations to move to Washington, Pennsylvania, over the weekend if Newark wasn't cleared by then. He knew that once Caruso relayed the message to Bill Young, who would then inform the studio, all hell would break loose. He was starting to feel superstitious: maybe they shouldn't have started filming on Friday the thirteenth after all.

De Palma didn't want to be available when the executives got the latest news from the courtroom front. He spent the afternoon at a café near the New York University film school, drinking cappuccino after cappuccino, eavesdropping on the conversations of the students at nearby tables. He reminisced about lost locations from other movies. The day he and Vilmos Zsigmond had arrived in Florence to film "Obsession" they were informed that all the church interiors they'd planned to shoot in were no longer available. A French film company had used a church for a pornographic movie, and the Vatican had banned further filming in churches. De Palma had regrouped quickly. He had spent a summer years ago bumming around Italy on a motor scooter and knew just where to find a good stand-in for the forbidden locations. Without delay he moved his operation down to San Gimignano.

When De Palma finally checked his watch that Thursday afternoon, it was 4:30, only one half hour until dailies were scheduled to be shown up on Forty-fourth Street. He decided to disappear altogether, and headed over to the Angelika Film Center on Houston Street, a multiplex specializing in foreign and avant-garde films. The theaters had been built below street level; the dark basement lobby had a queasy purple fluorescent glow and rumbled when subways passed by. As De Palma descended into the dark, he was feeling a little belligerent. Let them wonder where I am, he thought. They're going to panic. Let *them* find a courthouse in New York without me.

By 5:15 Caruso realized De Palma simply wasn't going to show up for the dailies. He put in a call to the director's home and, after leaving a message on the answering machine, told the editors to go ahead with the dailies without De Palma. Caruso wasn't able to pay attention. He couldn't believe that De Palma had disappeared. What was going to happen tomorrow out in the Hamptons? Was the director going to grace them with his presence?

When he walked out of the Technicolor building, Caruso glanced up and broke into mirthless laughter. The sky was ominously overcast. Of course! thought Caruso. Of course it would rain; after all, the one scene they could film the next day — the golden crumbs scene — was scheduled to be shot outside. Caruso drove downtown to the Tribeca Film Center, where he checked the weather forecast. As predicted: rain.

Caruso knew he had to do something. Even with all the chaos they hadn't yet missed a day of shooting, and this wasn't the time to start. Bill Young had just informed him that if a courtroom weren't found by the first thing Friday morning — in about twelve hours — Lucy Fisher and Mark Canton were getting on a plane and flying to New York. Caruso had finally come up with a budget — of $38.5 million, $10 million more than Warner Bros.' original estimate, and the executives didn't want it to go one cent higher. Caruso decided that since De Palma had gone AWOL, he'd take matters into his own hands. They had to shoot something the next day, and Caruso wanted that something to be inside.

He called Eric Schwab into his office and asked him if there were any possibilities among the Park Avenue lobbies De Palma had rejected. He knew Schwab had a better sense of what the director might like than anyone else working on the film. In the locations room they dug up the "maybe" file and pulled the best candidate, 77 Park Avenue. Schwab and Sylbert headed uptown to find a co-op official or building manager who could give them permission to film the next morning. At 8:00 P.M. Caruso finally reached De Palma at home and told him that because of the weather forecast they would be shooting the next morning at 77 Park Avenue.

"I hate that lobby," De Palma grumbled.

"Don't worry," Caruso said. "Vilmos said he's going to make it beautiful."

"I hate beautiful," said De Palma. But he didn't say no.

At 7:30 the next morning Karl Slovin, De Palma's p.a., maneuvered his 1978 green Saab up Park Avenue in a daze. He was late and exhausted already. Thinking they were going to shoot the golden crumbs speech, he'd driven out to the Hamptons the night before so he could have De Palma's coffee ready for him on time. He'd gotten word of the schedule switch late that night, so he waited until morning to make the two-hour drive back to the city.

Slovin pulled up to the curb at Thirty-ninth and Park and asked one of the parking coordinators where the orange cones were that designated crew parking. A curly-headed young man told him he'd have to park in a garage because the mayor's office required twenty-four-hours' notice before issuing parking permits. As Slovin pulled away, the young man asked him if he thought it would be all right for him to talk to a reporter from *Premiere* magazine who was writing an article about parking coordinators. Slovin looked at him as though he were being addressed in Senegalese.

Eddie Iacobelli, the head of Local 817 of the Theatrical Teamsters Union, was telling his drivers that, like Slovin, he'd gotten word of the schedule switch late the previous night. "Tom Hanks's camper was already at the Hamptons when we got the word. The director's camper, two wardrobe trucks, and Kim Cattrall's camper — they were on the road when we got the word. This is not normal. Because of the courthouse, we're all messed up, I'm told." In other words, Iacobelli's drivers had gone into serious overtime because they went where they were supposed to go — before the location was suddenly changed. Now that they had finally reached their proper destination, Iacobelli and his men would spend most of the day the way they usually did — standing around, because the rules of Local 817 prohibited drivers from doing anything but driving.

Inside the lobby, Sylbert, dressed in his khaki hunting gear and Topsiders, was slowly walking back and forth while the gaffer orchestrated the placement of lights. Sylbert wasn't wild about this lobby. There were longer lobbies and more beautiful lobbies, but they couldn't get clearance to shoot in any of them. This one had a nice series of arches and decent columns in the Regency style and chandeliers; the arches provided convenient recesses for the lights.

Like almost everyone else on the set that morning the production designer was feeling dyspeptic. The thrill of this challenging picture was diminishing fast. Here they were in this second-rate luxury lobby instead of the Hamptons, and the predicted rain hadn't even arrived. And there still wasn't a courthouse.

"This Chinese fire drill has been going on for weeks now," Sylbert said with disgust. "It's a matter of opinion whether Morgan Freeman is right for the part. It's a matter of opinion whether you think he's going to make the picture better or whether it's the kind of casting that would give rank opportunism a bad name." He squinted at a light shining in his eyes. "But it's not a matter of opinion that everybody has built a courtroom for the last thirty years to shoot in. You have to be extraordinarily lucky to find one in a major city, and then you have the lighting problem because all day long the sun is moving. We started to build one and then they cast Morgan Freeman, and when they cast Morgan Freeman they had only three weeks at the most to do something."

The more he thought about it, the more indignant he got. "The biggest scene in the movie. The finale! Why put a movie at risk like that?" He shook his head and answered his own question. "Demented optimism!"

From the end of the lobby's corridor, Chris Soldo, the first assistant director, yelled, "Clear for rehearsal. Clear for rehearsal."

One of the residents of the building, a stylishly dressed woman in her forties, tried to make her way through the throng blocking her path to the front door.

"Lady, could you move back," said Soldo. She looked startled, then ashamed. She apologized for trying to walk through the lobby of her own building.

The script notations for the lobby scene were general:

> INT. McCOY APARTMENT BUILDING —
> LOBBY — SHERMAN — NIGHT
> pulls Marshall out of the elevator.
> MARSHALL SQUEALS and drags his nails across the lobby . . .

Tom Hanks, wearing a hand-tailored suit and a raincoat, was standing by with a small dachshund named Brody, also in a raincoat, a smart little plaid. Brody was not the only dachshund on hand. Three dogs had been lined up to fill the role of Sherman's dog, Marshall. Dapper Dan, the dachshund wagging his tail at Chris Soldo, was the lunger and tugger. A dog named Maggie would play Marshall planting his feet and refusing to walk. Brody would lie on his back while being dragged.

Soon after the rehearsal began, De Palma arrived on the set, outfitted in raingear from head to toe. No one asked him where he'd been the night before when he was supposed to be at dailies. He watched the rehearsal without a word, then left Zsigmond and the gaffer to prepare the lights for the next shot. Fred Caruso and Chris Soldo stopped him before he left to discuss the logistics of heading for Pennsylvania over the weekend. Soldo told De Palma he'd had Pete Runfolo send a casting person out there already to find the extras needed for the courtroom scenes.

"It isn't going to be easy to find a lot of black and Puerto Rican people in Washington, Pennsylvania," said Soldo, pulling on his baseball cap. "There's police standing around, the judge's assistant, a lot of people in front of the railing who have court business." The usually soft-spoken Soldo had an edge in his voice. "If we go to Waspy Pennsylvania I don't know how many Bronx types there are."

De Palma sounded exasperated. "Pittsburgh's forty-five minutes away. What's in Pittsburgh?"

Soldo said, "Unemployed steel workers."

De Palma buttoned his raincoat. "They must have *blacks* in Pittsburgh." At 8:30 A.M. he disappeared.

When Ann Roth, the costume designer, came looking for De Palma two hours later, the antique furniture from props had replaced the lobby's original antique furniture and the lights were set up.

When she asked Caruso where the director was, Caruso shrugged. "Is he coming?" he asked sarcastically.

Roth looked bewildered. "Of course he's coming. It's his movie."

"It wasn't his movie last night when he didn't show up for dailies," said Caruso.

De Palma did plan to return to the set, but he was in no hurry. He had a leisurely breakfast at E.A.T. up on Madison Avenue, then had his driver drop him at an electronics equipment store. He wanted a new Walkman to drown out the babble on the set. As he was paying, the salesgirl compared his signature with that on his platinum American Express card and asked him for identification because the signatures didn't match.

He pulled out his driver's license. "Wait until you sign fifty checks a day," he said to her. "Your signature will start to look different every time, too."

His next stop was a music store, where he bought a number of tapes for his new machine: *Madame Butterfly, La Bohème,* Debussy's *La Mer,* and the Philip Glass soundtrack from the movie "Mishima." When De Palma returned to the set around 11:00 A.M., Hanks and the dogs were ready for shooting to start. For the rest of the day De Palma sat between takes with a faint smile on his face, his headphones planted in his ears.

Doug Rushkoff, the AFI intern, soon became bored with the dachshunds and asked Eric Schwab if he could join him and his location scout, Bruce Frye, when they left to check out yet another rooftop view for one of Schwab's shots.

Rushkoff's curly hair was flying loose as he sat in the back seat of Frye's car, sulking as they drove uptown.

"Brian obviously doesn't want to share anything with me," he said, his thin, sensitive lips quivering. "I'm thinking of calling the academy and asking for another director."

Schwab was irritated by Rushkoff's impertinence. "That's him," he said brusquely. "Sit and watch the dailies. Watch how he sets up the shots."

Rushkoff shrugged. "He doesn't really talk to the actors much. I've gotten a little discouraged by his isolation from the company, by the kind of conversations I'll hear him having with the actors. They only talk about the given circumstances of the scene. Sometimes I think he's just trying to find the coolest shot he can do."

He shook his curls. "Of course I realize we've only been doing these big exterior scenes —"

Schwab interrupted him. "Look, there won't be much of a relationship. Just watch. He's hurt my feelings a lot of times."

On the rooftop of an East Side co-op, Schwab pointed to one of the highest steel girders of the Fifty-ninth Street Bridge. "I climbed up that," he said.

Rushkoff was suitably impressed. "Wow! Was it scary?"

Schwab said nonchalantly, "Not as scary as the Brooklyn Bridge." He handed Rushkoff his viewfinder. The intern pressed his eye to it. With his face hidden, he confessed, "I had a secret fantasy that Brian would like me and get close to me. Be my mentor."

He handed the viewfinder back to Schwab. "I feel sad."

Of all the shots Schwab had been assigned, two preoccupied him the most: the Concorde shot, and the expansive opening title shot, the image that would set the tone for everything that followed. De Palma had delegated both conception and execution to Schwab, who had spent months dreaming up a vision of Manhattan that was fresh and that fulfilled the possibilities he saw in the brief description laid out in the script:

FADE IN:
EXT. MANHATTAN SKYLINE — NIGHT
MOVING IN FAST MOTION — a kaleidoscopic jewel box — glittering, shining, and speeding PAST our eyes.
ANGLE
MOVING south TO north FROM the Battery and the World Trade Center, streets and buildings FLIPPING FAST like black diamonds spilling INTO our peripheral vision and DISAPPEARING as we SPEED uptown TOWARD . . .
FIFTH AVENUE—NIGHT

Bruce Frye, his location scout, had spent months contacting the operators of more than fifty buildings all over Manhattan, arranging for the best spot to sight the "kaleidoscopic jewel box." They were getting a reputation around town as the weirdos from "Bonfire" because Schwab liked to check the view by hanging off the edge of skyscrapers.

The quiet Frye, who with his black-rimmed eyeglasses and chubby face looked like a desk man, not a daredevil, enjoyed these outings as much as Schwab did. Frye had found working on this movie exhilarating and discouraging. He would remind Schwab they were making a movie, not building a monument, and Schwab would retort that they weren't making "Teenage Mutant Ninja Turtles," the kiddie action picture that Frye had worked on. Frye's reply to that was that "Bonfire" would be lucky to make as much money as "Turtles," which had turned out to be one of the year's biggest hits at the box office. But soon the location scout got caught up in the idea of "Bonfire" as a prestige project — as the biggest and the best — and began approaching his job with the fervor of a religious convert. After all, he was working hand in hand with De Palma's chief disciple.

Climbing the Brooklyn Bridge had been a sobering experience for both of them. A construction worker had led the two film people up the cable but had neglected to outfit them with the proper climbing belts, and they found themselves twisted in rope cables 250 feet above the East River.

When they relived the glorious terror of that daredevil feat, Schwab assured Frye that De Palma would expect nothing less of himself. "I've worked on so many films with him and he's never said, 'That's too difficult,' " said Schwab. "We've climbed up mountains, a snake crawled — no, really scurried — right through Brian's legs. There was this hill we were all sliding down, and that was before he lost weight, and Brian never once said, 'This is too difficult.' "

Satisfied that the day's shooting was under way, Fred Caruso and Pete Runfolo returned to the office to prepare for Monday's shoot. Either they'd be in Washington, Pennsylvania, or, if a local courtroom came through, they'd be at the housing project in the Bronx currently on the makeshift schedule. They had to be ready for either, which left Caruso in the uneasy position of having to telephone Bruce Willis's agent to tell him to have his client poised to fly East for the housing project scene without being able to assure him that the star really was needed.

Pete Runfolo was also a former music teacher from New Jersey, and he and Fred Caruso had known each other a long time. He left Caruso with a sympathetic nod and headed to his own office. Runfolo operated one floor below Caruso at the Tribeca Film Center, in a huge utilitarian office on the sixth floor. His end of the operation didn't even rate the functional indoor-outdoor carpet they had up on seven; the concrete floors were painted a bluish green. This was the housekeeping department. This was where bills were paid, food was ordered, schedules were distributed. The big decisions were made upstairs on seven; they were put into action on six. Salaries were negotiated on seven; complaints about overtime pay were registered on six.

When Runfolo walked into the office Friday afternoon, his two assistants were working the phones, making arrangements to move the 150-person crew and 40 actors to Pennsylvania over the weekend. One of them swallowed a couple of Pepto-Bismol tablets as she talked to a travel agent about airplane reservations.

"I have to fly first class," Runfolo said to her. "My fat ass won't fit coach."

The assistant gulping Pepto-Bismol gave him a sour look. "C'mon," said Runfolo as he lowered himself into the chair at his desk. "The way we've been pissin' away money here, what's one more first-class ticket?"

As the travel arrangements continued, teamster captain Eddie Iacobelli walked in. Iacobelli, a trim, handsome man with short gray hair, liked to brag that he'd known Runfolo when the big shot was still a gofer. The two men fell into a routine, a kind of burlesque the point of which was always the same: the artistic types running the show would be lost if the pragmatists weren't around to keep their feet on the ground. "We're treatin' this movie like it's Michelangelo," snorted Iacobelli. "Why don't we go to Italy and film it there?"

Iacobelli admired the stack of messages on Runfolo's desk. Here, as in every outpost of Hollywood, one of the many measures of power was the thickness of the daily message pile. "I got my tit in a wringer here," Runfolo said as he attached a lightweight telephone headset to his ears to begin returning calls.

As he was waiting on hold after several calls, an assistant reported that Melanie Griffith was on her way from the airport and she needed an extra car for her luggage. "She really is Maria," another assistant snorted. A fax had arrived the day before asking the production office to outfit Griffith's room at the Regency with a highchair, a stroller, and a walker for her seven-month-old baby. It was stipulated that "above items should be TOP OF THE LINE" and that "MG will reimburse the company."

All afternoon Runfolo fielded phone calls. There were complaints about unpaid overtime and questions from everybody about where to go Monday. He had flights booked for Pennsylvania for the lighting technicians, so they could start preparing the courthouse there. But he told Ann Roth to have costumes ready for the big scene at the housing project in the Bronx as well.

Runfolo leaned back in his chair, his headphone curled under his massive chin, and began opening up bottle after bottle of pills while he talked on the phone. He lined up a white capsule, a brown pill, another brown pill, two small gel pills, one large gel, two enormous white capsules, and a huge orange capsule. There was a stress complex vitamin with extra vitamin C; Kyolic Aged Garlic extract powder; adrenal concentrate, vitamins A and D; B-complex 100; and something called EthiCal, "World's Best Bone Builder." He pulled out a box of Ziploc freezer bags and filled each bag with a complete complement of vitamin pills — preparation for future stress — before pressing it shut.

Later that day Fred Caruso convened a meeting to discuss the courtroom dilemma. Ron Smith and his boss Bill Young, the men from Warner Bros., were there, along with Schwab, Sylbert, and one of the location scouts. Caruso had left word on De Palma's answering machine, warning him that the executives were on their way East and to ask him what he wanted to do about the courtroom.

Caruso tapped on a bottle of stress tablets and grinned at the group sitting on the floor next to the producer's desk staring bleakly at photographs of courtrooms. "Grown men," he said, looking down at the group squatting on the floor. "Multimillion-dollar decisions."

Caruso started with the bad news. "Newark is dead. The word just came in from the judge. We were about to sign the contract, then the chief judge of the Third Circuit Federal Court of Appeals got into the act." Nothing would change his mind — not even a call from chief corporate counsel at Warner Bros.

Bill Young, a square man with short gray hair, hoisted himself to his feet. "Why are they dickin' around with us?" He stared out the window, exhausted from the fruitless search for a courtroom. He had spent the afternoon with Caruso and Sylbert up in White Plains, only to find another candidate that wouldn't work. His mission to New York had been a failure. After ten days he'd only succeeded in agreeing with the filmmakers that finding a court-house was very difficult indeed. He shook his head and said mournfully, "I've got my executives flying in over the weekend."

Sylbert held up a photo of the Essex County Courthouse, a state court building that was also in Newark. It was an elegant structure, designed by the same architects who'd built the U.S. Supreme Court in Washington, D.C. Sylbert felt certain they could get Essex County because they'd already used that building the previous Friday night, to film the scene in which Abe Weiss, the district attorney, orders his flunkies to find his Great White Defendant, the man who hit the black kid, Henry Lamb. Of course, that scene was shot on a staircase, not inside a courtroom. And it was a one-night shoot; it didn't disrupt the ordinary flow of business for several days, possibly a couple of weeks, the way the Kovitsky scenes would.

"This is it," Sylbert said. He knew that De Palma had already rejected that courtroom because it was too small for the large action scene he had mapped out as part of the finale. But maybe he'd feel differently now that they were desperate.

Caruso wasn't so sure. "I look at these pictures, but I'm not a director. I'm not a production designer. All I know is the difference between going to White Plains and the difference between going to Washington, Pennsylvania, is the difference of between $500,000 and $1 million, and they don't want to spend a million fuckin' dollars. On a business level you say White Plains. On a creative level you say Pennsylvania."

Schwab started to say something about "aesthetic distinction" and Caruso interrupted.

"If someone put a gun to your head and said shoot it, you'd shoot it. You know what the studio is saying. You started off at $29 million, you went to $32 million, then you went to $34 million, then to $36 million, then you went to $38 million, and now you want to push $40 million."

Caruso informed the group that the word had come down from the very top: Robert Daly, the chairman of Warner Bros., had dictated that the studio was not going to spend $1 million or even $500,000 to move the production out of New York.

Pete Runfolo, who had come upstairs to join the group, heaved himself up from his chair and began to mumble. "Shit or go blind," he said. "Shit or go blind."

Caruso continued with the exuberance of a preacher hitting his stride. "At what point do you stop? Do you stop?"

Now Runfolo was nodding his large head, up and down, and he chimed in the chorus. "Shit or go blind. Shit or go blind."

He looked at Schwab, who was identified in everybody's mind as De Palma's surrogate. "It's just like that thing on Park Avenue."

Schwab held up De Palma's defense. "That's right, but that was, Pete, small . . ."

Runfolo waved his giant hand dismissively. "Eric, there was a lot of pressure on that. There was just as much pressure on the lobby as there was on the courtroom. We shot in there because somebody said, 'Shit . . . or go blind.' "

Schwab was exasperated. Didn't these people understand the difference between a one-day shoot in the lobby that was only one segment of a larger scene, and the background for the most important sequence in the entire film?

"That's right," he said. "You make that compromise where you can."

"It's not my decision," said Runfolo with a shrug.

Schwab narrowed his eyes. "No, it's not your decision."

It was 6:30, and Caruso still hadn't heard from De Palma. He called Willis's assistant, Clare Leavenworth, to let her know he didn't know what was going on. A few minutes later Willis's agent checked in just to make sure Caruso had been in touch with the actor.

Caruso looked at his watch. It was almost 7:00 P.M. Just then, the phone rang. It was De Palma. Caruso gave him a run-down on the day's events: The executives were coming to town. Bruce Willis was ready to fly in for the housing project scene Monday. The Newark federal courthouse was definitely unavailable. Washington, Pennsylvania, was definitely available. Yes, they could find blacks and Hispanics in Pittsburgh because an HBO movie had just been filmed there with a cast that was 75 percent black and Hispanic. Lucy Fisher would be in the office at 11 A.M. the next morning, and she wanted to see her director.

Caruso listened for several minutes, while the others watched. He hung up the phone, shaking his head with admiration.

"Great fuckin' guy," he said.

"What's the story?" asked Schwab.

"He listened; he said, 'Okay, Freddy, okay, we'll try to figure it out,' " said Caruso, looking relieved. "He'll call me tomorrow. 'We'll figure something out!' No yelling; just, 'Okay, okay, fine.' "

Caruso headed for home. Saturday night he and his wife were throwing a big dinner party for friends he hadn't seen for years, even though they lived around the corner from him. He had a mountain of pâté de foie gras in the refrigerator, a giant risotto, and several kinds of pasta in the works. He was in a jaunty mood. Still, he wouldn't lay even a small bet on where he'd be the following Monday.

That evening De Palma took Kim Cattrall, the actress playing Judy McCoy, and a jazz fan, to hear Bobby Short sing at the Carlyle Hotel and to the Blue Note. Because her scene had been postponed indefinitely, she'd flown in from Los Angeles for nothing, and De Palma felt he should do something to make it up to her. It was a welcome break for him as well. There was little variation in his routine. He saw a few close friends, usually for cappuccino or dinners at the same handful of restaurants, went to movies and occasionally the theater, and played computer games. Though he'd lived in New York on and off for almost thirty years, just a few blocks from the Blue Note, he'd never been there before. He enjoyed the diversion.

But it was only a brief respite from his anxiety about the movie. He rarely slept through the night once a project had begun, and that night he felt under siege. For all his bravado he didn't enjoy confrontation. He wanted to solve the problem of the courtroom before he had to face Fisher the next morning. He kept running the different elements of the courtroom sequence through his brain, trying to figure out how to make it work in the spaces available to him. He'd been in this position before. On "The Untouchables" he'd originally staged Eliot Ness's big moment — capturing Al Capone's bookkeeper — as a long, complicated train chase. That too had been deemed too expensive by the studio executives. Borrowing from the Russian filmmaker Sergei Eisenstein's "Battleship Potemkin," De Palma had come up with a solution that had become the picture's cinematic showpiece: the slow-motion shootout that took place around the baby in a carriage bouncing its way down the train station steps.

Finally, De Palma found the answer to the "Bonfire" dilemma — an answer whose simplicity seemed absurd, once he found it. He could break the final scene up and move the action sequence out of the courtroom. That way the physical layout of the courtroom wouldn't matter so much. The sword fight part of the scene could take place out in the hallway. As he dozed off before dawn, he formulated the strategy for his new plan as though there had never been a problem at all. Maybe they could use the staircase at the Essex County Courthouse in Newark again. He'd loved the curve of the stairs.

Saturday morning De Palma met Eric Schwab for breakfast at E.A.T., and De Palma laid out his ideas for reconfiguring the courthouse scene. Sylbert joined them after breakfast and helped them refine De Palma's plan to divide the action between two locations. By the time Lucy Fisher showed up at the Tribeca Film Center at 11:00 A.M., there was nothing left to discuss. Fisher was thrown by De Palma's unusually warm greeting. He felt giddy now that the burden had been lifted. That Saturday morning he felt as if he'd been given a reprieve from the tunnel and was breathing free air again. He playfully grabbed Fisher's arm and led her outside for a stroll around Tribeca while he explained the changes he'd worked out with Sylbert and Schwab. They could use one of Judge Roberts's courtrooms for the trial scenes and Essex County for the sword fight. The crisis was over.

Monday was a perfect spring day, sunny and in the sixties, and "The Bonfire of the Vanities" was back in the Bronx. With the crisis past, Lucy Fisher had flown back to L.A.; Canton and his bosses, Terry Semel and Robert Daly, remained in New York for the Time-Warner annual meeting.

The crew's spirits were revived by the weather and the sense that a firm schedule was about to be posted. Also, the night before "The Untouchables" had been aired on network television, and almost everyone had watched it. The film renewed their enthusiasm; it reminded them that the solemn man who never said good morning was a director of imposing talent.

On Monday, the man himself was not in such a great mood. *New York* magazine had run a three-page spread on "Bonfire," suggesting the ways different directors might have cast the movie. What bothered De Palma was the caption that accompanied a sinister photograph of him: "The self-styled gore auteur makes twisty, homage-ridden thrillers and blood-drenched explorations of violence."

He couldn't escape it. How many movies would he have to make before the media would stop using words like *blood-drenched* to describe him. Though six years and three movies had intervened since "Body Double," his last thriller, they were still pigeonholing him as the misogynistic horrormeister. Had he ever defined himself as the heir to Hitchcock? In the end, it seemed, celebrity was celebrity, and once your celebrity had been defined it was very difficult, maybe impossible, to alter.

Despite his gloomy mood, De Palma was grateful that Fernando Ferrer's attack on the movie appeared to have been forgotten by residents of the Bronx. At this location, the housing project at 171st Street between Fulton and Third, just west of Crotona Park, the only demonstrators had been put there by the movie people. The sequences to be shot here had little to do with advancing the plot but were meant to deal with a subject at the heart of the book: the manufacturing of news for political purposes.

In this scene the opportunist Reverend Bacon — played by John Hancock, a towering actor with a sonorous voice — stages a demonstration protesting the system's failure to find who hit Henry Lamb. He has invited Robert Corso, the TV journalist played by Geraldo Rivera, and Peter Fallow, the tabloid journalist played by Bruce Willis, to "cover" the event. Bacon was to lead Annie Lamb from her real home — in a comfortable, low-rise public housing project that looked like a suburban apartment complex — across the street to a giant lot bounded on one side by forbidding apartment buildings, and on the other two sides by burned-out hulks. The whole thing is Bacon's setup. His flunkies have littered the lot with tires, trashed cars, and burning debris, and have brought junky clothing for the demonstrators to wear for the television cameras. Bacon has also brought his own choir, to provide music for his staged demonstration.

Once again, De Palma's inspiration for the scene had come in the middle of the night, the day before filming was scheduled to begin. He'd figured out a way to underscore how a political animal like Bacon can exploit the media. He'd decided to shoot the sequence for a split screen. On one side of the screen the audience would see what would appear on the TV news and in the tabloids, the demonstration itself. On the other side of the screen they'd see the real story, the ingredients being dumped into the mix: Bacon lead-

ing Annie Lamb across the street away from her modestly comfortable home to the bleak lot where she would appear on camera; the
demonstrators changing their clothes; the television make-up people touching up Annie Lamb's and Bacon's faces. To complicate it
all a little more, the director decided to film the two sets of action
simultaneously. Doug Ryan, the operator, would disguise his Vista-
Vision camera as a TV camera and film the "demonstration."
Larry McConkey, the Steadicam man, would circle around to
capture the behind-the-scenes action.

More than 250 people — the crew and the extensive cast of
principal actors and extras for the demonstration — gathered in
the Bronx shortly after sunrise. Most of them would spend most of
the day sitting around while De Palma on the spot choreographed
this complicated shot.

There was a surreal beauty in that empty lot bounded by sorry
brick edifices, those Bronx ruins. The set dressers had enhanced the
desolation with a pile of tires and a bulldozer moving car hulks
from here to there. People from the neighborhood observed from a
distance. A small group stood on the roof of the high-rise projects
across the way, and a girl in a red jacket sat cross-legged on the fire
escape of one of the grim buildings at the lot's boundaries, looking
down at the wreckage like some tourist at Pompeii.

Chris Soldo was trying to organize the extras cast as demonstrators. "Ladies and gentlemen!" he shouted through his megaphone. "Listen up. Quiet. When Bruce Willis walks through here,
don't pay any attention. Never look at the Steadicam moving
around. Look at the newsmen. This camera is invisible. It does not
exist."

Ann Roth darted up to a quartet of black women dressed as if
they were going to church in the South circa 1965.

"Sensational!" she said.

One of the women, wearing a pink straw hat with cloth flowers
and pink earrings in the shape of flowers, muttered, "I'm not
sensational. She's got me in this Easter Bunny hat with Easter
Bunny earrings." But she wasn't really angry. She admired Roth's
earrings: an engagement ring was dangling from one lobe, a wedding ring from the other.

"I want these ladies to have their white gloves," Roth called out to one of her assistants. "I *love* the way these girls look!"

She ran over to Doug Ryan and pulled off the bright green jacket he was wearing, his own jacket. She handed him a brown suede jacket so he would look like a real cameraman; he would appear in McConkey's Steadicam shot. The costume designer gazed over at Geraldo Rivera, posed by the side of the road.

"Doesn't he look like the groom on the wedding cake?" she asked.

Les Lazarowitz, the New York sound man, poured nine vitamins into his hand and swallowed them. He saw Nancy Hopton, the script supervisor, watching. "You know who sells these things?" he asked. "Sharper Image. They're made for decathlon athletes or film people who work eighteen hours a day. These things you never dreamed of. I only take them once a day."

Nancy Hopton was an athletic woman who flew airplanes in her spare time. "I only take fourteen pills a day," she said.

Everyone dreaded falling ill; the hours and constant exposure to changing weather almost guaranteed sickness, and the timetable didn't allow for days off.

The sound man held up his vitamins like a sideshow hawker. "All I know is I haven't had a cold in at least three days," he said.

Because two cameras were filming simultaneously, the sound man had to watch two video monitors at once, mixing the sound for both. "This is crazy. With my left ear I'm mixing what's on that screen, with my right ear I'm mixing what's on that screen," he said. "It's a little confusing." The sound man had to record everything so De Palma and the editors would have all the sounds from the set available to them when they edited the scene. The conflicting sounds transmitted into his ears from the people holding the boom mikes out by the actors were driving him crazy enough. Compounding his agony was the monotonous repetition of loud *whooshes* from above. The projects were directly under La Guardia Airport's flight pattern. Every thirty seconds an airplane flew overhead.

From the chaos emerged a rehearsal. Extras threw jars of mayonnaise. A choir in golden robes walked across the street. One of the "demonstrators" sprayed the ABE WEISS FOR MAYOR poster with paint.

"Stop spraying!" screamed the second assistant director. "Stop spraying! It's a rehearsal."

As the activity became more frenzied, De Palma appeared even grimmer than usual. Under normal circumstances he would have plotted out this complicated shot step by step. But because he'd dreamed it up at the last minute he had to do his planning publicly and under an immediate, insistent deadline.

Still, he relished this kind of spontaneous creative gesture. If he could pull it off, he would have proved to himself, once again, that he held a rare power in his hands. He could *illuminate* an idea in a way almost no one else could.

Soldo announced it was time for lunch, and De Palma practically ran to his trailer. Almost immediately a little black kid climbed into the director's chair.

"Take your places *now* or you're all fired," the kid shouted.

Pete Runfolo smiled at the kid and resumed clipping his finger-nails with the tiny scissors on his Swiss Army knife. A minute later he was joined by a skinny woman with long blonde hair, faded jeans, and a friendly smile. She lived in the high-rise projects bordering the vacant lot.

"It's really great you're filming here," she said. "At one point these projects were great for low-income people who was working. I've lived here almost all my life, for twenty years, since I was twelve. It's become really bad. The drugs. Especially the crack."

She was interrupted by three young boys. "You in it?" one of them asked her.

"Shouldn't you be in school?" she retorted.

"I gotta get out of the city," she said. "To Jersey. Somewhere." She shook her head. "Every night they're shooting somebody. There's somebody dead. Saturday night we hear shots and my husband looked out the window with his binoculars and saw the police pull a body from behind the trash."

Runfolo nodded. The woman watched a group of children pose for a picture of themselves standing next to Bruce Willis's chair. The woman smiled at Runfolo and said, "I'm glad they're making a movie about the Bronx that's not about drugs."

*　　*　　*

Just before the half-hour lunch break was over, Karl Slovin, De Palma's production assistant, ran up to Schwab, looking quite pale. Melanie Griffith had been brought to the set for a hair and make-up test. She would be put together in the make-up trailer, and at some point during the afternoon the results would be filmed. Slovin began to chatter. "Melanie came by while Brian was taking his nap. She wanted to see him. I didn't want to wake him up. Finally he got up and I told him and he said, 'I can't deal with it now.' But Melanie wants an *answer*. What do I do?"

Schwab excused himself from this dilemma. He didn't even ask what Griffith wanted an answer *to*. "Go talk to Fred," he said.

Slovin looked around a little frantically and spotted Caruso and ran over to him, panting. Caruso regarded Slovin with amusement. "I know this isn't the biggest thing you have to deal with," said Slovin to the coproducer, "but Melanie doesn't like her camper."

Caruso's expression — attentive but unrevealing — didn't change. "She came over to me and looked at Brian's and said, 'I bet his is nice.' " Slovin took a breath. "Do you have a slightly bigger camper?"

Caruso glanced at his watch. It was 1:30. He had a meeting at 2:15 with Judge Roberts to talk about courtrooms. He started to walk away and turned around. "Don't worry," he said to Slovin. "We'll get Melanie her camper."

De Palma couldn't nap. He kept recapitulating the scene over and over in his mind: move Bacon and the demonstrators across the street; watch the demonstrators change clothes without breaking the flow; Bruce and Geraldo watching, talking; the choir; the television camera dutifully recording the staged scene; the Steadi-cam making ironic comment on it all.

As he returned to the set Slovin told him Griffith had arrived and wanted to see him. The director ignored the p.a. The last thing De Palma needed to contend with right now was Melanie Griffith. He knew from his experience with her on "Body Double" that she needed constant tending. She needed a lot of things to make it work. Her sensitivity always threatened to undercut her intuitive brilliance. When she exposed herself, she took on a Marilyn Monroe kind of vulnerability. If she detected a flicker of animosity she would concentrate on that distracting criticism — real or imagined — to the exclusion of everything else.

Yet she had guts. Not an actress in Hollywood had been brave enough or foolish enough to audition for Holly Body, the porn queen in "Body Double." Griffith was the exception. She didn't flinch from the crude language or from having to simulate masturbation in front of the camera. And she pulled off the role with remarkable success. Only Griffith had been exempt from the critical scorn — even revulsion — the film received. For Griffith, "Body Double" was a coup; it was the movie that helped pull her out of obscurity.

De Palma knew it was crucial to let Griffith know how important her well-being was to him. She had a lot more baggage now than she had back on "Body Double." She'd divorced actor Steve Bauer and remarried her first husband, Don Johnson, the star of the "Miami Vice" television series that had been popular a few years back. Griffith's career had been on the ascent since "Body Double," while Johnson's was stagnating. In addition, she had brought along three children: the child she'd had with Bauer, Johnson's child, and the baby they'd had together the previous October.

De Palma knew Griffith was under a lot of pressure, and he planned to check in with her first thing every day she was on the set. He knew he should go soothe her right away, but until he was certain the shot was going to work, Griffith was going to have to deal with her insecurities by herself.

De Palma returned to the set with tension etched into his face. Another rehearsal began. By 3:30 not a foot of film had rolled. It hadn't yet come together the way De Palma envisioned the scene.

The sun was baking the actors' make-up to clay. De Palma stared at the blank monitor, rerunning the rehearsal he'd just watched through his head. His shoulders relaxed a touch, the only indication that he was finally satisfied that he might pull off the split screen.

Then, without warning, De Palma vaulted out of his chair and started to run up the block. Karl Slovin grabbed the coffee Thermos and ran after him. Nancy Hopton looked at the director's disappearing back and turned to Vilmos Zsigmond. He shrugged. "This is definitely not a film by committee," he said.

Slovin returned a few seconds later and explained. "He went to talk to Melanie. Just to say hi."

A small man wearing large clothes showed up on the set at 4:00 P.M. He had on an oversized jacket, baggy pants, a blue shirt, a bold paisley tie, and round sunglasses, the sum of which spelled "Hollywood." Charles Mercuri, the Willis wardrobe man, giggled. "You can always tell who they are. The clothes on their backs cost four thousand dollars. Their sunglasses cost seven hundred dollars." Within seconds the whispered conferences among the crew had established that the Hollywood man was Mark Canton, executive vice president of worldwide picture production for Warner Bros.

Canton crouched behind the video monitor and put his hand on the back of De Palma's chair in a companionable way. As McConkey did his gracefully clunky Steadicam walk, De Palma explained the shot to Canton. This was the first take. Canton looked at his watch. It was 4:10. The sky had grown cloudy as the afternoon wore on. Yet as the choir sang, "The storm is passing over," the sun peeped through.

"Looks good, man, looks good," said Canton to De Palma. He stretched out the words, for emphasis. "Looooks, gooooood."

At 4:25 Canton checked his watch again. The crafts services woman brought out another snack, miniature Nestle's Crunch bars. Canton thanked De Palma and headed back for Manhattan.

That evening Tom Wolfe was one of the featured speakers at the Coro Foundation's "Commitment to Leadership Dinner," along with Spike Lee, the young black filmmaker whose skills as a director and willing interviewee had elevated him to celebrity status. The Coro Foundation was a heavyweight public service charity with a high-minded mandate: "To identify and prepare leaders to effectively and ethically meet the challenges and rigors of public responsibility."

Brian De Palma had received a handwritten invitation to the dinner from Coro's chairwoman, Meredith Brokaw, wife of NBC anchorman Tom Brokaw. In her letter, Brokaw told De Palma that the speakers, Tom Wolfe and Spike Lee, would be joined by "some of the most influential people in the city." As testament to the Coro dinner's importance, Brokaw also noted that it had been mentioned in Liz Smith's gossip column, where it was described as "the networking get-together of the year." De Palma had chosen to ignore Brokaw's invitation.

Wolfe wore white; Lee wore black. And there did seem to be, as Liz Smith promised, a great deal of "networking" taking place in the Pierre Hotel ballroom that evening — a great deal of it taking place among the heavy contingent from the media. The *Daily News* publisher, James Hoge, was there with his wife, Sharon, as well as a full representation from network television: CBS chairman Laurence Tisch and his wife, Billie, Jane Pauley and Gary Trudeau, Bryant and June Gumbel. Judge Roberts was in the audience, though Fernando Ferrer left after cocktails.

Wolfe and Lee treated each other with tedious politeness as they sat on-stage fielding questions from the panel of Coro fellows. The young scholarship winners were too intimidated to press for follow-up answers. The audience tolerated Wolfe's learned dissertation on immigration patterns in the Bronx, and applauded when Spike Lee said, "I don't make my films for the Academy members."

In all, the evening was a snooze until Lee asked Wolfe if he had read the script for "Bonfire." When Wolfe said he hadn't, the filmmaker proceeded to denounce the ending shot when Henry Lamb recovers from his coma and walks out of the hospital (instead of dying, as he does in the book). Wolfe said he couldn't comment on a script he hadn't read.

"You write a great book and you don't care what they do with it? You just take the money?" Lee asked incredulously. "I can't believe you haven't read the script or been on the set."

Wolfe never deviated from his tone of detached amusement. "In actual life they never blame the writer. It's always: Look what they did to his book! And if the movie is better than the book, the book gets caught in the updraft," he said. "There are good people working on it and I have high hopes."

The next morning De Palma found a histrionic message waiting for him on his answering machine from Peggy Siegal, the persistent P.R. woman. "Have you read the *Daily News*? Spike Lee gave away the ending to the movie and Billy Norwich printed it!" When he didn't call her back, Siegal called the production office. She was determined to get on this picture and would continue to try to prove that without her, nobody would know anything.

The occasion of the Coro dinner had escalated to grand proportions by the time the newspapers finished with it. "A racial 'Bonfire'; Spike Lee, Tom Wolfe in hot debate," teased the *Oakland Tribune* on its front page. "The audience at the sixth annual Coro Foundation leadership dinner, which includes the likes of Walter Cronkite, Tom Brokaw and Bryant Gumbel, leans forward as a panel begins asking questions," began a gushing article in the *Los Angeles Times*.

Appalled by what she was reading in the press, Lucy Fisher put in calls to Tom Wolfe and to Spike Lee to find out what had happened at the dinner. Fisher was constantly phoning Wolfe, even though he'd made it clear from the beginning that he had no interest in having anything to do with the movie. But Fisher admired him, and, she would admit if pressed, she wanted him to admire her. Every time the script went through a major change she called him so he wouldn't hear about it from somebody else. When De Palma wouldn't let her into rehearsals, she passed some of the time while she was in New York having drinks with Wolfe. But she hadn't had a chance to fill him in on the new ending, the Henry Lamb coda that De Palma had dreamed up as a final touch of irony to show that Lamb, the person who started the "bonfire," had been forgotten about.

When she finally got through to Wolfe, the issue was settled with a brief, polite exchange. Spike Lee, however, was another matter altogether. He wasn't an outsider like Wolfe. No matter how hard he worked at posing as the last angry black man, he made his films with Hollywood money. That made him part of the community and subject to its rules.

"How would you like it if you had a movie and someone else got up and started talking about the end of the movie and it was in the paper?" Fisher snapped at Lee. "How would you like that?"

Lee's apology was sufficiently deferential to Wolfe, De Palma, and Warner Bros., though Fisher wasn't entirely satisfied. She would have liked to yell at Lee a little more, but she hoped someday to make a movie with him and didn't want to press her luck.

* * *

De Palma didn't pay any attention to the Coro affair. In two days he was to begin filming the courtroom scenes with Morgan Freeman, and not a minute too soon.

Once again, Judge Roberts, who couldn't resist the lure of the movies, came to the aid of the film crew. After it was decided that the new requirement for the courtroom was proximity to the New York production office, Brett Botula, the location man, started negotiating with the judge about using one of his courtrooms. Roberts studied the calendars of his judges trying to find a schedule that could best accommodate the movie people.

But when he found out that Botula was also talking to another judge down at Centre Street in Manhattan, Roberts was furious. Did they think he had nothing better to do than work for them? Botula sped up to the Bronx and got a glimpse of what Roberts must have been like as district attorney. "Look at me in the eye when you talk to me!" he screamed at the location scout. "Did you lie to me? Did you lie to me?" Then the judge called Fred Caruso and told him that he and all the rest of the movie people were nothing *but a bunch of eels*!

In the end, though, Roberts came through. He decided to turn a courtroom on the sixth floor of the Bronx County Building over to the movie crew. They'd have to shoot at night, leaving the courtroom open for business during the day. At 5:30 P.M. on May 9, the Bronx County Building was almost empty except for the security guards in the lobby, waiting for the movie people. Judge Roberts was up in his chambers, ready to greet them when they arrived.

Chapter 10

WIRE WITHOUT A NET

While Judge Roberts waited in his chambers for the film crew to show up, the streets remained curiously empty. Only the orange cones set up by the parking coordinators earlier in the day hinted that something unusual might be about to happen. But at 5:45, just fifteen minutes before the crew was scheduled to arrive, there was no sign of the campers and cars "Bonfire" dragged with it wherever it went.

At 5:46 a van and an Oldsmobile convertible drove up. A skinny young man in jeans and a T-shirt and a pale young woman wearing a long black skirt and a black beret began picking up the cones and handing them to a third man in jeans, who stuffed them into the back of the van. When they'd collected all the cones, they got back in their vehicles and left.

The three were members of the "Bonfire" parking crew and their destination was the new site for the courtroom scenes: the Queens County Courthouse. The decision to change courtrooms had been finalized exactly one hour before the crew was expected to start setting up in Judge Roberts's courtroom.

The Queens courthouse had been one of the prospective candidates from the beginning. This modestly noble example of 1930s architecture seemed grand only by comparison with the run-down little buildings that surrounded it on Sutphin Boulevard. But it had one major advantage over the Bronx County Building: its available courtroom was on the second floor, four floors lower than the courtroom in the Bronx. Because the courtrooms were being used during the day, all the Kovitsky/White scenes had to be shot at night. To create the illusion of day during these night shoots, cranes would have to lift the lights to the windows from the outside. The condor cranes required to reach the eighth floor added five thousand dollars to the budget, every day.

The court officials in Queens had been indecisive. But at 4:00 P.M. they sent the word: their courthouse was available. Fred Caruso sent Eric Schwab out to the courtroom to have a look. At 5:00 P.M. Schwab called De Palma, who was watching dailies, and De Palma gave the order: move to Queens. At that moment Schwab felt as though he were back at U.C.L.A., working on a student film, where it was common practice to decide where you were going to shoot an hour before shooting began. But the decision made by U.C.L.A. students didn't require the notification and transportation of three dozen vehicles and 150 people.

The crew arrived in Queens in small groups, parking their vans and campers in the lot behind the courthouse, the sole occupant of which by early evening was a bus holding a load of prisoners.

The movie people walked hesitantly around the bus, aware that its inhabitants were watching their every move. "Yah yah yah," a voice cried out. "Fuck you, man," said another.

At 7:00 P.M. the crafts services crew arrived and set up a table of snacks near the door. Next came the cinematographer, Vilmos Zsigmond, and the gaffer, Colin Campbell, with their identical canvas bags and their identical green jackets, acquired on their last film, "The Two Jakes." They headed up to the set, the courtroom on the second floor. By now there should have been a bustle of preparation, the noise of many walkie-talkies crackling. Instead, the room was nearly empty and there was silence.

Campbell and Zsigmond looked around and made the evening's first creative decision: every one of the courtroom's six giant chandeliers contained fifteen lightbulbs, and all ninety bulbs needed to be replaced with forty-watt bulbs.

As the technicians arrived and began changing the bulbs, Eric Schwab and the production designer, Richard Sylbert, slumped in the first row of spectator seats and watched.

Schwab told Sylbert he'd seen him liberally quoted in the press recently. In *Premiere* Sylbert had said unflattering things about

Robert Evans, the producer of "Chinatown"; in *Esquire* he had commented on Warren Beatty's sex life ("Warren used to scan the trade papers, looking to see who was getting a divorce. He was great with wounded birds . . .").

Sylbert was looking quite pleased with himself. His wilted safari suit needed to be cleaned, but his perspective was crisp. "All that publicity is thrown into the hopper of celebrity gossip, which is currency today in America," he shrugged. "If you're witty you can get away with a lot."

"Yeah," said Schwab. "You'd be obnoxious if you weren't witty."

Caruso walked up and winked a wink that had the makings of a nervous twitch.

"I have to get outta here," said Sylbert to the producer. "I have fifteen gorgeous locations ready for this picture in Los Angeles. I don't need to sit here and watch you fail."

Caruso walked away to do some pacing in the aisles.

A few rows back from Sylbert and Schwab, Ann Roth and Vilmos Zsigmond had settled in to watch the changing of the lightbulbs. With a simple question, Zsigmond dispelled the prevailing sleepy mood.

"Have you talked to Melanie about her make-up test?" he asked the costume designer.

Roth leaned forward in her seat, having picked up the undercurrent in the cameraman's seemingly innocuous question. Roth said tersely, "She doesn't have a problem."

Zsigmond's sandpaper voice sounded even hoarser than usual as he registered amazement. "She doesn't mind those lines around her eyes? Those *bags?*"

The conversation caught Caruso's attention. He stopped pacing and joined the group.

Roth looked at the coproducer. "I told you I thought she looked great. I tell you right now no make-up in the world will hide that." *That.* "My God. The woman is almost thirty-four years old."

Roth felt sympathy for Griffith, whom she had worked with before on "Working Girl." The men, however, were brutal in their analysis of the star's looks.

"Use Preparation H." Caruso laughed. "That'll shrink 'em."

"My feeling is she looks great," said Roth. "The woman is thirty-three years old, and she looks one thousand times better than she looked in 'Working Girl.' " The consensus had already been established that in "Working Girl" her face was puffy and she was fat.

Zsigmond's face had the impish glee of a cartoon chipmunk. "I bought a laser disk last night to see how she looked in 'Working Girl.' Ballhaus [the cameraman] must have used a number ten diffusion. The camera never went closer than this." He held his arms as far apart as they would go. "I think Ballhaus was doing the photography to work around *that girl*."

Caruso's innate chivalry kicked in. "She looks gorgeous now."

Zsigmond frowned. He'd been irritated by the choices for the women's roles in this film from the moment he'd been hired. He thought to himself, How could Sherman McCoy be in love with Maria if she looked like *an old bag*. He was going to have to use all kinds of trick lighting and filters to make Griffith look like anything but *an old bag*. He'd had the same problem with Kim Cattrall. How was he to believe that Sherman McCoy would be married to *an old bag* who looked the way Cattrall looked when Zsigmond first tested her on film. He almost quit when he saw these *old ladies* De Palma was giving him. He thought to himself, *Jesus! What did I get into?*

Roth was saying, "Get an eighteen-year-old boy if that's what you want. I think those lines are divine." She paused a minute before throwing in her trump card. "Look, Brian has his own idea of what's sexy."

Zsigmond waved his hand dismissively. "To me, that German girl, Uma — when she showed up the whole crew went wild. I think this movie would have needed something like this."

Roth changed the subject by pulling out a notebook to go over her request for additional costume money with Caruso. The repeated changes in this movie had forced her to go over budget for the first time in twenty years, and she was not happy about it. She had one final word for Zsigmond. "Look, we don't have a Jewish judge, we don't have Uma Thurman, and we have two Disneyland boys playing the black boys."

Caruso put on his bifocals and studied Roth's list. "Melanie's agent called today. She was so happy at how well she's being treated. She told me she wasn't treated well on John's movie." (Griffith had just finished filming "Pacific Heights" with John Schlesinger.)

Still looking at Roth's budget request, Caruso said someone had told Griffith to come to Queens at 2:00 A.M. — De Palma's "lunch break" during the night shoot — just to show the director the make-up and hairdo being considered for her scenes. "She said she didn't feel comfortable coming out at two in the morning," he said. "I don't blame her." They'd agreed to have her show up at 10:00 P.M.

Just then the teamster captain, Eddie Iacobelli, joined the klatch. "Hey, what's with Melanie?" he asked. "She looks awful skinny. She was nice and chubby in 'Working Girl.' "

Caruso was feeling tense. Just when he'd thought his problems with these courtroom scenes were over, he'd been hit with fresh troubles in New Jersey. Earlier that day he'd lost the Essex County Courthouse, which he'd figured was in the bag for the sword fight scene, the section of the courtroom material De Palma had moved out into the hallway.

Everything had been set. The chief administrator of Essex County was delighted to have the film company return, especially since Warner Bros. had agreed to contribute $250,000 toward the courthouse's renovation. He hadn't anticipated the intervention of New Jersey's chief justice, Robert Wilentz, who said "Bonfire" couldn't use the Essex County Courthouse to shoot scenes that showed "black persons acting in a riotous, lawless and life-threatening manner." Justice Wilentz deemed the film "prejudiced," issued an injunction against the movie production company, and ordered the county sheriff to arrest Caruso if he stepped inside the building. Caruso was tantalized by the idea of being arrested. But the Warner Bros. executives, Bill Young and Ron Smith, restrained him. There had been enough trouble already. Meanwhile, the Essex County chief administrator was furious that he was losing his $250,000 renovation fund. He cried "censorship," accused the chief justice of political opportunism, and took steps to have the injunction lifted. But the legal action couldn't be resolved in time to help Caruso.

It was starting to seem like some kind of cosmic joke. Here they were, filming the movie version of a book that had uncannily proved to be a predictor of real-life events. Now, once again, the real world seemed to be taking its cues from Tom Wolfe. Less than three weeks after the "Bonfire" crew had filmed in the Essex County Courthouse, Wilentz suddenly decided that it was inappropriate and that unless the offending scene was rewritten it wouldn't be filmed in New Jersey.

So Caruso found himself back at the bottom of the hill, with ten days to find someplace to shoot the sword fight scene. He'd much rather worry about the bags under Melanie Griffith's eyes.

By 10:00 P.M. the Queens County Courthouse was starting to look like a movie set. The parking lot was jammed with campers and cars; the bus containing the convicts was gone. Cranes had been set up below the courthouse windows to bring lights up to the second floor; a maze of electric wires shimmered in the sky. The lights went on; day was finally emerging out of night.

Ann Roth dropped by Brian De Palma's trailer to ask him what he thought should be done about Griffith's face.

"Vilmos and I are getting a copy of 'Blue Steel' to see what that guy did with the light. It has to do with patterns across faces," Roth said.

De Palma said sarcastically, "The problem with Melanie is simple. There are lines under her eyes."

Roth nodded. "We can solve it. We'll get her some sensational sunglasses. And in a lovemaking scene she can toss her head way back —"

She was interrupted by a knock at the door.

Karl Slovin stuck his head in. "Melanie's here," he said. "She's in the make-up trailer."

Roth excused herself, and De Palma took a bottle of Evian water from the refrigerator into the bathroom — the water wasn't working in the camper, and he wanted to brush his teeth before greeting his star.

He walked to the make-up trailer through the narrow corridor formed by the sixteen campers parked behind the courthouse.

He found Melanie Griffith sitting on a chair in front of the camper's mirrored wall, wearing jeans and a plain T-shirt. She looked fragile — pale and thin. The facial lines that had been discussed so thoroughly were emphasized by the trailer's harsh light. Though they had seen each other two days before, Griffith and De Palma locked eyes with an intensity that implied reunion after a long absence. It was a theatrical moment, director and star meeting in this sterile camper after dark, preparing to go into battle together.

"How are you?" De Palma asked gently.

"I'm much better," she replied, her cotton candy voice sounding especially tenuous.

"Yeah?" His tone had the loving solicitousness of a father applying gauze to his adored child's wounded knee.

"Yes," she said ever so softly, and they hugged.

De Palma returned to his trailer to try to nap while the lights were prepared. Monica Goldstein intercepted him, reminding him not to forget to autograph the photograph of him standing with his arm around Judge Roberts.

Every day for eight days the Queens County courtroom was filled with real plaintiffs and defendants by day and with movie people by night. Every dawn the entire set was packed up and taken away, and every dusk it was put back together again. As a practical matter, this meant that it took twice as long to do one half the amount of work for double the cost it would have required to do the shoot during the day. To convert night into day, night after night, required an extra crew of fifteen grips and electricians, who, along with the rest of the crew, were paid double time.

It would take an additional six days to film the courtroom scenes that De Palma had moved out into the hallway — once they found a hallway. Because all these scenes would be shot at night, that meant that those fourteen days would equal twenty-eight days' pay.

Had the scenes been shot as originally planned, on a sound stage in Los Angeles, they probably could have been contained within the five days originally scheduled. The sound stage would have been dressed and lit and kept that way until the scene was completed. Everything would have been cheaper. It automatically cost $30,000 a day less to shoot in Los Angeles, where extras were getting $40 a day, compared with $200 a day in New York, with a night premium of $25–$30.

These expenditures eclipsed the $100,000 spent for the courtroom set left unused on the Warner Bros. lot, as well as the $30,000 for Sylbert's elaborate murals depicting the Bronx for the make-believe courtroom. Those beautiful murals were now lying in boxes somewhere.

It would take a while to sort out all the costs — incidentals like flying in actors for scenes that wouldn't be shot. At that moment Caruso estimated the decision to cast Morgan Freeman, instead of Alan Arkin or Burton Roberts or even Walter Matthau, was running at about $2 million.

The first thing Brian De Palma saw when he walked across the parking lot at the Queens courthouse on May 11 at 9:00 P.M. was Melanie Griffith, looking stunning as she stood in the soft light illuminating the trailers and vans surrounding her. The waif had been transformed into a statuesque blonde wearing a tailored brown jacket and pants that ballooned at the thigh like jodhpurs, her hair done up in an elegant pile. A delicate blonde woman in her fifties stood next to her. The two of them looked like royalty who had stumbled into the servants' quarters.

"You remember my mother, Brian," said Griffith with confident poise. There wasn't a trace of the jittery woman who'd locked eyes with De Palma in the make-up trailer two nights earlier.

Now it was the director who was hesitant and shy. "Yes, hi," he said, hugging Griffith's mother, Tippi Hedren. She'd starred in two of Alfred Hitchcock's films, "The Birds" and "Marnie," and it was generally believed the director had been infatuated with her.

Griffith tilted her head. "Do you like my hair?"

De Palma examined it for a long time before he said, "It's lovely."

"Doesn't she look beautiful?" Hedren asked. "Don't you think her hair looks just like mine did in 'The Birds'?"

De Palma accompanied the mother and daughter into Griffith's trailer, where Griffith proceeded to tell him how upset she was that when she went down to the Regency's lobby to be picked up at 6:00, no one was there. She'd had to wait, which was bad enough.

What infuriated her, however, was the fact that no one at the production office wanted to take responsibility for the mix-up. She wanted De Palma to get to the bottom of this.

The director emerged from the trailer looking unusually animated. He collared Aimee Morris, the production assistant who'd gotten him up from his nap.

"Who is responsible for Melanie's car?" he asked.

Morris was nervous. Every production assistant on the set had gotten the word that Griffith was on the warpath about the mix-up. "Nobody was informed," she said nervously.

De Palma looked at Morris as though he were seeing her for the first time. She looked cute with the walkie-talkie hanging off her belt, as if she might have a sense of fun.

He nodded for her to follow him into his trailer and sat her at the little kitchen table by the portable phone. "Let's see what Aimee's made of," he said, grinning at the assistant.

De Palma registered her look of confusion. He saw that she didn't understand that he was bored to death with these stupid courtroom scenes. He hated courtroom scenes. They all looked like "Perry Mason" to him. After two days he was sick of watching Morgan Freeman repeat the Great White Defendant speech over and over again, waiting for him to get the inflection just right. And Freeman wasn't all that exciting. De Palma had started to wish he'd gone with Roberts after all. At least that would have been *unique*.

Morris looked at him curiously as he asked her, "You think it's fun watching us shoot Kovitsky's point of view looking at Kramer saying the same things he said last night? This is a director's nightmare." With a conspiratorial glimmer he said, "We're going to have so much more fun running down the missing communications link. Melanie is . . . oooooh. These kinds of things throw her off."

Morris caught on to the game quickly and lit a Camel Light. De Palma lit a Players. They sat and smoked, and De Palma explained the facts of life to Morris. "Little things like this get your star upset," said De Palma. "And she comes to the set upset and you're in trouble. You have to keep your star anxiety free."

De Palma left Morris in his trailer to use his phone to track down exactly who forgot to have a car waiting for Griffith at the Regency. Morris was shrewd enough to capitalize on this opening into the director's good graces. She called Griffith's assistant back at the hotel, and the production assistants at the Tribeca Film Center, and determined from them that she would have to talk to the hair and make-up people and Ann Roth to get all the details.

She left De Palma's trailer to find Roth on the set. As she was leaving she almost tripped over Karl Slovin, who was running to the trailer to make some decaffeinated coffee for De Palma. Slovin wondered briefly what Morris was doing there but didn't have time to pause. The director needed his coffee.

After a week of night shooting, the crew and cast were ragged. The only person who seemed to be enjoying himself was Morgan Freeman. For this actor, who had only recently ascended to movie star status, the whole thing was a lark. He'd read the book and wouldn't have dreamed of casting himself as Judge Kovitsky — not, that is, until he'd heard who had been cast for the other lead roles. Like everyone else, he'd cast the book in his own mind, and the only one of his fellow actors he would have chosen himself was F. Murray Abraham — and he would have cast Abraham not in the role of Weiss but in his own part, that of Judge Kovitsky.

Freeman had shaved his head to play Kovitsky without consulting anyone. He wasn't Jewish and he wasn't white and he wasn't old, but he could be bald.

Freeman started rehearsals for *Taming of the Shrew* during the second week of shooting "Bonfire." He'd get back home to the Upper West Side of Manhattan from Queens by 7:00 A.M., sleep for three or four hours, then head off for afternoon rehearsals. But "Bonfire" was a breeze compared to Shakespeare. He didn't even bother to learn the lines until they were shot. He'd just look at the page and do it and eventually there would be a good take.

In between takes, the first team kept to themselves, hardly even mixing with the two hundred–plus extras who were on hand to play the demonstrators and hangers-on watching Sherman's trial. Willis and Griffith generally headed for their trailers. Hanks spearheaded a nightly card game; he'd invite the crew to join as well as other actors.

But Freeman circulated. Between takes his shiny head would

appear above the crowd, and he looked as if he were running for office. Besides being a sociable fellow, he felt an obligation to mingle. Many of the extras were New York actors he'd known for ten or, in some cases, twenty years. Acting was a tough profession and even tougher if you were black. Freeman was well aware that his success was a major standout. That very week a television promotion for "Brubaker," the Robert Redford movie, declared the picture "starred Morgan Freeman." He'd been in that movie for a couple of minutes! He still could ride his bicycle to the Shakespeare rehearsal without being recognized by anyone, but there was no denying it. He'd become a star.

But if the extras loved Freeman, his charm was having less effect in front of the camera as he stumbled his way toward perfecting the justice speech. After take two, the cameraman approached De Palma. "Why are we putting this into the movie?" Zsigmond asked. "This is a speech. It's boring."

De Palma didn't answer, but he was wondering the same thing. He was irritated that Freeman hadn't prepared. They'd kept shooting and shooting while the actor learned his lines. Meanwhile he had $30,000 worth of extras sitting around waiting.

Yes, he could cover him, and he would. But he knew very well Freeman wouldn't dare pull this stunt with *Taming of the Shrew*. He wouldn't fumble his way through Shakespeare while ten actors were watching him. He'd seen it over and over again with these stars. There was something about the money and the fame and the adulation that made them stop doing the boring work they did automatically when they were struggling. Everyone tells them they're great, and they start to believe it.

He liked Freeman personally, and appreciated the fact that the actor acknowledged his disapproval and tried to improve his performance as the night wore on. But his voice was getting hoarse, and he was wasting it even more by chatting up the extras between takes. Why wasn't he in his trailer resting, or learning his lines? Didn't Freeman know he was being paid $650,000 to pull off the justice speech, the most difficult acting feat in the entire movie? Didn't he know that exhaustion was the perpetual enemy? That's why De Palma was so prickly about his naps.

The director had grave doubts about this speech. It was a playwright's speech, and no matter how good it might be, De Palma felt, it could cast an uncomfortable pall, like having a friend start lecturing about the environment just as you've passed out the paper plates at a picnic. Speeches tended to weigh movies down. He'd had this problem before, with the speech Michael J. Fox delivered in "Casualties of War." Almost every critic had singled it out as a leaden moment, an unnecessary recapitulation of the movie's themes.

But the Warner executives loved the justice speech and so did the screenwriter, Michael Cristofer. So De Palma would shoot it and they would put it together and when it was all done they'd see how it played.

On May 15 Eric Schwab was walking down Forty-fourth Street to buy a brisket sandwich for Monica Goldstein before dailies started at Technicolor. While the courtroom scenes were being shot, dailies usually started at 6:00 P.M. He bumped into De Palma on the street, and in a casual way the director told Schwab that because the Metropolitan Museum had backed out, he'd thought of a new idea for the opening of the movie. He wanted the journalist Peter Fallow to enter the awards dinner after a walk through a long corridor, besieged by sycophants, the way you'd see the Beatles before concerts, the way Jake La Motta did in "Raging Bull." Fallow, the celebrated writer, would appear like a combination of Truman Capote and a rock star. He'd be drunk, stumbling his way past admirers until finally he hit a wall of flashbulbs. De Palma could pick up on the flashbulbs again at the end of the movie, as reporters close in on Sherman at the courthouse, and bring the story back around to Fallow.

De Palma's enthusiasm was lost on his second unit director, who wasn't certain how to take what he was hearing. Was this new beginning going to eliminate Schwab's opening vision, the "kaleidoscopic jewel box"? He couldn't bring himself to ask. He left De Palma and solemnly walked to the corner for Goldstein's sandwich.

At dailies the group watched the 360-degree pan of the courtroom. As the camera circled the room, the face of almost every principal actor appeared briefly on the screen — a huge collection of star power and talent. One by one, there they were: Hanks, Griffith, Abraham, Freeman, Willis. As De Palma watched the faces on the screen, only one thought went through his mind: How much were they paying for this assortment of actors? *What insane amount of money were they paying?* He wanted to tell the editors to stop the film and get out the adding machine.

Schwab couldn't concentrate on the dailies either. For two hours he had had to consider the fact that De Palma's new idea for the opening almost certainly meant Schwab's opening sequence was about to go out the window. Back in November or December when he and De Palma had discussed the beginning of the movie, De Palma had agreed to let Schwab do the whole thing. He could hire the special effects house, come up with the shots, and figure out how to cut them together. It was a big responsibility; the opening set the tone for the whole movie.

Now Schwab was ready to go. He had a special effects crew scheduled to fly in from Los Angeles in a few days. Frye had already cleared thirty-eight of the locations they would need for the fifty angles on Manhattan that Schwab had arrived at after months of planning. The paperwork had been massive: letters asking permission, arranging for insurance, and taking other legal precautions.

Schwab thought of the stacks of books on architecture and cityscapes he'd combed through back at the office. He thought of his storyboards. He'd laid out this three-minute sequence of colliding images as though it were a feature film. In some ways, though, he hadn't been too careful in his planning. With grips, teamsters, the camera crew, and the special effects people, the shot would have cost more than $250,000 — as much as De Palma's first five films put together.

If the opening were canceled, the only big challenge left for Schwab on the film would be the Concorde shot. Certainly he wouldn't have chosen a shot of an airplane landing to make his imprint on any film, but since that was what he'd been given, he felt more determined than ever to make it something spectacular. He'd figured the budget for the shot at $80,000; if it didn't work out, he'd be a fool.

As he sat there he already felt like a fool. What did his access to

De Palma mean outside of this little world, where that access was regarded as a rare privilege. Outside it meant nothing. All his work was supplemental to De Palma's; it could be obliterated at a moment's notice, without consultation. No one on the outside knew what he did. They didn't know that he'd canvassed thirty states to find the bridge for the scene with the Mounties in "The Untouchables"; that he'd flown to Australia and Mexico and all over Thailand to find the bridge for "Casualties of War," finally settling, ironically, on a bridge over the River Kwai.

He didn't blame De Palma. It was just becoming clearer to him daily that he no longer wanted to be subject to someone else's whim — no, to someone else's power.

After one round of dailies of the justice speech the next day, Vilmos Zsigmond stood up in the front of the screening room and yawned. "I hate this," he said. "You go to sleep and it's dark and wake up and it's dark. I feel like I'm filming in Iceland."

He dragged himself up the aisle and noticed Caruso. "That speech was really something," said Zsigmond, shaking his head. "I didn't think it was so big while we were shooting it."

There were two sets of dailies that day; De Palma had settled in back with the editors for the second round of dailies as Zsigmond left. The projectionist rolled the takes of the justice speech again. Each take was long: two and a half minutes. Freeman delivered the speech with a great deal of feeling and a spirit of nobility. But something was missing. Freeman didn't have the raw passion of Judge Roberts, and the scene lacked the inherent edge of a white judge lecturing a black mob.

Michael Cristofer had come to dailies specifically to see this speech. De Palma had never worked with a writer as closely as he had with Cristofer. Since the director had lost his producer, he frequently turned to Cristofer to act as his sounding board.

The writer was enthusiastic about Freeman's performance but was noncommittal in his commentary. "Maybe we should play it for an audience," he said.

De Palma couldn't shake the feeling that the speech was making an announcement: this is the *message* of the movie. The movie was twenty-seven days into production, and De Palma felt as if they'd been in that courtroom forever. Now these speeches: the judge castigating the mob, then telling them to be decent. The studio executives kept saying it could all be fixed in the editing room. De Palma felt fairly certain that when they put it all together, something would have to go.

The lights went on, and Schwab brought De Palma drawings of the Palm Court at the Winter Garden, where the opening scene of Fallow's Pulitzer Prize banquet would now be shot. While De Palma studied the drawings, Schwab dug a ginseng capsule out of his pocket. Like everyone working on the film, he fortified himself against illnesses with zinc, garlic, ginseng, and an assortment of vitamins.

Schwab was trying not to sulk openly. His Thai girlfriend, Lek, could take a vacation only once every six months and had wanted to come for a visit in May. Schwab had told her not to come because he would be working on the opening shot. Now it was canceled and Lek had already given up her vacation.

He had spent this entire gloomy day in the bowels of the World Financial Center, looking for a corridor that could work for the opening shot De Palma had sketched out for him. Almost against his will he was excited about what he'd seen beneath the marble palace. A maze of concrete hallways led from an underground parking lot to an elevator. The elevator opened near one of the elegant shopping strips that fed into the Palm Court. He'd had Brett Botula, the location scout, push him through the corridor in a garbage cart while they filmed a videotape to show De Palma.

When De Palma finished looking at the sketches of the space, he examined the jacket Richard Sylbert had designed for Fallow's Pulitzer Prize–winning book (which bore a close resemblance to the jacket of *Bonfire*). A giant replica of the jacket was to hang from the Palm Court ceiling.

"Should the jacket face the audience the way it would in real life?" Schwab asked.

"No!" said De Palma. "The image is for us. The camera. I want it like the sign at the AFI dinner. As vivid as that sign in 'Citizen Kane.' "

Schwab understood immediately that he was referring to the

running-for-governor scene in Orson Welles's classic movie.

Schwab folded his drawings, and Roth stepped up for her consultation with the director. "Do you mind Bruce Willis's hair?"

"What's wrong with it?" De Palma asked.

Roth said, "It's *painted*. If you don't mind I'm going to speak to his hairdresser. His scalp is painted."

Her tone warned De Palma that he didn't dare laugh. "It's a sensitive subject," she said. "I think he's attractive without this painting. It's like vaudeville to me. I don't want to get into it with him or that little person who does it for him, if you don't mind."

"That little person" was Josee Norman, a small, attractive woman with a French-Canadian lilt to her voice. She had been doing Willis's hair for six years. Like all of Willis's entourage, she saw her job as fending off the boobs and incompetents who were doing their best to make her boss look bad.

Norman stayed as close to the camera as she could when Willis was being filmed. Whenever the light shone so that his scalp peeked through his thinning hair, she would complain to Zsigmond, "Back light. Take it out." That bald spot obsessed her.

Finally they hit upon an idea: they would spray Willis's head with black face powder. This presented a new set of problems. During the courthouse scenes, every time Willis took his glasses on and off, the powder would rub off on his face.

That evening De Palma mentioned the matter of the painted skull to Willis. Quite cordially the star suggested to the director that perhaps he shouldn't be lit so harshly from above.

Just before dawn on May 18, a weary Morgan Freeman leaned against the judge's bench with his arms folded and recited the justice speech while one camera pointed at Saul Rubinek, the actor playing the assistant district attorney, and another camera pointed at the spectators. Freeman's voice was raspy.

This was "coverage," the filming of the same scene from a variety of angles, with two or more cameras. This would provide the editors with options when it came time to put the scene together. If the justice speech seemed to lag, they could give the audience a moment of comic relief by cutting to Saul Rubinek's face, which resembled a caricature. Each new angle required a different arrangement of lights. To pass the time, Tom Hanks was reading *The New Yorker* in the judge's chair. Freeman began singing "Pretty Woman."

De Palma held his face in his hands. He loathed coverage. To him it was obscene, no matter how necessary. Any *moron*, he would say, could set up three cameras and have people talk. That was television's curse and the reason, he felt, so few actors knew their craft. No one worried about getting it right because they knew if one actor made a mistake, the cameras could cut to somebody else.

De Palma felt weak as he rode back into Manhattan, just as the sun was rising. His boys — he thought of Karl Slovin and Doug Rushkoff as a unit, whose name he couldn't remember — had forgotten to restock his trailer with his diet drink. He was determined to keep his weight down; after 6:00 P.M. he ate nothing except his Dutch chocolate diet drink. At four this morning he'd needed something to spur him on. He wanted to get out of the courthouse and on to the next location by tonight. He needed his Medifast, and it wasn't there.

He was annoyed at Monica Goldstein. If she didn't want to work as his assistant on the set, that was fine. But she should have found a replacement who was as competent as she was. He liked the film students well enough. They seemed like bright fellows. They seemed like nice kids. But when he was working he needed a servant, not a student. He needed someone who could anticipate what he wanted when he wanted it. He wasn't demanding a lot: his water, his coffee, his diet drink. From now on the film students could hang around and watch him if they wanted to. But he wanted a new assistant, tonight. He'd been checking out the p.a.'s and narrowed the choice down to three: the girl with the hat, the guy who was someone's son, and Aimee Morris.

By the time he reached the Village, he'd decided on Morris. He'd been impressed by the way she'd handled interrupting his nap. She'd checked with both Goldstein and with Chris Soldo, the first assistant director, about what to do. Soldo had stood up for her and had taken responsibility for her; Morris had been hired on his recommendation. That had impressed De Palma as well. Soldo hadn't been intimidated, and he hadn't tried to pass the buck. Morris followed up with an apology.

Tom Hanks, Melanie Griffith, and Bruce Willis.
Copyright © 1990 Warner Bros., Inc.

Producer Peter Guber first approached Tom Hanks about playing Sherman McCoy at the 1989 Academy Awards ceremony.
© *Alex Berliner/Visages*

Brian De Palma with Judge Burton Roberts outside the Bronx County Building. De Palma didn't think Roberts was "likable" enough to play the judge Tom Wolfe modeled on him.
© *Steven Sands*

Tom Wolfe kept his distance from "Bonfire" after he sold the rights to his best-selling novel. © *Steven Sands*

Lucy Fisher, who became the highest-ranking woman executive in Hollywood, was in charge of Warner Bros. "prestige" projects. "Bonfire" was the biggest movie that had ever come her way. © *Mark Hanauer*

Warner Bros. production executives Bill Young and Ron Smith bring their boss, Mark Canton, executive vice president of worldwide production, to the Bronx for a day of filming. © *Steven Sands*

Brian De Palma and cinematographer Vilmos Zsigmond decided there would be no ordinary camera angles in their movie, that they weren't a couple of "old fogeys." © *Steven Sands*

Production designer Richard Sylbert and the McCoy apartment on Stage 25 of the Warner Bros. lot. *Copyright © 1991 Warner Bros., Inc.*

Fred Caruso (*right*), the line producer who always expected to be the "fall guy" if "Bonfire" failed, goes over some sketches with one of the film's art directors. © *Sara Krulwich*

Monica Goldstein (*right*), Brian De Palma's personal assistant for five years; and Aimee Morris (*left*), De Palma's production assistant on "Bonfire." © *Sara Krulwich*

Randy Bowers, Bruce Willis's stand-in. © *Sara Krulwich*

One of Bruce Willis's two bodyguards. © *Sara Krulwich*

Above: The sword fight scene that didn't make the final cut of the movie. *Below, left:* Kim Cattrall and Tom Hanks. *Below, right:* Morgan Freeman as Judge Leonard White, formerly Judge Myron Kovitsky. *Copyright © 1990 Warner Bros., Inc.*

Melanie Griffith and Tom Hanks.
Copyright © 1990 Warner Bros., Inc.

Beth Broderick played the critical part in a risqué scene involving a Xerox machine, a scene invented specifically for the movie by screenwriter Michael Christofer.

Beth Broderick and Bruce Willis in the Xerox scene.
Copyright © 1990 Warner Bros., Inc.

Brian De Palma's protégé Eric Schwab directed the movie's opening shot, a view from one of the Chrysler Building gargoyles. © *Sara Krulwich*

That night Slovin was preparing De Palma's trailer for the midnight trek from Queens into Manhattan for the next shoot, when the director showed up with Morris in tow. Without explanation, he ushered the young man out, saying only that Morris would be doing his job that night. Slovin hung around the set that night in a state of shock. He'd never been fired before, and this was completely unexpected. Thursday night De Palma had even been friendly, chatting with Slovin about the dynamics of the scene.

Finally, five hours later, Chris Soldo approached Slovin. "I'm sorry, Karl," he said, tugging his baseball cap over his eyes. "Brian wants Aimee for the job." Soldo offered Slovin a job as lockup p.a., to guard the perimeter of the set and make sure no interlopers trespassed. That wasn't what Slovin had signed on for. He'd been willing to do menial labor for De Palma because he wanted proximity to the director and the camera. He wasn't going to learn anything about the way the set worked out at the farthest boundary.

He decided to quit. Doug Rushkoff had already given up on "Bonfire." The AFI student had just left for Los Angeles to work on a music video for Virgin Records. He'd invited Slovin to join him, and now Slovin decided to take him up on the offer.

As Tom Hanks was heading for Queens earlier that evening to film the final courtroom scene in which Sherman McCoy goes free and the Reverend Bacon leads the spectators into a demonstration, the radio announced that a verdict in the Bensonhurst case had come in. For months the city had been obsessed with this racially charged case involving a gang of white teenagers who were charged with killing a young black man who'd ventured into the largely Italian Bensonhurst section of Brooklyn.

The radio announcer described the scene. When Keith Mondello, one of the defendants, was declared not guilty, the Reverend Al Sharpton leaped to his feet and screamed, "You're finished!" The reporter described the ensuing melee in the courtroom and then concluded breathlessly, "The tension in the courtroom was overpowering — it was as though we were watching the courtroom scene from *The Bonfire of the Vanities*."

Well, why not? Hanks thought. Why not.

* * *

Shooting Hanks's scene in Queens went smoothly, and during the "lunch" break that night, just after midnight, the "Bonfire" crew left Queens. By 1:30 A.M. the cameras were being readied to roll again, this time at the surrogate court in Lower Manhattan. There was some irony to the ease of this transition, as nothing else about these two locations had come easily.

The action against "Bonfire" by New Jersey's Justice Wilentz had roused the press once again. The Newark *Star-Ledger* had given the story front-page play. Newspaper and television editorialists all over the country became defenders of "Bonfire" and Warner Bros., invoking the First Amendment. The *New York Times* designated Wilentz "New Jersey's Chief Film Critic." As the journalists reported and pontificated, the surrogate court came through. And in the end it wouldn't matter. After the agony of finding a place to film this scene, and the difficulty it would take to shoot it, the sword fight would be left on the cutting room floor.

In the sword fight scene Sherman grabs the judge after he delivers his speech and leads him out of the courtroom into the hallway, to escape the rioting mob inside. They find themselves pursued by the mob from within, and by a mob of reporters waiting outside. As the two groups press in on Sherman and the judge, a statue of blind justice falls to the floor. The judge is blinded by the plaster dust. Sherman picks up the sword that has broken away from the shattered statue, and pulls the judge through the mob. In slow motion he slaps at his enemies with the sword, one by one: Abe Weiss, Kramer, and finally, Peter Fallow. De Palma had dreamed up this scene to revitalize the movie after the courtroom speeches, to rouse the audience to applaud Sherman's triumph and redemption. It was the kind of Grand Guignol De Palma loved — a broad, operatic melodrama.

With its sweeping marble banisters and grand staircase leading up from the main floor, the surrogate court was perfect for the slow-motion heroics of the sword fight scene — except there was no way to light it. The antique glass ceiling was off-limits. Colin Campbell, the gaffer, came up with an ingenious solution. He floated five giant white helium balloons on the inside of the vaulted ceiling; the light could bounce off the balloons.

*   *   *

Morris had taken her station next to De Palma's station on the set quite naturally. Though she was uncomfortable with her "promotion," she'd decided to make the most of it. She'd studied film at Emerson College in Boston and was eager to work her way up through the film business. She'd just celebrated her twenty-third birthday, and she was full of energy and self-confidence. She wasn't afraid to ask De Palma questions.

When Monica Goldstein dropped by the set that night and saw Morris laughing and flirting with De Palma, she was furious. Why didn't he laugh with *her*? Didn't he think she was intelligent? No matter what she did, she couldn't seem to earn his respect. And now Morris just waltzed in and acted as though she and De Palma were equals. It occurred to Goldstein that she was being replaced even as she watched. This was like a scene out of "All About Eve," and she was Bette Davis, watching a younger woman connive her way into her place.

But Goldstein couldn't deny that she had gotten her job, back on "Wise Guys," in much the same way. She'd made a point of carrying the "Monica bag" with her everywhere — a snack bag holding the raisins and nuts De Palma liked to munch before he'd lost weight. One day, driving back into Manhattan from New Jersey, he'd asked her if she'd like to be his assistant. Oh, yes, she knew how it worked.

Geraldo Rivera was scheduled to appear on camera that night, as part of the reporting mob Sherman attacks with his sword. Rivera couldn't resist the opportunity for self-promotion disguised as news. As De Palma worked out the details of his shot inside the surrogate court, pacing back and forth, whacking an imaginary sword through the air, Rivera set up for a live feed to KCBS in Los Angeles outside. It was 10:30 P.M. in New York, and there was an unusual amount of traffic downtown on this warm spring night.

A van drove by. "Geraldo!" screamed the driver.

"Hi," he said, his hands in his pockets. Over and over, horns honked. "Geraldo!" The trim man with the mustache smiled and gave the thumbs up to his fans.

Rivera's cameraman set up his lights, and Rivera chatted with the L.A. anchor through a hidden microphone. "Life is a sweeps," he said. "I'm a let's-go kind of guy, and this week is 'let's go.' " He laughed. "During this night shoot I brought along my wife. She's in the trailer."

The cameraman indicated they were about to start filming, and Rivera adjusted his face to the earnest expression familiar to his fans. He explained that he played a TV newsman in the film. "This character is a lot more cynical than I would ever be, and certainly a lot more ruthless," he told KCBS. Then he summarized the plot, inaccurately describing Melanie Griffith's character, Maria, as Sherman's "slightly nymphomaniacal wife" instead of his mistress.

After a sentence or two more about "Bonfire," Rivera warmed to his next subject: himself. He discussed his book contract and his show, and said that the show he'd done on child labor was his favorite show of the season. The show he'd liked least, he assured KCBS viewers, was the one that had won the highest ratings. That was his show about celebrity imposters. Six Geraldo Rivera look-alikes had appeared with him; "Geraldo" had beaten "The Oprah Winfrey Show" for the first time that season.

Rivera concluded the interview by returning to "Bonfire." "It's an exciting, violent happy ending," he said. "I love you too. Bye-bye." He blew a kiss to the camera. The lights went off. Rivera's smile disappeared.

De Palma was shooting all night for several nights and meeting with Michael Cristofer by day, trying to put the beginning and the end of the film together. Under De Palma's new strategy, the film would open and close with Peter Fallow. A long Steadicam shot would introduce the writer as a celebrity. De Palma was hoping for a daredevil feat: a single take that could run as long as five minutes, tracking Fallow as he staggered his way up to the Pulitzer Prize banquet where he was being honored for his book, *The Real McCoy and the Forgotten Lamb*, his account of Sherman McCoy's story. They'd have to come up with some dialogue to accompany the action, which would culminate with the drunken Fallow stumbling onto a stage and being blinded by flashbulbs. This would lead into the narration, the story of "Bonfire." Then, at the very end, Sherman's sword fight would end with reporters flashing pictures, bringing the film back around to where it started, with Fallow at the banquet.

The studio executives weren't happy when De Palma broke the news about the new opening, three days before he was going to film it. Though he explained the Steadicam shot in as much detail as he could, they wanted to see it written down. But Cristofer hadn't had a chance to work the scene out yet. Most of it was still being developed in De Palma's head.

During dailies on May 23, Mark Canton and Lucy Fisher put in a call to De Palma to air their concerns about this production. De Palma took the call in the screening room, in front of Schwab, Morris, Caruso, the editors, their three assistants, Goldstein, and Cristofer. "Bonfire" was six days behind schedule and $1,670,187 over budget.

Fisher complained that the book jacket Sylbert had designed for *The Real McCoy and the Forgotten Lamb* too closely resembled the cover of Tom Wolfe's book. De Palma assured her no one would remember that cover; most people read the paperback, which had a different cover. They discussed locations, Griffith's hair, and the cost of sending the second unit to Philadelphia to scout for a location for the cemetery scene. De Palma explained why they still didn't have pages for the new opening.

"We're moving locations because the publicity has shut us out of locations. If we had the Met and I could zoom through the window, my life would be one hundred times easier, okay? Yesterday I saw the location for the first time. Yesterday! Do you think this is fun?" His tone was weary but firm. "Give me some advertising and trailer material. I'm trying to delegate this to you, Lucy . . . I *am* tired. We're dealing with a whole bunch of stuff. Night after night after night."

His tone softened. "Thank you. Bye-bye."

He hung up and turned to Schwab. "They're complaining about you going to cemeteries. You're out of control, Eric."

Schwab looked worried. "Ron Smith had a fit because Bruce Frye and I drove to Philadelphia to find a cemetery. You know what our expenses were? Gas!"

De Palma began to tease. "There have got to be fall guys, Eric. You and Fred Caruso are mine."

Schwab laughed, but Caruso, standing near the door, didn't crack a smile.

* * *

On the way down to surrogate court for that night's shoot, De Palma turned to Aimee Morris, who was riding in the back seat. "I don't want to go to the set, Aimee," he said in a friendly, flirtatious way. "Let's go to L.A." To the teamster driver, he said, "Let's keep driving."

Instead, the driver let them off at the trailer, where De Palma sat at the little kitchen table eating popcorn while Morris fixed espresso. Chris Soldo dropped by to tell De Palma his ideas about background for the opening sequence, which was scheduled for shooting Saturday night of the coming weekend, Memorial Day weekend. Soldo had determined they'd need twenty-four actors to play paparazzi with flashbulbs, a limo driver for Fallow, and uniformed guards; and they'd need an ice sculpture and a jazz combo, perhaps, to play in the tunnel.

"You should dress your p.a.'s as security people. Let's put them on camera," said De Palma.

Soldo continued down the list: hors d'oeuvres, a giant salmon mousse, champagne glasses, a diplomat and his wife and their pretty daughter.

De Palma laughed. "Let Fallow try to make the diplomat's daughter when he falls into the elevator and sticks his hand in the salmon mousse."

"Yeah," said Soldo. "Just as the waiter is arranging the parsley."

De Palma warmed to this exercise in improvisation. "Let Bruce go around the corner, let his wardrobe guy —"

"Charles."

De Palma nodded. "Have Charles whip his clothes off so he's a total mess. Have a seltzer bottle spritzing."

Soldo was animated too. "And the paparazzi —"

"No, no," said De Palma. "They should be like all those pathetic people with Brownies outside the Broadway theater."

He and Soldo continued improvising for several minutes. After the first assistant director left, Morris piped up, "I have an idea."

De Palma rolled his eyes and laughed. He was amused by Morris's obvious ambition and aware that the crew was watching her every move. "All right, Eve Harrington," he said, referring to the manipulative young actress in "All About Eve" who schemes to supplant her idol and mentor. "Go ahead."

Morris spoke confidently. "When you and Michael were talking about that scene with Sherman in the courtroom, how about a dissolve?"

De Palma stopped smiling. He'd missed bantering about films with friends over cappuccino since this film had begun, but he had no patience for ill-conceived ideas.

"A dissolve?" His tone was cutting.

Morris stumbled as she tried to articulate what she meant. De Palma bore down on her, and she stammered through a shot sequence.

Red-faced, she fell back on charm. "This is how I learn," she said. "I say what I say and you rip me apart. I can't wait until you see my film."

De Palma laughed. "I have seen your film."

A couple of days earlier, Morris had brought him a video she'd made at Emerson College. Tired as he was, he'd taken a look at it. De Palma was always looking for talent and was willing to help those he liked if he thought they had potential. He liked playing the part of the catalyst. Morris's work wasn't bad, but it wasn't inspired. "To me it's a music video." He shrugged.

"It *is* a music video," said Morris defensively.

De Palma rolled his eyes. "Visualizing what these nitwit lyrics say is not interesting. This is not Cole Porter here. You want to find a metaphoric analogue that is not just a duplication of these half-witted lyrics. In and of itself, music video is an imbecilic profession. 'I love you,' and somebody kisses somebody. You did it perfectly."

Morris took in the critique without flinching. "That's what my teacher said. I never wanted to get into music video anyway."

De Palma softened. "As a music video it's fine. It just falls into all the clichés of that genre. The question is, what do you want to do?"

Morris pulled hard on her cigarette. "I want to be . . . more creative."

De Palma looked disappointed. "C'mon, Aimee. You're starting to sound like a space cadet."

Morris concentrated. "I want to learn more about how to use a dolly. How to combine shots so it's not disrupted —"

De Palma had grown impatient. "Take an idea that has to be told in visual images. That's what I always tell my students. It can be

Super 8. Take any cliché — somebody killing somebody. Pure action, but make it original."

Morris perked up. She still had a chance to prove herself. "A mugging."

De Palma waved his hand dismissively. "Don't tell it to me. Draw me a series of shots of someone being mugged. That's how you learn. By looking through a camera and shooting things."

Once again, Morris tried to win his approval. "That's what I would do with photographs. We were supposed to do a landscape, but it couldn't be an actual landscape. I threw sticks on the esplanade and took a picture. I took a picture of bark on a tree."

De Palma looked annoyed. "What does that have to do with anything? You have to learn to tell a visual story."

Morris sighed. "Okay," she said. "I'll work on this mugging thing."

De Palma's impromptu class on film theory and practice was dismissed when Ann Roth popped by the trailer to discuss the details of moviemaking in the real world. "Let's talk about something unpleasant," she said. "My two phone calls from Lucy Fisher." Roth looked disgusted. "She doesn't like Melanie's hair."

"Lucy said she liked the Ivana Trump/Brigitte Bardot look that's being featured in *Vogue* and *People* magazine." Roth paced in the tiny kitchen. "Good God! *People* magazine! I told her *People* is not what we are striving for."

De Palma held his hands palms up. "I did talk to Bruce Willis about his hair," he said.

Roth looked impressed. "Did you?"

De Palma laughed. "I don't think it made a difference."

Roth patted him on the arm. "Still, good for you." She poured herself some of De Palma's espresso.

That night was scheduled for filming the sword fight scene. The director went through several takes shooting Tom Hanks charging up the hallway on the mezzanine waving the sword of justice and whacking the other actors, with an emphatic whack for Bruce Willis. The hallway was packed with extras and the Willis entourage. Hanks's wife, Rita Wilson, who was six months pregnant, dropped by with Hanks's two children from a previous marriage.

In between takes, Willis and Hanks sat on their canvas chairs and watched themselves on playback, on the video monitor. Hanks looked bored as Willis droned on about how his work on "Moonlighting" improved his ability to play to the camera. Suddenly, Hanks leaned forward until his face was just inches from the video monitor.

He examined the close-up on Willis, whose image was wearing the wise-guy smirk that had become a subject of much mocking commentary among the "Bonfire" cast and crew over the past few weeks. "Big, shit-eating grin I see there on the monitor," said Hanks jovially. Willis showed no sign of registering the comment. Hanks peered at the monitor again. "Yup," he said. "There it is."

Just then the Willis entourage converged around their boss. Hanks kept staring at the monitor.

By Friday afternoon the previous night's filming at the surrogate court seemed like ancient history. De Palma was completely charged up, thinking about the opening Steadicam shot. He'd briefly visited the location under the Palm Court and realized just how tricky the long shot was going to be. In order to offer running commentary to the actors and the camera operator during filming, he would have to insert himself into the shot because there was nowhere to hide from the camera in the narrow corridor. He decided to shave his beard so he wouldn't be recognized. Unlike Hitchcock, De Palma rarely made cameo appearances in his own films. He had played a part in "Greetings" because somebody didn't show up and had inadvertently appeared in "Scarface" in a reflection.

Everything about the Steadicam shot was coming together at the last minute — including casting. At 5:00 P.M. casting began at the Tribeca Film Center for the receiving line at the Winter Garden dinner for Peter Fallow. They needed actors to play a diplomat, his wife, and their daughter. In just a few hours rehearsals were to begin for the scene that would be filmed the next night. As De Palma went over the parts with Jeff Passaro, the New York casting man, he kept muttering with excitement. "Wire without a net," he said. "Wire without a net."

Eric Schwab walked in, looking drawn. He and Frye had just spent two hours in the Holland Tunnel, on their way back from an unsuccessful scouting trip to New Jersey. They still hadn't found a cemetery for the shot leading to the funeral scene for Arthur Ruskin, Maria's husband. De Palma told Schwab to take notes on the auditions, since Nancy Hopton, the script supervisor, wasn't there yet.

Passaro ushered in a group of distinguished-looking middle-aged men and women, and De Palma asked them to introduce themselves to the video camera. Then he cordially moved up the line, acting the part of someone going through a receiving line. "Hi, I'm Brian De Palma," he said. "Nice to see you." When he reached the end of the line he waved the group out the door. "Go on out and let me look at it."

He repeated the mock receiving line with a group of young women, only this time he was flirtatious, putting his arms around them and trying to nuzzle their faces with his, the way the drunken Peter Fallow would. Then, matter-of-factly, he walked away, and the young women were dismissed. The video monitor played back the scene. De Palma watched himself grappling with the young women on the video monitor and laughed.

He went through the scene with another batch of diplomat's daughters, and then he auditioned a woman for the part of the P.R. lady who would accompany Willis on the golf cart underneath the Winter Garden. The woman wasn't quite right, but De Palma had an idea. What about casting Tom Hanks's wife, Rita Wilson, in the role? Wilson was brisk and funny, the perfect type for an overeager public relations person. He even liked the fact that she was pregnant.

When he called Wilson up, the actress was intrigued with the idea but hesitant. This was one of the few weekends Hanks wasn't scheduled to work, giving them a rare chance to see one another in daylight hours.

While she thought it over, De Palma auditioned some more diplomat's wives. The phone rang. De Palma's face brightened. Wilson had agreed to play the part.

He told Caruso, who'd come in during the auditions, to have Hanks's trailer down at the Winter Garden by 8:15 for Wilson to use. "So the gal from L.A., we'll do something else with her?" said Caruso gently.

De Palma turned red. He'd completely forgotten they'd already hired an actress for the P.R. lady, and she was en route from Los Angeles at that minute. "Oh? Oh. We'll put her somewhere at the party." It was 7:00 P.M., an hour before the all-night rehearsal would begin.

The shot De Palma conjured up for the Winter Garden would prove a major test of Larry McConkey's skill with the Steadicam. The first part was relatively simple: Bruce Willis and Rita Wilson would ride through the first 380-foot passageway on a golf cart, facing McConkey and the camera on a golf cart in front of them. Then McConkey would get out of the cart and move backward on foot. Always walking backward, he would have to maneuver around the cart holding the giant ice sculpture, and end up in the elevator. The stretch from the corridor to the elevator was 234 feet. Upstairs, there was a further 250-foot stretch from the elevator to the Winter Garden.

De Palma wanted to accomplish all of this in a single take that would last nearly five minutes. In film time, that was an eternity.

By Saturday night everything was set. The Palm Court was decked out for a glorious ball; each of the thirty-five tables was adorned with a $150 flower arrangement. A five-foot salmon mousse that cost $750 was on hand; $30,000 of new lightbulbs had been installed. A twenty-five-by-thirty-five-foot banner depicting the book jacket for Fallow's *The Real McCoy and the Forgotten Lamb*, hung alongside the north wall. Gold papier-mâché palm trees had been mixed in with the real palm trees, and the extras were dressed in a variety of black, gold, and silver dresses. Everything glittered.

The fake party inspired a rare feeling of festivity among the tired crew. One of the editors dropped by with his wife; Sylbert brought two of his daughters. An assistant showed up with a baby.

Randy Bowers, Willis's stand-in, stood at the top of the stairs wearing a tuxedo. Tonight he would have his shot; he and Willis's make-up man and wardrobe man would appear on camera, helping Fallow slip into clean clothes after he smears salmon mousse all over himself on his way upstairs. Bowers was wearing a tuxedo and a diamond stud in his left ear; Willis had given him the earring as a gift on his thirty-fourth birthday a few weeks earlier. Bowers had pierced his ear two years before for Willis, to match Willis's pierced ear when he stood in for the actor in "In Country."

Nearby, Sylbert was admiring his handiwork, the giant book cover. "It's better than the original," he was saying, referring to the cover of Tom Wolfe's book. "Take a look at the original. What was it? A glass coffee table with a reflection of the city and an awful Persian rug."

While the actors and extras waited for the Steadicam shot to be completed down below, F. Murray Abraham lectured his captive audience on *Cyrano de Bergerac*.

Finally, a large man in a security guard's blue blazer, with a soft chin and thin lips and a smooth face, appeared at the top of the marble steps to survey the glamorous landscape below.

"Doesn't he look younger?" Aimee Morris asked Schwab. Schwab couldn't bear to look at De Palma in his new guise. The director looked entirely different without his beard, less formidable, even vulnerable.

De Palma disappeared downstairs, where everyone was at their stations. The shot began. McConkey propelled himself backward, as De Palma hustled to keep up with the actors so he could hear their dialogue. As McConkey started to back around the ice sculpture near the elevator, a huge crowd had to move with him: De Palma, McConkey's assistant, the two sound men, and two assistant directors, in addition to the actors. The move had gone smoothly during the rehearsals the night before, when the cart that now contained the ice sculpture had been empty — and light.

Now the actors continued to move at the quick pace established during rehearsals. But the cart was slowed down by the mass of ice. Suddenly McConkey heard a sickening noise. Something was being squashed behind him. But the rule was, don't stop until someone says to stop. He kept moving backward and fell right on top of his assistant, who had collapsed against the slow-going ice sculpture. McConkey rolled over him, clutching his equipment like a seventy-five-pound baby.

De Palma ran up to the two men. "You okay?" he asked. "Larry, you okay?" Then, in a panicky voice, he asked, "Is the camera okay?" It was established that McConkey and the camera were fine. The assistant, however, had to be taken to the hospital for stitches; when McConkey and camera rolled over him, his face was smashed into the concrete floor.

De Palma looked at McConkey in complete amazement. "I've never seen you fall," he said, as though even the *idea* were impossible.

Catastrophe seemed to lurk everywhere. The night before, De Palma had had to write lines for the scene because he couldn't find Michael Cristofer. Now this accident just as they were starting to film. Then, in the middle of it all, the actress playing the diplomat's daughter had an anxiety attack while five hundred people waited to finish the scene. She became feverish and started throwing up. To calm her down, De Palma took her into his trailer parked in the loading dock under the Winter Garden. For twenty minutes he rehearsed her lines with her and listened to her life story, how she almost got a job on the sequel to "Blue Lagoon" but lost it because she wouldn't do nudity.

At that moment De Palma felt a thrill, as he realized what a miracle the whole thing was. This incredible production could be brought to a halt . . . just . . . like . . . that.

The festive mood that prevailed during the shooting of the party at the Winter Garden quickly dissolved into the feeling of exhaustion and gloom that had shrouded the crew since night shooting had begun. By the Tuesday following the Memorial Day weekend, it was back to business as usual. The executives were panicking. They felt their influence had slipped away entirely. Yes, the new opening worked, but what if it hadn't. They wanted to move this operation back to their turf, back to Los Angeles, as quickly as possible.

The faxes increased in number and intensity: Shoot Maria's apartment on the back lot. Don't shoot outside Rockefeller Center. Don't shoot on Prostitute Street, even though the second unit portion was already on film. Over and over the executives sent out the message: This picture is out of control. We're shutting it down.

There were telephone calls in the middle of the night, from Fisher and Canton to Bauer to Caruso to De Palma. De Palma read the faxes and tried to figure out some way to compromise that wouldn't compromise his movie. This was a movie about New York, and he needed exterior shots of the Bronx and Manhattan. He wanted to accommodate the executives, but there was one thing he wouldn't do: he wouldn't shoot the Bronx in Los Angeles.

On June 6 the "Bonfire" crew was back at Prostitute Street in the Bronx, the final night of shooting in New York before the show moved to L.A. They'd spent a week under the Third Avenue Bridge, done the Merrill Lynch bond room over the weekend without a hitch, and filmed outside Rockefeller Center.

People from the neighborhood crowded against the barricades and the rooftops of the stores lining the street to give the "Bonfire" crew a suitable sendoff. The p.a.'s patrolling the boundaries of the set looked particularly grim as they explained to the mostly black and Hispanic onlookers why they couldn't slip by the blue police barriers. The babble of the crowd and the blare of radios was punctuated by small, flat sounds. *Ping. Ping. Ping. Splat. Ping. Splat. Splat.* The spectators were pitching eggs and lightbulbs from the perimeters.

The crew pretended to ignore the chaos at the edge and concentrated on the chaos they were manufacturing. The "set" was crammed with garish cars and actors playing pimps and hookers and junkies stumbling up the street. Doug Ryan, the camera operator, was perched on a Titan crane; he wore a raincoat and held an umbrella to protect himself from flying eggs and glass. De Palma, whose pants leg was wet with egg slime, didn't like what he was seeing on the street in front of him; Ann Roth had dressed the extras like circus performers. He could see he had to do this shot fast — make the point that Sherman and Maria were lost in a world without white people and get out. He didn't want to give the audience time to figure out they were looking at a clichéd caricature of the Bronx.

As the eggs went splat and the noise amplified, De Palma pushed himself as far back into his director's chair as he could and covered his ears with his new headset. At the perimeters a few fistfights erupted, and the policemen assigned to the set intervened. But the police said they couldn't do anything about the lightbulbs and eggs.

Fred Caruso decided to enlist the help of Gino Lucci and Colum-
bo Saggese, who operated Picture Cars East, the company that
provided all the cars for the film. Lucci and Saggese, both of whom
had sunglasses hanging from their shirt collars even though it was
midnight, had also hired members of the Ching-a-ling motorcycle
gang as extras for "Bonfire." When Caruso asked the partners for
help with the rowdy onlookers, Lucci and Saggese put the Ching-a-
lings to work. The Ching-a-lings wore their hair and beards long
and were liberally decorated with complex tattoos. Lucci assured
Caruso that the bikers only looked like Hell's Angels. "They wear
the same jackets and smell the same way," he said. "But they're
docile like babies if you treat 'em like human beings and not
submorons." Within an hour after the Ching-a-lings started patrolling the rooftops for egg and lightbulb throwers, the pelting
stopped.

Just after midnight, Chris Soldo instructed the p.a.'s to escort
Melanie Griffith and Tom Hanks to their chairs, which were set up
in the middle of the street. When they were settled, Soldo shouted
through his megaphone at the female extras waiting for instructions. "Girls, start shucking and jiving."

Griffith, in a trim, mustard-colored suit, and Hanks, in his
hand-tailored suit, looked suitably misplaced. Griffith glanced at a
passing Ching-a-ling and admired his tattoo. The actress lifted a
slim leg and tilted the heel of her high heels. "I have a tattoo," she
said to Hanks. He glanced down at the tiny heart on her ankle.

Then Griffith leaned against Hanks and whispered, "I have
another one on my ass."

Hanks drew back in his chair. "Don't show it here," he said in a
distant, light tone.

A few minutes later, a p.a. came by to lead the stars back to their
trailers. Zsigmond and De Palma weren't ready for them.

Griffith was furious. She'd been sitting out in that trailer since
6:00 P.M. like some second-rate stand-in. They'd had her get on a
plane to New York the day after she'd finished "Pacific Heights"
and then made her wait nine days. Night after night in the Bronx
she had waited around in wardrobe for six hours and someone
would tell her, "C'mon, get ready, you're on," and then nothing

would happen. Sometimes, thought Griffith, the more money they have to work with, the more fucked up things get. If they have only a small amount of money, they have to be so careful and so organized. With a ton of money they can kind of wander all over the place and know that their asses are covered.

She'd complained before and she would complain again.

PART III

The Los Angeles Shoot

Chapter 11

HOLLYWOOD WAY

The Warner Bros. water tower was a big, old-fashioned structure that looked like a giant barrel on stilts, a replica of the water towers in Hollywood Westerns signaling to travelers from a distance that they were approaching a frontier town. In this case, the town was the Warner Bros. lot, and both town and tower had become relics of another age. The tower no longer contained water, and most movies were made off the lot. Still, the tower remained a potent symbol for the glory days of the studio, when this 140-acre sprawl on the Burbank side of the Hollywood Hills really was the physical plant for the factory of dreams.

For the last two decades, Warner Bros. had shared the lot with Columbia Pictures as part of the retrenchment of the 1960s. During that period, the real estate originally acquired in 1928 by the founding Warner brothers — Harry, Albert, Sam, and Jack — had lost its individuality if not its value. For twenty years the two studios shared sound stages and screening rooms under the generic rubric of The Burbank Studios. The Warner Bros. logo on the water tower had been replaced by the initials TBS.

But in the summer of 1990, the year the studio celebrated its fiftieth birthday, Warner Bros. had regained its lot as part of the $1 billion settlement of the breach of contract suit Warner filed against Sony Corporation for hiring Peter Guber and Jon Peters. In return for its 35 percent interest in the Burbank Studios, Columbia received the old MGM lot in Culver City, which Warner owned. Warner emerged triumphant: not only had its historic boundaries been restored, but the Burbank property was worth about $50 million more than the Culver City land.

The water tower had been refurbished to reflect the new order. The TBS was replaced by a freshly painted Warner Bros. logo: a bright white WB glistening against an electric blue shield. The symbolism was lost on no one: the lot was once again stamped with the familiar mark that identified every piece of company property — from Bugs Bunny cartoons to "Batman" to "The Bonfire of the Vanities."

The "Bonfire" crew was happy to report to work in this cloistered world on June 12. After the frantic uncertainty of New York's streets, the rigidly enforced security of the lot was comforting, as was the five-day-a-week, days-only shooting schedule. Every morning crew members turned onto Hollywood Way, the street whose terminus was Gate 4 of the Warner Bros. lot, where guards closely inspected entry passes before allowing anyone — no matter how familiar the face — to enter the grounds.

Behind the gate stood the tower, silhouetted against the grizzled Hollywood Hills. Giant buildings resembling airplane hangars lined up to the east and north of the water tower. These were the sound stages where entire apartments, offices, and subway systems could be built and dismantled as needed. Rows of one- and two-story buildings sprawled across the rest of the lot. These housed offices and storerooms for canisters of film. Warnings from the Federal Bureau of Investigation regarding copyright infringement were posted everywhere.

With its high-level security and utilitarian structure, the lot at first blush resembled an army camp. However, nestled between the stark offices and the sound stages were enchanting streets lined with two-dimensional buildings. This was the back lot. There stood comfortable clapboard houses, a Main Street. There were banks and saloons and a pretty town square. The make-believe spirit was enhanced by the sight of security guards pedaling around the lot on bicycles. There was the sense that everything anyone needed was available. People who worked there didn't even have to worry about their cars being dirty. An outside cleaning service came onto the lot and washed the cars under little tents while their owners went about their business.

This place felt so safe, so completely removed from the rest of the world that it was possible to leave the keys in a car all day long without fear that either keys or car would be stolen. It felt so safe that Bruce Willis showed up for work without his bodyguard.

Only Brian De Palma found no comfort in the safety of the lot. In fact, he felt suffocated. The regularity of the schedule and predictability of the environment — and the proximity of the executives — only made the tunnel seem narrower to him. Even now, the script was in flux, and shooting was nine days behind schedule. De Palma kept running the movie through his mind over and over, trying to see how — or if — it would all fit together in the end.

Worst of all, De Palma still smarted from having been fired from this studio on his first Hollywood picture twenty years before. Now he did his best to keep to himself. He rarely used his office in Producer's Building 5, the two-story cement and brick building "Bonfire of the Vanities" shared with the "Life Goes On" television series about a young boy with Down's syndrome and with three independent production companies. The offices were dismal, with fake wood paneling, ugly brown carpet, and harsh fluorescent lights. De Palma's car only infrequently could be seen in the space reserved for him out front. There was meager evidence that he'd stepped inside the place: a March 1, 1990, version of the "Bonfire" script, and two packs of Players cigarettes in a desk drawer. In another drawer was an unopened box with a gold bow from Prestige Wine and Spirits, containing a bottle of Cristal champagne and a note from Peter Guber that said, "All the joy and success in the world to you. Congratulations."

This was the third office De Palma had occupied on this lot. He frequently pointed out his headquarters for "Get to Know Your Rabbit" as he drove to and from the various sound stages. In 1983, after "Scarface," he'd signed a three-picture deal with Columbia Pictures. As production began on "Body Double," the first film in the package, the studio installed De Palma in "permanent headquarters" on what was then the TBS lot. De Palma recalled the studio executives — who'd long since left Columbia — expressing a great deal of concern about his office. How did he want it decorated? How much square footage did he need? Naturally he was given a personalized parking space.

Three weeks after "Body Double" opened to awful notices and even worse ticket sales, Columbia canceled his multipicture deal and asked him to vacate his office. The name on his parking space was painted over when the grosses for "Body Double" came in.

Warner Bros. had already taken precautionary measures to allocate blame for the cost overruns. During the last week of shooting in New York, Bill Young had put in a call to Ron Smith to tell him that after he finished overseeing Schwab's second unit he was off the picture. A new executive, Penelope Foster, would be the on-site production person in Los Angeles. Smith thought his removal was unfair and had been describing himself as "Bonfire"'s Oliver North. At the studio, the executives described Smith's departure from the picture as a "vacation." By the end of the summer he would cease to be a Warner Bros. employee.

Warner Bros. didn't make any effort to give the filmmakers a warm welcome — and no one else did either. A few weeks before "Bonfire" left New York, one of Peter Guber's assistants had called Monica Goldstein about arranging a date for the welcome home party Guber wanted to throw for De Palma and the "Bonfire" principals. Many phone calls went back and forth between assistants: Guber's assistant kept offering new dates, which Goldstein kept accepting after she'd cleared them with De Palma. Shortly before the production moved to the West Coast, the phone calls from Guber stopped coming. No one from his office said the party was off. The date was simply left in limbo.

Tuesday, June 12, was the first day of filming in Los Angeles, and the action took place in Sound Stage 25. The bedroom of Peter Fallow's small, messy New York apartment had been constructed beneath the catwalks forty feet above. Just around the corner from the apartment was the set for the jail where Sherman would be incarcerated; a few steps away from that was the interior of a stuffy French restaurant, authentically pretentious, from the deep red banquettes to the starched white tablecloths and fussy serving pieces. As the schedule moved forward, different sections of the sound stage would light up, like exhibits in a funhouse.

That day the lights were on in the set for Fallow's bedroom. The scene would show the reporter lying on the floor of his apartment, unable to get up and go to work — unable to do anything. He gets the telephone call from the lawyer working with the Reverend Bacon that will give the reporter his big story: the story of the white man leaving a hit-and-run accident in the Bronx.

Originally Fallow was supposed to have this conversation at his office, after he staggers across Liberty Park. De Palma made the change to emphasize how morally bankrupt Fallow had become; he was in such bad shape that he couldn't even drag himself to his office. The change also meant that the footage from the first day's filming was no longer needed; it was no longer necessary to show Fallow in Liberty Park because he was no longer going to his office.

The director couldn't resist a visual elaboration on even the simple image of a drunk lying on the floor of his apartment. There simply would not be any conventional camera angles in this film. He and Zsigmond had become obsessed with the *unique*, like two bright film school students who were bursting to show what they could do. Sometimes, as they evaluated a shot, they wondered whether they were going too far. That had happened when they filmed the Merrill Lynch bond trading room with a ten-millimeter lens. No one would dare try such a thing. They had chosen the ten-millimeter lens, the widest lens possible, to allow the audience to take in the panorama of that giant trading room all at once. But using the lens was dangerous because it provided no room for play; every time the camera moved, whatever was at the edge of the frame became distorted on film. Desks would bend at the corners; people would look like gargoyles. Zsigmond and De Palma speculated whether the effect would be too cartoonish, and then De Palma ended the discussion. "What are we, Vilmos, old fogies? Let's go for it!" Zsigmond was exhilarated by De Palma's enthusiasm and his daring.

Though the crane shot over Fallow's apartment was far less extraordinary, it would require the full attention of Zsigmond, Doug Ryan, the operator, and Geary McLeod, the first assistant cameraman. The camera was propped up on a crane. As the platform was lowered, the camera would turn slowly as it swooped down on Willis lying on the floor talking on the phone. To make the turn, the camera had to spin on a special rotating head. All three cameramen had to crowd onto the platform of the crane; Ryan tilted and panned while McLeod pulled the focus, and Zsigmond slowly rotated the camera. Two grips gently lifted the fulcrum of the crane to lower the platform.

The crew huddled in front of the small set, watching this intimate piece of theater. Willis had his usual entourage there — except for the bodyguards. One of his brothers arrived on the set and stood next to Randy Bowers and the rest of the Willis group. Charles Mercuri, the star's wardrobe man, kept touching the ugly red mark under his nose; he'd been mugged in New York's Pennsylvania Station the day before he left. Josee Norman, the hair stylist, commiserated. Willis, who refused to fly commercial airlines, had given her a lift back to Los Angeles on the Warner Bros. jet Friday night. The flight was nightmarish; they encountered turbulence that caused the plane to drop four hundred feet. Norman was already frazzled. She'd been forced to plan her daughter's wedding while she was on location in New York. As if all that hadn't been enough, just before they left, her clothes had been stolen out of her room. They all agreed: it was good to be back.

Marty Bauer, De Palma's agent, headed out to the Burbank lot that afternoon to mediate at the meeting scheduled between his client and Rob Friedman, chief marketing man for Warner Bros. A half hour before the meeting, he stopped by the "Bonfire" set. De Palma glanced over and gave his agent a brief nod; Bauer settled into Fred Caruso's canvas chair, then glanced around looking for a familiar face while he spritzed breath freshener into his mouth. He made a point of visiting De Palma on every set. The agent and his wife had even traveled to Thailand when De Palma was making "Casualties of War" — though they cut their trip short and left after five days. While he waited for De Palma he reminisced about that trip with Monica Goldstein, who had walked over to pay her regards when she spotted him. "We had to get out of there. It was 120 degrees outside," he told Goldstein, who had been in Thailand during the entire shoot. "Awful!"

Marty Bauer's two prize possessions were Brian De Palma and Sunny Blossom, his thoroughbred gelding sprinter. One of Sunny Blossom's trophies sat on a coffee table in Bauer's office, but it was De Palma's name that assured his agent good tables in restaurants.

Like so many of the New York Jews who moved to Hollywood,

Bauer never seemed quite comfortable with his life there, with the endlessly glorious weather that seemed the perfect metaphor for the deception that was at the heart of his livelihood. Day after day he would drive his blue Mercedes to the office through the sunlit glare along the palm-lined streets of Beverly Hills. As he was driving, the radio would announce that the smog count was dangerously high. The sun and the trees and the blue sky inviting him to inhale deeply the poisonous air were like an alluring vixen, or a chocolate cake — sweet temptations lulling him into forgetting that Hollywood would inevitably ruin his health.

He complained about the business and philosophized about it. He liked to characterize agents as dealmakers and translators, the "bridge" between the artists they represented and the studio executives who put up the money. "They speak in Greek, the filmmakers speak in Italian, and I translate the conversations" was how he described his job, adding, "I'm talking metaphorically."

Bauer's loyalty to De Palma never wavered. To be sure, it was a loyalty cemented by the 10 percent the agent took out of De Palma's salary, but genuine affection and admiration went into the mix as well. Bauer was intelligent enough, and possessed of enough residual guilt, that he wanted to believe his life's work wouldn't merely add up to how many millions of dollars of schlock he could move around. He believed in De Palma as an artist; if he could get $3 million for his favorite client for his next picture, so much the better.

Without a producer to take the heat, Bauer had found himself more of a middleman on "Bonfire" than he'd wanted to be. "A great agent is a bridge builder," he would say. He meant the studio executives could vent their frustrations on him, and then he'd figure out some way to let De Palma know what they were angry about — all the while trying to encourage his favorite client to understand the studio's point of view.

Bauer knew De Palma's rational side *did* understand the studio's point of view. The director could articulate quite convincingly all the reasons he should follow the studio's wishes. Then, in the next breath, just as convincingly, he would denounce the studios as the Evil Empire. Bauer had to admit that he agreed with De Palma, *on some level*. On some level they were the Evil Empire. Their job was to turn out pap, to rein in the artistic independence of filmmakers. Their job was to try to turn everything into "Head of the Class" or "Mork and Mindy."

Bauer had convinced himself that De Palma, working with Cristofer, had changed an unacceptable script into a script he would hear himself describing as "brilliant." He didn't know whether or not he'd been caught up in the self-delusion that almost inevitably sets in, once a project — a *major* project — was in motion.

At that moment, Bauer was most worried about the negative vibrations he felt out of New York. He'd always expected trouble from the media back East, but not this early in the game. From the beginning he'd felt the critics were going to bury the movie. "The only way they wouldn't bury this movie would be if Brian made it true to the book and it grossed twenty dollars and twelve cents," Bauer would say. "You cannot make this movie with Brian De Palma's salary, and Tom Hanks's salary, and Bruce Willis's salary and be true to the book."

Already he'd felt the snobbery beaming across to the Coast. He'd put in a call to Tom Wolfe's agent, Lynn Nesbit, generally thought of as the diva of literary agents. He just wanted to let her know that De Palma wanted Tom Wolfe to *feel good* about the movie. "So if you want to get in touch, give me a call," he'd told her. Bauer was disturbed by her response. He interpreted her quick termination of the conversation as a brush-off, and bristled when he recalled her words: "I told Tom he just has to give up on it."

Irritating as they might be, Bauer wished his problems with "Bonfire" were limited to dealing with the aesthetic sensibilities of the Eastern establishment. He knew he was sensitive to the opinions of people like Nesbit. Bauer had grown up in the Bronx, taking what he read in the *New York Times* as the word of God. He'd spent the formative years of his adult life trying to become part of the Eastern establishment himself, when he worked out of the New York office of the William Morris Agency.

Right now, however, he had a practical problem to contend with. According to the rumor that had become Hollywood wisdom by the beginning of June, "Bonfire" was out of control. Hollywood worked very much like the New York Stock Exchange: rumors and perception were as important as reality. Just as a negative rumor could send a company's stock into the tank, so could bad vibes about a project lower the value of everyone associated with it. Rumors became their own reality.

Bauer found "Bonfire"'s production problems plaguing his negotiations for De Palma's next project. He'd been talking to Paramount Pictures for more than a month to sign De Palma for "Ghost in the Darkness," an African adventure story De Palma nicknamed "Jaws in the Veldt." Kevin Costner, who had become a star in "The Untouchables," had indicated he was eager to make the picture with De Palma.

Paramount's initial enthusiasm had been damaged by the publicity out of New York. The studio was already contending with several big budget pictures that seemed unlikely to recoup their costs: "Days of Thunder," the Tom Cruise picture about a race car driver; "Another 48 Hours," the sequel to the Nick Nolte–Eddie Murphy buddy picture; "The Godfather, Part III," which was plagued with its own production problems. The last thing the Paramount executives wanted to commit themselves to now was sending Brian De Palma — a director with big budget problems — to a remote continent with Kevin Costner to make a brutally difficult film.

As if all that weren't enough, Bauer had to contend with Fred Caruso. He'd signed Caruso on as a client that spring and was constantly having to field the studio's questions about the co-producer. Fisher had been infuriated by Caruso's unswerving loyalty to De Palma. Every time she thought about *that courtroom* she got mad all over again, and she wasn't shy about letting Bauer know how she felt.

Fisher would go at it over and over again: When Caruso said, "Yeah yeah yeah, we have a courtroom," she never knew whether it was 99 percent done or 80 percent done. All she knew was that in the end they shot at night, it was expensive and unwieldy, and she felt she never got a straight answer.

Fisher's complaints complicated Bauer's relationship with Caruso, who wasn't his favorite or most important client. Bauer was less than thrilled to get a call from Caruso, shortly before he arrived in Los Angeles, saying that, after all the tension and last-minute maneuvering he'd had to deal with back in New York, he'd decided to ask De Palma for more recognition. In addition to his "co-producer" credit Caruso wanted to share top producer billing, to see his name on the screen on the same line as De Palma's.

It wasn't the kind of thing Caruso felt comfortable asking De Palma directly. Would Bauer mind relaying the message?

Rob Friedman, Warner's chief marketing man, loved to postulate theories about why filmmakers needed him. "Filmmakers don't necessarily think with their marketing hats on," he liked to say. "They're thinking with their egos. We think with our marketing hats all the time."

De Palma thought Friedman was condescending and unresponsive. Earlier that spring, De Palma had repeatedly asked Friedman to put out a survey asking potential moviegoers what the name *Bonfire of the Vanities* meant to them. For weeks Friedman had stalled. Now it was June, only six months from release, and De Palma still hadn't heard a single idea from Friedman about the ad campaign or about a teaser trailer — a brief spot that would run in movie theaters during the summer simply to herald a major event "Coming this Christmas."

Friedman's agenda was simple. He had two pieces of news for the filmmaker at the meeting with De Palma and Bauer: "Bonfire" wouldn't have a teaser trailer or a New York benefit première, even though studios often tied a major film's opening to a charity function. Friedman assured De Palma that the studio planned to celebrate his picture with gala openings in both New York and Los Angeles. But the studio executives had agreed that a benefit could be problematic with a movie as potentially controversial as this one, the marketing man explained. "Most people who can afford five-hundred-dollar-a-plate or thousand-dollar benefits are over fifty and don't go to movies anyway. And the minute the wife hears 'Fuck you' or something else they go, *Ahhhhhhhh,* and sit on their hands."

Neither Bauer nor De Palma raised any objections, so Friedman moved on to his next subject: why he didn't think a teaser trailer would work for "Bonfire." This was a tricky subject because, he'd found, many filmmakers believed that the absence of a teaser trailer indicated the studio didn't think much of their film.

That wasn't the case at all, said Friedman, as he launched into a detailed explanation of why he didn't want to run a teaser trailer. "*Bonfire of the Vanities* means something to few people in America. Specifically those people who read it, which is not a vast percentage, and then those who haven't read it but who have heard of it, which is a bigger percentage but still not a vast percentage. And the minute you say something in a nonspecific informational fashion using the cast that we have it might communicate something the movie is not," said the marketing man. "And you don't want to work backward. You always want to move forward."

Friedman left the meeting feeling that he had gotten his point across as lucidly as possible. De Palma's impression of the meeting was that the man at Warner Bros. in charge of publicity and advertising didn't like him very much.

Not everyone working on "Bonfire" had made the move to Los Angeles. On June 12 Schwab was still in New York, finishing up the second unit. He had a lot to do, much of it filming the scenery various characters would see from the inside of moving vehicles. He directed shots of the greenery along the Connecticut Turnpike; of cars moving over the Triborough Bridge; of the interiors and exteriors of subways and subway stations.

A few days earlier he'd taken a crew of twenty and directed a scene in which fifty limousines drive through a cemetery. This would be the lead-in to the funeral of Maria's husband, the rich entrepreneur Arthur Ruskin. The shot had to be composed without the New York skyline so the angles of different takes could be matched; Sylbert would fill in a fake skyline on a matte painting back in Los Angeles.

Schwab was using the operator who had been on standby for Zsigmond when the first unit was in town. The next day, when Schwab looked over the footage, he was furious at what he saw. His carefully plotted shot had been ruined. The operator had allowed the frame to drift above the skyline.

In his entire career, Schwab had never been in the position of having to deal with an employee who wasn't doing a good job. He'd only had responsibility for the second unit on a couple of films and had been lucky enough to be satisfied with the people working for him. Yet he agreed with De Palma that it was more important to have the job done right than to have people like you. He remembered how cold and detached De Palma had been when he'd fired their camera operator in Thailand. He'd told Schwab he couldn't worry about whether he was thought of as a nice guy.

When Schwab saw how bad the footage from the cemetery was — by his standards — he didn't hesitate. He called Caruso and asked him to get him a new operator. He was surprised at his own ability to have a man fired without remorse, without much emotion at all, one way or the other. He couldn't afford any mistakes on the Concorde shot — the shot De Palma had bet him a hundred dollars couldn't possibly be good enough to include in his movie.

So on June 12, as the first unit had settled into its Los Angeles routine, Schwab would find out whether his long calculations for the Concorde shot were going to work or not. Now that the opening had been changed, this picture of the New York City skyline would be his only chance to create the vision of the urban "jewel box."

All through the spring, Schwab had dragged his location scout, Bruce Frye, to Kennedy Airport every couple of weeks to find the right spot to set up the cameras to film the plane landing. Frye had never worked so hard on a movie, though he'd been dubious when Schwab kept insisting "Bonfire" was going to be even better than "The Untouchables." Except for "The Untouchables" and "Blow Out," Frye didn't really like De Palma's movies. He and the other location scouts had actively disliked Schwab when he first arrived in New York and belittled everything they showed him. They mocked his Prussian perfectionism and started to call him Eric von Schwabheim.

But soon they saw that Schwab was hardest on himself. Frye became caught up in Schwab's excitement and convinced himself that Schwab's obsessive seeking of perfection would be worth it. The location scout soon believed it himself: they were part of a great enterprise.

So when he and Schwab weren't climbing to the tops of buildings for the opening shot, which had been canceled, they were standing on different runways out at JFK. Frye would get the clearances from the airport and then watch Schwab stare at the sky for hours, as he tried to conceptualize a way to make "planes taking off and landing" seem interesting.

Schwab needed Frye's enthusiasm to keep himself pumped up. Anything less than monumental for this shot would be dreadful, a nice commercial for Air France and nothing more. Working on his special calculator, Schwab figured the sun would be exactly where he wanted it to be about two minutes before sunset on June 12. He would have thirty seconds from the time the sun appeared in the camera frame until it dropped below the city skyline. As Schwab masterminded this shot — a shot that verged on the impossible — Frye had to convince the Port Authority, the Federal Aviation Administration, and Air France to do their part.

Schwab would need a plane manned by pilots who not only could guide their plane onto the runway with split-second timing, but could also adjust their longitude and latitude to fit the frame of his cameras. He needed the cooperation of the control tower, which would have to clear the plane for landing at exactly the right moment. On April 30, the Port Authority, which operates the airport, gave the go-ahead, providing Warner Bros. arranged for insurance liability for not less than $2 million. But the airport authorities were dubious. They told the Warner Bros. people the chances of the plane's appearing in the sky at such a precise angle at such an exact time were maybe a thousand, maybe a million to one.

Schwab, Frye, and the second unit director of photography, Andrew Laszlo, spent the day before the shot was scheduled at the airport watching the regularly scheduled landings of Concordes through a variety of lenses. Schwab realized the plane looked smaller than he'd anticipated. He asked Caruso to have longer lenses shipped in from Los Angeles overnight. This last-minute discovery put Schwab on edge. What else had he overlooked? He was especially nervous about timing the dropping of the sun; clouds had obscured the horizon that evening. He and Frye also met with officials from Air France. The airline was so excited about this promotional shot it was flying in a brand-new plane from Paris, staffed by an ace crew. At the end of the meeting one of the Air France officials gave Schwab a tiny model Concorde.

That night Schwab couldn't sleep. He had discussed the shot with Zsigmond only once since the cameraman had told him about the special calculator back in February. Zsigmond disagreed with Schwab's decision to photograph the Concorde from the front as it landed. The cameraman thought it would look better shot from behind.

Schwab was worried about going against the advice of the celebrated Zsigmond. He kept reviewing every possible angle but couldn't quite re-create the look of the plane in his mind. At 2:00 A.M. he remembered the model Concorde that he'd stuck in his jacket pocket that afternoon. He propped the little plane on the dresser in his hotel room and placed a small weight on its tail to make it tilt the way the Concorde would as it descended. For the next hour he peered at the miniature Concorde through a variety of lenses, front and back, trying to imagine it against an orange sky. He decided to stick with his original plan. At 3:00 A.M. he finally went to sleep. As he dozed off one final worry crossed his mind: What if it rained?

The morning wake-up call at the Regency always included a weather report. Schwab woke up to good news: clear skies were forecast. He and Frye met the camera crew out at the airport. At the last moment, Frye had convinced airport officials to let them film at a different spot on runway 13L, closer to where the plane would be landing.

They would be using five cameras that day. Much of the morning and afternoon passed in a search for the best place to aim for the magic spot in the sky. Schwab wanted the extra cameras for insurance: they were using such powerful lenses that they risked producing the image of bright light and nothing else if the sun fell directly in line with a camera's eye. One camera shot in Vistavision; if the timing proved to be off, matte artists could paint in the sun or the plane or both. The cameras contained only one load of film. If they missed the shot, there was no going back.

That afternoon the special plane and crew arrived from Paris. The pilots were cocky, eager for the chance to prove that they could do the impossible. Schwab, Frye, and Laszlo met with the pilots and the Air France officials to coordinate everything: which direction to make the approach; where to start turning; at what spot on the runway to land. The FAA had agreed to give the plane clearance approximately ten minutes before sunset, weather permitting. Once the Air France people on the ground got the word, they'd tell the movie crew to prepare to film.

The Concorde took off about twenty minutes before the shot was scheduled and rapidly disappeared from view. Schwab scanned the sky intently through a pair of binoculars. He couldn't see a thing. Ten minutes before the designated landing time the Air France people hadn't heard from the control tower. The sun was dropping, and there was no plane in sight.

As the minutes went by, Schwab had the feeling his $80,000 shot wasn't going to happen. Then someone from Air France started screaming, "It's coming! It's coming!"

Five cameras pointed at the sky, and five cameras started to film. The sky glowed orange. Schwab peered through the binoculars so intently it seemed a blink would cause him to explode. The plane was coming closer, the sun was sinking fast. Suddenly Schwab realized the Concorde was too fat! The sleek plane should look pencil-thin, and this plane was noticeably bulbous. This plane was not the Concorde. It was a 747.

"Cut!" he yelled. "Cut."

He was starting to feel panicky. Sunset actually seemed to be accelerating.

Then, there it was. The plane popped up on the horizon, just a few degrees away from the Empire State Building. Once again the cameras started to roll.

And once again they stopped. Three times the dot in the distance revealed itself to be a 747 as its outline became discernible. Three times the cameras were turned on and turned off.

It was all happening so fast there wasn't time to feel discouraged. Yet the warm late spring evening seemed to have become uncomfortably hot. Schwab kept staring through the binoculars, willing the Concorde to appear. He was beginning to think it was too late. It was possible that if the plane showed up now, the sun would already have plummeted out of the frame, into the skyline. Why was it falling so fast?

Then the Concorde materialized in the late evening sky. The strange-looking plane, floating like a mythical creature, seemed to drift down to earth. In fact, it seemed to be descending at such a leisurely pace Schwab now felt certain the sun was going to disappear before the plane could land.

"C'mon plane, c'mon plane, c'mon plane," he muttered, over and over again, clutching his binoculars. For three minutes he willed the plane to beat the sun, and they were the slowest three minutes he'd ever endured. The plane seemed stuck, as though gravity had been suspended, leaving the Concorde to hang in the air forever — while the sun disappeared entirely.

Then Schwab realized the plane had made its turn and was landing. Its wheels were hitting the runway exactly at the second they were supposed to. No one screamed hallelujah or said anything at all. The cameras kept rolling as the wind and noise died down and the plane taxied to a stop.

For several moments, the Air France officials and the camera crew continued to watch silently, like a sophisticated audience at the symphony who knew better than to ruin the finale by clapping before the final note ebbed into silence. When the Concorde had come to a complete stop, the camera operators started talking to each other and to Schwab. They'd never seen anything like this before in their working lives. Through the long lenses of their cameras they'd witnessed something that, at that moment in June, seemed nothing less than miraculous. It had been eerily beautiful; this shimmering image had transcended the cliché of its separate parts: a plane, a Hallmark card sky, the New York City skyline.

In a daze, Schwab took in the congratulations of the Air France officials and his crew. Then, when he was able to think, he called Caruso from the runway to tell him they'd completed the shot, that the line producer's faith had been rewarded. The money had been well spent.

Only then did Schwab realize how exhilarated he felt. After all the disappointments of the spring, he had accomplished something memorable. He wasn't deluded. He knew that this was, in the end, just a second unit shot of an airplane landing. But he also knew what it had taken to get it. His elation surged again the next day when he stopped by Technicolor to look at the footage.

All alone in the screening room he watched the Concorde floating through the smoky orange sky like some giant Aztec bird. It seemed to pause over the Empire State Building, hovering as though trying to decide where to go next. The plane actually looked alive. The city appeared the way it had always looked in Schwab's imagination: like a jewel.

The thought crossed his mind that De Palma had lost his bet and would be happy to lose it. Schwab hadn't spent seven years working for the man without being able to predict what his reaction would be to this technical achievement. Unless he didn't know anything about anything, Schwab felt certain there would be a plane landing in "The Bonfire of the Vanities."

When De Palma watched the Concorde shot during dailies in the screening room on the Burbank lot, he'd started to howl. Nothing registered his approval more unerringly than that cackle. "Vilmos," he called down to Zsigmond, "we can retire now. This is a young man's game. Look at *that*!" And he started to howl all over again. Maybe his boy Schwab would make it after all.

In all the years Schwab had worked for De Palma, the highest praise he'd gotten was "That's fine, Eric" or "Good, Eric." So he was shocked to find a message waiting for him at his hotel room in New York shortly before he returned to Los Angeles: "You're doing a great job. Brian."

Schwab was still glowing as he returned a call from Goldstein. When he got her on the line, he made her repeat what she'd said to be sure he'd heard her correctly: Lucy Fisher's office had called. *Lucy Fisher* had seen the Concorde shot and wanted to set up a meeting with Schwab as soon as he got back to California.

Fisher had started to appreciate Schwab back in May when she'd flown in to settle the courtroom problem. De Palma had always been generous toward his second unit director and told Fisher that Schwab could explain the problems they were having with locations. She felt as though she could talk to Schwab; he seemed so straightforward and uncomplicated. This came as a relief after dealing with the erratic De Palma and an ameliorator like Caruso.

She and the other executives were dazzled by the Concorde shot. It was spectacular, yet it wasn't jarring or outrageous, like so many of the movie's other spectacular shots. The Concorde shot was soothing; this pretty vision of New York struck a sentimental chord in the executives, who retained romanticized associations with the city from their youth. Fisher called Marty Bauer and told him he should sign Schwab on as a client. She didn't know if the young man could direct, but he certainly knew how to shoot. It was unusual to see second unit footage that was as good as the first unit footage, especially when the first unit director was Brian De Palma. It would be worth finding out if Schwab could go to the next level.

On June 21, the forty-ninth day of production, the crew gathered for the second day of shooting in the French restaurant that had been built on Stage 25. In this scene the reporter Fallow meets with Arthur Ruskin, Maria's elderly husband, on the pretext of doing a story about business entrepreneurs.

As the shot was being set up, Bruce Willis remained aloof from the crew, as usual. He had mastered the straight-ahead stare that eliminated most people from his sight line. He concentrated on *not* thinking about whether people were watching him, though of course it was impossible not to think about it. He would talk about wanting to be thought of as an ordinary person, though the only way he could accomplish this was through extraordinary action: by secluding himself in his trailer, by flying in private jets, and by shielding himself with bodyguards.

He was defensive about his celebrity. "I want to be able to scratch my ass in public. If people want to make a career out of writing that down — 'Bruce Willis scratched his ass' — who's the asshole?" As he'd become more and more famous, he'd become more and more antagonistic toward the press — perhaps because he seemed to monitor his success by the medium he claimed to loathe. "It's a fact," he would say. "You know there was a study done a couple of years ago that if you put my picture on the cover of a magazine it would sell more magazines than if you put somebody else's picture on it."

Yet he worried about the quality of his celebrity, and recognized that he was most famous among readers of the supermarket tabloids. "I've become a commercial for the *National Enquirer* or the Daily Cocksucker or whatever these things are," he said. "If you put my picture on top of some lurid story, people will put their money down to read that story. If some advertising company tries to use my face to sell a product, I can sue them. I can take them to court and I'll win because they are using my services without compensating me. These bullshit newspaper guys decide my life is news, and there are no laws to stop them."

When "Moonlighting" made him a phenomenon just five years earlier, he'd thrown some wild parties and more than a few punches — including a couple at some policemen. He didn't handle his liquor very well. The tabloids did love him; he'd become a regular feature in the *Star* and the *National Enquirer*. His celebrity was magnified with the success of "Die Hard"; the police detective he played in that supersonic action picture differed only slightly from his TV persona. In just five years he had become more famous and far richer than he ever could have imagined.

Willis knew exactly how valuable he was and how much he was being paid, but he wanted more. He wanted respectability. He said that was why he hired a bodyguard: to protect himself from unruly fans and to protect his fans from him. Without that human barrier, when some guy yelled an insult, Willis couldn't overcome his natural inclination to pop the assaulter. Now that he'd become important — and had done some jail time for his fits of temper — he couldn't afford that kind of direct contact with his public.

He wanted "Bonfire" to anoint him with respectability, to show the world that he was an actor of serious intent — that he could play an antihero like Peter Fallow. But by now it had become clear to everyone that whatever Willis's intentions, he was trapped by the limitations of his range. He simply couldn't turn off that insinuating smirk. Much of the rewriting of the script over the past several weeks had been done to accommodate Willis, to make Fallow conform to what the star projected. More and more, their dissipated parasitic journalist was resembling a self-effacing tough guy with a troubled conscience.

Under the lights set up all over the French restaurant set, it was hot and the air smelled of salmon that had been lingering on platters too long. Every little detail had been attended to: the elaborate floral arrangements, the supercilious waiters dressed in short tuxedo jackets, the fussy chandeliers. Even the food — the salmon with asparagus and rice, and the pasta primavera with shrimp — was genuine. Only the luscious fruit tarts were plastic because the crew and extras had kept poking their fingers into the real desserts.

For this scene, Willis and Alan King, the comedian playing Arthur Ruskin, were seated in that most awkwardly intimate of luncheon positions, side by side on a banquette. Ruskin starts gulping Courvoisier and proceeds to tell Fallow a long-winded story about his new venture: flying Arabs to Mecca. Ruskin wheezes and drinks his way through the tale of primitive people and modern technology; suddenly he is overtaken by a coughing spasm, and his head slams down on his plate. Fellow diners notice and make a commotion; the maitre d' walks over and looks annoyed. He motions for two waiters, who yank the table out. Ruskin slides down. One Good Samaritan comes over to give the Heimlich maneuver, but he drops the dying man when the maitre d' hints at possible liability. Fallow catches him, and, as he holds the dead man in his lap, the maitre d' brings the check. He informs the reporter that the restaurant doesn't accept credit cards.

Alan King delivered Ruskin's monologue with raspy gusto, take after take after take. As he took a gulp of his drink, the camera drew closer on a dolly track. The scene required split-second timing; King's delivery had to be synchronized with the camera movement. Then, after he collapsed, the waiters had to swoop in and swoop out at a staccato pace. Willis had nothing to do but to sit at the banquette and appear attentive yet bored. The pace had to be perfect. The scene had to capture the absurdity of the situation without lingering on it. King's speech was tricky: it could seem hilarious or it could seem like an unnecessary digression.

De Palma sat unobtrusively at a banquette a few feet away from the actors while King delivered the monologue. Every time the actor completed Ruskin's tale of the Arabs who thought it was usual procedure to land a plane by crashing into the desert, De Palma burst out laughing. After twenty-seven takes, the director felt he had captured the essence of the comedian's schtick. He was delighted with what King was doing with that monologue. But he could see that after the speech concluded, there were too many other things going on in this scene; too many people had lines to speak that were slowing down the action. During rehearsal and during the first few takes he wanted to run through the scene as it was written and try to figure out where the jarring notes were.

When a scene depended so much on timing, the way this one did, you could almost hear the rhythm. He could figure out what was throwing things off balance only by seeing the whole thing through.

As the crew rearranged the lights and cameras for the next part of the scene — the waiters rushing in and the Heimlich maneuver — Chris Soldo gave directions to the extras: "The table has been quite loud, quite obnoxious. Look over at this man keeling over like you're annoyed at this disturbance and want the little people to take care of it."

One of the actors playing a waiter came up to De Palma, who was sitting at a banquette, and suggested adding a line.

"May I say, '*Il est mort. C'est vrai. Mais quelle audace!*' " The "waiter" looked at the director expectantly.

De Palma stared without comprehension at this man speaking French. He shook his head, as though waking from sleep. "We'll see," he said. He handed Aimee Morris his cigarette, and she snuffed it out.

They rehearsed Alan King falling into Bruce Willis's lap and the waiters rushing over to pull the table away. An actor popped up from the next table, yanked King up by his underarms, and started squeezing his chest to affect the Heimlich maneuver. Willis sat and watched.

The whole thing was repeated again, this time on camera. After the first take of the Heimlich maneuver scene, King asked the British actor playing the Good Samaritan not to squeeze so hard. "I almost lost a nipple," he coughed.

As the camera was moved back into place, Willis suddenly spoke: "I think it should go twice as fast." Though he spoke softly, many crew members standing nearby glanced surreptitiously over at De Palma.

"We're dyin' here," said the actor.

No one said anything, but that simple stage direction injected a queasy feeling in the air. The ruling order had been unbalanced. Actors were free to express their opinions to directors. This, however, was something else. Willis had circumvented the director's authority altogether. He was speaking directly to his fellow actors, telling them how to play the scene and doing it with the most casual assumption of power.

Willis knew he was breaking a code, but if he felt confident about anything, he felt confident about his own comic timing. All he'd done in "Moonlighting" for four years was deliver fast, funny patter. He knew that his job was to service De Palma's vision of the film. He also knew what his position in show business was at that moment in time, and that he was valued at $5 million and De Palma wasn't. Five years ago he wouldn't have dared to open his mouth like this, even if he had been every bit as certain he was right as he was now.

De Palma decided to ignore the incident. Then, after the next take, Willis piped up again. "First half of that take was really good," he said to the waiters. "The second half was a little slow." He turned to the maitre d'. "I think you should move faster."

The actor turned to the camera, which was being reloaded. "Will you see that?" he asked Doug Ryan, the operator. "The wet spot at the far corner of the table?"

Ryan assured him the spot wasn't showing up in the frame, and the maitre d' began to rehearse yanking the table out. Willis watched him, pursed his lips, and said brusquely, "Can I show you one time?"

He stood up and yanked the table out fast.

De Palma took all this in with a mild sense of shock. Unlike Tom Hanks or F. Murray Abraham or Morgan Freeman, who approached their work with calm intellect, Willis operated on instinct. In that sense, thought De Palma, Willis was like Griffith, like the little girl playing the daughter, like the dog. They could do what they did very well, but you had to hang in there waiting for them to do it. Occasionally they could be brilliant; you just had to wait and see where their instincts guided them.

Once De Palma had gauged the boundaries of Willis's skills and limited his own expectations, he had no quarrel with the actor's instincts and had been happy to listen to his suggestions — in private. This was completely unexpected — to find himself short-circuited before he could work out the problems with the scene. As director, he was accustomed to being treated as king of his little dominion. When he put out his hand someone automatically put a cup of cappuccino in it. But Willis was reminding him in a very vivid way of just how ephemeral his power was.

He had to make a fast calculation. It was important to establish the fact that he, not Willis, was in charge. He also knew that his was a borrowed authority. Once a major star started throwing his weight around he couldn't be stopped. The financial structure determined the real chain of command. Every time it came down to a struggle between a director and a star, it was the director who would be replaced. His only intrinsic power came from the actors' belief that he could make them look good. Once he lost that, he was finished.

De Palma decided to make a symbolic statement. He hoisted himself out of his banquette and walked over to the table where Willis and King were sitting. He sat next to Willis and looked at the waiters standing by for instructions.

"Come in quick," De Palma said.

"Yeah, fast," said Willis.

De Palma sat next to the actor while the waiters rehearsed the scene, then returned to his banquette behind the camera. After the take, he and Willis watched the scene on the video playback, and De Palma asked Willis to step off the set with him for a few minutes. They took a little walk around the sound stage, and the director told the actor how much he appreciated his ideas. However, he said, he needed time to evaluate the entire scene before he started making adjustments. Willis shrugged his shoulders and said, "It's your picture. I'll do whatever you want."

De Palma didn't want resignation either. He needed the actor's good will and cooperation. They talked for a few minutes about the dynamics of the scene, and what was bothering Willis. The actor explained that he felt ridiculous just sitting there with King lying in his lap for what seemed like forever waiting for the waiters to come, waiting for the Heimlich maneuver. He just wanted the action to move along faster. De Palma assured him his ideas were being taken into consideration.

Willis returned to his banquette on the set. King was complaining about being squeezed by the Heimlich maneuver over and over. Willis indicated that he was in good spirits by making a little joke. De Palma proved that he had indeed taken Willis's suggestion into consideration by shooting the next take with fewer lines.

*   *   *

One half hour before the afternoon lunch break, during a pause to reload the camera, a shaggy little man with a beard and dark sunglasses walked onto the set, glanced around, and walked over to Zsigmond. The two men hugged. A space automatically opened between them and the extras and crew members milling around during the break. Many people kept glancing at the visitor, trying to pretend they weren't staring.

Steven Spielberg was there to have lunch with Brian De Palma. Dropping by the set of friends, colleagues, and clients was a moviemaking ritual. In New York, Michael J. Fox had shown up one evening to hug De Palma and chat for a few minutes. Jeffrey Katzenberg, chairman of Walt Disney studios, had paid a visit to see Tom Hanks, who was under contract with Disney and allowed to make "Bonfire" only at Katzenberg's discretion. The agents of almost all the principal players would make an obligatory visit sometime during the shoot.

Spielberg slid into a chair at one of the tables and greeted everyone who came up to him in a friendly way. He chatted with one of the actors, whose child attended the same preschool as Spielberg's son Max. Spielberg told the actor Max was taking swimming lessons and loved the water but refused to take off his water wings.

At 2:30 lunch break was called, and De Palma and Spielberg walked through the sound stages to the commissary. "This is a nice lot," said Spielberg, who had the look of an impish boy even though there were streaks of gray in his beard.

"Oh, yeah," said De Palma with a snort. "This is where I shot 'Get to Know Your Rabbit.' The last time I was in this commissary I think I saw John Wayne there."

"John Wayne?" Spielberg looked at De Palma to see if he was teasing. "John Wayne is dead."

"Yeah," laughed De Palma. "The last time I was in this commissary was in 1970."

Spielberg found this impossible to believe. "You mean you don't eat lunch in the commissary."

De Palma said, "I go to my trailer and sleep."

"I don't take a trailer, and I don't use it if I'm given one," said Spielberg. "I like to hang out with the actors on the way back to the set."

De Palma rolled his eyes.

Spielberg laughed. "I enjoy this process more than you do."

The friendship between Spielberg and De Palma mystified a great many people in Hollywood. Spielberg was Mr. Industry; he didn't shy away from the black-tie circuit and enjoyed the company of studio executives. His other close friends were Sid Sheinberg, the MCA president who discovered him; Steve Ross, Time-Warner chairman; Terry Semel, Warner Bros. president; and George Lucas, a fellow filmmaking entrepreneur. De Palma, on the other hand, was still regarded as the interloper from the East. He was a provocateur, and he wasn't sociable. Aside from Spielberg, none of his closest friends was a major player in the business.

Spielberg had become identified as the contemporary Walt Disney ever since his "E.T.: The Extraterrestrial" became the most popular movie of all time. "E.T." had been one of those pictures that transcended the usual boundaries. Nearly everyone loved "E.T." — children, adults, intellectuals, and innocents. Spielberg's production company, Amblin Entertainment, specialized in fantasy and adventure films. Spielberg was Disney with techie razzmatazz. Of course, everyone in the business was aware of the hard side. The public might think of him as Peter Pan, but anyone who had ever negotiated with him knew Peter Pan dictated a mean deal memo. He was said to believe in the 99–1 split: he took 99 percent and his partners took 1. It was known that Spielberg could guarantee that a picture would get made, and in return he wanted things done on his own terms, and they were always favorable to him.

He and De Palma needed each other for a variety of reasons. At the top of the list was the fact that very few people understood exactly what they did. Smart people could critique them, and help them, but only a small cadre of filmmakers worked at such a rarefied level of visual skill. Other directors might make movies that were more dramatically cohesive, or intellectually challenging, but few directors could think of more interesting ways to use a camera to tell a story than these two men could.

Spielberg valued De Palma's opinion because it was guaranteed to be critical, and few dared to criticize Spielberg anymore. He was a little intimidated too by the older man's Eastern intellectualism.

De Palma read all the time; he enjoyed browsing in bookstores as much as in computer stores — and he loved computer stores. Spielberg freely admitted he didn't read books.

De Palma respected Spielberg's judgment almost as much as he appreciated his loyalty. Spielberg was intimidating as well. De Palma had been raised to respect men of stature, and in the world he operated in, no one carried more weight than his friend. There would always be a slight awkwardness about their respective places in the industry; they had learned to accommodate themselves to that fact of life over the years.

There was one other key to their friendship's endurance: they didn't do business together. On the few occasions they tried, the deals fell through. So they had that rare thing in Hollywood, a personal relationship that really was personal.

When they reached the commissary De Palma rushed ahead. The place was almost empty. A waitress greeted him and said she was sorry, they were closed. De Palma looked at her blankly. Another woman, the manager, walked toward them and started to repeat, "We're closed."

Just then Spielberg caught up to De Palma. The manager took one look at the new arrival, and without taking her eyes off him she said to the waitress, "We're open."

De Palma had a salad and a glass of his diet drink, and Spielberg had a bowl of matzoh ball soup. He tasted De Palma's drink and said he'd recently lost fifteen pounds himself. Spielberg told De Palma about the various projects he was working on, and De Palma told Spielberg what had happened with Willis in the French restaurant scene. They discussed the delicacy of handling actors with few words and many sighs and much raising of eyebrows.

On the way back to the set Spielberg nodded at the handsome gray and black trailer parked outside the sound stage.

"Nice camper," he said. "Yours?"

De Palma laughed. "No," he said. "Bruce's."

In many ways their relationship hadn't changed since they met in 1971, when they were both novice filmmakers. Spielberg was visiting New York and was introduced to De Palma by a mutual friend, who brought him to the hotel where Spielberg was staying. Spielberg remembered his first impression: he answered the knock on his hotel room door, and before he could say hello a large man brushed right past him and walked into the room and checked out the furniture. Spielberg felt as if his surroundings were being inspected. Nothing had changed; even now, when De Palma drove to Spielberg's estate out in the Pacific Palisades, David Selznick's old home, he'd barely greet his host before heading directly for the huge home's coziest room — the one with the giant television and electronic equipment. He'd sink into a comfortable chair and stay there for hours.

De Palma moved back to California in the mid-1970s, before either he or Spielberg made a breakthrough film. The two filmmakers would double-date and generally found they had more in common with each other than with their female companions. Their dates weren't always amused to find their evenings recorded on videotape; De Palma used to carry his camera with him all the time.

They loved their gadgets. Through one of the executives at Universal Pictures, where Spielberg was a rising star, Spielberg was given one of the first mobile telephones in town. One evening he and De Palma parked in the driveway of a young woman's house and called her to ask if she'd like to get a friend and go out with them. They thought it was just hilarious to see the shock on her face when they rang her doorbell seven seconds later.

The two men made the movies that catapulted them out of obscurity within a year of one another. In 1975 "Jaws" would set Spielberg on a road toward fame and commercial success unparalleled in Hollywood history. A year later "Carrie" made the filmmaking establishment acknowledge that De Palma couldn't be dismissed as an avant-garde weirdo. The film, a horror movie, attracted too much critical attention and box office return. But De Palma couldn't resist following his own muse, no matter how offbeat and offensive it might be, and that voice repeatedly removed him from the industry's embrace.

For years Spielberg had watched his friend battle his demons. He liked De Palma's quirky sensibilities but kept hoping he would move into the mainstream. Spielberg found it so comfortable there. He was delighted with "The Untouchables," De Palma's most conventional film. Spielberg argued that there was nothing safe about "The Untouchables," that De Palma had managed to insert his personality into the material. Audiences could accept the outrageousness because it came in a recognizable package.

As "Bonfire" progressed, he became uneasy watching the tense maneuverings between De Palma and Warner Bros. He knew De Palma still smarted from "Get to Know Your Rabbit" and that the experience had been so horrible it almost kept him from returning to Los Angeles. De Palma didn't seem to differentiate between those executives who had left Warner Bros. years ago and the current regime.

Spielberg understood the executives' attitude toward De Palma. "He's got twenty, twenty-five years of independent filmmaker habit to assimilate or set aside or what have you," Spielberg would say. "Brian, from the executive standpoint, has the scent of *film noir,* maverick, auteur, upstart European — even though he's from Philadelphia. He's extremely New York, extremely single-minded, and a lot of these executives remember how Brian got his start, making Brian De Palma movies. Now suddenly Brian is making a Warner Bros. picture directed by Brian De Palma.

"That's different from a film that Brian writes, produces, and directs, that comes from his soul, that comes from who he is. Brian now has to take who he is and superimpose it on a movie that could have been made by Sidney Pollack, or Robert Benton, or Roman Polanski, John Schlesinger. It could have been made by Sidney Lumet. And each of these people would have made it different, but they all could have made 'Bonfire of the Vanities.' None of those people could have made 'Obsession.' None of those people could have made 'Dressed to Kill' or 'Blow Out' or 'Sisters.' None of them."

Spielberg knew that conflict between the studios and De Palma would be inevitable. De Palma wasn't afraid to shock them with camera angles nobody would dare to try. But he was playing in a different arena now from that of ten years before. He'd asked the studio to back him for a film that wasn't necessarily uniquely his. That changed the nature of the game entirely. "Brian is stepping into shoes that can be worn by other filmmakers. When he does that, he's caught up in the machinery of the studio system," Spielberg observed. "And he has to live with it. I live with it. We all do."

Chapter 12

LEADING LADIES

A crowd of torsos stood lined up in the corner of the wardrobe department at Warner Bros. These headless, limbless dress forms made from steel and cloth were suspended at different heights on metal stands to exactly replicate the heights of the actresses whose names they carried. Some of the forms were fifty years old; some were new. Right in front was the most petite of the torsos: that was Debbie Reynolds. Next to her was a larger form, marked Julie Ewing, and another simply designated as Dianne. At the end of the row was Demi Moore, the wife of Bruce Willis. Her form was shoved up against a torso marked Jean Simmons. On a still summer day, they seemed like ghostly witnesses to the dreams that had been manufactured in this place over the years.

There was a time when the wardrobe departments at the Hollywood studios were a mecca for dress designers and seamstresses from all over the world. Warner Bros. was no exception. In the final extravagant days of the big studio musicals, anything could be made there. The Jewish refugees out of Vienna were still working then, extraordinary seamstresses caught up in the romance and art of movie costuming. They approached their craft with a zest that bordered on insanity. If a designer needed a complex piece of lace, they'd make it. If white seed pearl sewn on the zodiac was the order, they'd make that too. This was the wardrobe department that created the exquisite gowns for "My Fair Lady" in 1964 and embroidered pumpkin seeds for "Camelot" in 1967.

Wardrobe, of course, was only part of this great machine, this massive cottage industry that required the specialized skills of vast numbers of people. When labor was cheap, the studios turned out illusion efficiently and profitably. Eventually, however, the business changed. The founding moguls died or sold out to conglomerates, and the workers organized into a powerful force. The studios could no longer afford to bankroll elaborate detail. "Camelot" and its embroidered pumpkin seeds capped Warner's decline in the sixties, foreshadowing the retrenchment of the seventies. After that, illusion was still very much at the heart of the movie business. But how it was created and by whom had changed; most of the costuming work, like everything else, was done by independent contractors.

The wardrobe department still existed in the summer of 1990, though it seemed more like a mausoleum than a vibrant workplace. Closets and cardboard boxes contained the remnants from hundreds of movies and television shows — everything from housedresses to Roman sandals. A handful of women from Poland and Armenia were on hand to do alterations for the four Warner productions then under way on the lot: "Trickhouse," "To My Daughter," "The Rookie," and "Bonfire." They operated out of a large room that seemed locked in time. The heavy irons and bulky sewing machines were solid relics of another era.

On June 21 Ann Roth met with a seamstress to discuss a problem with the black strapless evening dress designed in Paris for Kim Cattrall, the actress playing Judy McCoy. De Palma had asked her to drop fifteen pounds for the part, and she had complied. Now her dress was three-quarters of an inch too large across the bias and needed to be taken in. Roth told the seamstress that Cattrall was very slender now. The seamstress nodded and pulled over the Debbie Reynolds torso for the alteration.

Cattrall's evening gown was one of dozens Ann Roth and her crew were preparing for the Museum Ball, the society party Sherman and Judy attend the night before Sherman is to be arrested. Tom Wolfe had set the scene at a dinner party and used it to give readers a peek inside this exclusive, rarefied world. For Wolfe, the events at the party — Sherman finds himself at the same party with both his wife and his mistress and tries to tell his mistress what is happening to him — were less important than the setting and the clothes. From the vases to the silverware to the apricot soufflé, Wolfe laid out the requirements for such a gathering in delirious detail. He lavished an entire paragraph on the apricot soufflé alone.

Roth had been preparing for the party scene — which would be a huge ball in the movie — for months, starting back in the garment district atelier in New York where she and the dressmaker had dreamed up Melanie Griffith's golden gauze evening gown, the centerpiece for the scene. Now, with shooting only four days away, she and her crew had to outfit 275 guests.

None of the robust California extras she'd seen so far remotely matched Wolfe's description of the women in Sherman's social set. These actresses all had high, unnaturally round breasts; they had admirably toned biceps; and they had a great deal of bleached blonde hair and very leathery skin. Moreover, they weren't social X-rays. "You can see lamplight through their bones . . . while they're chattering about *interiors* and *landscape gardening*," wrote Wolfe. There weren't even any lemon tarts — "women in their twenties or early thirties . . . the second, third and fourth wives or live-in girlfriends of men over forty or fifty or sixty (or seventy), the sort of women men refer to, quite without thinking, as girls." Roth felt that the actresses she saw were pedestrian, businesslike yet unprofessional. They all seemed to know what movie grossed the most at the box office the previous week, but none of them had an inkling about what kind of shoes would match a certain dress. But Roth told herself she shouldn't expect more. No one at the studio, as far as she could tell, felt passion for anything — except the subject of how much things cost.

On June 21 Roth and her two assistants were outfitting the extras in two unfurnished apartments a few blocks south of the studio, one for the men, one for the women. Since Roth would allow only a few of them in at a time, the extras had to line up outside under the unclouded summer sky. The temperature had climbed into the high eighties, and there was no escape from the sun. By the time the extras walked in the front door, hot and perspiring, they were in no mood for Roth's acerbic assessment of their manners and their attire.

The living room contained three chairs, a full-length mirror, and three long racks of evening gowns. Piles of high-heeled pumps and bras obscured the pale blue wall-to-wall carpeting.

The eighty-first woman to walk in the door that day introduced herself as Patty. Patty was a short, solid woman with spiky brown hair and facial lines that indicated she wasn't an ingénue. She was wearing a Star of David as well as a cross around her neck. She explained that she worked as a movie extra to supplement her other work. At the moment she was also a waitress, a maid, and a nurse's aide.

Patty was staring at herself in the full-length mirror and tugging at the unyielding blue and black evening dress she'd been stuffed into. Roth, also regarding Patty's reflection, told Gary Jones, her associate, to open the bodice and loosen the back. Patty grumbled, "This makes me look fat."

"It'll look fine," said Roth dismissively. Then the costume designer tilted her head back and looked at Patty instead of at her image. "Actually, it'll look fine," she said in a comforting tone.

Patty was sent into the next room to change. She was replaced by a fleshy woman of indeterminate age who was wearing tight jeans and a T-shirt. Her skin was leathery, her hair a brittle blonde.

"Are you wearing underwear?" Roth asked.

The woman looked startled. "Yes," she said.

Roth had pulled a bright yellow evening dress over the woman's head and looked at her bustline sadly. Jones saw the look and asked the extra her bra size. The extra said she had a strapless bra in her bag and turned her back to Jones while she put it on. After she'd readjusted the dress with the new bra, she looked hopefully at Roth.

"This bra is useless," said Roth.

Roth pulled a sturdy strapless bra with an attached girdle out of the pile. As she adjusted the blonde's undergarment, Patty came back into the room to ask about jewelry.

"I want expensive, important jewelry," Roth said. "The kind of jewelry wealthy women collect to make part of their lives. Important sapphires. Important emeralds."

Patty looked dazed.

Roth patted her arm with one hand as she finished hooking the blonde extra's bra with the other and assured Patty that her jewelry would be fine. "It's the kind of jewelry none of us own," Roth said. "Just don't bring any flashy show-biz stuff."

One after another the women came into the room, casually pulling off their shirts. Gary Jones — the only man in the place — politely tried to avoid seeing them nude but frequently couldn't avert his eyes in time.

A great many of the extras weren't wearing underwear. Roth was more perturbed by the general absence of proper shoes. She simply couldn't see how experienced extras failed to understand that she couldn't evaluate how they looked in evening gowns when they were wearing sneakers or boots. Roth was always comparing California extras unfavorably with those in New York. In New York the extras tended to be members of the Screen Actors Guild, whereas in California most extras had no other theatrical aspirations. In other words, the extras in New York tended to bring shoes.

Finally she asked the three women who happened to be in the room at the time whether they made their living as extras.

"Yes," they all said, looking ready to talk further in their friendly California way.

"Then you must come prepared," Roth said in her most indignant schoolmarm voice. "With pantyhose. With shoes. You can't look like you've just come off the tennis court."

A narrow blonde woman with a hard face and thirteen years of experience as an extra looked particularly chagrined by Roth's comment. Her name was Georgina, and she had brought with her a raspberry pink dress she'd bought at a thrift shop for ninety-five cents.

"I ride horses," she said to Roth apologetically. "That's why I have muscular arms." All the extras seemed eager to please Roth, especially after she scolded them.

"I never wear bras," Georgina added.

"I know," said Roth. "You should have brought shoes." Her voice softened. "But don't feel bad. Every other one didn't."

After four dresses were thwarted by Georgina's muscular arms, Roth solved the problem by eliminating sleeves from the equation. As Georgina slid into a strapless, plum-colored dress, Georgina said, "I've been at fittings for years and have never been asked to wear shoes."

"Well," said Roth. "They don't know what they're doing."

They, to Roth, represented everyone in the business (she loathed that expression as well: *the business*) who settled for the slipshod and the not-quite-right. More and more, it seemed to her, that *they* were the business.

At 5:00 P.M. Kim Cattrall arrived for her fitting, and she was ushered upstairs to one of the bedrooms. Cattrall had been chosen to play Judy McCoy after De Palma couldn't find anyone else, abroad or in New York. The actress had graduated with honors from the London Academy of Music and Dramatic Arts and had frequently appeared on-stage — in serious dramas, like *A View from the Bridge, The Three Sisters,* and *Twelfth Night.* Her film roles had been mostly forgettable and had been given to her mainly because she photographed well without her clothes on. Her movie career hadn't progressed much from "Porky's." Now in her mid-thirties — a dangerous age for an actress — she was thrilled to have been chosen to play Judy. A serious role in a serious movie could change entirely how she was seen by the industry — if the movie were successful.

Ann Roth followed Cattrall upstairs, where she found the actress standing alone in the stark little room in front of a mirror. Cattrall looked quite slender in the black taffeta evening gown. She had been dieting obediently for the past two months, at De Palma's suggestion, and now she was suitably bony to portray a social X-ray. Her hair was stiff and colored an unnatural black.

"Your hair is very interesting," said Roth.

"I cut it," said Cattrall in a faint voice that had the slightest British accent, a remnant of her childhood in London.

Roth wrinkled her nose.

"What jewelry do I need?" asked Cattrall, hesitantly. All the actresses were intimidated by Roth, though they tended to like her a great deal once they became accustomed to her piercing and immediate reactions.

"None," said Roth. "You show up and I'll put it on you."

Cattrall stripped down to her Calvin Klein briefs as though she hadn't noticed Gary Jones's arrival. Jones turned his back when he saw she wasn't wearing a bra. He, Roth, and Cattrall unanimously rejected a flouncy purple dress. Cattrall replaced it with a frumpy, knee-length brown dress with a velour bottom and a spangly gold top — Roth's suggestion for the dinner party scene.

"This is so anal-retentive, this dress," said Cattrall, looking pleased at her reflection in the full-length mirror. "It's very Judy McCoy." She addressed herself to Jones, a gentle, unobtrusive man.

"I love that description!" said Jones. "It's also very *Town and Country* to the hilt." Roth saw the actress was relaxed with Jones and decided to leave the two of them alone. She returned to the extras downstairs.

Cattrall slipped on a bland emerald green dress and Jones said with admiration, "You really are down to a size four." Cattrall's eyebrows knotted slightly, the only movement in her face as she stared at herself in the mirror.

"You look great." Jones's tone was encouraging.

Cattrall turned around and hugged him. "It's been hard," she said. "The waiting and the dieting." Her voice was shaky as she repeated. "It's been hard."

Roth had been fitting evening dresses since 7:30 that morning. At 7:00 P.M., as she approached her 120th fitting of the day, she was still scolding the actresses about proper shoes. When she finally left at 8:00 P.M., she was exhausted and disgusted. "I never saw so many augmented breasts in my life," she said later.

For the first time in her life, Roth felt mortal. Friends were dying, her husband was seriously ill. She referred to his illness with deceptive lightness. "Harry's grouchy," she would say. One day she said, without provocation, "I hate being a senior citizen." No one could quite match that idea — senior citizen — with Roth. She seemed ageless.

Roth was proud of the work she was doing, but it seemed more difficult than it needed to be. She was frustrated by what she saw as a steady decline of standards in the business, by the new generation of stars who lacked professionalism and a sense of craft. She liked to discuss what she was doing, with actors who didn't find their profession — *being actors* — an embarrassment, the way, for example, Bruce Willis apparently did. She could imagine explaining why Fallow was dressed the way he was if, say, Robert De Niro were playing the part. She'd say, "This suit comes from a certain amount of narcissism, the kind of guy who would work for *Interview* magazine. I know a lot of guys who don't have any money who wear thirty-five-hundred-dollar suits." But she found Willis completely unapproachable. She felt certain that he simply didn't understand the process.

And De Palma wasn't making things any easier. He remained aloof, as though he were making this picture alone. Roth found his attitude irritating. She had the feeling she wasn't part of a well-oiled machine, that there were a lot of tentative people working in what she thought of as a "vaguely constipated way."

Like Ann Roth, Dick Sylbert had been preparing for the party scenes for months. At the outset the production designer and De Palma had agreed to transfer Wolfe's dinner parties to grander settings. For the opera party, Fred Caruso lined up the Los Angeles County Museum of Natural History. Sylbert admired the museum's open dioramas where no glass separated the displays of stuffed wild animals from the public. For the party, Sylbert designed his own diorama showing hyenas disemboweling a gazelle. He loved the juxtaposition of this image against the society crowd. "When you think about animals, and these people, you realize that's what they are," he said. "Beautifully dressed animals."

Sylbert had set up shop in a nondescript double trailer at the corner of the parking lot next to Producer's Building 5. He always worked out of a trailer rather than an office. He was a nomad and felt it was appropriate to operate like one. Besides, this way he could park his car just outside the door. His office was cluttered with drawings and boxes of crackers and newspaper clippings. Warren Beatty's film version of the Dick Tracy comic strip had just opened and Sylbert's pop art design had been widely praised.

He was almost finished with his part in "Bonfire." All the set dressing was ready to go for the museum, and his showpiece — the $500,000 Park Avenue apartment that had been built on Stage 22 — was just about completed.

From the beginning the production designer had endorsed De Palma's vision of the movie. He felt the movie had to be exaggerated because the book was an exaggeration. "It's cardboard figures, it's all journalese, New Journalese — *Ay yai, ay yai, ay yai, ay yai!* kind of writing," said Sylbert. "It's a parody, it's a restoration comedy about the Wasp descending, and you need somebody with a lot of visual style who's interested in overdoing it. Because the book is overdone. The book is three hundred pages too long, and the book is very cold." He liked the way De Palma was forcing the thing all the time with complicated shots and strange angles. He too felt that if they didn't do that, they'd be left with a miniseries for television reduced to two hours.

Sylbert could see that the movie was going to be as overdone as the book was. "You have to do it," he would say. "You have to push your luck. Not ridiculously. You can't turn this thing into a cartoon, or a parody, or an out-and-out comedy. What Kubrick did with 'Strangelove.' "

He was satisfied that "Bonfire" would show a version of New York that had never been shown before. "If that city isn't tired, no city is tired," he said. "This is going to be a very rich version of New York, almost the way the book is written. You're talking here about capital letters. Park Avenue Duplex. Big capital letters. Billboards. Otherwise, you'll have no style at all."

He never deviated from his cultivated attitude of weary enthusiasm. He could talk about his set pieces with the energy of a young production designer who'd never been in charge of a picture before. Then, without missing a beat, he became the jaded Hollywood veteran, the man who had seen it all a million times. The cast, the script — these things were outside his authority. Maybe Hanks could give the picture an emotional pull the book didn't have and didn't intend to have. He wasn't sure. He wasn't certain that banking so heavily on these highly paid stars was a good idea. "With the right material it can pay off," he'd say philosophically. "Paul Newman said it a few years ago: 'A movie star cannot make a movie work, but a good movie can make a lot more money with a movie star.' "

Just then his six-year-old daughter, Daisy, a worldly imp with long blonde hair, ran into Sylbert's tiny office and reported that the tooth fairy had just given her three quarters for a tooth, complained that it was too hot in the trailer, and asked if she could have a lollipop. Her slender, gray-haired father hugged her, told her she couldn't have a lollipop, and sent her on her way. "See you tomorrow, precious," he said.

At 9:00 A.M. on June 25, the first day of shooting at the Los Angeles County Museum of Natural History, the temperature was already pushing ninety degrees. The little road leading to the giant rose garden along the side was packed with campers and trucks carrying the movie paraphernalia. A giant tent had been set up on the lawn where the hair and make-up people were tending to the 275 extras. Men in tuxedos and women in evening gowns dragged folding chairs to the shady spots on the giant lawn, and sat around drinking coffee from Styrofoam cups and reading newspapers. The morning air smelled of hair spray.

Inside, where it was cool and dark, lights were being prepared in front of the diorama Sylbert had built. Hanks was standing where hors d'oeuvres had been arranged, on a buffet set up in the middle of tables covered by tablecloths with zebra stripes which Sylbert had designed. Andre Gregory, the actor-raconteur, had been dressed in a foppish velvet tuxedo with an ascot; he was playing Aubrey Buffing, the poet with AIDS who wanders through the party preaching hellfire and brimstone.

In this scene, as the camera zeroes in on Sherman's face, Buffing is analyzing the predicament of the protagonist in *Don Giovanni*, the opera the partygoers have just attended. The scene is meant to show the pressures building on Sherman: he wants to seek out Maria to discuss his predicament. The Steadicam would follow him as he quickly moved from the room with the diorama into the brightly lit rotunda, where he would find Maria and Judy chatting in a group. The museum's rotunda was splendiferous, the gowns and the flowers suffusing the room with color.

Zsigmond wanted the camera to pass slowly by the ravaging hyenas before settling on Hanks's face. As Hanks stood impassively in front of the hyenas, and De Palma scanned the set from his director's chair, Zsigmond said to the operator, Doug Ryan, "Just take your time. A nice, slow, beautiful move."

Melanie Griffith had vanished after her last scene in New York, three weeks earlier. When she had reappeared on the lot the previous day to try on her evening gown, the costume people were surprised by what they saw when she undressed. Word quickly passed around the lot: Melanie had new — larger — breasts.

There was much speculation about why she did it. The favored story attributed her decision to a desire to please her husband, the actor Don Johnson. Johnson had been a phenomenon of the eighties, playing a detective on "Miami Vice," the television show that had been heralded as part of the New Wave. This series spoke directly to the generation nurtured by MTV; it was a show whose dramatic pulse came from music, clothes, and color. Johnson turned the combination of loafers and no socks and pastel T-shirts under blazers into a fashion statement; he rivaled Bruce Willis as the favorite cover boy of the supermarket tabloids. By the end of the decade, however, "Miami Vice" was history, and so, it seemed, was Johnson.

Griffith, whose career had been flourishing, took care to mention her husband and her children whenever she could. She would even talk dreamily about doing "normal things" — like making the beds, or going to the supermarket — with the reverence reserved to those who didn't actually have to do them.

De Palma and the executives took Griffith's reconstruction in stride. Cosmetic surgery had become commonplace not only in Beverly Hills but in wealthy enclaves around the country and among men as well as women. In Griffith's case, the only problem was timing; her physical realignment might be noticeable in scenes that had been started in New York and would be completed in L.A. Luckily, she was fully clothed in all of those. All her lovemaking scenes with Hanks — which required her to strip to her underwear — were to be shot on the lot.

Lucy Fisher, in her fifth month of pregnancy, was especially sympathetic to Griffith's decision. "She had a baby, give her a break," was the executive's reaction to her star's reconstructed breasts. "They look great. Now they're back to where they were before. She looks fantastic."

When Griffith arrived at the museum for her first day of shooting in Los Angeles, everyone's eyes moved to chest level as she walked through the dark exhibition hall toward De Palma. Griffith thwarted their curiosity by wearing a baggy black shirt that hung loosely over her tight black jeans. Her hair was pulled up in a casual knot on her head. Without her camera make-up, her face appeared grainy and tired. She slipped into the canvas chair next to De Palma's. Without taking his eyes off Hanks, De Palma rubbed her back. Griffith patted his leg, then leaned over to kiss his cheek. He didn't move his hand from her back.

The camera stopped rolling, and Griffith jumped out of her chair and walked swiftly to Hanks, greeting him with a hug. She kissed Zsigmond and then planted herself in front of De Palma's chair, facing him. From the elevation of his director's chair, his nose was directly parallel with Griffith's chest. Without warning, she leaned toward him and pressed her breasts against his face.

"How do they feel?" She giggled.

He looked uncomfortable. "How are you, Melanie?" His voice was gentle.

"Good," she said brightly. She stared at him as though he'd contradicted her. "Good," she said again.

When Griffith went off to be dressed and made up, the cameraman discussed the scene with his operator. Zsigmond said to Ryan, "You can make that pan smoother, Doug. Before was nice and smooth. It's floating. The whole shot is floating. Float through it smooth."

Most of the shots were designed to catch the expression on Hanks's face. Sherman is trying to maintain his aimless party grin when he hears the poet Buffing ranting about the descent of Don Giovanni into hell. The grin contorts into a grimace.

The stage directions were precise. "Tom should move an inch forward," said Zsigmond, examining the video monitor.

Hanks took an imperceptible step. "That's good," said Zsigmond.

A large man wearing a purple sport shirt and baggy shorts and sneakers waved at Zsigmond. "Hi," he said. "We're doing videotape today. Just so you know who we are."

"We" were the video crew from Pattyson Productions. Over the course of the production they would spend eight days on the set — three days in New York, five days in Los Angeles — filming interviews with the stars and taping snippets from the movie. This "behind-the-scenes" footage would become part of the studio's E.P.K., the electronic press kit, which would be distributed to network, local, and cable television stations all over the country.

Like almost every other aspect of the motion picture business, the promotion of movies was both the same as it had always been and very different. The studios were founded by salesmen, entrepreneurs who'd made their fortunes in *schmatta* and real estate. They understood packaging and readily transferred their skills to the marketing of filmed fantasy.

From the beginning, the studios were adept at manufacturing "news" about movie stars and their lives for the media. More serious journals like *Look* and *Life* and *The Saturday Evening Post* carried their share of predigested Hollywood lore. But the movies opened up a new industry: the fan magazine. In 1930 the first issue of *The Modern Screen* magazine was published. It was 132 pages long, sold for ten cents, and featured an actress named Kay Francis on its cover. The articles included "Garbo's Hiding Place," "An Open Letter to Clara Bow," and "Hollywood Wardrobes," an inside look at Fay Wray's "personal closet."

In the early days the public wasn't given much information about the mechanics of filmmaking. The publicity focused more on what stars wore, what kinds of food they liked, their family lives. The actors and actresses were presented — and accepted — as models for everyday Americans.

By the time "Bonfire" was filmed, movie news had to satisfy a more skeptical audience and tried to do so by taking on more and more of the trappings of "respectable" journalism. The *Los Angeles Times* kept a weekly scorecard of how movies were performing at the box office. The public now tended to talk about how movies were doing the way they'd discuss baseball. "Entertainment Tonight," a syndicated television show about show business that mixed gossip, financial intrigue, and information in a breezy format, became a popular follow-up to the evening news. The movie studios adapted quickly to the requirements of this publicity machine. They understood the trick was to help provide material that journalists could present as reportage.

John Pattyson of Pattyson Productions saw the future in "behind-the-scenes" coverage back in 1983, when he produced a feature on the making of "Dune," a science fiction film. That early experiment in the genre helped introduce the studios to the idea of creating "news features" to promote their movies. Rather than clutter their movie sets with independent producers whose footage couldn't be monitored, the studios preferred to oversee their own behind-the-scenes production shot by someone they could trust.

"A certain decorum is required," explained Pattyson's cameraman, the man in the purple shirt. "You won't see a news crew here. They don't know how to do it without disrupting the flow of work. I know Vilmos. He feels comfortable. A news crew comes in, they won't feel comfortable. A news crew might do something like shoot Melanie without make-up. Really stupid."

Pattyson conducted interviews, produced, edited, and directed the segments, then sent them to the studio, which hired him for re-editing. Pattyson's featurettes lasted five to six minutes and cost between $30,000 and $100,000. For the top-of-the-line "Bonfire," his crew had spent eight days on the set, three in New York and five in Los Angeles — twice the usual number of shooting days.

A compact man with small, even features and thinning curly hair, Pattyson described what he did as "infotainment" and used the word as though it had been part of the lexicon forever. Infotainment was part of the revolution in mass communication. Language itself had changed to accommodate hybrid forms of information, entertainment, and advertising. *Docudramas* told real stories in fictional forms. *Advertorial* sold products in articles that looked like features. *Infotainment* combined it all.

Infotainment could probably be traced back to its print antecedent, *People* magazine, whose presentation of fact and gossip as news had altered the nature of celebrity and of journalism in America in the seventies.

The emergence of infotainment as a regular feature on local news shows resulted in a complex symbiosis between the studios and the journalists who followed the film industry for television. The journalists liked to think of the E.P.K. as nothing more than a video press kit, no different from the background information that all businesses routinely distributed to the press. Because television news relies heavily on pictures, the studios, which provide the pictures, could control video stories much more easily than print. Infotainment was efficient public relations.

John Pattyson had his crew set up their lights and camera in the North American Mammals room, where he planned to interview Melanie Griffith for the E.P.K. A few hours after she dropped by to say hello to De Palma, Griffith reappeared in the museum as a glittering gold apparition, swathed in the dress Roth and her designer had been working on for so long. With some difficulty, she jumped up on the high chair Pattyson had set up for her in the middle of the room.

While Willis seemed to see nobody, Griffith had a tendency to absorb everything and everyone. When Sylbert passed by she straightened up in her chair and called out to him, "Congratulations on 'Dick Tracy.' " She beamed a bright smile in his direction. A second later she drew a sharp breath and asked the make-up man and the hairdresser to get out of her line of sight.

"I'm nervous enough as it is," she snapped.

Pattyson sat in a chair facing Griffith and in a quiet voice asked her what it was like to play Maria.

Griffith bit her lip and leaned forward in a way that made her recent surgery impossible to ignore. Her voice became lighter and more childlike than ever.

"She's fun! It's really *fun* to play her. My husband keeps saying, 'You're not really like that.' But it's fun. A really flamboyant character. I like playing her." She looked a little uncertain. "I wouldn't want to be like her. There's a lot of lies."

Griffith knew that her job here was simply to be sexy and charming, and that no one expected her to analyze the transformation of book to film. Still, she was worried she would be asked the question, and she didn't want to have to tell the world that she hadn't actually read the book all the way through. She'd wanted to finish it after she got the part, but she was making "Pacific Heights" and she had only one day between the two films. So she read the Maria sections and then tried to slog through the rest of it in New York. She was relieved when she heard from other people that it wasn't what they would call a very quick read. She could tell it was *great*, but it wasn't *quick*.

Pattyson droned on. "Why is this role a challenge."

"I think any role is a challenge," said Griffith dutifully. "It's not easy to go out there and possibly make a fool out of yourself. Maria is so outrageously Southern and wild. Fun . . ." She looked quizzically at Pattyson. "Am I making any sense?"

He assured her that she was.

Then she told him about her feelings for De Palma. "He's kind of . . . godlike, Brian is to me. I just adore him. He's wonderful." Her eyes started tearing. "He's an extremely creative, intellectual icon . . ."

Before she could continue Pattyson asked her what separated De Palma, in her mind, from other directors.

Griffith's eyes narrowed. "That's so unfair," she whined. "I don't know why you guys ask that." In a firm voice she said, "To me Mike Nichols is a god. Brian is a god." Her tone indicated the subject was closed.

During a break in filming while the lights were being reset, De Palma had his chair set up outside, at the top of the museum steps. Sitting alone having a cigarette, he stared down at the extras walking slowly through the baking air and blew smoke up at the sky.

His moment of peace was interrupted by a cotton-candy voice. "How do I look?" Griffith asked him.

She pirouetted in her skin-tight strapless evening gown with the graceless charm of a young girl balancing in ballet slippers for the first time. De Palma smiled.

Griffith leaned over and stole a cigarette, then grinned at the director, like a coconspirator. "I did the press kit and told them how wonderful you are."

Griffith stood next to De Palma for a moment. Together they stared out at the museum's front lawn; then Griffith was led off by a p.a. A few minutes later Alan King joined the director outside. He was wearing his own tuxedo with a monogram on the sleeve: ALAN. His thick make-up started to cake almost immediately on contact with the stiff afternoon heat. "I'm not trying to pad my part," he said to De Palma, "but I was thinking, at the party, when Maria's looking at the Italian, I should say 'ciao.' " He laughed, a loud, wheezing laugh. "Ciao!"

De Palma looked at him and laughed. Thus encouraged, King launched into a spontaneous monologue. "Remember when all the yuppies were saying 'ciao'? I call my son, and at the end of the message on his answering machine he says, 'Ciao.' " He coughed and wheezed and leaned toward De Palma in the classic stance of the comedian delivering a punch line. "So I say to the machine, 'This is your father. Ciao. Give me a call. Ciao. Hope all is well. Ciao.' "

With that, King disappeared, the diminishing volume of his wheezing laugh marking his progress back into the museum.

In condensing the book's vast plot, De Palma and Cristofer had given a small but crucial role to Caroline Heftshank, the trashy British woman who travels with the drunken hedonists of Peter Fallow's circle. In their version, when Maria runs off with Caroline's lover, an Italian painter, Caroline takes her revenge by telling Fallow that Maria was in the car with Sherman McCoy when they hit the boy in the Bronx.

The main requirement for the actress playing Caroline would be her ability to carry out one of Cristofer's innovations: pulling off her panties and plopping her naked bottom onto a Xerox machine for photocopy reproductions. She would also appear in the party scenes in suitably sexy dresses.

Lynn Stalmaster thought this sounded like a part for Beth Broderick. This lithe woman with the deep, throaty voice and dark hair and eyes would joke that she'd spent most of her film and television career wearing nothing but a bra and panties and carrying a gun. She'd done dozens of guest star appearances on television, usually as some variety of tough sister. She gave the impression of being indomitable. Her commanding voice and the hard look in her eye in combination seemed to say, "C'mon. Just try it."

But on this sweltering Monday afternoon Beth Broderick seemed quite vulnerable as she sat outside the museum during a break, her strapless plum and pink evening gown draped daintily over the edge of a folding chair. She was smoking a cigarette and trying not to cry. At the beginning of the break she and De Palma had been discussing the scene and the director had pulled her onto his lap. They were sitting in that familiar fashion when Melanie Griffith showed up. Griffith made it quite clear that she felt that she — the star of the movie — had been evicted from her rightful place by a bit player. De Palma slid Broderick off his lap. Without a nod at Broderick, Griffith wrapped her arms around De Palma's neck. "Brian, you pat everybody's ass," she whispered.

Broderick's pale face was flushed. She wasn't quite sure what to do, and so she just stood there. Griffith's assessment of their relative status vis-à-vis the director was particularly devastating because for the past four months Broderick and De Palma had been having an affair. Though it wasn't exactly a secret — they'd sat at the table next to Tom Hanks and Rita Wilson the other night at the Ivy, a popular show business restaurant — neither one of them was eager for the cast and crew to know.

De Palma had never completely recovered from his divorce; his four-year marriage to actress Nancy Allen had officially ended in 1983. He had always attributed the difficulties in their marriage to the competition that frequently arises in show business families, and to their inability to come to terms with the fact that his career was much more successful than hers. They'd met on "Carrie," and then he cast her as the leading lady in three films. Perhaps in a foreshadowing of things to come, De Palma chose to end "Blow Out" with the death of Nancy Allen's character. He placed the beginning of the end with "Scarface" and his decision to hire Michelle Pfeiffer instead of his wife to play the woman the gangster married.

As for Broderick, she had enough uncertainties about being an actress without the additional dilemma of sleeping with her boss, the director. She'd moved from California to New York at the age of eighteen and had done the theater circuit for four years. Frustrated with the business, she left to work as a restaurant consultant for a few years. She started doing volunteer work with AIDS patients and ended up running a program that distributed food to people too sick to leave their homes. She was also resuming her acting career with voice-overs for commercials and small parts in off-Broadway shows. Finally she decided the jobs were in L.A., and she moved back West.

She'd been cast as Caroline Heftshank the previous December. When she arrived in New York in March for rehearsals, De Palma took her to a bookstore after she'd gone through her lines one day. He asked her to dinner, and now, four months later, she was wondering if they might marry. He seemed determined to have a family, and the idea appealed to her. They spent most evenings together. When they had separate plans, she would often go to his house up in the Hollywood Hills to spend the night. He would wake up with the most terrible dreams, and the vulnerability she saw in this powerful man had a frightening pull on her.

Still, Broderick was shrewd and sensitive and tuned in to the way she was perceived by De Palma's well-placed friends. They'd gone to dinner at the Spielberg house a few times. She was treated cordially, always, but with reserve. Broderick invariably left these occasions with the feeling that she was regarded as the rebound girl.

Broderick always said what she thought, and she dressed provocatively as well. Sometimes it was suggested to her that perhaps men made insinuating remarks to her on the street or at the gym because her clothes were so . . . skimpy. Broderick would dismiss that idea with a philosophic retort: "Yeah, isn't that the ultimate debate for women in America. You wore that short skirt so you were asking to be raped." She'd shrug and take another drag on a cigarette. "You can't be less than who you are. I can't be less than who I am. In this business bright women are not looked on with great fondness. It's always, 'Ah, she's a bitch.' "

The main reason she kept her affair with De Palma under wraps was her memory of another film she'd worked on, where she and the other women would spend hours in the make-up trailer belittling the director. She remembered the way she and the others felt, at the end of the film, when they discovered that the make-up lady had been having an affair with the man they'd so relentlessly mocked in her presence.

Eric Schwab, who'd flown in from New York over the weekend, had shown up at the museum that morning looking crisp in his brand-new clothes. He was scheduled to meet with Lucy Fisher that afternoon and had bought new khaki slacks and a white shirt at The Gap. He consulted with Ann Roth, who thought the casual ensemble, even the sneakers, were fine, but suggested Schwab add a jacket to indicate he understood the importance of the occasion. Larry McConkey, the Steadicam operator, agreed with Roth. De

Palma, however, vetoed the jacket. Caruso didn't think it mattered what Schwab wore but advised him to check in with Marty Bauer before talking to Fisher.

Schwab had arrived back at the set at 4:00 P.M. His meeting with Fisher had been postponed until the next day. To calm himself down, he stopped at The Gap on the way back to the museum and bought another pair of chinos and another white shirt so he'd have fresh clothes for the next day's meeting. At 6:00 P.M. he left for the airport; his girlfriend, Lek, was flying in from Thailand for a weeklong visit. They hadn't seen each other since early spring.

By Tuesday, the next morning and the second day of filming at the museum, the heat had become unbearable. The temperature would reach 112 degrees in downtown Los Angeles, 14 degrees higher than the last record temperature, which had been set 107 years earlier. A high-pressure dome had settled over the Southwest — "like a lid on a Dutch oven, baking the entire landscape beneath it," was the way a *Los Angeles Times* writer put it.

Inside the rotunda of the Natural History Museum, what seemed like the longest cocktail party in the history of the world was dragging on. As Larry McConkey repeatedly lumbered after King, Griffith, and Cattrall, the extras milled about, forcing their faces into the overbright animation required for this kind of formal occasion. Every time Chris Soldo, the first assistant director, yelled "cut," the extras crowded in front of the fans set up at strategic spots on the floor.

"This is a cocktail party, not a funeral," Soldo called out to the sweating cast. "Look like you're having fun."

Like so many of these technically precise shots, this one required a great deal of repetition, and a great deal of waiting between takes. The Steadicam shot was followed by an equally difficult dolly shot. By lunchtime the temperature was into the triple digits. The extras wilted, eating rice and grilled chicken outside on long picnic tables. A make-up man shook his head as he looked at all those naked arms and backs broiling in the sun. "What if we have to shoot an extra day?" he wondered out loud. It occurred to him that halfway through the scene it would appear that the guests at a party taking place in New York in the spring had broken out with a mysterious rash that bore a remarkable resemblance to sunburn.

Back inside, Griffith moved around the rotunda in her startling dress like a jittery cat on the prowl. She seemed to be readjusting her antennae almost as frequently as she tugged at the bodice of her gown. When Soldo told her she had ten minutes until she was needed on camera, she turned to De Palma. "They always say it's ten minutes, then it's six hours." Her giggle didn't dispel the effect of the frown she turned Soldo's way.

Soldo pulled on his baseball cap. "Ten minutes, six hours, it's all the same," he said with a smile, and walked away. Griffith tottered over to Tom Hanks, who was sitting on a chair in front of the video monitor. He'd gone to his first Lamaze class with his wife that weekend; their child was due in August. Griffith crawled onto his lap and asked him if he was nervous about their love scenes.

"Not at all, no," he said, pulling his head back stiffly. "You know, Melanie," he said in a bantering tone, "I saw your husband on television. He was on a large boat looking very small." Griffith looked at him uncertainly.

De Palma joined the actors and laughed. "You'll sit on anyone's lap," he said to Griffith.

Griffith got up as she spotted a new face. Michael Cristofer was in town to go over with De Palma the narration Bruce Willis had to recite over the opening Steadicam shot; he was also scheduled to meet with the producer David Geffen about another project. Cristofer introduced himself to the actress. She leaned over, holding a smoldering cigarette in one hand.

"Hiiii," she said. "What a thrill . . ."

Cristofer looked pleased at the recognition. He started to say something. Griffith, however, had taken on a businesslike tone. "When Boris pours the champagne, do I have to say, 'Eat your ass'?" she said. "It's so crude."

The screenwriter looked nervous. He glanced over at De Palma, who wasn't looking his way. "It's supposed to be crude," he said quietly.

"Couldn't I be crude without being so gross?" Griffith's voice was sliding into a whine.

Cristofer didn't know how to cope with this barrage of pouty charm. Griffith grew impatient with his hesitancy and walked back over to De Palma. She repeated her complaint.

"What's wrong with it?" said the director, caressing her as he said no.

He excused himself and walked over to talk to Cattrall.

By 6:30 the scene, the purpose of which was to bring the principal players through the crowd to the place where Sherman and Maria meet, still hadn't been completed. Griffith's patience had evaporated. "What are we doing next?" she screamed up at Soldo, who was standing on the balcony above. He shouted back, "It's basically a geography shot. Bringing you around to wherever you're talking to the Russian and Sherman."

Griffith turned to Nancy Hopton, the script supervisor, and said in a small, hurt voice, "Is that a really outrageous question to ask?"

De Palma met his lieutenants up at Burbank at 8:45 that evening to look at dailies of what they'd shot at the museum the day before. Eric Schwab slipped into his seat in the back of the small theater, just in front of De Palma. He still couldn't believe the day he'd had. He'd met Marty Bauer at 3:00 P.M., and Bauer handed him over to one of his young agents. A half hour later Bauer popped in and said, "You're an unmitigated genius. Lucy, unprovoked, said you're an unmitigated genius. So what can we use to sell you. A reel? A script? Let's do it! Let's do it! Welcome aboard."

From there Schwab had gone to his appointment with Fisher. She was direct and attentive and very complimentary about his Concorde shot. All he could remember afterward was that she was wearing a dress covered with pink flowers.

Fred Caruso had seen another side of Fisher when she called him in for a tough meeting a few days before. She and Canton were apoplectic about the cost overruns. The picture was now $4.5 million over budget. They were not at all pleased that the decision to cast Morgan Freeman had now cost a multiple of his salary — and all the bills weren't in. Caruso was feeling the pressure from other quarters as well. Willis had to be finished by the end of the next week because he was about to start another picture, "Hudson Hawk." F. Murray Abraham had a scheduling problem and still was insisting that he didn't want his name on the movie if he didn't get billing as prominent as that of Morgan Freeman.

De Palma was adding another demand. "We must find a production assistant for Melanie," he said to Caruso at the end of dailies. "Someone has to be with her all the time. This is not easy. You need someone who has a lot on the ball. She'd like Aimee, but I have Aimee. Melanie's a very delicate girl, and if things aren't handled right we'll always be standing around for forty-five minutes."

Zsigmond interrupted. "An hour and a half we'll be standing around."

"Waiting for her," continued De Palma.

Caruso and Schwab walked across the lot together toward the production office. It was 9:30 and peaceful on this hot summer night. "Did you see 275 extras in that shot?" Caruso asked Schwab. "How many of them did you actually see? Fifteen? Twenty? Did you see the ambassador and his wife and their daughter? We had to fly them in from New York for this scene."

Schwab didn't say anything. The truth was, he hadn't been paying all that much attention during dailies. He'd been thinking, This is such a shitty projection room. I hope this isn't where they show the dailies of my movie. What a heady day it had been. He couldn't pull himself away from the lot, even though he knew Lek was waiting for him at his apartment. De Palma hadn't asked him how his meeting with Fisher had gone, but Schwab didn't mind all that much. Already he was feeling more confident, less dependent on the evaluation of his mentor.

Caruso started laughing as he thought about how much waste there had been and the price he was already paying. He lightly punched Schwab on the arm. "That's why I like to work with young directors, Eric," he teased. "You can say no."

By Wednesday the heat was bearing down with ominous force. Fires were breaking out all over tinder-dry southern California, spread by erratic gusts of wind. Several hundred homes would go up in flames in Santa Barbara that day; an arsonist started a fire that seemed to skip from roof to roof. The temperature finally settled at 109 degrees in downtown Los Angeles, 3 degrees shy of the record set the day before. By early afternoon, Charlie Saldana, the West Coast key grip for "The Bonfire of the Vanities," observed that he'd consumed three giant bottles of mineral water since breakfast and hadn't been to the bathroom yet, he was sweating that much.

They were still at the museum. The seven scenes scheduled to be shot there were taking far longer than expected. They'd be lucky to get out in three days instead of two. The problem wasn't so much getting Hanks from here to there, as Sherman moved through the party in search of Maria. The difficulty was in orchestrating the faces around him as the Steadicam walked with him: making sure there were no shadows, that somebody's nose wasn't sticking in the frame, that Hanks got off his mark exactly on time.

The flowers were holding up only slightly better than the extras; everything and everyone had withered long ago. Griffith's dress clung so tightly she had a hard time sitting, and her feet hurt from wearing those ultrahigh spiked heels. She rested on De Palma's knee during a break and called out to Soldo, "Chris, a chair."

The first assistant director had grown weary of being treated like a valet by Griffith. He asked a p.a. to bring her a chair.

Soldo had started in the film business as a p.a. himself, nineteen years earlier, during summer break between his junior and senior years of high school. He worked on an obscure Sophia Loren film memorable to Soldo because that was where he'd met Fred Caruso, who owned the company handling the production services for the film. Peter Runfolo was the location scout.

The first assistant director came from a show business family. His father, a flutist, worked on Broadway shows and as a studio musician for NBC. As a boy, Soldo had sat in the orchestra pit while his father played the music for Sammy Davis doing *Golden Boy*, for Robert Morse in *How to Succeed in Business Without Really Trying*.

Soldo went to film school at U.C.L.A., always working on movies during summers as a production assistant. He had worked on "Sisters" with De Palma, "Serpico" with Sidney Lumet, and "Taxi Driver" with Scorsese. He had quit school his senior year for a job on "New York, New York." He finally completed his degree requirements in 1980, when a Screen Actors Guild strike forced him to stop working. He made a few eight-millimeter films, but his heart was in producing, not directing. He was an organizer and a mediator. Being the man in charge scared him. He hoped in time to be somebody's powerful Number Two, to attach himself to a director who would rely on him to help shape things. De Palma gave him a lot of leeway but would never confide in him the way a younger, less experienced director might. Soldo wanted to be in a position that would force people like Melanie Griffith to acknowledge that he might have something to offer besides his ability to find her a chair.

Griffith remained firmly planted on De Palma's knee, even after her chair was set up next to his. De Palma patted her backside, and she snuggled against him.

When Michael Cristofer arrived on the set, though, the actress once again made a point of greeting the screenwriter with a warm hello.

"I'm very excited," she said. "My husband is coming back. He's been gone two days."

Cristofer looked a little confused and smiled politely. Soldo walked over and shook Cristofer's hand. The assistant director had worked on "The Witches of Eastwick," the John Updike novel Cristofer had adapted for the movies.

" 'Witches' paid for the down payment on my house. This one's paying for preschool," said Soldo. "Keep writing."

Alan King joined the group, and he and Griffith took alternating drags on the same cigarette. The camera was ready, so Griffith handed the cigarette to Cristofer while she walked to the center of the room, to the spot where Maria is standing when Sherman catches sight of her at the party. This scene, which required Sherman to walk a good distance through a crowd of people, had to be pieced together bit by bit. Griffith's job at that moment was to stand next to King for a few seconds while the camera recorded Maria's boredom. That done, Griffith returned to Cristofer who handed her back her cigarette. She held the cigarette in one hand and put the other on Zsigmond's back; he'd taken the chair next to Cristofer's. The cameraman stood up and walked away.

"I don't think he likes me," said Griffith. "Every time I put my hand on his back he moves."

Griffith's intuition was correct. Zsigmond found the only nice thing he could say about the actress was that he was relieved she looked much better in the movie than she had in her initial screen test. He much preferred Kim Cattrall. "I love Kim," he would say. "I love her voice. She has a great voice. She is really that ball-breaking woman who tries to dominate Sherman McCoy." He had been most surprised — pleasantly so — by Tom Hanks. "He has exactly the right flavor for comedy and also seriousness. You feel sorry for him," Zsigmond had said. "I think that's what is going to save this movie. We have a great star, and he is going to carry this movie."

The group had now moved to the center of the rotunda, for yet another angle on the party guests. Tom Hanks sat at a table and filled out a crossword puzzle with Nancy Hopton, the script supervisor. Tippi Hedren, Griffith's mother, showed up on the set in a smart little knit dress, carrying a Louis Vuitton bag. When the necklace of one of the extras came unhooked, Hedren automatically reached up to refasten it for her, without removing her eyes from her daughter. Even in a crowded room like this, Griffith commanded — and demanded — attention.

Griffith stayed near De Palma after the cut, oblivious to her mother's attempts to grab her attention. Finally their eyes connected.

"Have you had lunch?" Hedren asked, as she delicately chewed a piece of gum.

Griffith pressed her lips together. "Do you want to have lunch with me?" She tugged on her dress and asked Zsigmond if he'd met her mother. They shook hands while Griffith seemed to search for something.

She spotted Aimee Morris hovering at De Palma's elbow and asked her to find someone to take Hedren to Griffith's trailer. She looked coolly at her mother.

"Sammy will fix you something," Griffith said. As Hedren was escorted off the set, Griffith's face relaxed. In an affectionate tone she mentioned that her mother was acting in a soap opera, "The Bold and the Beautiful," and that she kept lions and other wild animals on her ranch.

Then she sat at one of the tables and took out a cigarette. In between drags she took long sips of water out of a large glass. Hanks asked her what she was drinking.

"Oh, vodka," she said. She saw that Hanks didn't know whether she was joking or not.

"I was just kidding. It's water. It used to be vodka," she said. Morris was sitting nearby and drew closer. Griffith elaborated. "For four years on and off I'd have a glass of vodka in the morning. Then I'd get going with cocaine." She told Morris she'd gone to AA meetings on three separate occasions. She'd get off the stuff for a while, then go back on it again. Now she was forbidden to drink even a glass of wine.

She laughed. "Don says he can't wait for the day there's an injection that lets us drink again without getting hooked."

Griffith then began musing about whether drinking was perhaps a genetic problem set off by something chemical. Soldo interrupted to get the actors in place for the final take of Alan King's scene. "Artists, please," he said. "Mr. King. Madame . . ."

After the shot was completed, Soldo yelled, "Alan King, finished in the picture." The extras applauded, acknowledging the actor's final scene with the traditional sendoff. The numbing effects of the heat and the boredom were dispelled for one brief instant.

Vilmos Zsigmond was frustrated and he was tired, but he was also optimistic as he watched the dailies every night. He was curious to see how the movie would all piece together, yet as the final phase of filming approached, he had a good feeling about it. Better than good. "I really think we have the smell of a great movie here," he said. "I really think so. I feel it inside. We have all the ingredients in there for a great movie."

Zsigmond had grown increasingly tense as he tried to do his job and everyone else's as well. De Palma had brought in Doug Ryan to operate the camera when the studio refused to hire the operator Zsigmond normally used. The first time Ryan met Zsigmond, the little Hungarian got right to the point: he told Ryan he was concerned that he would act as De Palma's operator, not his.

Ryan, who had served in the Marine Corps in Vietnam and had spent his early years in the film business reconciling himself with his past, had tried to develop a Zen attitude toward work. He assured Zsigmond that the best way for him to serve De Palma would be to follow Zsigmond's wishes. He would do his best to compose shots the way Zsigmond wanted him to.

But Zsigmond couldn't resist second-guessing him every step of the way. During every setup, the cameraman was torn between his desire to tell the gaffer exactly where he wanted the lights to go, and his urge to watch the video monitor to see what Ryan was doing every instant.

Ryan tried not to feel belittled by Zsigmond's imperious attitude. Now that they were back on home turf he could release some of the tension by surfing on weekends. During the day, when Zsigmond would peer through the camera until shooting began instead of letting Ryan analyze the composition, Ryan would try to follow the advice of philosopher Joseph Campbell: "You have to follow your bliss," he'd think. But then he'd think, what was his bliss? Working was his bliss. So, he reasoned, if working was bliss and he was working with Vilmos Zsigmond on "Bonfire of the Vanities," then bliss involved a lot of tension and anxiety.

The operator had looked forward to "Bonfire" as a challenge that would propel him toward his goal of being a cinematographer instead of an operator. But he was convinced that he would remember the picture as purgatory, his penance for an earlier sin. He had hoped to have a chance to learn from Zsigmond, but the camera-man wasn't interested in discussion. He never said to him, "Doug, this is where we are and this is where I want us to be." It was always: "This is how you connect the dots. From *a* to *b* to *c* to *d*." Ryan saw composition as a brushstroke, the thing that connected what he saw with his eye, his mind, and his heart. It wasn't connecting the dots.

After working fourteen hours a day for so many weeks, he felt alienated from his own camerawork. He felt as though it weren't his. He felt hollow.

That afternoon Melanie Griffith would have to utter the words she'd asked Michael Cristofer to change the day before. In this scene, Sherman finally corners Maria at the opera party and wants to tell her he is about to be arrested. Maria wants to distract him and introduces him to another guest, Boris Karlevskov, a Russian ballet dancer. She assures Sherman that Boris doesn't understand English and proves it by smiling at the dancer and saying, "Boris, darling, would you like me to eat your ass?" Boris, in French, asks her if she wants more champagne.

De Palma had asked Griffith to chatter with "Boris" in French at the start of the scene. Rummaging through her schoolgirl French, Griffith remembered something she thought would be appropriate and improvised.

"*J'aime toucher ton gros zizi,*" she said flirtatiously to the actor playing the Russian. Translation, roughly: "I like to touch your big dick." Apparently Griffith had overcome her inhibitions about crude dialogue.

Before Griffith allowed the cameras to roll, however, she leaned over and said something to De Palma. De Palma called Soldo over and told him to clear the set of everyone who didn't need to be there.

Soldo slowly turned in a circle, taking in the hundreds of people crowded in the rotunda. Dozens of extras were required for this scene, as well as numerous electricians and other technicians to manage the lights, the cables, the fans. Evicting a few of them seemed pointless and a little cruel — it was murderously hot outside.

"This is ridiculous," muttered Soldo, who rarely displayed his irritation. "Why is the eyeline clear so important now?" he asked, referring to the area the actors could see when they were performing. But in a very loud voice, he said, "No guests. No visitors. Step out of the room please."

Griffith didn't care if she seemed unreasonable. She was always measuring every situation, weighing how people were responding to her and evaluating what they wanted from her. If six people were standing around with their arms crossed watching her and she sensed they didn't need to be there, she didn't want them there. She *noticed* the gawkers. She could feel them watching her.

She felt it was embarrassing and unnecessary to have people critiquing her work while she was doing it. She'd get enough of that when the movie came out.

For the first few takes she said "eat your ass" so inaudibly her voice barely registered on the sound man's equipment. Then, on the tenth take, something started to happen. Griffith started to push the line. Her voice got higher, louder, and she was grinning.

De Palma sat up in his chair. "Keep the pace up," he said to the dolly operator, moving the camera toward Griffith as she talked.

"Giddy and giggly," he instructed Griffith.

By take nineteen she'd completely loosened up. The line's vulgarity had now become a joke. As a giant roomful of people tiptoed around, Griffith devoted herself, take after take, to "giddy and giggly."

The next day the crew returned to Stage 25 on the Warner Bros. lot, where another actress would be asked to lose her inhibitions for the camera.

Beth Broderick and Bruce Willis were appearing together in scene 250, in which Broderick's character, Caroline Heftshank, lures the reporter Fallow into the office at Leicester's. Leicester's was the restaurant Tom Wolfe described as the place where "the Brits — members of the London *bon ton* now living in New York — come and go, to have a few . . . and hear English voices." Since the Fallow character was no longer British, the restaurant's persona had become more amorphous.

In this scene, the drunken Heftshank decides to take revenge on her boyfriend and Maria, by implicating Maria in the hit-and-run accident. Cristofer invented a bit of action to accompany Heftshank's revelation to Fallow. The screenwriter's stage directions read:

> She switches ON the MACHINE, which starts PHOTOCOPYING her twat.

After Heftshank and Fallow finish their conversation, Heftshank hands the reporter the photocopies and tells him to give them to Maria and her lover, as a "gift."

The small room built to house the Xerox machine in the corner of Stage 25 was secluded from spectators by plywood and drapes. The sound man and the video monitor operators sat outside, as did the make-up and hair people. Only the most necessary members of the crew were allowed to watch as Broderick pulled off her panties and jumped up on the glass surface of the photocopier over and over.

As the day wore on, Broderick's face darkened. "My basic goal was to try and keep from crying," she said. "It's very difficult, you're very embarrassed. There's no getting around it. It's not like you agree to do this and you have no feelings about it. I agreed to do it so I have to give it up. I can't worry about who's seeing what. That's Brian's job. All I can do is do what I have to do to get it over with."

It was understood that Broderick's naked crotch would never appear in the final film. She was accustomed to doing far more outrageous nudity on the set than would ever be used. It was standard practice to reveal everything in order to give the director footage that convincingly suggested the revelation of everything.

Broderick said she appreciated the comedic value of the scene. Besides, she felt, she had no choice. "If you look at the roles for women that are available, the only way I can be interpreted is based on what I look like. You take someone like me, who is sexy — okay, let's face it, I am. I'm built a certain way and that's the way it goes. There's this allure in my voice. So that's what I have to sell.

"But I'm also very intelligent and very quick, and capable of doing the things women are never given the chance to do. A lot of people don't trust that. Intelligence is considered a drawback in an actress. Particularly in pretty actresses. What you hope and bank on is that with your training and your other qualities you'll get a chance to exercise them, if you do this first."

Beth Broderick would emerge from nine hours of filming the Xerox scene with bruised buttocks and thighs and feelings of humiliation quite unlike anything she'd experienced before in her professional life.

De Palma was grim and even more silent than usual during the filming in Broderick's scene. Watching Broderick's discomfort pained him in many ways. He was sympathetic to her embarrassment and aware that he was complicit in it as her director. And, because of their relationship, he was vividly reminded of the days when he was married to Nancy Allen, and the woman parading nearly naked in front of him and his crew was his wife.

He had filmed a great deal of nudity over the years, and it always made him feel uncomfortable. He would talk at length about the brutality of the system's treatment of women. Yet there was a contradiction between his words and the depiction of women in his films, where they tended to be sex objects or saints. He had created strong, spirited women, like Holly Body in "Body Double," or Liz Blake in "Dressed to Kill," but one was a porn star and the other a prostitute, women defined by their sex.

Over the years De Palma had been asked repeatedly about his treatment of women in films, and his response was always the same. "I'm saying what I've said a thousand times before," he'd say. "Women are more vulnerable than men. And I like photographing women." It had never occurred to him to excise the Xerox scene, which hadn't been in the book and which wasn't critical to advancing the movie's plot. He refused to censor himself because of the public's perception of his view of women. Besides, the Xerox scene was a mere drop in the river of concerns he had about "Bonfire."

Chapter 13

NICKEL AND DIMING

Proximity didn't alleviate the tensions between the executives and the filmmakers. If anything, the executives felt even more frustrated at their inability to rein this movie in now that it had moved into their backyard. Fisher was angry at Caruso for all kinds of things. Big things, like never letting them know the exact status of the courtrooms. And little things, like Griffith's perquisites.

Warner's lawyers had carefully delineated which of Griffith's demands the company would pay for. They'd agreed to the voice coach, for example, but had balked at her choice for a driver. Sam Conigliari had worked for Don Johnson when he was filming "Miami Vice" down in Florida. Though Conigliari's official status was driver, Griffith wanted him to operate her trailer because she liked the way he cooked. Warner Bros. refused to ship Conigliari to New York because he wasn't a member of the teamsters local there and wouldn't be able to drive. Griffith had been unhappy about that and asked Caruso if Conigliari could join her in L.A. He agreed. The Warner executives, however, were furious when they received word that Caruso had agreed to pay Conigliari's airfare, his rental car, his hotel, a $75 per diem fee, and $10,000 salary for five weeks' work. They were even angrier when they discovered Conigliari wasn't a Los Angeles teamster either and Griffith would be needing a driver as well. Conigliari was being paid to clean Griffith's trailer and cook her macrobiotic meals.

On three occasions Lucy Fisher and Bill Young, the Warner production executive, called on Marshall Silverman, the Warner lawyer assigned to "Bonfire," to ask him how to fire Caruso legally. Silverman, who had worked with Caruso in New York on and off over the years, defended the production manager and told the executives to give him a chance to explain. Shortly after arriving in L.A., Caruso met with Fisher and Young. Reluctantly, Fisher conceded that Caruso's explanations for the cost overruns were convincing enough for him to keep his job. They didn't convince her, however, that she could trust him.

Though the executive offices were a short walk from the sound stages, Fisher and De Palma didn't see each other much. She had recovered from the insult of having been banned from rehearsals in New York, back when the movie was getting started. After that, she felt that De Palma paid attention to her suggestions and tried to be reasonable. "I like him a lot, and I think he likes me," she said of their relationship. "We respect each other and we're . . . I would hesitate to use the word because it's his prerogative to use it or not . . . but I would say he is . . . collaborating. He may not want anybody to know that. But he's very open to intelligent suggestions. He likes a good idea and he doesn't care where it comes from. With a lot of them [other directors] you have to wait three days so they can pretend the idea was theirs."

She knew that circumstances had led to last-minute changes, like the Steadicam shot that opened the film. But now "Bonfire" was on the lot, and she and her boss, Mark Canton, the studio chief, still felt excluded from decisions. By June 27, 1990, the production was nine days behind schedule and Christmas suddenly seemed just minutes away. So the Warner executives fired off a memo across the lot to De Palma and Caruso:

> BONFIRE OF THE VANITIES is now at $4,200,000 over budget, with additional costs to come on 2nd Unit. We are aware that most of this overage was due to scheduling problems with Morgan Freeman and the Courthouse. However, it is our concern that the overages are going to continue if we do not immediately address the remaining potential scheduling problems.

Fisher and Canton offered several suggestions for ways to speed things up, either by cutting characters from certain scenes or by taking out dialogue. The executives also dictated that the opera scene, in which Sherman and Judy McCoy attend *Don Giovanni* the night before Sherman's arrest, "will definitely not be shot."

Fisher didn't realize it, but with this directive she and Canton had issued the opening salvo in what she and De Palma would come to call the opera fight. As usual, the fight wasn't really about whether or not to film the opera scene. It was a matter of control.

When De Palma received the Fisher-Canton memo, the only thing that registered was that ultimatum: the opera scene "will definitely not be shot." De Palma felt that the scene, which shows Don Giovanni's descent into hell and Sherman's reaction to it, was an important prelude to the party scene that follows and to Sherman's own incarceration the following day. At the opera Sherman watches Don Giovanni being consumed by the flames of hell. As he reads the libretto he sees the words *repent, repent.* Then, at the party, he identifies again with Don Giovanni when he meets Aubrey Buffing, the poet with AIDS, who pontificates on Don Giovanni and warns Sherman that "justice will not tarry."

Perhaps De Palma wouldn't need the opera scene in the end, but he wanted the option of using it in the movie. He was willing to cut the golden crumbs scene instead — the scene in which Judy McCoy belittles Sherman by explaining his profession to their daughter in demeaning terms. But he was told that Terry Semel, the Warner Bros. president, adored that scene and didn't want it taken out.

What infuriated De Palma about the Fisher-Canton memo was its nonnegotiable language. He read the words *definitely will not be shot* as a direct insult and unpardonable manipulation. The executives, he felt, were using the opera scene to force him to adhere to the schedule — insinuating that he wasn't trying to do that himself. From the beginning he'd told them he'd need seventy-eight days to shoot the film, and they'd said that was impossible. Finally, he capitulated. He'd try to finish in sixty-six days, he told them, always knowing that the schedule would be impossible to meet. They'd be lucky if they finished in seventy-five days.

When the memo arrived, De Palma had been watching Broderick's ordeal on the Xerox machine for several hours, and he wasn't in a diplomatic frame of mind. He was too exhausted to debate and wished someone else could take his place. Besides dealing with Griffith and Broderick he was working with Cristofer by phone, trying to tighten the remaining scenes. At the same time, he couldn't ignore the pressure emanating from the pretty bungalows across the way. Fisher and Canton had let him know they'd prefer that he edit the movie in Los Angeles instead of New York, where he always did postproduction on his films. He was starting to feel as though there were no end to this tunnel.

All this was weighing on him when Fisher called him in to discuss the memo the following day, on June 28, during a break in the Xerox scenes. She waited for the director in her large office on the second floor of the executive building, decorated in white-on-white.

As De Palma walked into the building he told himself that Fisher was just doing her job and he intended to endure their meeting calmly. But as he climbed the stairs he started to feel angry. She's got executives to answer to, he thought, and I've got the world to answer to.

The thirty-minute meeting started off pleasantly enough, as Fisher explained why she and Canton thought they could eliminate the opera scene and how they could save some time by using voice-overs while the second-unit footage of scenery going by played on-screen. De Palma listened as she continued to elaborate on the points she'd made in the memo. Suddenly he heard himself shouting that the only way the executives would see pictures of cars driving by with voice-overs would be "over [his] dead body." He told Fisher she and Canton should figure out an alternative, and concluded by accusing Warner Bros. of "nickel and diming" him, and acting like a low-budget schlock distributor. With that he abruptly walked out the door.

Shortly afterward, a package arrived for De Palma at Producer's Building 5. It contained a second copy of the June 27 memo and a note from Mark Canton. It said:

Dear Brian:
Apparently you left Lucy's office without taking your notes . . .
   Since we don't consider ourselves to be "nickel and diming" you, and indeed welcome your creative input and suggestions to make these things work, perhaps you should at least have a copy of the notes.
Best,
Mark

Fisher wasn't thrown off guard by De Palma's outburst the way she had been back in New York. She wasn't shocked and she wasn't angry. When De Palma called her three days later saying, "I'm sorry, Lucy. Really, I'm sorry, Lucy. I'm so sorry," she was happy to accept his apology, convinced she had the moral edge.

Mark Canton wasn't at all pleased with the way things were going in the biggest picture on his slate for 1990 — but he didn't like face-to-face confrontation. On July 2, just before he left town for two weeks, he sent a stern memo addressed to Caruso alone, with copies to Brian De Palma, Marty Bauer, Lucy Fisher, Bill Young, Penelope Foster (who had replaced Ron Smith), Terry Semel, and Bob Daly, Warner Bros. chairman. It said:

> In addition to our memo of June 27th, regarding the $4,200,000 over budget expenditures, we received budget overruns last week of another $175,000 (including an extra day at the museum). And, we have just received word of additional overages from New York, of $150,000 that we didn't previously know about. Costs continue to escalate. This cannot continue.
>
> Henceforth, all production decisions will be made between you, Fred Caruso, co-producer, and me, Mark Canton, Executive Vice President, Warner Bros. Inc., Worldwide Theatrical Production, with either Penelope Foster or Lucy Fisher serving as my emissaries. We can no longer allow for any variances from the budget that are not approved by myself or one of the aforementioned people. For instance, even after our most recent conversation, you doubled the Screen Actors Guild Ruskin family at the Funeral without any notification or conversation.
>
> We stand by the memo of June 27th. In addition, we want to make the following points:
>
> 1. We need to see approved locations for the Southampton location and Conference room location by the end of next week (Friday, July 13th).
>
> 2. In addition to the fact that it has never been in the budget, we, in no way, feel the Opera Scene is necessary. The Aubrey Buffing AIDS jokes will play as is. The Aubrey Buffing repentance speech will also probably still play (whether or not he and Sherman have just come from a Don Giovanni opera — which the average person does not know, or care about). A poet who is dying of AIDS would certainly be given the license to expouse [sic] a philosophical monologue about coming to terms with a corrupt lifestyle before it is too late.
>
> 3. Michael Cristofer is available and he has already been paid in case you need him to come back to help shorten the party and McCoy

apartment, Funeral or whatever else you want. However, it seems like work that could be done over the telephone. At any rate, he is willing and able to cooperate.

4. The alternative to Los Angeles post-production schedule comes to over $250,000. Therefore, we will reluctantly keep the post-production in New York and the film (or a dupe) will come to L.A. for viewing whenever necessary.

Please study the June 27th memo (reattached for your convenience) and these additional points, and call Lucy Fisher, with your binding affirmation no later than 6:00 P.M. on Thursday. We feel that none of these suggestions will hurt the integrity of your already excellent movie, and we trust that a constructive spirit of cooperation will now prevail.

Thanks, Mark [in handwriting]

The budget kept climbing. On June 28 Bob Anderson, the L.A. production manager, sent a memo to Penelope Foster, notifying her that "the special effects on process, subway and McCoy house have become bigger than life." This brought the week's total "overages" to $44,600.

Anderson and Caruso tried to clamp down. They issued memo after memo about the necessity of getting approval for petty cash and all purchases and rentals of equipment and props. Caruso felt a special need to bring things under control. De Palma had turned down his request for a more significant producing credit. He didn't feel that Caruso had protected him from the executives the way a producer would have, nor did he rely on him for artistic advice. He appreciated Caruso for what he was, and that was a line producer, the one who supervised the production once the creative decisions were made.

Caruso had taken the rejection in stride. It hadn't come as a surprise. He had been hired as line producer, and it would have been uncharacteristic of De Palma to change his status. After years of working with the director, Caruso had come to expect neither bile nor generosity from De Palma. His real concern now was to try to undo some of the damage that had been done to his relationship with Warner Bros. — and that meant reining in the budget.

The crew started complaining that the pinch-penny atmosphere made them feel as though the studio thought they were all liars.

Warner wanted a big-budget picture, then they complained about every nickel spent.

"They have taken on the Disney mentality," complained Gary Jones, the costumer. "They treat people terribly. When we started I did a breakdown on the film with Ann. Fred asked, what did I think it was going to cost. I said, $400,000. He said that can't be. Warner has said I can give you only $250,000. I said at the very least it'll be $300,000. At some point it worked its way back up to $400,000."

Jones was particularly upset because he and Roth had a good track record. They'd finished their last picture for Warner Bros. $35,000 under budget.

"I had no interest in lying," he said. "We told them what it would cost and they didn't want to hear it. They've treated us like second-class citizens from day one. Like stupid second-class citizens."

At the same time there was a general complaint about the way Warner Bros. kept re-evaluating individual contracts. Nearly every member of the crew had had a dispute over salary with Warner Bros. People learned after they started work that their deal memos had been changed, usually to specify a lower salary base. The studio assured the various crafts people that the difference could be made up in overtime.

Nancy Hopton was appalled. "They want you to put in all this fake overtime. But we're putting in so much overtime already you can't put in fake overtime. They want me to pretend that I'm only being paid what I got paid four years ago so they can say to people they hire in the future, '*We* only pay this.' "

The crew came to expect problems with their checks almost every week. For Chris Soldo, the first assistant director, the money disputes added up to about two thousand dollars over the course of the shoot. "They don't care if an electrician or an assistant director or a prop man gets upset. They can't afford for Melanie Griffith or Bruce Willis to get upset," Soldo said. "I know at this studio every time I get a check it's wrong. It's such a little amount of money on the one hand. But it would pay a lot of bills. I find the whole thing very distracting."

* * *

Money had lost its meaning in Hollywood. Hyperinflation had given the movie industry the ephemeral feel of the Argentinian economy. A script sold for $3 million in June 1990, a sum that would have been unimaginable a year earlier. Powerful agents were making salaries of more than $1 million a year, and top studio executives had become multimillionaires. Terry Semel and Bob Daly each earned $50 million on the Time-Warner merger; Disney chairman Michael Eisner took home $40 million in 1989.

Money didn't seem to mean anything, and yet it meant everything, and the executives weren't quite sure what to do. They felt they couldn't scrimp on stars and scripts, so they cut where they could.

Hollywood had always been seen as the land of opportunity. Its founding fathers were Jewish entrepreneurs, mostly immigrants, who saw in the movies a way to build fortunes in a new world where they could create the rules of respectability. Back East these rag peddlers from Eastern Europe would never be accepted either by the Wasp establishment or by the German Jewish elite. Hollywood, however, was virgin turf for a new class system. They built an industry that captured the country's dreams and transformed them into a powerful collective fantasy. Having been excluded from the traditional corridors of power, the moguls built their own world and made themselves its rulers. The most beautiful, fantastic people had to kowtow to them.

By 1990, however, a new breed had invaded. These new entrepreneurs were refugees not from Russia but from Wall Street. They were the young M.B.A.'s and lawyers who had come of age during the eighties, men and women who had never built or run a company but who thought nothing of buying and selling them — before they were thirty. They were variants of Michael Milken — and Sherman McCoy — people who didn't concern themselves much with what the companies they traded did. It didn't matter whether they made food or furniture, or if the food or the furniture was any good. The companies were merely components. The thing that mattered was the deal. Deals had become the source of hunger and satisfaction for the Wall Street hotshots. These kiddie warriors put companies together and took them apart like Tinkertoys.

By the end of the eighties it was over. Milken was facing criminal charges, and Donald Trump was in financial difficulty. However, the young crop of M.B.A.'s and lawyers found a fertile ground for their talents in Hollywood, which was booming. Hollywood was competing — quite successfully — with Wall Street for Ivy League graduates. What could be better for a well-educated man or woman with a good education and a bent for commerce? They could make a lot of money — an obscene amount of money — and convince themselves that they hadn't wasted time with those literature requirements.

The studios enlisted the M.B.A.'s for their marketing and research departments; the big agencies welcomed the former tradertrainees from Salomon Brothers and Goldman Sachs.

Though no one could pinpoint exactly when the insanity had begun, everyone agreed that Steven Spielberg and George Lucas were somehow responsible. When "Star Wars" and "E.T." broke the $100 million mark at the box office, studios became obsessed with the big score. A string of modest successes would no longer be satisfactory — not with the lure of the jackpot.

So studios started to pay more for "elements" that might assure huge numbers. Stars had always come with a big price tag, and, in recent years, so had star directors. But the studios still controlled the stories. They'd hire writers who came to them with ideas or drafts and pay them a modest development fee to write a finished script. Only a fraction of these deals resulted in movies. Writers could spend years in development hell, the Hollywood version of research and development. It was common for scriptwriters to earn a reasonable living working on scripts without ever once having one of those screenplays made into a movie.

But one day the agents — the dealmakers — figured out that every element could be sold as the thing — the possible thing that would turn into the next megahit. Why shouldn't writers cash in as well? Someone came up with the idea of the "spec" script, a completed screenplay offered to the studios at auction. Instead of paying a relatively modest sum to option a finished product, the studios could see what they were buying right from the start. But in return for this certainty, they paid dearly. In April 1990 the Geffen Film Company bought "The Last Boy Scout," by Shane Black, for

$1.75 million. Less than three months later, Carolco paid $3 million for "Basic Instinct," by Joe Eszterhas.

The trader mentality began to dominate big agencies like Creative Artists Agency and International Creative Management, and smaller ones like Bauer Benedek. Each deal was contingent on the next deal, and bidding wars became routine. A "flop" immediately became "yesterday's lunch."

Richard Sylbert was amused by the studio's constant nattering about money. In his mind, the entire point was excess. How could they re-create the world of the Master of the Universe if they scrimped? The production designer simply ignored the memos and kept working on his masterpiece, his tribute to excess: the six-thousand-square-foot Park Avenue penthouse apartment he was building on Stage 22. After the courtroom, this was the single most important set of the movie. Nine days of shooting were scheduled to take place there, covering thirty-two scenes.

From the outside, the McCoy apartment looked like a giant plywood hulk, looming up in the dim light of the cavernous sound stage. To reach the entrance required careful maneuvering around the ropes and cables needed for the sound and light equipment. But inside, the place gleamed. Sylbert had spent $350,000 stocking his make-believe palace — which had cost $500,000 to build — with the trappings required by Tom Wolfe. "It was the sort of apartment," wrote Wolfe, "the mere thought of which ignites flames of greed and covetousness under people all over New York and, for that matter, all over the world."

The walls were lacquered (four layers thick to achieve the right glow), the vases were Chinese, the chairs were Chippendale, the floors were parquet, and the couches were covered with flowery Mark Hampton prints. Sylbert had loaded chintz on chintz, detail on detail. An eighteenth-century Aubusson carpet covered the floor of the master bedroom. The library was stocked with the requisite George Stubbs hunt scene and leather-bound books. "Dogs and horses," said Sylbert. "They like dogs and horses better than their children."

The production designer had visited every antique shop in Los Angeles to find lamps, paintings, and bric-a-brac — all the little details that would make the place the perfect home for Sherman and Judy McCoy. He was proud of his work there, and happy to repeat the spiel he delivered to writers for the *New York Times* and *House and Garden*.

"Anglophilia," he said. "It's a recipe, like a cookbook. In the case of Wasps and Jews but not Continentals. A rich Persian wouldn't want to be English. French, maybe. But Wasps, especially the new crowd who have no claim to be English, they want to be Lord and Lady somebody. Almost everything in this place, every piece of furniture, is English," he said. "Good English."

Sylbert loved to lead his visitors up the curving staircase in the foyer, dropping names at every step. "Judy did their apartment, but she would have had Mark Hampton," he said, referring to the prominent interior designer. In the McCoy master bedroom he'd placed *the* book on design for the Park Avenue crowd: Chester Jones's *Colefax & Fowler Today*. Sylbert would nod at the book and give a knowing wink. "This whole thing is sort of a pleasant well-meaning takeoff on Colefax & Fowler. Their red is *the* red, their yellow is *the* yellow." He'd stare at the curtains and muse, dreamily. "The first time I saw these curtains was at Pauline Rothschild's apartment in London."

Sylbert enjoyed leading tours through this showcase, which both celebrated and mocked the Park Avenue strivers. "What I did was become one of those guys. Mark Hampton is my guy," he'd say in his gentle Brooklyn accent. "I became a cross between Hampton and Mrs. McCoy." He would make sure, before shooting began, that the appropriate vases were stocked with his favorite flower, the delicate phalenopsis orchid, purple in the study, white in the living room.

For the next week the movie fell into a lulling routine that dispelled the sense of urgency. Most of the time was taken with "process" shots. The actors climbed into limousines or subway cars set up in front of a movie screen and pretended to be riding along while previously filmed scenery was projected onto the screen behind them.

By July 10 the temperature had dropped from unbearable to merely hot, rarely dipping below the ninety-degree-mark in the daytime. Even though the picture wouldn't be finished until the end of the month, people were already starting to look ahead. Bruce Willis was gone, off to Europe to begin shooting his next picture, "Hudson Hawk."

But Griffith and Hanks were still at work, pawing at one another, again and again, in Maria's apartment, the little New York flat — with fireplace — that had been built on Stage 23. To make sure that Griffith's eyeline would be clear, the set was closed. Griffith and Hanks would occasionally emerge from the plywood enclosure, tugging at their clothes.

During these scenes Aimee Morris was barred from her usual spot next to De Palma because her presence wasn't absolutely necessary. She sat on the floor outside the set reading the novel *White Palace* and wondering what she was going to do next. She had no connections out here in Los Angeles, and De Palma seemed to have completely lost interest in her career. There hadn't been any film classes since they'd arrived in Los Angeles. He was on the set until 7:00 or 8:00 P.M. every night and at dailies for forty-five minutes or an hour after that. Then he slipped into his blue Mercedes and was gone.

Chris Soldo, the first assistant director, was bored as well. Two actors repeating the same dialogue over and over didn't require his attention. This wasn't like orchestrating the movement of 150 actors playing reporters in the Bronx, or a couple of hundred extras at the museum. He was astounded at De Palma's ability to concentrate. Soldo found the repetition positively numbing.

Everyone was starting to prepare to move on to the next thing. Monica Goldstein had become engaged to a man she had been dating for five years, and she and her fiancé were talking to producers, to agents, to writers, trying to find a script they could help turn into a movie. She still hadn't asked De Palma whether he would give her associate producer credit. The right moment to broach the subject never seemed to arrive.

Fred Caruso mostly felt relieved that the two days scheduled for the scenes in Maria's apartment were actually going to take two days. He was praying that they'd sail through the next two or three weeks without a major mishap. He would be "exclusive" to "Bonfire" until the crew was off the payroll and all the call sheets and camera reports were in order. Though he could take another job after that, his final payment wouldn't come through until after postproduction, when the assembled movie was delivered to the studio.

Meanwhile, he was working the phone, keeping up with old contacts and making new ones, reading scripts, and even thinking about writing one.

But even as everyone else working on the film was thinking about moving on, Peggy Siegal, the P.R. woman, continued to try to insinuate herself into the picture. She inundated De Palma and Rob Harris, the unit publicist, with suggestions and pitches. Her latest: Italian *Vogue* wanted to put De Palma on the cover wearing his own clothes.

De Palma continued to ignore her calls and faxes.

Shooting had begun on the jungle scene, the scene Uma Thurman had read for her audition. Sherman and Maria have just returned to Maria's little apartment in Manhattan after the incident in the Bronx. Sherman is still shaken by his suspicion that they hit a boy with his car. Maria finds the whole thing sexually exciting and seduces her lover.

Griffith was finding the sex scenes surprisingly difficult. It wasn't Hanks; she liked him well enough. But something was different for her: sex was different. She wasn't a single, sexy, flamboyant young woman anymore. She couldn't be the sassy free spirit she'd been in "Body Double" or in "Something Wild." She wasn't twenty-seven. She wasn't even twenty-nine. She was thirty-three years old and married. She'd given birth to two children and was mother to three.

In the past she'd barely hesitated before diving into the naughtiest part. But she was finding it traumatic to play Maria. No one knew the torment she went through every night before she was going to shoot one of these scenes. No one knew, she thought. No one knew except her and — maybe — De Palma. But as Griffith opened her blouse and murmured for the ninth time, "Don't think, Sherman. Don't think. Just fuck," De Palma had other things on his mind, and he was having trouble concentrating on whether Griffith was throwing her head back just right and whether

Hanks's face carried the right mixture of distress and lust.

What De Palma kept thinking about — or trying not to think about — was next week's meeting with Terry Semel, the executive who was second in command at Warner Bros.

After De Palma's stormy session with Fisher and the ensuing memos from Canton, their boss, Terry Semel, had decided to impress upon the director how important it was to contain costs. For the first time since shooting had begun, Semel would have a face-to-face meeting with the director. Cristofer was being flown in from New York, not only for the meeting but also for final adjustments in the script. Now, on the sixty-third day of production, with the budget moving toward $50 million, the chief operating officer of Warner Bros. had decided to make it clear that the studio wasn't a patsy. The company wasn't going to spend $75,000 on a scene that wasn't *necessary*.

As De Palma thought anxiously about the meeting with Semel, Griffith kept bungling her lines. She would be off the picture in two days, and De Palma knew it was going to be a very long two days. As her scenes had become more and more intensely sexual, she had become more and more frantic. He wasn't oblivious to the problem. "Here's this bright, sensitive woman who always ends up in movies with her clothes off, saying, 'Fuck me,' " he said later. "It's that old problem. She wants to be treated as more than that, but then when she sees she is treated like a sex object she goes with it."

His job with Griffith was to clear the way and to wait, and even then he could never tell exactly what was going to happen. With Hanks, he'd know. He could discuss the scene, Hanks would tell him what he was going to do, and then he'd do it. Griffith couldn't calculate what she was going to do. She didn't have a handle on it herself. It was nerve-racking, sitting and waiting for something to spark.

Eric Schwab was in an exciting kind of limbo. He didn't have much to do except be on hand if there were questions about the footage he'd filmed for the process shots. So he had plenty of time to think about his career, which seemed to have been set in motion by the Concorde shot. After his meeting with Fisher, he got a call from one of the younger production people at Warner. Schwab met with him and was introduced to some of the other people in the development department. The same people who didn't want to hear from him when he and Kuwahara had been peddling "Chasing the Dragon" a year ago were now telling him they had scripts they wanted him to read, that they were enthusiastic about working with first-time directors. A month earlier he'd been thinking about how he might try to raise money independently to make a movie, and now one of Fisher's lieutenants was asking to read his script. The development man told Schwab he'd spent some time in Thailand and asked to read "Chasing the Dragon." Schwab had sent the script right away. Now Schwab was doing what most aspiring directors, actors, and writers did every day in Hollywood: he was waiting for a phone call.

Meanwhile, De Palma kept finding directing chores for Schwab. He needed a close-up shot of Maria packing up the painting on the wall of her lover's hideaway. The painting, the work of her new lover, the man she'd stolen from Caroline Heftshank, is a nude with Maria's face. In an earlier scene, the nude had Caroline's face. Schwab was to direct the portfolio cover flopping over the painting.

Schwab looked sheepish as he rehearsed the prop man who had to shut the portfolio holding the painting. Everyone went about their business with a bit of a giggle. Zsigmond measured the distance from the painting to the light; Nancy Hopton squatted, holding her note pad on her lap. The rest of the crew had evacuated the sound stage.

"On the bell," said Chris Soldo in a teasing tone.

Schwab gave his instructions to the prop man in a deadpan monotone. "Okay, you want to shut it."

Soldo snorted. "Okay guys, listen up. Before we shoot the painting I'd like the eyeline clear."

Zsigmond laughed. "This is my favorite shot," he said. "Love it."

Schwab's hazing continued through Griffith's last day on the picture, July 12. The actress was heading off to the south of France for a family vacation. She and Hanks had spent the previous day sitting in a silver Mercedes-Benz parked in front of a movie screen. As the footage Schwab had shot from the Bronx was projected onto the screen, Hanks and Griffith, Sherman and Maria, are trying to find their way back to Manhattan. Two grips gently rocked the car to simulate motion. The atmosphere was relatively relaxed on Stage 21.

The only thing left for Griffith to do, on her last day of work, was to step on the gas from the passenger side of the car. The only part of her that would appear on camera would be her leg. In preparation, her legs had been waxed the day before in one of the make-up campers parked outside.

For the first time in a while, De Palma was smiling that morning. He called Schwab over and told him that it was time he learned how to direct actors. He would shoot Griffith's foot pressing down on the accelerator.

Schwab started to laugh. He'd grown up in a prankster household and knew when he was being razzed. De Palma put his hand on Schwab's shoulder. "Remember, Eric, you have to stroke actresses," he said with a grin.

While Griffith visited the make-up trailer so one of the stylists could teach her how to put together casual hairdos while she was on vacation, De Palma enlisted Schwab to help with Hanks's part of the scene. Hanks sat in the Mercedes with the camera pointed at his face. De Palma watched footage of the passing scenery on one video monitor, while Schwab kept an eye on Hanks's face on the other. De Palma told Hanks what was going on outside the car and at the appropriate moment Schwab said, "Tom." That was Hanks's cue to react with a shocked expression.

After capturing Hanks's reaction on film, they were ready for Griffith. De Palma snickered to Soldo, "I want to watch Eric handle Melanie." Schwab remained by the video monitor, feeling like an apprentice once again.

Griffith slipped into the sound stage and stood by a little awkwardly as the shot was prepared. She wasn't wearing make-up, and her hair was limp. She caught De Palma's eye and walked over to hug him. She whispered something into one of his ears, turned his head, and whispered into the other.

"Thank you," he said.

Griffith slid into the Mercedes, and Schwab said stiffly, "Okay, Melanie, you can do it now."

Nothing happened.

Chris Soldo walked over to Schwab and whispered, "Say 'action.' "

Schwab flinched. "Action," he said.

Griffith's foot slammed down on the gas pedal, and the grips pressed hard on the Mercedes's trunk to make the car appear to be lurching ahead.

Finally, when the foot and the lurch were properly synchronized, Griffith got out of the car. She nodded politely at Schwab and hugged De Palma again.

As she leaned against him he rubbed her backside. "It's been a pleasure working with you, Melanie," he said in a light tone.

Griffith pulled back and stared at him. "I can't tell if you mean it," she said.

Hanks joined the group, and Soldo announced the conclusion of Griffith's role. "Ladies, gentlemen. Finished in the movie. Melanie Griffith."

Griffith looked around a little uncertainly. Only a bare-bones crew was on hand for this simple scene, and most of them were milling around, eating and talking. There was a smattering of applause. Griffith grabbed Hanks and hugged him tightly. "Goodbye," she said, and disappeared out the side door.

The week of July 16 would be devoted to scenes set inside the McCoy apartment. The apartment's grandeur was diminished considerably once it was packed with lights, cameras, and electrical equipment. There was something eerie about that large plywood structure sitting in the middle of Stage 22, pulsing with the muffled sounds of bodies and machinery moving in a space that now seemed cramped. Yet there was an undeniable Hollywood magic to it all: a plywood box on one side, Park Avenue splendor on the other.

On July 17, however, De Palma's minions were far more aware of the drama that was about to take place outside the sound stage. At 3:00 P.M. the director was scheduled to meet with Lucy Fisher and her boss, Terry Semel. The opera fight had escalated to the upper reaches of the studio hierarchy. Semel would decide.

De Palma had arranged the day's shooting schedule so that the lights would be reset between 3:00 and 4:00 P.M., so the crew wouldn't be put on hold while he met with the executives. The entire crew seemed aware of the meeting and its importance, even though only a few people on the set actually knew what the meeting was about. As the hour approached, the sense of urgency in the air intensified.

The p.a.'s out by the front door of the sound stage were standing by with walkie-talkies, on alert to notify Aimee Morris that the executives were approaching. Morris had her walkie-talkie attached to her belt and kept checking to make sure it was on. For the first time since New York, the group snapped with military precision. The executive visit was being viewed with trepidation, like a diplomatic mission from a country with which the nation had an uneasy alliance — or like a parental incursion into the secret clubhouse.

At 2:30 De Palma called Morris into his trailer. She found him emptying ashtrays. "Let's clean this place up," he told her. She helped him straighten up the trailer, then radioed the second assistant director, who was inside Stage 22 at the McCoy apartment.

"Michael Cristofer around?" she asked. Cristofer had been scheduled to fly in from New York for the meeting, and then to rewrite the script if adjustments were needed. Hanks was on standby as well, to offer his opinion if the executives wanted to hear it. Cristofer had become important to De Palma, both as a sounding board and as a connection with the studio.

The writer had just arrived on the sound stage. He stood in the foyer of the McCoy living quarters and stared at the winding staircase in awe. "Man," he whistled. "Maybe Dick could do my apartment!"

Morris strolled into the apartment at 3:00 P.M. holding her walkie-talkie. "Hi, Michael," she said. "The meeting's been moved to 3:30. Brian wants you to see some footage before the meeting. There's a car outside."

De Palma remained in his trailer while Cristofer was whisked off to the screening room across the lot. Morris stood guard outside.

At 3:30 her walkie-talkie crackled. A production assistant from the office notified Morris that Terry Semel hadn't returned from wherever he'd been. Morris relayed the message to De Palma, who was furious. They'd been putting him under all this pressure to make sure they didn't go further over schedule and now they were *late.* He stewed for fifteen more minutes before he opened the trailer door and asked Morris to find out if there was an update on the executives' whereabouts. She radioed back to the office and was told that no one knew where they were.

De Palma bounded out of the trailer and walked quickly back into the sound stage. He told Soldo to call the actors for rehearsal. Ten minutes later the walkie-talkies were activated again. The message passed from one assistant to the other: the executives were on their way. They'd left the executive building and were headed across the lot on foot.

De Palma left the set and joined Cristofer in his trailer. A few minutes later Lucy Fisher, now noticeably pregnant, turned the corner at the far side of Stage 22. She was accompanied by Terry Semel, a small man with black hair, slicked back. They walked quickly to De Palma's trailer, knocked, and were ushered in by the director.

The tone of the meeting was cordial. Fisher and Semel complimented their writer and director on the film's progress, as they went over the scenes that still needed to be filmed. They praised the dailies and reiterated their high hopes for the picture. Semel explained why he felt the golden crumbs speech was necessary, to give the audience a sense of the difference between Sherman and his father.

Nearly an hour into the meeting, De Palma and Cristofer offered the reasoning behind the opera scene. They explained how important it was to indicate Sherman's frame of mind when he encounters the fire-and-brimstone rantings of Aubrey Buffing at the party. De Palma assured the executives that a simplified version of the scene could be shot on a sound stage and wouldn't cost more than $75,000.

Semel smiled at De Palma. He told the director to go ahead — if he would guarantee the scene wouldn't cost more than $75,000. The Warner Bros. president and chief operating officer had discussed his interpretation of "guarantee" with Lucy Fisher before the meeting. If De Palma cared so much about the scene, he should put it in. But they were willing to pay only so much for it, and they were willing to let the $75,000 estimate be the amount. They merely wanted De Palma to demonstrate to them that the shot was *meaningful* to him. They wanted to make it *personal* to him. Those were the words they used among themselves. *Meaningful. Personal.* For the most part the money wasn't personal to De Palma. He didn't have to spend the extra millions out of his pocket. They agreed that the reasonable thing, from their point of view, was to let De Palma shoot the scene at the cost he promised. They would pay $75,000 and not a penny more.

De Palma sat listening politely across the small kitchen table in his trailer. That word — *guarantee* — seemed to hover in the air in front of him. It hadn't yet sunk in what, exactly, Semel meant by *guarantee*, even as the smiling executive amicably explained. De Palma's answering smile was frozen as he listened to Semel saying that since he, De Palma, cared so much about the scene, of course he wouldn't mind paying for any excess cost. Surely, he thought, Semel was joking.

With smiles locked in place, everyone shook hands and the executives left the trailer, happy to be working with such a reasonable man. Fisher was in a fine mood when she called Marty Bauer afterward. She told him how well the meeting had gone and that Semel would be sending over a letter for De Palma to sign, confirming that the director would pick up any overages on the opera scene.

A few minutes later Bauer got a call from De Palma. "This is a cheap shot," he yelled. "It's not going to work. They don't give a damn about the people who work for them. Do they think we can be bought and sold? I thought they were joking. I'm not going on the line for overages. I'm not an investor in this movie. I'm not going to accept those terms. I'm going to tell them I'm not going to sign any piece of paper. It's absurd."

He couldn't calm himself. "How much did it cost when they're an hour late for a meeting? I had a crew sitting around for an hour because of them. And they didn't even explain why they were late for the meeting."

He was tempted not to show up the next day. Let them pay a crew to sit around and wait for *him*. But he knew he wouldn't be able to do it. He would force himself to behave like a professional. Executives came and went, in this industry, he reminded himself, but he was always there.

To soften the insult, Fred Caruso assured De Palma that the scene could easily be shot for $75,000. He was surprised but not shocked at the executives' request. It wasn't common practice, to be sure, but it did happen when a movie was over budget. He was sorry that De Palma had to take the punch on this one. That was usually his job: to take the jabs from the studio and then soften the blow for De Palma. He couldn't imagine the executives actually hitting De Palma up for $5,000 if the shot went over budget. On the other hand, these were among the worst relations he'd ever experienced between a production company and a movie studio, especially as the executives claimed they loved the footage. They loved the footage, but they didn't love the price. He could only hope that the success of the movie would make everyone forget about all of this.

Marty Bauer responded to De Palma's phone call by arranging a meeting between his client and Fisher the next day. As he did in every conversation with the executive, Bauer opened by saying, "Lucy, I know it's been really hard for you on this movie . . ."

Fisher interrupted him this time. "Marty, please stop patronizing me," she said. "I can't take it anymore. Brian and I have our ups and our downs. I've been on worse. Remember, I worked at Zoetrope." Zoetrope was the studio Francis Ford Coppola built in the seventies to free himself of Hollywood control; within a few years, he had to file for Chapter 11 protection from creditors.

Bauer relayed a message from De Palma to Fisher: the director would not sign any guarantee. She agreed to meet again with De Palma the next day to resolve the matter of keeping the opera scene within budget. The meeting was set for 6:00 P.M. in De Palma's trailer, outside Stage 22.

At 5:45 on July 18 Lucy Fisher walked out of the executive building to get into her car. Though the sound stage was within walking distance, it was hot and Fisher planned to go home directly from the meeting. As she drove alongside the sound stages toward Stage 22, she decided to return a phone call to someone she'd been trying to reach all day. She didn't expect him to be there, but figured she'd leave one last message.

To her surprise, her call was answered. As she talked on the car phone, she parked her blue BMW next to Stage 22 but kept the motor running so the air conditioning could function. She was so engrossed in conversation that she didn't notice the time until she heard someone pounding on the door. Fred Caruso stood outside, pointing at his watch. It was 6:10. She signaled that she'd be there shortly and tried to wind up her call.

A few minutes later, there was another loud knock on the BMW door. This time it was Marty Bauer.

Bauer had arrived on the lot at 4:30, where he was greeted by Caruso. "I'm here to figure out the shape of the trailer," Bauer had joked. He'd wandered around the sound stage, which was being set up for yet another shot in the McCoy apartment, while De Palma went to watch dailies during a break in filming. Bauer was enjoying the backstage glamour and nodded when Kim Cattrall wandered by, looking pale and lovely in her elegant gown. At 5:45, just as Fisher was leaving the executive building, De Palma returned and invited Bauer to join him in the trailer while they waited for the Warner Bros. executive. When Bauer saw how tense Fisher's tardiness was making De Palma, he decided to go out to her car.

Aimee Morris and Chris Soldo were camped across the road from De Palma's trailer, trying not to burst out laughing at the comedy they were watching, this unexpected break in the tedium. The second assistant director emerged from Stage 22. "Vilmos wants to know if he can go home and come back later," he said, grinning.

Five minutes later, at 6:20, Bauer escorted Fisher the fifty-foot distance from her car to De Palma's trailer. De Palma was waiting for her at the kitchen table.

Fisher told De Palma she could understand why he didn't want to sign a piece of paper on principle. But he had to understand something as well. "This movie still has four or five months to go and there'll be many things you're going to want from us on this movie," she told him. "All I want is your word of honor that you will stick to the budget on this scene. That will be the same to me as signing a piece of paper. If you shake my hand and look me in the eye and tell me that you understand it to the same degree as if you signed a piece of paper."

He smiled, and she stuck out her hand. But she warned him, "It'll be a good idea for you to stick to this."

He took her hand and looked her in the eye and told her he promised he would shoot the scene for $75,000.

Fisher emerged from the meeting with a smile on her face. She was even more pleased the next day when De Palma called to check whether her production people's estimates matched the numbers Caruso was giving him on the opera scene. Cause and effect, she thought.

For the next eight days De Palma concentrated on the complicated setups in the McCoy apartment, especially the party scene in which Sherman goes half mad and disperses his guests by shooting in the air with a shotgun. One day the crew moved out to Pasadena, where the golden crumbs scene was shot in the back yard of the large home that had been chosen to represent the Connecticut country house of Sherman McCoy's parents.

De Palma still wasn't sleeping well. His rest was disrupted by fears that were both precise — will this shot merge smoothly with that shot? — and global — will the movie succeed or fail?

On July 26, the night before the last day of shooting, De Palma was able to relax just a little. Three relatively easy scenes were scheduled for the last day, and then he planned to take a brief vacation with Beth Broderick before plunging into what he knew would be a frantic postproduction schedule. He indulged in a small celebration by dining at one of his favorite restaurants, the Ivy. The comfortable bustle and rustic decor were deceptive; this was a Hollywood power center. There was an *A* room and a nobodys' room, and one sensed that the seating plan was put together with the latest *Variety* on hand.

De Palma was clearly an *A* customer. He was ushered immediately to his table. Shortly after he was seated, Uma Thurman spotted him from the next table. In her sleek dress and elegantly blunt haircut, she looked older and more self-assured than she had when she'd auditioned to play Maria, just six months earlier. She slipped from her seat and came over to kiss De Palma and ask him how the movie was going. "Great," he said. "Fine." Thurman nodded and returned to her table. A former studio chief dropped by to pay homage, then an actor whose career was on the decline. They were followed by a number of other people whom De Palma didn't recognize but greeted warmly. They were agents or former studio heads or independent producers. It was difficult to concentrate on the well-prepared food. There were so many people to see and to consider seeing during this ritualistic homage to power that masqueraded as the dinner hour. De Palma didn't stop by anyone else's table.

De Palma loved the Ivy and its rituals — as well as the food — but claimed he used the restaurant as a base for his ongoing study of Hollywood anthropology. "It's a fascinating world to watch," he said. "A kind of Disneyland. Living in this value system makes you think like a deranged king. You start to be affected by what I think is a very unhealthy way of looking at what you do in terms of what is important and what is not important."

He looked around the faces glowing in the Ivy's warm light. "You get your aesthetic judgment swamped," he said. "But that's the nature of movies, which is art and commerce, only here the commerce is God. You look at these guys, they get eaten up by the business. One day I'm going to say, 'What am I doing this for?' Wrestling with these people trying to do something unusual and different, and they want something mediocre and stupid! You always know you'll lose your power base one day. You won't have the physical strength to keep on top of this game. One day I won't get that opera scene."

He paused to nod hello to someone whose name he couldn't remember, then continued. "You sit in New York and say, 'That's a piece of junk. Why do they make movies like that?' Then you come out here, and you can begin to understand how they can make movies like that. The fact is, people pay money to see them."

On July 27, the seventy-fifth and final day of filming for "The Bonfire of the Vanities," the weather was deceptively clear and cool in the morning as the crew reported for work. By noon, however, the temperature had risen into the nineties. A last-minute attack of nostalgia for the film had overtaken the crew, partly because in a few hours they'd all be facing unemployment once again.

The crew prankster, a tall grip who liked to pin clothes hangers to people's shirts, had big plans for the day. He had enlisted Chris Soldo and Aimee Morris to help him make a video about De Palma. Morris's assignment was to ask De Palma if he would participate, and to give him his line, which he wasn't to speak until the final wrap.

When De Palma walked onto the set that morning, everyone on the crew said, in unison, "Good morning, Brian."

He looked startled, then smiled. He saw the prankster in the corner and briefly wondered whether he could have fun doing this if he were that guy. No, he answered himself, and kept moving toward his chair.

All three scenes were to be filmed on Stage 23, on modest sets that had been rigged the day before. The day began with the conference room scene, in which Sherman and his colleagues speak to their boss, who's in England, by speakerphone. Sherman describes the multimillion-dollar risk he has confidently taken on behalf of the firm; his boss barely listens, distracted by the cricket match he's watching. After months of trying to find a space whose boldness would match Sherman's bravado, De Palma decided to save money by shooting the scene from above. The camera would circle above the Master of the Universe as he spoke to his disembodied employer. The dizzying effect would be accentuated by the rug they were standing on — Sylbert had designed the bright geometric patterns.

Next, they'd move to another corner of the sound stage for the controversial opera scene. Kim Cattrall, Tom Hanks, and two minor players would sit in the opera box and react to the imaginary *Don Giovanni* playing in front of them. At the moment Sherman realizes the parallel between Don Giovanni's fate and his, two grips would hold a large orange cloth and wave it in front of a giant light, thus casting a fiery hue onto Hanks's face.

Finally, they would film the opera itself. A tenor who'd never sung opera before had been cast as Don Giovanni. He and his fellow singers would play the scene showing Don Giovanni's descent into hell on the makeshift set that had been constructed at the far end of the sound stage. It consisted of a couple of fans, some lights and pieces of cloth, and two giant cell doors that would clang shut.

There was an uncharacteristic feeling of affability on the set as these modestly constructed scenes were filmed. Hanks stood with his fellow players on a rug spread on the concrete floor, and the camera spun above. On the monitor, the shot appeared bizarre, unsettling.

At 11:00 A.M. Peter Guber paid the visit he'd been talking about paying since filming began on April 13. The new chairman of Columbia Pictures arrived wearing faded jeans and moccasin loafers and a blue work shirt. Lynn Nesbit, Tom Wolfe's agent, held his arm. She was wearing a patterned knit dress, a pink sweater, and open-toed shoes. Her toenails were painted red.

Keeping a respectful distance from De Palma, they watched the crane move the camera lower, and they smiled when De Palma laughed. When the shot was completed, everyone converged by the carpet with handshakes and smiles. Nesbit asked Hanks if he'd met Tom Wolfe.

"No, no, I wouldn't know what to say except to fall over him," said the actor, with boyish politeness.

Nesbit tilted her head. "Oh, no, everyone's expecting this formidable person and he's really this very nice man."

Guber put his hand on De Palma's shoulder. "Brian! Who are you getting for that voice, Sherman's boss?"

Before De Palma could answer, Guber said, "Brian! This is the Master of the Universe talking up there. A voice without a body. He's Sherman's boss, this man! He's created this whole thing and now he's in England for an escape! This is Vesco in Costa Rica! This has to be the voice of the ultimate Master of the Universe! Get George C. Scott in for fifteen minutes, or Jason Robards!"

Guber was interrupted by the publicity photographer, who gathered the group together for a photograph, arm in arm: Nesbit, Guber, Hanks, De Palma, Zsigmond. Then, Nesbit and Guber were gone.

Guber was pleased with the suggestion he'd given De Palma about the voice in the conference room. "If I'd been with him, I'd have hit him over the head with a million different things." He sighed. "That's what producing a movie is *about*! It's giving somebody the chance to say, 'Look, look, look over here!' or 'Well, that's interesting,' or 'This is what's interesting.' It's saying, 'Stand back!' "

His brief visit to the set confirmed what he'd always known. "This picture has to operate between a nine and a ten. It can't operate at a seven and succeed. Straight comedies, or action, they can operate at five. But this one — nine! Probably closer to nine point five! To really work and really bring in the audience, it has to be unique in all its qualities. This is the film that will put the cap on the eighties."

He didn't really have a sense of the film yet. He'd never been invited to dailies, nor had he asked to be invited. He'd decided he didn't want to see any of the film until the première. Back in his office, which overlooked the Warner Bros. lot, he said, "I don't normally go to premières." Then he smiled broadly. "I never go to premières, but there's no way I'm going to miss this one."

Back on the set, filming had resumed. After take fourteen De Palma asked Zsigmond, "Anything else we can do with this turkey?"

Zsigmond chuckled. "Why don't we do a good one."

Everyone laughed, and De Palma said, "Let's do one more."

They did.

"Is it over?" Hanks asked De Palma.

De Palma shrugged.

"I guess the game is over," said Hanks. He shrugged and went off to change for his next, and final, scene.

In between setups De Palma sat in his trailer as usual. In just a few hours he would wrap his twentieth movie. He'd seen himself on film the other day at dailies; the camera had kept rolling after he'd already said "cut" and had walked out next to the actors.

He'd been amazed at what he'd seen. He still thought of himself as a kid. He still *thought* the way he'd always thought. He certainly didn't think of himself as a middle-aged person. When he saw himself up there on-screen, he thought, My God, that's . . . What's that *thing* up there? Who's that old guy? Is that me?

Seeing himself on film was always a shock because it was the only time he felt he really saw himself objectively. He hated what he saw. He hated to watch himself walk; he felt he walked at a tilt. He didn't even like the way his voice sounded — thin, gravelly.

This he saw with his own eyes. Otherwise, he had to gather how other people perceived him from what they said, and he knew what they said: He's distant. He's cold. That wasn't at all how he saw himself, but he knew there must be truth to the assessment. He'd heard it too many times.

He merely thought he was focused. He knew the minute he allowed himself to be distracted by even an ordinary pleasantry he could miss something. And that would be the worst thing that could happen.

"Once it's recorded on film, forget it," he said. "It's there. Locked. It's in celluloid forever. You are really writing in concrete that is hardening as you stroke. When it works, it's great. When you catch that moment, it's great. And if it's off the mark, it's there forever."

Tom Hanks had been associated with "Bonfire" longer than any other actor, so long that the picture was starting to feel like government work. Now it was about to end, almost entirely without ceremony. He always liked to say it was just a job, but he knew very well that it wasn't just another job as he gazed around Stage 25, this vast barn where he'd been pretending to be Sherman McCoy these past weeks.

After a brief break Hanks joined De Palma and Kim Cattrall and the actors playing the Bavardages, the McCoys' companions at the opera. De Palma gave the actors their instructions. He told the women to look caught up in the thrill of the opera and Hanks to look miserable as Sherman hears the chorus urging Don Giovanni to repent.

Seven takes later they had it, and for them, the actors, the picture was over. "Finished in the movie," said Soldo grandly, waving at the actors.

The crew yelled bravo and waved. Hanks kissed Cattrall's hand with a flourish.

All that was left was the opera itself. At 6:40 De Palma watched the singers performing the "Repent" aria from *Don Giovanni* on a makeshift set, and he burst out laughing. "This is worse than a high school play," he said.

The singer playing Don Giovanni, he was told, specialized in musical theater, not opera. He didn't speak Italian and was having difficulty deciphering the cue cards the grips held up for him.

So the filming of "The Bonfire of the Vanities" concluded with the director and his crew watching one of the worst renditions of *Don Giovanni* anyone could remember seeing, ever.

At 8:30 the lights came on. "Check the gate," called Soldo.

Zsigmond and De Palma patted each other on the back.

Then the prankster approached De Palma with a video camera. Monica Goldstein, who had come to watch the final moments, glanced apprehensively at Eric Schwab. He shrugged.

"Brian De Palma," said the grip. "We just finished shooting seventy-five days of 'Bonfire of the Vanities' at a cost of $40 million. What are you going to do now?"

The crew looked at De Palma, curious to see how he would react to this uncharacteristic intrusion into his privacy. It was well known that when "The Untouchables" wrapped in Chicago, De Palma left without saying a word to anyone.

De Palma stared at the grip, then grinned. "What was my line?" he asked.

Someone whispered in his ear. De Palma looked directly at the video camera and flashed a big smile. "I'm going to Disneyland," he said, and proceeded to shake the hand of every single person standing nearby.

PART IV

Post-production

Chapter 14

"THIS IS THE BEST MOVIE
WE EVER MADE"

On Monday morning, August 13, Cara Silverman, an earnest woman with short brown hair, an open, friendly face, and a fondness for baggy clothes, clipped a long strip of film onto a metal bar. This strip of film was added to a collection of similar strips hanging like drying laundry over a large metal container lined with canvas. The basket, called a trim bin, was the place where the editors saved "trims," or outtakes — pieces of film that weren't yet being used in the movie being edited but which might be used later. The assistant editors labeled each trim — and there would be hundreds — and recorded it in a log so that it would be readily available if the editors decided they needed it after all.

Silverman was assistant to David Ray, one of the two editors working on "The Bonfire of the Vanities" in New York. For months they'd been assembling the footage from the dailies into coherent scenes, using De Palma's storyboards and Hopton's notes for guidance. They worked in messy little rooms, hunched over splicing machines, cutting film and putting it back together again pretty much the way it had been done since motion pictures began.

The two editors, their assistants, and two apprentice editors had been working steadily on "Bonfire" since filming had begun in April. Now the pressure was really on. A test preview for a public audience was just a month away, on September 12, one day after the Warner executives were to see the film for the first time.

The editors and their assistants had been moving as fast as their methodical work would allow, preparing a "rough cut" for De Palma to see when he returned from his weeklong holiday in the Caribbean. The rough cut was a version without music and without refined sound, the equivalent of a final rough draft. Before De Palma left he had seen "assemblages" — individual scenes cut together — on the flatbed, the editing table, but he hadn't yet seen the movie as a whole on the screen. The film was already twelve minutes shorter than it had been when he'd seen the assemblages — two hours and thirty-three minutes long, still half an hour longer than the studio wanted.

The editors hadn't had much time themselves to stand back and look at the film as a whole. Normally, the director would look at a rough cut and discuss the problems with the editors, who would then re-edit the picture for the "director's cut." If the director liked that version, they would screen the film for the producer, make the changes he wanted, and then present the film to the studio. The studio's ideas would be incorporated in the film, and then it would be shown to a preview audience.

For "Bonfire," the director and the producer were the same person, thus eliminating the producer's cut. And a preview had been scheduled for the day after the studio screening, so yet another opportunity to refine the film before subjecting it to audience review was gone.

Because of the tight deadline, two editors had been hired for the project. One of them, David Ray, didn't like the way studios now rushed pictures through production: "When I started in the early seventies, you'd take three or four months to film, then a year to edit." Now, he said, for financial reasons having to do with the huge up-front investment studios made for each movie, the studios rushed the films out to bring in compensating revenue as soon as possible. "A lot of problem films can be saved, just given the time," he said on the day he and his coeditors were screening the film in rough cut for De Palma. "But we're not given the time to edit them. Very often you're not making the film better the way it should be, by rushing it out. You don't have the chance to live with a film, to let it evolve."

Throughout filming, the editors had been piecing the film together, scene by scene, worrying about how the various angles would cut together to compose an individual scene. They rarely discussed among themselves whether the entire film would be any good or not; they found themselves concentrating on the parts — the mast, the sails, the rudder — not on where the ship was going.

Besides the pressure of time, the editing of "Bonfire" had also been colored by the initially uneasy relations between the coeditors, David Ray and Bill Pankow.

Ray was an intense, slender British man with an acerbic sense of humor that seemed at odds with his soft voice and thoughtful manner. He held a master's degree from Columbia University's Graduate School of Journalism and had begun his career working for Fred Friendly, the journalistic pundit, as a broadcast lab supervisor. He had moved into film in 1972, working as an associate editor on films like "Network," "Equus," and "The Taking of Pelham 123." He'd worked with De Palma only once before, as the editor on "Scarface."

Bill Pankow, a solid man with a degree from the New York University Film School and a mischievous mustache twisted like a Hungarian hussar's, had worked on nearly every De Palma picture since "Dressed to Kill," either as associate editor or coeditor with Jerry Greenberg. He'd been the sole editor on "Casualties of War."

Originally De Palma had wanted Jerry Greenberg to work on the picture, but he had already signed on for "Awakenings," Penny Marshall's film version of the book by psychiatrist Oliver Sacks. Pankow, too, was busy, finishing a Paul Schrader picture called "The Comfort of Strangers." Greenberg recommended Ray, who had been his assistant on "Scarface," and De Palma hired him in October to start work in January. Then, to accommodate Melanie Griffith's schedule, the start date for "Bonfire" was delayed, squeezing the entire schedule. Although Ray hadn't asked for help, De Palma brought in Pankow — who'd finished with Schrader's film by then — as coeditor, to help meet the deadline. Though both men had worked in collaboration with other editors in the past, this was different. Both had worked with Jerry Greenberg, for example, and had willingly deferred to the more experienced editor. However, their experience was roughly commensurate; neither one assumed that the other, simply by virtue of experience, had a more compelling point of view.

The brainy Englishman and the down-to-earth New Yorker were quite different — as people and as editors. Pankow had learned his craft from De Palma and adhered to De Palma's rules of film grammar. For example, if the camera was looking at something through a particular character's eyes, De Palma liked that character's face to appear on-screen first, to let the audience know whose point of view they were seeing. He knew too that De Palma didn't like overlapping dialogue — having people speaking simultaneously — and he didn't like for a character to start speaking while on camera and to finish off camera.

Ray, however, had trained under a number of different directors and preferred a more varied approach. Though he knew De Palma liked his crane shots to run uninterrupted, he would occasionally cut into them. And he would include off-screen voices speaking at length if he thought it made a point. For example, in the golden crumbs speech, Ray felt the point of the scene wasn't really for Judy McCoy to explain bonds to the daughter but to humiliate Sherman in front of his parents. As Judy talked, he kept Sherman and his parents' faces on-screen, to show how Judy's words were affecting them. De Palma had him re-edit the scene, putting more of Judy and the little girl on-screen.

Ray and Pankow divided the scenes and edited them separately. Ray worked on the third floor of 1600 Broadway, the Times Square building where De Palma leased editing rooms, and Pankow worked on the ninth. Soon they began to notice that there was a distinct divergence of style. At some point, they tacitly agreed to adjust to one another: Pankow would occasionally break one of De Palma's rules of film grammar, and Ray tried to do so less often.

Ray had been disappointed when Pankow was hired. "Bonfire" was a big, prestigious film, certainly his biggest solo effort. He came to appreciate his partner, however, especially now, when they were feeling the crunch. Even before, it would have been difficult for Ray to accomplish the task without help. Ray's second child was born the first day of shooting, and shortly afterward he moved his family into a new apartment in New York. Without Pankow, he'd have been working every weekend and evening throughout the shoot — and he didn't know what he would have done at this point, because both of them were now editing every weekend and every night.

Editors learned early on that it wasn't good form to question the film they were working on while they were working on it. Ray Hubley, Bill Pankow's assistant — they'd met on "Dressed to Kill" eleven years earlier — remembered his first film, "The Wiz." Hubley had been so excited to be part of a film directed by Sidney Lumet. Then, the night before he started work, he saw the Broadway musical on which the film was based and thought, This is really dumb. But he admired Lumet as a director and thought the cast was talented, so he told himself that the movie would have to be better than the play. As filming progressed and the footage came in, though, the young apprentice began to have his doubts. When he expressed his concerns to other, more experienced editors, they'd equivocate. "Oh, it'll be fine," they said. Soon Hubley realized there was an ethic of blind faith, that it was necessary to believe in what you were working on or you wouldn't be able to concentrate on how to make it better.

Later, this idea was crystallized for him by Jerry Greenberg, De Palma's editor on "Dressed to Kill." "If it's terrible, you can make it bad. If it's bad, you can make it mediocre," Greenberg explained. "If it's mediocre you can make it good. If it's good you can make it very good."

Hubley hadn't liked Tom Wolfe's book and had doubts about Cristofer's script, and he suspected that it might be a struggle to make this film work. But he knew he could be wrong. He remembered that he had felt embarrassed to be working on "Dressed to Kill" — which turned out to be a hit — and when he had helped piece together "Kramer vs. Kramer" he was sure it would be a flop. Hubley knew what he liked, and he knew how to edit film, but he felt far more confident about picking racehorses than about picking hit movies.

"Bonfire" had been a problematic film from the start, to be sure, but it didn't feel like a debacle — and Hubley knew what real trouble felt like. He and Pankow had worked for a month on "Heaven's Gate," and even in their New York editing rooms they could smell the smoke on that one. He felt this film might be an embarrassment, but it could also be one of those movies that are so strange they're entertaining.

At 10:40 A.M. on Tuesday, August 13, De Palma arrived at the screening room on the second floor of 1600 Broadway. His face was a healthy pink, and he looked relaxed from a week of snorkeling and reading.

De Palma sat in the fifth row, with Ray a seat away on his right and Pankow a seat away on his left. Both editors held long yellow legal pads.

De Palma watched the film quietly, laughing here and there. His comments to the editors were cursory: "Cut to Mrs. Lamb when Reverend Bacon points. The introduction to the split screen isn't clear."

When it was over, he said, "Very good, guys. You did a great job. I'll meet you after lunch."

The meeting after lunch was held in Ray's editing room on the third floor. The room was cluttered with the boxes containing the sixteen reels of "The Bonfire of the Vanities," splicing machines, a leather couch, a table covered with papers, and dozens of Post-it notes dangling from shelves. But there was plenty of light, both from the fluorescent lights above and from the window on the south side. The adjacent building to the south had been knocked down as part of the Times Square renovation, and, temporarily, there was a spectacular downtown view.

Cara Silverman, Ray's assistant, pulled the curtains shut, and De Palma seated himself in front of the editing table. The two editors and their assistants sat nearby as they prepared to go through the film reel by reel. De Palma had them stop the film when he had a question or comment.

"Do we need 'Do you want to go wee-wee in the rain'?" was his first question, which he answered himself. "I don't think we need that."

As he stared at the film, he told Ray and Pankow that Dave Grusin, the composer, would be coming into town the following week and needed to see the film.

They discussed where they might need more narration and whether Kim Cattrall as well as Tom Hanks should be in a shot in which Judy says, on the telephone, "Sherman, if you want to speak to someone named Maria, why do you call me instead?"

At one point, when Sherman's boss says on the speaker phone that he is watching a cricket match at Tottenham Park, Ray said quietly, "Do you intend to keep this? Tottenham Park is a football stadium, not cricket."

"What?" said De Palma in mock horror. "Tom Wolfe is wrong?"

In his precise way, Ray repeated, "Tottenham Park is football."

De Palma laughed, and said in a friendly but sarcastic tone, "Thanks, David."

Some directors liked to engage in an extensive dialogue with their editors, analyzing the merits of a given scene's positioning and what it does or doesn't do to advance the film's story and themes. De Palma liked working with the editors and was relaxed in their company. Still, there wasn't much discussion. De Palma generally pieced the film together in his mind before he shot it. Most of De Palma's editing instructions came in the form of his tapping on the table and saying, "This should be longer" (*beat, beat, beat*), or, "This should be shorter" (*beat, beat, beat*).

He stopped at the scene in which Annie Lamb, mother of the hit-and-run victim, starts to realize just how much she can profit from her son's accident.

Ray asked, "How valuable is that whole thing?"

De Palma said, "Not essential to the story. Obviously we can take out the Annie Lamb thing. The first thing I'd like to do is dump Annie Lamb."

The "Annie Lamb thing" takes place in the hospital where Henry Lamb lies in a coma. The Reverend Bacon tells Mrs. Lamb she can sue the hospital for negligence and collect $10 million in damages. At that moment, Annie Lamb is transformed from a genuinely grieving mother to just another greedy opportunist. "I could use a few things," she says, then asks the lawyer to have his limousine pick her up in the morning. "I could do some shopping."

At 5:00 P.M. De Palma, Ray, and Pankow were halfway through the film, and De Palma was bleary. He watched Griffith saying something he couldn't understand, and he muttered, "Cut all this babbling out. Melanie babbling. It doesn't make any sense." He stood up. "That's it for today, guys."

* * *

At the end of August De Palma had to fly to Rome with Pankow to "loop" Willis, who was filming "Hudson Hawk," an adventure film. The actor also recorded the new narration Cristofer had written for "Bonfire." Beth Broderick had gone along with De Palma to Rome for a brief vacation. The vacation went well. The looping was disastrous. The Italian studio had antique equipment and Willis was exhausted. By the time he showed up for the looping session after working all day, his voice was weak. They'd have to rerecord much of his narration.

Meanwhile, De Palma was growing increasingly worried about the publicity campaign. He felt he couldn't get Rob Friedman to do anything. From the beginning he'd felt the Warner marketing man wasn't on top of things. For months De Palma had tried to shake him up. He'd asked him repeatedly to test the title and was still after him to put together sample trailers. Friedman's people had put together one trailer over the summer and it hadn't tested well. People who'd read the book thought the trailer was too frivolous.

De Palma knew he had a selling problem. How should "The Bonfire of the Vanities" be presented? As a satire? A drama? A comedy? He hadn't figured out the answer, but he knew it was crucial for deciding how to position the movie. He didn't have time to figure it out himself; he had a film to finish. But Rob Friedman's group wasn't coming up with anything, and he was worried. Friedman had been stalling, saying he couldn't do anything until he saw the film. De Palma felt as if it was the opera scene fight all over again, the studio's way of pressuring him to finish faster — as if he and everyone else weren't already working from morning until night. The instant De Palma sensed someone was trying to manipulate him he crawled into his shell, and Friedman struck him as manipulative through and through.

He would sit sipping cappuccino and replay his conversations with Friedman, taking both parts: the beleaguered filmmaker just trying to do his job, and the sluggish, arrogant studio executive De Palma liked to refer to in the plural, as "they."

"*Yesterday I said, 'Maybe we should have Bruce narrate the trailer to position the tone of the material.'*

" *'Great idea,' they said.*

"I said, 'I'm going to Rome to record his stuff. Let me know if there's additional material you need.'

" 'Great idea. What are you going to record?'

"I say, 'The voice-over material that's in the script.'

" 'Oh. Could you send it to us?'

"I said to Monica, 'Pull out the voice-over material and type it up and send it to them. Literally, we have to do it for them.' I've never seen anything like this. When I made 'Dressed to Kill' I saw fifty ad campaigns. Completely drawn, illustrated ad campaigns. Fifty!"

De Palma especially disliked Friedman's condescending attitude. He acted as though "Bonfire" were De Palma's first picture. Friedman was a public relations man, start to finish, De Palma felt, the kind of guy who always says everything's fine when nothing is fine. But there was no way around him.

Friedman was aware of De Palma's impatience, and he was getting tired of the filmmaker's insinuations that he wasn't doing his job. He thought he'd been doing his job. A picture of the three stars and a blurb had run in the "People" section of *Time* magazine, thanks to him, and that same picture was scheduled to appear on the cover of *People*'s fall preview issue on September 3.

What else could he do until he'd seen the film? He'd asked De Palma to see it over and over again, and De Palma refused to let him see it until the production executives had seen it.

Friedman simply didn't understand De Palma's reluctance. The marketing department at Warner *always* saw the film before the production people did. Not the whole department — just Friedman and his head of advertising. Yes, De Palma had a tough schedule to meet, but Friedman thought the director was unreasonable to hold things up just because the movie wasn't as tight as he'd like it to be before he let the marketing people see it. Friedman had told De Palma again and again that he could trust them to see the movie even before Lucy Fisher did. They weren't there to judge the movie, he told him, just to see what they could use to sell it.

"Every movie we ever see is the greatest movie we ever saw," Friedman said, explaining how it was his professional duty to lie about what he really thought about movies. "Because it's the only way we can have the filmmaker's trust that we don't go to our management and say, 'It's shitty, it's great, you got problems, it's too long, you gotta make it this and this.' We don't do that. The filmmakers have to have trust in us."

He knew, however, that De Palma didn't trust him, and that irritated him. He considered Spielberg a friend and couldn't understand why that friendship didn't seem to impress De Palma. The director had liked the trailer they'd tested; it was . . . *sassy* was the word Friedman liked to use. Satirical. His bosses — "our management," Friedman called them — weren't crazy about the tone, however, and they were vindicated by the market research, which showed that people were confused by the test trailer.

Like De Palma, Friedman wasn't sure how to position this film, though he was aware that his job was to figure it out. Was it funny? Serious? Controversial? He knew that this movie, more than any other, wasn't just playing to an audience. This movie was playing to the media. It had to play to the sophisticated reader, but it also had to play to Middle America. Friedman knew what his problem was. "To be commercially viable it has to work in Middle America, where they don't know about the book and they don't know about the excesses of the eighties personally," he said. "And yet the movie can work for them on a different level — on a satirical, humorous commercial film level." He certainly knew what the problem was. He just didn't know how to solve it.

One day in August, just after Saddam Hussein marched into Kuwait, Rob Friedman met with Mark Canton, executive vice president of Warner Bros. Worldwide Theatrical Production. Canton excused himself a few minutes into the meeting, which took place in his office, to take a phone call from Warner chairman Bob Daly; he used the telephone in the bathroom for privacy.

When he returned to the room, he accepted a cup of hot tea from an assistant and picked a tall pretzel stick from a cup on the coffee table by his comfortable couches. He told Friedman he'd been watching television that morning and was disgusted to see Saddam Hussein being interviewed.

"But then, Robbie," he said, "I saw the most amazing thing." Canton leaned forward on the couch and bounced with excitement, like an eager boy.

He told Friedman that Saddam displayed his British hostages to the TV interviewer and brought a little boy in front of the camera. " 'Aren't we giving you milk?' Saddam asked the little boy."

Canton leaned on his knees. "The little kid looked terrified and nodded yes. 'And aren't we giving you corn flakes?' Saddam asked him. And again, the kid nodded yes."

Friedman looked attentive, waiting to see where the story was going. Canton started to grin. "And then Saddam moves on to this next kid who's really tough looking. I mean, ferocious. This kid looks like Johnny Depp. And I see he's wearing . . . a Batman T-shirt."

He started to laugh and couldn't stop. "And I swear . . . to . . . God . . . that Saddam skipped over him because the kid was too tough. I don't want to exploit this . . ."

He and Friedman doubled over with laughter.

"I don't want to exploit this, we don't need the credit for having Batman on there . . . But you can imagine at that point I felt like calling *USA Today*, like calling everyone . . ."

Canton wiped his eyes. "What a world."

Friedman was now fully at ease with Canton's line of thinking. He sat back in the couch and grinned. "My job is never over," he said. "The Batman shirt was easy. The tough part was getting Saddam to go into Kuwait."

The editors had trimmed seven more minutes from "The Bonfire of the Vanities" by August 20, when Dave Grusin, the film's composer, arrived for the "spotting" session. After watching the film all the way through, Grusin would sit with De Palma and the editors in front of the flatbed — the editing table equipped with sound — and decide where music was needed, and what kind.

De Palma hadn't met Grusin yet. The composer specialized in light contemporary music influenced by jazz — a departure for De Palma, who almost always hired composers with operatic inclinations. Bernard Hermann, Hitchcock's composer of choice, had scored "Obsession," which turned out to be the composer's last film. In recent years, De Palma had mainly used the Italian composers Pino Donaggio and Ennio Morricone.

But the director felt the satirical tone he was aiming for in

"Bonfire" required something urban, jazzy, and Grusin specialized in commercial jazz. He'd scored nearly forty films and dozens of television shows, and won Grammys and an Oscar. His credits included film scores for "The Graduate," "Reds," and "Heaven Can Wait"; and the theme songs for the television series "Maude" and "St. Elsewhere," and the daytime soap opera "One Life to Live." He'd played piano for Andy Williams and arranged the music for the singer's television show. Dave Grusin wasn't just another composer; he was a favorite son of Hollywood, even though he lived in Connecticut.

De Palma appeared tense when he arrived for his meeting with Grusin at the Brill Building, 1619 Broadway, just across the street from the editing rooms. Built in 1934, the building was a product of machine age architecture, with a sleek facade of stainless steel and brick, with inlays of black and clear glass. Duke Ellington had once kept an office in the building, which had been refurbished not that long ago, and it was now occupied by various providers of film services. The building included sound editing rooms, screening rooms; the P.R. woman Peggy Siegal had an office there.

De Palma's healthy Caribbean glow had faded; he looked sallow. The weather was rainy and unseasonably cold. He was wearing green khaki fatigues beneath his raincoat. The screening for Grusin was scheduled for 2:00 P.M. in the fifth-floor screening room. This was a popular place to screen films for the New York critics. The plush dark green chairs were so comfortable the critics joked that one test of a movie was whether it could make them forget the temptation to curl up and fall asleep.

De Palma and Grusin shook hands and sat in the last row. Grusin was a pleasant-looking man, with a broad, square face, and a flat, mellow voice. He was wearing pleated black pants and a beige linen sport jacket over a short-sleeved dark-blue and black patterned shirt. When he was growing up in Littleton, Colorado, he'd thought of becoming a veterinarian. One could imagine a sick and frightened puppy relaxing in his gentle presence.

They were joined by the editors and by a small group of people from the sound department. David Ray, carrying his yellow pad, asked De Palma if he could sit next to him to take notes. De Palma nodded yes.

Before the picture began, De Palma said he already had some ideas for the music. "There are some places that are obvious. A long opening sequence with Bruce Willis and a sword-clobbering scene."

Grusin asked, "Do you have anything there?"

The director said he'd had the editors mix in music from other movies at certain spots in "Bonfire" to indicate the mood he wanted. "I have this straight Western stuff," De Palma said. "I have some 'Silverado' and 'The Natural' — triumphant stuff. It's pretty obvious. I need some more ironic stuff." Usually De Palma prepared an entire "temp track," a temporary score for the entire picture. For "Bonfire," however, there was no time.

As the film began De Palma seemed anxious. He repeatedly cracked the gum he was chewing quite loudly. As Grusin watched the film he occasionally clapped his hands and laughed. The editors watched silently; from time to time they wrote something on their pads. When the movie was over, De Palma told Ray that he and Grusin were going out for a cup of coffee and would meet the editors across the street in a half hour.

David Ray and Bill Pankow spent the time setting up the first reel of film on the flatbed. They agreed that the film still needed to be "tightened," though De Palma had told them he thought it played well now. The editors knew the music would make a difference, and they also knew how decisions about the music would be made. "All kinds of adjectives get thrown around," Ray said, laughing, "but it really comes down to the composer sitting at the piano."

Pankow sighed. "Usually by the time we put the music in we've seen the movie so many times it's easy to know where there are gaps, where music is needed. This time we don't have that luxury."

Grusin and De Palma returned at five o'clock. An assistant set up chairs for them by the flatbed and handed De Palma a cappuccino in a cup marked BRIAN. Pankow told Grusin they'd prepare a cassette of the film for him, and asked the composer if he'd like each scene measured by a digital counter so he'd know exactly where the music cues should start and stop. Composing for film added yet another layer of exactitude; each piece of music had to fit precisely, to the second.

"Cool," said Grusin. "Great." He pulled out a long note pad.

The editors began rolling the film across the flatbed. As they watched the scene where Sherman takes Marshall the dog out for a walk and drags the reluctant animal across the floor, Grusin laughed, as he had the first time he saw it.

"Now you'll get the animal rights people on you," he joked.

The editors laughed too. Their laughter seemed to prompt De Palma, who was concentrating on the images on the flatbed screen. When he realized Grusin had made a joke, the director laughed perfunctorily.

They continued watching the movie in silence, until the scene in which Sherman enters the bond trading room.

"Do you think we should have some triumphant music here, to show he's Master of the Universe?" De Palma suggested.

Grusin nodded, and asked one of the editors to "zero" the spot, to indicate on the film where the cue should go, designating where music should begin and where it should end.

As the reel came to the end, Cara Silverman, Ray's assistant, quickly stepped up with the next reel, and Ray slipped it onto the flatbed spool. De Palma and Grusin discussed where to insert music when Sherman and Maria get lost in the Bronx, and whether to give Maria a cue when she sees the tire or whether they should have music up to that point and then stop it.

For the scene in which Sherman and Maria return to Maria's apartment and congratulate themselves for their bravery in the Bronx, De Palma went with his operatic inclinations. "Let's do a mock Tristan and Isolde here."

Grusin seemed to like the idea. He laughed and wrote something on his legal pad.

De Palma seemed relaxed for the first time since they'd started the spotting session. "This is the love theme for Sherman and Maria," he said. "Forty-five minutes of Wagner."

As they went through the next few scenes, De Palma occasionally paused to praise the editors. When they reached the split screen sequence and watched the Reverend Bacon shake hands with Fallow and Corso, the TV journalist played by Geraldo Rivera, Grusin chuckled.

"So you got Geraldo to really be sleazy," he said.

Pankow laughed. "It was a stretch," he said.

"He worked hard at it," added De Palma.

As the reels were changed, Pankow flipped on the answering machine to see if there were any messages. A woman's shrill voice announced that she was Peggy Siegal and she was looking for De Palma. "Someone in my building saw him and I'm trying to track him down," she said.

Pankow asked De Palma if he wanted the number.

De Palma shook his head. "No, no, no, no, no, no, no."

Pankow laughed. "I think she pays the elevator guys to keep watch for you."

The rest of the session went quickly and smoothly. De Palma said he wanted "Rossini farce kind of stuff" for the scene in which Sherman wires himself to get a taped confession from Maria, and Grusin joked about De Palma's request for music to fade from the opera scene to the cocktail party scene.

"Is there anything from *Don Giovanni* that's nice and cocktailish?" De Palma asked.

"Oh, yeah," said Grusin with a smile. "The cocktail party scene from *Don Giovanni*."

For the scene at Arthur Ruskin's funeral, De Palma told Grusin they'd wanted to play "If I Were a Rich Man" but couldn't get the rights from the *Fiddler on the Roof* people. For the scene where Sherman's father visits his son and offers his support, De Palma requested "el sobbo father-son music," and when Morgan Freeman appeared as the judge, preparing to deliver the decency speech, De Palma said, "What do you think? Should we cue him at all?" He giggled. "The integrity cue?"

Grusin shook his head. "If this were a conventional film I would do it. But with this one, I don't know."

They spent several minutes discussing how to score the final moments of the movie, which had four closing scenes: the judge giving the decency speech; Sherman pulling the judge in slow motion through the mob, waving the sword of justice at the crowd; Fallow back at the awards banquet, where the movie started; and the coda of Henry Lamb getting up from his hospital bed and walking unnoticed onto the street.

They discussed where the music should go and where THE END

should go, and Pankow suggested putting THE END in the scene when Lamb gets out of bed, to cover up the fact that he gets up without unhooking himself from the intravenous feeder.

"What!" shrieked De Palma.

"Henry Lamb is hooked up to an intravenous and then all of a sudden he gets up without unhooking it," said Pankow. "That isn't realistic."

De Palma rolled his eyes. "Please," he said. "You guys have been watching this movie too long."

He said they should put THE END just before Henry Lamb's eyes flicker, and Grusin said that's when he would put a music cue. It was 7:45 and they were done, two hours and forty-five minutes after they'd begun. Grusin said he'd start writing the music in a month or so. First he had to go to Los Angeles where he'd be scoring the Sidney Pollack picture "Havana," starting on September 15.

Grusin stood up and gathered his things. "That's the quickest spotting session I've ever done," he said. The editors escorted him to the door, and he turned and shook De Palma's hand. "I really liked the movie," he said. "It's really surprising. I'm in shock."

Having discussed the end of the movie with the composer and the editors, De Palma next turned his attention to the beginning. Before he'd left for the Caribbean he'd discussed the movie's very first opening shot with R/Greenberg Associates, a special effects group that created movie titles. The firm had designed the impressive opening credits for "The Untouchables," where ominous shadows form the letters for the name of the movie and its principal actors and creators. After canceling the original opening of "Bonfire", the "kaleidoscopic jewel box," De Palma asked Greenberg to come up with a graphics design that would capture the intent of Schwab's canceled shot, something that would immediately telegraph the sense of New York as a stronghold of power.

The designers at Greenberg drew up a storyboard that showed a panorama of New York, shot from daybreak to night by a special computerized motion-control camera that would collapse the passage of time. As night fell, the city's lights would start bouncing around and, through a special effect, seem to spin off the windows and start forming the words of the title: THE BONFIRE OF THE VANITIES.

De Palma liked the idea but wasn't impressed with the New York vista the special effects group came up with, a view from Rockefeller Center facing in the direction of the Empire State Building. He'd seen this clichéd angle on New York a thousand times, on every picture postcard.

He knew Eric Schwab was flying back to New York to finish a few second unit shots: an aerial view of downtown New York that would zoom in on Fallow's limousine as it entered the building just before the opening Steadicam shot; another aerial shot of Sherman's silver Mercedes driving across the Triborough Bridge; and an exterior view of Fallow's apartment building.

De Palma called Schwab and told him he had another assignment for him. He would direct the title shot for Greenberg, and he would be responsible for coming up with an interesting panorama of New York. This wasn't the "kaleidoscopic jewel box" — he wouldn't be able to splice fifty different angles together. He had to find one view — just one — that would say it all, and say it in a way it hadn't been said before on film.

Schwab flew back to New York over Labor Day weekend, just after De Palma had returned from Italy. They met at E.A.T. on the Upper East Side and drank cappuccino and mulled over the *spectacular* possibilities. They ruled out a helicopter shot — too tired — then discussed interesting building tops that could anchor the shot. De Palma thought Adolph A. Weinman's statue of Civic Fame — perched on the imposing Municipal Building, just north of City Hall Park — might work as a stand-in for a statue of justice.

Then the subject turned to gargoyles. "These people are gargoyles," De Palma said, referring to the characters in the movie. He wanted to find the best gargoyles in the city to serve as visual analogues. Schwab suggested the eagles jutting out from the Chrysler Building. He'd frequently admired the metal monsters from the vantage point of neighboring rooftops.

De Palma wanted to see what the Chrysler gargoyles looked like, so he and Schwab hopped into a cab and headed downtown to the Doubleday Bookstore on Fifth Avenue to find a photograph. They couldn't find one there, so they walked over to Rizzoli, where they found a picture of the gargoyles in a coffee-table photography book about New York. It was impossible to tell from the photo how the view would look on film, or whether they'd be able to set up cameras there. But one thing was certain: they were great gargoyles.

Schwab set to work on the assignment immediately. He had lost his location scout Bruce Frye, who'd been hired to work on "Godfather, Part III," so he was using a young man named Darren Wiseman, who'd scouted for the first unit in the spring. Schwab depended on Wiseman to arrange permission for them to climb to the tops of skyscrapers in order to find the views they needed for Schwab's shots. Wiseman, who usually knew how to slip someone twenty dollars when he needed access to a roof (and almost always had to borrow the twenty from Schwab), was an imaginative manipulator. He wrote his request in the form of a haiku to a Japanese bank, and as a plea for civic responsibility to another building owner, observing that the movie industry "brings literally billions of dollars each year into our economy."

While they waited for clearance from the Chrysler Building, Schwab and Wiseman made their way onto roofs all over town. As Wiseman watched Schwab snap pictures from one corner of the 245 Park Avenue roof, just up the block from the Pan Am Building, then run to the next corner and take some more pictures, he looked dismayed. "No matter what I show him, Eric is never happy," he said.

Schwab waved for Wiseman to join him. He pointed across Park Avenue at the ITT Building, which reflected the traffic from its mirrored exterior. "That's the title shot of 'North by Northwest' by Saul Bass," he said.

Wiseman rolled his eyes at Schwab's endless knowledge of film trivia.

With the budget pressure on, Warner Bros. had refused to pay for a rental car, so Schwab and Wiseman "roughed it." Sometimes they rode on subways and buses, but usually they got around in taxis. The line producer, Fred Caruso, had booked into a slightly cheaper luxury hotel, the Parker Meridien, instead of the Regency.

Schwab was glad to be back at work. After the film wrapped, he'd flown to Thailand and gone elephant trekking with Lek for a week. He'd had plenty of time to think, spending hours every day sitting on top of an elephant's head, riding from village to village with Lek, a guide, and the Italian designer who completed their group. Just before Schwab had left, Marty Bauer's assistant, Missy Malkin — who had worked as a trader at Salomon Brothers in New York before she moved West, to the movie business — had been elevated to agent trainee. This brash young woman was impressed by Schwab and by De Palma's faith in him, and she was aware that his success would be hers as well. She'd been sending his reel all over town. The reel contained the footage he'd shot on "Casualties of War" and the "Bonfire" second unit, including the Concorde shot. He'd already met with development executives at Warner, Disney, and two independent production companies. He was learning something about himself that was both exciting and depressing. When he had to, he could sizzle. The salesman genes were intact.

On September 10 De Palma stopped by his Greenwich Village office before flying back to Los Angeles. Schwab and Wiseman, who were using the office as their base, were there, waiting for another clearance to come through. Schwab followed De Palma into one of the back rooms and started talking very fast.

"Slow down, Eric," De Palma said with a grin.

Schwab slowed down. He told De Palma that the civic fame statue on top of the Municipal Building was unusable; the entire building was hidden by scaffolding. But he and Wiseman had gotten in touch with Black Clawson Company, the manufacturer of paper-making equipment. Just outside the Black Clawson offices on the sixty-first floor of the Chrysler Building was a terrace leading to the gargoyles. The chairman seemed enthusiastic about letting them film there. In exchange, he told Wiseman in a letter, he wanted only a contribution to the Lenox Hill Neighborhood Association. He also asked for "six tickets in the last ten rows from the back of the orchestra section for opening night," but, he assured Wiseman, "this is secondary to the charitable contribution." If Greenberg liked the gargoyle angle, and if Schwab could work out a way to do the shot the way he imagined it, there was no doubt about it, he assured De Palma. It would be spectacular.

De Palma laughed. "Better than the Concorde?"

Schwab hesitated. "Yeah. Better than the Concorde."

De Palma stuck out his hand. "All right, Eric, I have a proposition for you. Let's make another bet. Double or nothing on the hundred dollars I owe you for the Concorde."

Schwab hadn't seen the film yet, but he knew the Concorde shot — or at least a fraction of it — had made it into the rough cut. He had no idea whether he'd be able to match the Concorde.

"Double or nothing," he said.

On the morning of Tuesday, September 11, De Palma's fiftieth birthday, the director and the editors screened "The Bonfire of the Vanities" for the Warner Bros. executives on the Burbank lot. Lucy Fisher, Mark Canton, Terry Semel, Bob Daly, Bruce Berman — all the top people were there. Mark Canton brought his wife.

The reaction was intensely enthusiastic. David Ray, who had shown many films to many executives, said he'd never been to a more upbeat screening. Words like *masterpiece* were liberally dispensed at the end. Bob Daly, who had a reputation for never liking any Warner Bros. film, told De Palma that he loved it. There were hugs and handshakes all around.

The executives left the room and began making telephone calls. Fisher telephoned the stars, then Ann Roth and Dick Sylbert to congratulate them. She called Fred Caruso, who was in New York. "Fred, now we see what you were trying to do," she said. "It was hell, but all is forgiven."

Canton called Caruso as well. "De Palma's a genius," he told the producer. "This is the best movie we've ever made, even though it was a nightmare."

Then the phone started ringing at Marty Bauer's office. Fisher checked in, even Canton's wife called to offer her congratulations. Bauer was relieved. They were *wigged out.* They *loved* it. He was excited when Mark Canton called. "This is the best movie I've been involved with in the history of my administration," Bauer heard Canton saying. "In my ten years at Warner Bros., 'Batman' was my big commercial hit and this will be my big artistic hit. This movie summed up the eighties." Then, he said it again, "It's a great movie, and I'm proud to be involved in it."

* * *

Two hours after the executive screening, De Palma showed the film to Rob Friedman and Steven Spielberg. In some ways Friedman felt vindicated by what he saw. Though he would later say that he "loved" the movie, privately he confessed there were things in it that he "loathed." He hated the ending showing Henry Lamb climbing out of his hospital bed, and he detested the scene, which De Palma had already cut, where Annie Lamb, Henry's mother, shows herself to be a greedy opportunist like the Reverend Bacon and his lawyer.

But Friedman's job wasn't to have an opinion that was contrary to that of his bosses and the production executives. When the movie was over he stood up and said to De Palma, "You son of a bitch. You made a good movie, and it's going to be impossible to market."

Spielberg's reaction to the film was complex. He hadn't read the book and had no particular feeling about what the movie should be. He hadn't seen any of the movie or read the script since the first draft De Palma had worked on with Cristofer. At that time he'd felt the script was thin, that there wasn't a third act.

His first reaction to the movie was excitement, especially as he watched the four-minute, twenty-one-second Steadicam shot. "It's better than the shot Orson Welles did in 'Touch of Evil,' " he said. "It's the best sustained master shot I've ever seen."

As the film progressed, however, he began to feel the way he'd felt when, at seventeen, he saw Stanley Kubrick's "Dr. Strangelove" for the first time. "Dr. Strangelove" was a comedy about nuclear war, and Spielberg hadn't known whether to laugh at the buffoonery or be frightened by the real threat that some lunatic in government might actually use the bomb. In the same way, he didn't know how to react to "Bonfire." "There were parts that were very offensive to me," he said. "I was drawn and quartered by how my guts were telling me to behave and how my head was telling me to think."

He hesitated. "Let me use the word *uncomfortable*, not *offensive*," he said. "There were parts that were uncomfortable to me. The first shot of the Reverend Bacon. It was an exaggerated wide-angle lens that exaggerated his size, the size of his pulpit. That was the right approach. But because he was black it made me uncomfortable, like something you shouldn't do. If he'd been a white minister I wouldn't have felt put on the spot that way."

He was sorry that De Palma had cut a scene that had originally been in the script, in which Sherman and Judy serve dog food to guests, pretending it's pâté, and everybody eats it and says it's delicious. He felt that this moment, showing the McCoys united as a couple, was the only time they'd seemed human.

Spielberg couldn't say any of this to De Palma at the time. That wasn't why he was there. De Palma wanted to know the basics. Was it too long? Was it too short? Where should he cut?

At the end of the movie Spielberg turned to De Palma. "You've got a good cast and it'll probably open [do good business its first weekend] and then you'll see what happens," he said. "This is going to be a replay of 'Scarface.' You'll go at it with George Will on 'Nightline.' This is going to be really controversial."

Before she and De Palma had left for Italy in August, Beth Broderick decided to throw a surprise party for his birthday. She knew it was risky. She saw the pressure he was under. His nightmares didn't come as frequently as they had during shooting, but he seemed distracted much of the time. She knew he'd be showing the film to the executives on his birthday and to the preview audience the next day.

Broderick, a sentimentalist hiding behind a tough exterior, didn't want this milestone, this fiftieth birthday, to get lost in De Palma's obsession with the movie. It struck her that as close as she felt to De Palma, she didn't truly know him. He talked to her about his desire for a family, to be married, and, especially, to have a child. Part of his strong attraction to Kathy Lingg had been her little daughter. He'd videotaped the child visiting Disneyland and opening Christmas presents. His movies revealed a sentimental streak, an idealization of family relations. The Ness family scenes in "The Untouchables," for example, were unabashedly syrupy; and in "Bonfire," Sherman's reconciliation with his father was nakedly emotional.

Before going ahead with the party, Broderick consulted with Jared Martin, De Palma's old college pal who'd been camped out in the director's guesthouse for months. Martin thought a small party for De Palma's closest friends would be fine. Martin knew De

Palma didn't mind surprises. His wedding to Nancy Allen was presented to their friends in the form of a surprise party — though in that case, of course, De Palma was giving the surprise, not receiving it.

Broderick booked the back room at Madeo, a comfortable Italian restaurant in West Hollywood, where she'd eaten several times with De Palma. It wasn't a flashy show business place, and though its prices weren't modest, they weren't horribly expensive — a relevant consideration, because Broderick and Martin, two out-of-work actors, were footing the bill. Deciding on the menu and decorations was easy for Broderick. She had helped organize benefits when she was running the AIDS program back in New York, and she liked planning the details of a party. Faced with this intimidating crowd, she decided to make it fun, a little corny. She and Martin planned to meet at the restaurant before the party began to cover the table with streamers, noisemakers, toy guns, and funny hats. The room the restaurant gave them was way in the back, past the restrooms and the telephones. De Palma would never suspect.

The difficult part, she knew, would be inviting De Palma's friends. There wasn't enough time to rely on the mail, so she'd have to call. She dreaded putting in the calls to Spielberg, to Dawn Steel, the former head of Columbia Pictures, to Marty Scorsese. She could already hear the assistants on the other end of the phone saying, "Beth who?" Then she'd have to explain who she was and pray that if she did get through, De Palma's friends would remember who she was.

It all went more smoothly than she'd expected, and by September 11 everything was ready. Scorsese couldn't come because he was finishing up his film "GoodFellas," nor could Tom Hanks and his wife, Rita Wilson — their baby had been born just a few weeks earlier and they weren't going out. Schwab was in New York working on the opening shot. But Spielberg canceled a trip to Florida to make the party, and Dawn Steel and Art Linson, who had produced "The Untouchables" and "Casualties of War," had said they wouldn't miss it.

The ruse was simple. She and Martin told De Palma they were going to meet Linson and his girlfriend for dinner at Madeo at

8:30. They told the guests to arrive at Madeo no later than eight o'clock, to make certain the surprise would work.

At 6:00 P.M. Broderick and Martin met at the restaurant and had the waiters move the tables to form a giant square, seating twelve. They hung streamers and laid out the party favors, and then Martin went to pick up De Palma, leaving Broderick to greet the guests. She'd brought a Polaroid camera to take photos of each guest arriving for a little album she wanted to give De Palma as a memento of the evening.

Most of the guests arrived almost exactly at eight: Dawn Steel and her husband; Marty Bauer and his wife; Art Linson and his girlfriend; and Bart De Palma, Brian's brother. The men wore slacks and jackets; the women all wore variations on the same ensemble — long, form-fitting jackets with huge shoulders, and short, tight skirts that revealed fiercely muscular legs.

The guests didn't seem to know how to react to the Polaroid flash that greeted them as they walked into the room. They stood awkwardly by the table and counted the places, and wondered who was missing.

Bauer stared at the green and purple crepe paper and at the hats and toy guns and muttered, "What's the theme?" Bart De Palma began chatting to Barbara Bauer about Australia; the conversation seemed to make her relax. Marty Bauer announced that he was in a bad mood. He'd flown in from Kentucky that morning, where he'd been looking at racehorses, and he was exhausted.

Dawn Steel looked at the pretty woman with the exaggerated dark eyes and throaty voice who'd greeted her at the door and asked somebody who she was. When she heard that was Beth Broderick, the woman De Palma was dating, Steel gave a short laugh. "Well, at least I don't have to make this one's film." When De Palma was making "Casualties of War" for Columbia, where Steel was then in charge, the studio had distributed but not financed the film directed by the woman De Palma was involved with at the time.

By 8:15 there were fewer guests than chairs, and it occurred to everyone that Steven Spielberg and Kate Capshaw hadn't arrived. Linson wandered out to the front of the restaurant — twice. "They're not there," he reported back each time. Michael Cristofer wasn't there either, but no one asked about him. Broderick felt flushed and took another glass of wine. Where was Spielberg? His secretary had called that afternoon to confirm. Though no one mentioned anyone by name, the waiting guests talked about the *rudeness* of arriving late to a surprise party.

At 8:29 the headwaiter arrived with a breathless Spielberg and Capshaw in tow. They were animated and talking fast. "We went to *Matteo* in Westwood," Spielberg said. "*Matteo*," echoed Capshaw, who looked pretty in her white pantsuit, and slightly rounder than the other women. She'd recently given birth to Spielberg's child.

"We got there and they tried to seat us —" said Capshaw.

"And we asked about a party and they didn't know —" said Spielberg.

"We didn't know what to do —" said Capshaw.

"I called the office, and they told me it was Matteo, and then someone said, 'Maybe it was Madeo,' and they called and that's what happened and we raced —" said Spielberg.

"And we thought we saw Brian out front," giggled Capshaw.

A moment later somebody said to be quiet, De Palma was on his way. Broderick positioned herself near the entry, next to the bar where a television set had been left on. She seemed fragile and awkward, feeling the weight of her duties as hostess and like an outsider among these long-time friends of De Palma's.

Martin escorted De Palma in. He quickly grasped what was going on, and gave a big smile for the Polaroid and hugged Broderick. Spielberg and Capshaw took their places at the table. To Broderick's relief, they put their hats on and began shooting the toy guns. The waiters were slow to bring the food, but the wine was plentiful, and soon the prickly tension that began the evening dissolved.

Spielberg told De Palma he'd brought a forty-year-old bottle of wine, and then explained why it wasn't fifty years old. "I looked all over for a 1940 bottle of wine and couldn't find one anywhere. Finally I was told that all the vineyards in Europe were bombed that year," he said. "The war."

De Palma laughed. He was determined to get caught up in the warm spirit of the occasion, even though Martin had been wrong

— surprises did make him uncomfortable. He was accustomed to seeing his friends one on one; he didn't even care for small dinner parties. Having them all assembled together put him on guard. He felt responsible for them, for making sure they had a good time.

He also felt responsible for Broderick. He could feel her sense of alienation from the group and tried to include her in the conversation. He tried not to show his annoyance at the slow service and at the rudeness of the waiter, who brought a child to the table for Spielberg's autograph.

Watching De Palma's absorption in his friends, Broderick felt as though she weren't in the room. She drank more and more wine. De Palma seemed to disappear into a haze, even though he was sitting right next to her. Once again she felt as though she would never really know him, and that she would never be accepted by his Hollywood crowd.

De Palma noticed that Broderick was drinking a lot, and he put his arm around her. He was grateful to her for the surprise party, but his gratitude was mixed with anxiety. So much was riding on the preview in San Diego the next day. He wanted to forget about all that tonight, but Broderick's mere presence reminded him of it. She'd asked him if she could go to the preview; however, the executives had told him a few hours earlier that the Warner jet was fully booked. He suspected the plane wasn't full, but he didn't feel like arguing with them at this critical juncture. So now he was in the position of having to hurt Broderick's feelings after she'd done all this for him.

As the evening wore on, this mix of gratitude and anxiety began to feel a little bit like resentment. It was his birthday party, and he didn't want to worry whether Broderick was feeling included or not. He wanted to enjoy this celebration and the praise from the executives. He felt the way he had as a child, when his mother always managed to make herself the center of attention when he should have been. He didn't want to have to concern himself with Broderick's sensitivities, but he couldn't help it.

Spielberg raised his glass. "I want to make a toast," he said, "to this great movie I saw today: 'The Bonfire of the Vanities.' " The chatter stopped.

Spielberg, who would be joining the executives at the test screening the next day, continued the toast. "The movie I saw today was bright, satiric," he said. "It's like 'Dr. Strangelove.' "

Everyone raised their glasses to De Palma and joined Spielberg in a discussion of how to market the film. Spielberg said the ads should emphasize the satire, convey the mixture of darkness and comedy.

"No, no, no," said Art Linson, who'd had a couple of glasses of wine and was feeling expansive. "You want to show Tom Hanks and Bruce Willis. That's what they want to see. No one cares about New York outside of New York. Believe me, in Missouri they don't care about New York."

Capshaw piped up, with a grin, "Whoa, wait a second. I'm from Missouri."

Spielberg laughed and put his arm around her. "Here she is," he said in a teasing voice. "The lowest common denominator."

"Steven!" squealed Capshaw.

The other guests took this as a signal to end the discussion and broke up into separate conversations. Linson took a sip of wine and shook his head as he muttered under his breath, " 'Dr. Strangelove' didn't do so well."

The next morning De Palma went to the recording studio in West Hollywood to loop Griffith; nearly one hundred lines of her dialogue required rerecording. During filming, as she struggled with a North Carolina accent, she'd had a tendency to swallow her lines, a particular problem since Maria's malapropisms were one of the film's jokes.

De Palma was tense. Broderick was upset with him. She'd been insulted when he complained about the service at the restaurant and didn't believe him when he insisted that running down Madeo was a standing joke between him and his brother Bart. One of the things they liked about the place was complaining about it.

When she woke up grumbling that she had a hangover, he said, "No wonder, you certainly had enough to drink." Broderick was furious and hurt. She told him he'd ignored her all evening, that he hadn't even touched her, and now he was attacking her. De Palma felt bewildered. He distinctly remembered putting his arm around her. As they rehashed the evening, they felt as if they'd been to two different parties.

But he knew the birthday party wasn't what was eating at him.

When he finished with Griffith, he had to fly to San Diego for the screening before a preview audience.

The praise at the executive screening had done nothing to relieve his feelings of tension. Executives always said the film was wonderful — almost always. The MGM-UA executives hadn't said "Wise Guys" was wonderful. After they saw the film for the first time, they asked him to call in Garry Marshall, a director of popular comedies, to help him recut it, which he refused to do. But even when he showed his most controversial films to the studio people — "Scarface," "Body Double" — it was always the same: "Wonderful!" "A masterwork!" But, he always said, those same executives disappeared after preview audiences rejected the films. "You couldn't get anyone on the telephone."

On the morning of September 12 all he could think of was the Boston preview for "Casualties of War," a year and a half earlier. He'd flown in with Linson, who produced the film, Spielberg, and Dawn Steel. Bolstered by Steel's enthusiasm for the picture, he felt confident that this was the best picture he'd ever made. He was also nervous that its dark theme would unnerve the audience. His fears were confirmed by the results on the evaluation cards: an overwhelming abundance of "goods" and "very goods" and a distinct paucity of "excellents." Steel in fact didn't abandon him, but it didn't make any difference. The film failed at the box office anyway.

He drove to Burbank to catch the jet taking the executives to the screening, trying not to succumb to his feeling of impending doom. He tried to tell himself history didn't necessarily have to repeat itself. On the plane ride down, he noticed that there were plenty of empty seats.

San Diego had been chosen for the first preview screening because the executives wanted to test the film with an audience that approximated their idea of Middle America without having to fly very far from Los Angeles. It was felt that the prosperous southern California city would provide an "upscale" suburban audience that hadn't necessarily read the book; only 7 percent of the people who would attend the screening that night had read *The Bonfire of the Vanities*.

The studios had always tested pictures in front of audiences before final editing. In the past fifteen years, however, the research techniques used in advertising and political campaigns had been adopted by the industry. Research companies recruited audiences by age, movie-going history, and occupation to watch movies at various stages of completion. The test audiences were asked to rate the movie as "excellent," "very good," and so on, and to say whether they would recommend it. Then they were asked more specific questions about what they did and didn't like. The information could then be used to edit the movie and to market it.

Since the cost of making movies had climbed in 1990 to an average of $26 million per picture, and $11.6 million to market, the studios were relying more and more on the research. It wasn't foolproof, but it was a fairly reliable predictor of a movie's performance. A filmmaker could be fairly certain that if 90 percent of a preview audience rated his movie "excellent" or "very good," and a like percentage said they would recommend it, the movie had a good chance of being a hit. A low rating — 50 percent or lower in the top two categories — spelled disaster, or, at the very least, a difficult selling job. Much as filmmakers detested the idea of this pseudoscientific evaluation of their art, it had become a matter of course. And, even though the studios would always deny it, the previews were regarded as the moment of truth. Rather than rely on the vagaries of a director's imagination, or an editor's, the studios preferred to latch onto something more tangible. There was something comforting in the certitude expressed by an anonymous twenty-five-year-old man from San Diego who would firmly decree that he "liked Morgan Freeman" and that he "didn't like the sword scene — too confusing."

Before the movie began De Palma knew he was in trouble. He didn't know what "an upscale suburban audience" was, but the lack of ethnic and class diversity, the profusion of blond hair and golf slacks in the San Diego crowd, didn't look good to him. Much as he'd tried to downplay the executives' enthusiasm, he'd gotten his expectations up. He was willing to take their words at face value: he'd made a masterwork.

The funny thing was, he'd been to worse previews. Only five people out of five hundred walked out. The audience cheered when Sherman was exonerated. But he could see it and he could feel it:

There was a general lack of understanding. They didn't have a clue.

Marty Bauer too could see almost from the beginning that the movie was troubling the audience. "There was confusion," he said. "They seemed to be somewhat confused about it."

Steven Spielberg got the same impression. This was the twelfth time he had gone through the preview process with De Palma, though he had never invited De Palma to one of his own previews. He never invited other filmmakers to his previews. It was too terrifying for him. "I don't want to hear from filmmakers," he said. "I just want to hear from the audience. It's an experience I take very personally and very seriously. Sometimes I listen to the audiences too much. You have to go on your gut instinct. Your companion is your instinct. Your best friends can't help you. You start to distill your own vision."

During the "Bonfire" screening Spielberg kept his attention on the audience, since he'd just seen the film the previous afternoon. "I think the audience was with the film the minute Bruce Willis grabbed the salmon mousse off the plate and all the way through Tom Hanks dragging the dog down the hallway," said Spielberg. "The audience started to leave the movie the minute the car drove into the Bronx. Or was it Brooklyn?"

At that minute, said Spielberg, "I could feel the audience getting into the fetal position. I had that same reaction. I didn't know if I was supposed to be laughing or screaming."

Everyone's intuition was confirmed shortly after the screening. Only 59 percent of the audience said the film was excellent or very good, and only 49 percent said they would recommend it. The cards for "Casualties of War" had been better than that.

De Palma was pleasantly surprised by the follow-up meeting at Warner Bros. the next day. Everything about the Warner executives that had annoyed him, especially their insular sense of invulnerability, now seemed like an asset. They weren't thrown by the screening. None of them — not Daly, Semel, Fisher, or Canton — seemed to panic, the way he'd seen executives panic in the past. After the screening his feelings toward the Medici princes were warmer than they'd ever been.

He met with Canton and Fisher and analyzed the criticisms

they'd culled from the comment cards and from their observation of the audience. Some of the problems were minor. The French waiter scene seemed to go on too long; the split screen seemed to confuse people. Mark Canton said he missed seeing Annie Lamb joining in with the other schemers, a scene De Palma had cut out. That was one of the few scenes in which Bruce Willis, their $5 million star, appeared. He'd already been absent from the screen half an hour by the time the Annie Lamb scene came up; without it, he'd be gone even longer.

The audience's major attacks had been reserved for the ending — or endings. There were too many of them. There was the justice speech, the slow-motion sequence where Sherman grabs the judge and leads him down the courthouse corridor; Fallow at the awards banquet and the conclusion of the narrative; and then, as the closing credits roll, the coda that De Palma had added, Henry Lamb slipping out of his hospital bed and walking out onto the street.

The Henry Lamb coda drew the strongest negative reaction. The audience was angered by it, though not for the same reasons as Tom Wolfe, who'd been appalled at the implication that the hit-and-run accident might have been a sham. Instead, the San Diego audience, the upscale suburban audience, was infuriated that Henry Lamb — this thief who had threatened Sherman and Maria — was cheerfully walking off at the end.

Fisher summarized their discussion into a memo and left it to De Palma to decide what he wanted to do before the next preview, scheduled to take place in Boston in two weeks. He didn't know what to do. He had always felt that with "Casualties of War" he ended up cutting too much out after the Boston preview and that it made the movie worse. He consulted with Spielberg, with Bauer, and with Cristofer. All of them said the same thing: Don't cut anything out yet. Wait until Boston.

The next day he had to finish looping Griffith, and was feeling as though he'd swallowed a basketball, fully inflated. When she was finished, he drove home to the Hollywood Hills, took some Valium, and went to bed. An entire year had passed since "Casualties of War" opened, and he felt as though time had stood still.

De Palma didn't emerge from his house for five days except to meet with Eric Schwab to discuss the opening shot. Otherwise, he stayed indoors, monitoring all phone calls on his answering machine. Once again it was Bauer who pushed him out of his cocoon. "Get back to work," his agent told him. "It's not the end of the world."

De Palma got ready to go back to New York to oversee the next round of editing and the "premix" — the first round of putting together the movie's sound. The final mix would take place in Los Angeles, when the music would be scored.

Before he left, he met with Warner's publicity man, Rob Friedman, and with the studio's advertising director to see the publicity material he'd been waiting for since spring. When they showed him their poster design — the image that would be identified with this movie on billboards and posters, at bus stops, and in all the magazines — he couldn't believe his eyes. Their *big idea*, the thing they had to see the movie for, the campaign that had taken months to develop, was a photograph of Tom Hanks, Bruce Willis, and Melanie Griffith — in her sparkly gold dress — standing together.

When he saw their handiwork, De Palma silently resolved to remove himself from the advertising and marketing process. Snapshots of the stars! He couldn't believe this mediocrity. At that moment he decided he would simply be a good soldier. He would do everything he could to keep the studio's enthusiasm up and to encourage them to spend as much money as possible to open the picture.

Right now, he had one goal: to make it through the Boston preview and to get this movie finished. Then he'd think about what was really on his mind. There was less and less about making movies he enjoyed. So, he kept asking himself, "Why am I doing this?"

Chapter 15

IT'S IN YOUR BONES

On September 17 Bill Pankow stood bent over his moviola editing machine looking for the X that marked the location of take seven of scene 269. Both he and David Ray preferred editing on the upright moviolas to using the flatbeds, even though the sound was better on the flatbed. The assistant editors recorded the content of these trims in a log — backed up on computer. The film was filed by angle and by scene. That way, when the editors decided they wanted to structure a scene slightly differently from the way they had originally, they could easily find the piece of film containing, say, a direct shot of somebody's face.

Pankow was trying to figure out how to shorten the Ruskin funeral scene. At that moment, specifically, he was deciding where to put Sherman's cough. Sherman coughs when Maria discovers her lover has come to her husband's funeral wearing a hidden tape recorder, in the hope that she will say something incriminating.

The editor found the spot he was looking for and indicated to Ray Hubley, his assistant, where the film should be cut and spliced. Hubley said to one of the apprentices, "We're reaching a stage where everything that's creative Bill does in fifteen minutes and all the machinery that follows takes an hour and fifteen minutes." Every change required dredging up outtakes from the bins, then recutting the film and matching the sound. Each change had to be recorded in the log, so that when the next change came, the editors could easily find the pieces of film.

There were only eight days to go before the Boston preview. Pankow and Ray and their assistants were under great pressure to trim the picture on time. Meanwhile, the sound was far from completed. A relatively sophisticated sound mix had been put together for the San Diego preview by slipping in the relooped Willis narration at the last minute. But it would take weeks to finish the synchronization of the original sound, the looping, the sound effects, and the music. The technicians would be hard pressed to finish the mix in time for the December 7 release. Pankow and Ray had been told they'd have to move to Los Angeles in October for the final mix, which, even if everything went perfectly, wouldn't be finished until after Thanksgiving.

Pankow hadn't been thrilled to give that information to his wife. Less than a month earlier he'd gone to Rome with De Palma to loop Willis — a trip that had been for nothing, as it turned out, because the recording was too poor to use. A week after he and De Palma returned to the States, David Ray was dispatched to Rome to record Willis again.

Pankow's wife understood — up to a point — that travel was in the nature of the business. But it was difficult sometimes. When she'd been eight months pregnant with their fourth child, a year earlier, he'd moved her and their three kids from their home in Yonkers to Rome, where he was editing the Paul Schrader film. The apartment he'd rented was on the fourth floor of a walk-up — or eighty-five stairs up, as his pregnant wife kept reminding him. Pankow would joke that he was out of town so much his kids didn't even pay attention when he returned home. "They go right for the presents," he'd say.

David Ray was also feeling the crunch. Because the San Diego audience had reacted so negatively to the slow-motion sequence, De Palma had asked the editors to put it back to normal speed. This wasn't a simple matter. The sequence had been filmed for slow-motion projection — that is, the film had been shot faster than the standard twenty-four frames per second and then was projected at twenty-four frames per second. A scene photographed at forty-eight frames per second, when projected at twenty-four, will move at half its original speed, since each frame now runs for twice the length of its original exposure. Converting the scene to regular speed was a complicated and expensive process that involved snipping every other frame out of the film. The negative would have to be reprocessed and rephotographed, and even then it might have a jerky quality.

Ray didn't feel confident the conversion could be done smoothly. Though he was only forty-three years old, this process made him feel like a crotchety old man, wallowing in the past. "Quite frankly, I found the scene quite acceptable," he said, his clipped British accent emphasizing the disapproving tone in his voice. "Audiences today aren't very imaginative. When I was growing up, we were quite disappointed if things like this didn't happen. We would have been glad to see something strange, like the slow motion."

The short timetable made the working conditions for "Bonfire" especially difficult, and De Palma's terse style didn't make it easier. He was very specific about what he wanted, but not expansive at all. De Palma didn't bare his soul to his editors, the way other directors did. Sometimes a director would shoot a first version of a film that was just unwatchable — either because the director hadn't shot the right footage, or because his instructions to the editors were unclear, or because they'd followed his instructions incompetently — and then the director would work closely with the editors to refashion the film into something good.

De Palma didn't work that way. He gave his editors a detailed road map — the storyboards — right at the beginning. Then he'd look at how they put the film together and figure out by himself what he wanted done.

He certainly didn't want the editors talking to the studio executives. He asked Ray and Pankow to leave Los Angeles as soon as the screening was over. He discussed nothing with them until they were back in New York. Then he called Pankow and spoke to him for ten minutes about the changes he needed to make in the scenes he'd edited. He made a similar ten-minute call to Ray, and then one more brief call to Pankow.

Though Ray found the screening helpful as an editing tool, he was uneasy about the preview process. He knew an audience could help pinpoint what didn't play, but he was far less certain that it was wise to have audiences explain why they didn't like a film. If analyzing a work of art were so simple, wouldn't there be many more serious critics one could trust?

"To sit there when you've been intimately involved and to feel the vibes, to see that they're not reacting — it's almost painful," he said. "But I think the screenings are dangerous in one respect. It's an easy way not to use your brain, not to use your intuition. It's very scientific. Perhaps too scientific."

Though the editor made his living in this art form that relied so much on technology, he was saddened by the way the science part of the equation seemed to be smothering the art. To be sure, innovations like Dolby had vastly improved sound quality. But as he stared at the strips of film hanging over the bins while standing in the hallway just outside, he felt nostalgic. "I don't think we'll be using film in fifteen years," he said.

As he waited to hear from the lab doing the work on the slow-motion sequence, it occurred to him how little anyone knew about what he did. His brother, for instance, would say, "That must have been a fun film to work on," when in fact it had been, as Ray would put it, "sheer bloody murder." He never set his brother straight — in part because he didn't know how to explain it, and in part because he didn't want to dispel the mystique. "Everybody thinks about film, everybody knows films are made somewhere out there, and it's interesting," he said. "But very little is known about what goes on because all of us lie."

Across the street, in Studio J of the Brill Building, a thin, bearded man named Elisha Birnbaum, wearing sweat pants and a short-sleeved shirt, knelt and methodically beat two halves of a coconut on the floor. As he beat the coconut halves he watched a scene from "The Bonfire of the Vanities" playing silently on the movie screen in the front of the room.

The floor was covered with movable four-by-four squares made of different materials: one was concrete, one was wood, one was rubber, another was covered with sandpaper. The room was cluttered with rows of coats — raincoats, overcoats, army jackets, suit jackets — dozens of pairs of shoes, both men's and women's, and an assortment of odds and ends one would expect to find at a tag sale: old vacuum cleaners, salt shakers, cupboard doors, mops.

The bearded man kept tapping as he stared intently at the scene showing the demonstration in front of Sherman McCoy's apartment: men and women carried placards, black kids threw basketballs, someone escorted an elderly lady out of the building, and police patrolled on horseback.

Birnbaum was approximating the sounds of a horse's hooves with his coconut halves, which were wrapped in silver paper. While the mounted police rode across the screen, he tapped the shells with a *clip-clip* sound for fifty seconds to match the front legs, and then with a *clop-clop* sound for fifty seconds to match the hind legs. He knew exactly how long he was clipping and clopping because a large digital monitor glowed red just below the movie screen.

Birnbaum's performance was being observed by a man sitting behind a glass partition at the back of the room, and by another man sitting at a small table a few feet away from Birnbaum.

"I hate to tell you, Elisha," said the man at the table. "The front legs stopped earlier than the hind legs."

Birnbaum was the founder of Sound One, the company providing the sound effects for "The Bonfire of the Vanities." He was what is known as a Foley artist. Jack Foley was the one who figured out how to create sounds that would match the pictures on-screen, so the sounds he invented were called Foleys. Sound One would create 150 separate tracks for the premix of "Bonfire": footsteps, doors squeaking, the noise of the Concorde's landing. All those sounds would be recorded separately, then blended in the final mix with the music and the dialogue and background noise recorded on location. The effects were necessary because the original recording took in everything, always emphasizing dialogue, often to the detriment of the background clamor.

The man inside the glass booth rewound the film to the place where the mounted police appeared. Then, all three men watched the scene: the crowd of demonstrators, gawkers, and police officers on horses. The only sound accompanying this profusion of action, however, was the *clip-clop* of coconuts against concrete. Birnbaum nodded, and the film was rewound again. The scene appeared once again, but this time all the other sounds had been added. Now the tapping of coconuts seemed distinctly to be coming from the horse's hooves.

Birnbaum, who was born and raised in Israel, had started in the business as a sound mixer. One day he needed footsteps and recorded his own. He discovered that no one could create the sound of feet walking as beautifully as he could. He wasn't deluding himself. He knew how to hear. He heard things no one else did. He automatically isolated sounds. When people talked to him, he was acutely aware of the air whistling through their teeth, of the way material went *whoosh* when they crossed their legs. Birnbaum had worked in sound for twenty-one years in New York, and for twelve years before that in Israel.

In the past year he'd done the Foleys for twenty-five feature films, spending about two or three weeks on each. "Bonfire," however, would take him five weeks, the most time he'd ever spent on a picture. Usually Birnbaum was called in after a movie was completed, to fill in sound effects where they were needed. There wasn't time to wait on this one, though, so he'd been asked to do Foleys for every sound, just in case they were needed. It was going to take thirty editors, including assistants, and they'd have to be paid overtime on Saturdays and Sundays to make the deadline.

He'd found it difficult to work on "Bonfire" because he hadn't had a chance to see the entire film when he'd started. "I can't do my work mechanically," he said. "I have to know what it's all about. You must be able to concentrate 100 percent to do Foley, and you have to be an actor, to identify with the actor on the screen. So people can believe it's the character's footsteps, so it's not offensive. It's part mechanical and part acting. That's why it's Foley *artist*."

Birnbaum knew how to create a footstep that was authentic but not offensive. He used his props to *click*, to *clack*, to approximate the sounds of windows shutting, fans whirring, and doors opening. Sometimes he simply did what the actors on screen were doing, but more precisely. He inhaled, he exhaled. He specialized in kisses. He could kiss his hand in a way that, on a recording, would sound far more authentic than a real kiss would — and never offensive.

After Birnbaum was satisfied that the hoofbeats worked, he pulled a pair of open-toed women's pumps off the shelf and put them on, his black socks sticking out the front. The man at the table shook his head. "She's wearing flats," he said.

Birnbaum looked at the screen and saw that the woman whose footsteps he wanted to re-create was indeed wearing flats, and he changed his shoes. Almost all the shoes, both men's and women's, were Birnbaum's size: a man's 9½. Over and over he walked on the concrete square, creating footsteps for each person on-screen. He walked in sneakers, in men's dress shoes, in pumps.

Then Birnbaum took a basketball into the middle of the room and began throwing it up in the air and catching it.

"No, no, you're not getting the ring right," said an impatient voice.

Birnbaum raised his head to see who was talking. A stocky man with a mustache and a round face, a round body, and a round, balding head had quietly entered the room and was watching. He was Maurice Schell, the supervising sound editor for "Bonfire." He was responsible for coordinating all the movie's sounds. The two men had worked together on films for twenty years.

Schell walked quickly up to Birnbaum and grabbed the basketball. He stood a few feet away from the Foley artist and tossed the ball at him very fast. Birnbaum tossed it back. For several minutes the ball went back and forth between the delicate Birnbaum and the burly Schell. When Schell thought they had the ring right, he told the man in the booth to run the film.

Satisfied with the results, Schell had the projectionist move to the next scene: Sherman slipping out the side exit at the courthouse after his arraignment.

Schell became animated when he watched Hanks open the door. "Did you do something for the door?" he asked Birnbaum in a raspy voice. "I want a big metal door. This is a courthouse. You think it's wood? No, not wood. Metal. Have you ever been to a courthouse? Do you have something for a big, heavy sound?"

Birnbaum dragged out a large collapsible metal gate and pulled it open and shut.

"No, no, no!" shouted Schell. He began running around the room, rummaging through piles of stuff: the cupboard doors, the salt shakers, the bottles, the vacuum cleaners. "Elisha! I got it!" he cried. He dragged a giant wrench and an old box camera out to the middle of the room. He knelt on the floor and hit the wrench with the camera, achieving a sound that went *ka-clunk, ka-clunk*.

Breathing heavily, Schell pulled himself to his feet. "That'll be another component," he muttered, with obvious satisfaction. "Something that'll draw attention to him."

He walked back to the table. "You can do whatever you want to make the door close," he said. "I got my opening. I've got my sound now. It could have been just a door opening. This sound, it's just another thing to give it texture. But it's something. I want to *feel* something. Not a squeak. Every door squeaks. I want this film to have its own feel. Every film should have its own feel."

On September 24, two days before the Boston preview, De Palma was seeing "The Bonfire of the Vanities" for what seemed like the millionth time as he went over the premix with the editors. He sat near the mixer working the giant computer board that controlled the different tracks being folded together. Pankow stood in the corner of the screening room tossing darts at a board while they waited for the next reel to come up.

De Palma was watching Hanks and Griffith sitting in the Mercedes under the bridge in the Bronx. This scene had been looped, and the mixer had just replaced the original dialogue with the rerecorded dialogue. The motion of the actors' mouths didn't match the words they were saying.

"Good work, guys," said De Palma sarcastically. "It sounds like an Italian gladiator movie. Why don't we just put *looping* across the bottom."

The mixer nodded and scooted his chair to a distant corner of the control board and twisted a dial. This time, the voices appeared to come out of the actors' mouths.

De Palma tried not to let his eyes glaze over as he stared at the screen. He knew that like everyone else he was in danger of saturation. He liked the sound mix, in some ways. At one time it had fascinated him so much that he had made the main character of "Blow Out" a sound recorder. There was something surreal about watching actors walk across gravel and concentrating only on what the gravel sounded like. If he went to see somebody else's film while he was working on the mix, he would find himself completely distracted by footsteps, by the sound of a distant bird.

He knew he was reaching the point when he stopped looking at both the forest and the trees. In every film, a moment came when he started looking at the twigs, the grass, the pebbles, because he couldn't stand looking at the trees or the forest one more time. De Palma knew he was sick of this film, but he forced himself to stay focused, even though it was boring — agonizingly boring.

After the mixer added the car effect, he brought the Concorde shot on-screen. It had been cut to a few seconds. Every time he watched the plane landing and Griffith appearing on-screen in her Revillion sable, De Palma started laughing.

"Let's put in the theme from '2001' for Boston," he said. Pankow got on the phone and told one of the assistants to find a recording of "2001." While they waited, De Palma watched the Concorde land three more times.

The endless repetition reminded him why he couldn't bear to watch his own movies for at least a couple of years after they came out. He couldn't imagine what it would be like to go through all this for a *bad* movie.

On September 26 De Palma flew to Boston for the test audience screening. Spielberg joined him, as did an old friend, Jay Cocks, the *Time* magazine writer. Lucy Fisher couldn't come; she was in her seventh month of pregnancy and had been advised not to fly.

De Palma approached Boston in reasonably good spirits. Perhaps the movie would be appreciated better by an East Coast audience, a literate crowd. Forty-seven percent of the hand-picked audience had read the book, compared with 7 percent in San Diego. As he watched the audience watch the movie, his spirits rose even further. There was a palpable wave of enthusiasm. There was little rustling, and the audience seemed to get the jokes. When Sherman was exonerated, some people clapped.

But the charitable mood evaporated immediately when the judge's speech began. By the time Morgan Freeman was saying, "Decency is what your mother taught you," people were hissing. De Palma couldn't believe it. They were *hissing* at the decency speech. When Sherman grabbed the judge and began jabbing at the mob with a sword — the scene that Ray had converted from slow motion to normal speed — something else happened: the audience started booing as well as hissing. By the time Henry Lamb pulled himself out of his sickbed and walked out of the hospital, the friendly crowd had become hostile and angry.

Everyone who attended the special preview that evening was handed a standard letter-size questionnaire that asked the following questions:

1. What was your reaction to the movie overall? Would you say that it was ("X" one) . . .
Excellent. Very good. Good. Fair. Poor.

2. Would you recommend this picture to your friends? ("X" one.)
Yes, definitely. Yes, probably. Not sure. No, probably not. No, definitely not.

The next three questions required written answers: What did you like about the movie? What did you dislike about the movie? What did you like most and like least?

On the other side of the form were specific questions about specific performances, the story, the ending, the photography and settings, and the music. These were to be evaluated on a scale of "Excellent" to "Poor."

Then the questionnaire listed a number of words and phrases and asked the viewer to put an X by the words and phrases he or she thought described the movie. The words and phrases included "Entertaining," "Moved just right," "Different," "Held my interest," "Too slow in spots," "Not my type of movie," "Too choppy," "Depressing." After that, the viewer was invited to describe what, if anything, was confusing in the movie which wasn't explained by the ending.

The questionnaire also asked if the respondents had read the novel *The Bonfire of the Vanities*, and how the movie they'd just seen measured up to their expectations, whether it was "better than," "about as good as," or "not as good as" the book.

The questionnaire contained a list of twenty-one other movies — many of which someone involved with "Bonfire" had worked on — and asked the viewers which of those they'd seen "in a theater or drive-in" rather than on videocassette.

Finally, the questionnaire requested the age and gender of each respondent, and whether he or she had been "personally invited" or "came as a guest."

De Palma could barely force himself to read the response cards. Not surprisingly, most of the criticism focused on the endings. The audience members hated the decency speech, they hated the Henry Lamb coda. He was even more appalled by what they liked. The best scenes in "The Bonfire of the Vanities," according to the literate moviegoers in Boston, were that in which Sherman drags Marshall, the dog, down the hall, and the one where Beth Broderick's character pulls off her panties and photocopies herself on the Xerox machine.

De Palma was discouraged. He wasn't convinced that the preview process was helping at all. What was the point of changing things? The audience response scores weren't getting better and he didn't know what else to do. The big chip out was the justice speech. No one seemed to like it. As he'd suspected all along, it would probably have to go. After all the discussion among the professionals, in the end it was the moviegoers who would decide.

Only one outsider had been personally invited by the studio executives to all the previews for "The Bonfire of the Vanities." He was Joseph Farrell, founder of the National Research Group, the company widely credited — or blamed, depending on whom you talked to — for bringing the research methods of political campaigns to Hollywood. The studios had always tested films before preview audiences, although the executives at the movie studios, who had all used him since he began NRG in 1978, liked to pretend he didn't exist. He was contractually bound to confidentiality, primarily because the studios didn't want the public to think that movies were manufactured by research drones. When the *New York Times* mentioned NRG in one paragraph of an advertising column about new methods of movie marketing, Farrell was deluged with calls from angry studio executives. This small acknowledgment of his existence was enough to ruffle feathers.

In twelve years, NRG had grown to become the twenty-first largest research firm in the United States. It had 350 full-time employees in Los Angeles and 50 more in its London and Tokyo offices. And Joe Farrell drove a Rolls Royce.

In addition to putting together the test screenings and analyzing the audience comments, NRG had begun to provide all kinds of other information about movie-going habits. Every week over the course of a year, the firm recorded the "want-to-see" interest of a given film. NRG could tell a studio a great deal about a certain person of a certain age who saw "Batman" and liked it; what other movies the person had seen that year; how he or she had heard about it; what other movies this person would like to see.

Farrell tried to articulate exactly what good all this data did. "We don't forecast," he said. "This is too complex a field to get that precise. Not like weather reports — and I'm not even that sure about weather reports. This is a very big complex thing called a movie and a very complex series of perceptions that occur in moviegoers, the consumer. What you can do is get a sense of it from all the knowledge that you accumulate. Now you have the knowledge you have about a given movie in the context of the data bank you have. It begins to make more sense."

Farrell worked in semianonymity out of a pseudo-Gothic concrete and stone building in a seedy stretch of Hollywood Boulevard, an equal distance from the Burbank studios and from the Culver City and Hollywood contingent. The modest exterior was misleading. The interior of 7046 Hollywood Boulevard had been torn apart and re-created as a maze of futuristic offices, separated by curved walls painted bright pastels. Some of the playful furniture had been designed by Farrell himself under the name Giuseppe Farbino; he used the pseudonym, he said, because "who would buy furniture designed by an Irishman?"

Farrell was a shrewd dilettante who'd managed over the years to translate his various interests into profitable ventures. The transplanted New Yorker held a master's degree in fine arts and a law degree from Harvard. He alternated between Washington and New York, working as a lobbyist for various arts patrons, including the Rockefeller family and National Endowment for the Arts. Along the way he met Lou Harris, the poll master, and when political shifts put Farrell out of a job, he became the vice chairman of Harris's firm. To compensate for his complete lack of technical research skills, he took some courses in statistics — though his main job was to attend to the firm's business affairs.

In his five years with Harris, he learned how to wage a political campaign in a methodical way. He learned how research could help candidates figure out their "spin," and then how to exercise "spin control," the art of managing the way the media portrayed the candidates.

Farrell liked to say he got out of the polling business because he burned out. He moved to Los Angeles, hoping for a leisurely life. Then a friend who owned the rights to a couple of old television shows asked him to use his research expertise to see what the audience for the shows might be. Farrell quickly saw there was a wide-open market for what he'd learned in political campaigns.

It was 1977, and the movie studios had already started to take on the trappings of big business. The dynamics of the industry were divided. There was no central operation. Farrell saw agents, artists, studio executives, and exhibitors all approaching the marketing of a film with different interests. The old days were gone, when a mogul could make a movie succeed because he wanted it to succeed. In the very old days, before television, people simply went to the movies. You put a movie out, people went to see it.

Now, far fewer movies were released but at much greater expense. The studios were behemoths with huge fixed costs. They needed to put together a seasonal string of "product" in an orderly way, and the corporate parents wanted to know that something besides somebody's seat-of-the-pants judgment was involved in the process. Research provided comfort to executives working in an industry where the average tenure in a high-ranking job was a couple of years.

People called the movie executives paranoid. Joe Farrell would say, "I'm not so sure this industry is paranoid. Look at the job turnover in this town. I'm not so sure you're talking about paranoia. When you get into that state of fear, you tend not to do your best thinking. You tend to look for the worst. Research feeds back the public's minds to these people. And it makes them realize: Things aren't as bad as we thought. Or: Things are much worse."

As De Palma contended with editing and previews, Eric Schwab was consumed with the opening-title shot. After conferring with De Palma in Los Angeles, Schwab and Darren Wiseman went to the offices of Black Clawson, the paper manufacturing company, in the Chrysler Building to see if the balcony outside the company's windows would permit a view of New York that included a gargoyle. Schwab quickly saw the view he wanted: the camera would have to be set up just below the ornamental creature so that the fierce eagle would appear to be looking down on New York from Sherman McCoy's lofty vantage before his fall.

They would have to build a two-and-a-half-story camera platform to achieve the angle. Schwab and Wiseman appealed to Black Clawson's vanity by showing company officials a biography of Margaret Bourke-White, the photographer who had taken pictures of New York almost sixty years earlier from the space occupied by Black Clawson. The famous cover shot showed the celebrated photographer holding a camera in a daredevil pose, perched on the back of a stainless steel eagle suspended in air, sixty-one flights up. Walter Chrysler himself had hired Bourke-White during the winter of 1929–30 to take skyline photos from the pinnacle of the building while it was still under construction, hoping that her photographs would help justify his controversial skyscraper's existence. Her assistant took the shot of her sitting on the gargoyle, which was inspired by Chrysler automobile hood ornaments. Actually, her position wasn't quite as precarious as it seemed at first glance; Bourke-White was tucked into the space carved in the eagle's back to house one of the lamps that illuminated the Chrysler Building at night. Schwab and Wiseman told the Black Clawson officials that the view from *their* office, that famous view, had never been captured on motion picture film. This was their chance for immortality.

Schwab had called De Palma to tell him that they had clearance from the Chrysler Building tenants and that Greenberg, the special effects designer, was enthusiastic. They just needed approval from him; the shot would cost at least $150,000. The director's answer was waiting for Schwab back at his hotel: "Just do it."

"Just do it." Those simple words took on a larger meaning for Schwab as he worked out the details of the complicated motion-control shot with Greenberg's technicians, and thought about his career. His career! He'd never thought about work that way before. Even though he'd ended up learning something new on every film and had taken on additional responsibilities, he'd never had a plan before.

Now he had a reel, he had the cachet of working on "Bonfire," he had an entertainment lawyer, and he had an agent, Missy Malkin of Bauer Benedek, who was pushing him. Malkin had set up more meetings for him in New York. On September 24 he met with Norm Twain, a producer who had a production deal with Warner. Twain had achieved good standing with the studio after he produced the modestly budgeted "Lean on Me." That film, about the authoritarian school principal Joe Clark, which had starred Morgan Freeman, had made a healthy return relative to its cost.

Almost three years had passed since then, and Twain was eager to get another picture going. He had bought the rights to the story of John Cronin, an environmentalist who patrolled the Hudson River looking for polluters, and he had hired Michael Schiffer, who'd also written "Lean on Me," to write the script. The finished script of "The Riverkeeper" had been languishing in development at Warner for a year, and Twain was looking for someone to revive the project. He told Schwab how much he'd liked his reel and discussed "The Riverkeeper" with him at length. Schwab left the meeting feeling flattered and thinking Twain seemed awfully nice, very "un-Hollywood." However, he didn't think he had a chance at a studio film. Not as a first-time director.

He'd become acutely aware that, all the meetings notwithstanding, he was handicapped. Despite his experience, he was considered risky by the studios because he'd never directed a film before. He could impress development people with his ability to describe the way a story should unfold visually, and with his connection to De Palma. He couldn't prove, however, that he could direct actors and build a story on film. Studios were reluctant to gamble on new directors — especially a director who wasn't a writer and couldn't offer his own script — because of the costs. The budget for Schwab's Concorde shot surpassed those of De Palma's first three features put together. De Palma's tenth feature — "The Fury," made just fifteen years earlier — was the director's first film, the cost of which equaled his $2.5 million salary for "Bonfire." Independent production companies were only slightly less leery of novice directors, though they did offer opportunities if he didn't mind what he directed. Schwab wasn't willing to make a piece of schlock — not until that became his only option.

He was "uncredentialed," as his lawyer, Shelley Browning, put it. "Hollywood really is a network of linkages," she'd say. "So many uncredentialed, dishonest, and not-bright people succeed because a lot of it depends on who you know. Reality is irrelevant. Perception is everything." Schwab was "a relatively easy sale" because his reel was composed of high-visibility movies and he had the endorsement of a prominent, successful director. On the other hand, said Browning, "I can hear the studios saying, 'Well, it's one thing to do Brian De Palma's films. He's in a hotel room while Brian's getting it all set up.' It's hard. If five people present themselves, with all things being equal, they'll take the director who's done it before."

Schwab's feeling that his status as a first-time director made him about as desirable as a leper was confirmed the day after his pleasant meeting with Twain. Malkin had set up another meeting, this time with the son of a famous producer whose father had given him a job in development. They chatted for twenty minutes. Then Schwab was dismissed. "Hey, kid," said the twenty-nine-year-old producer's son, who did his hair in a chic ponytail and kept his feet on the desk for most of the meeting. "You've never made a film. We can't even give you TV."

So Schwab wasn't quite prepared for the call that came from Malkin the next day. After his meeting with Schwab, Twain told Malkin that he'd thought it over and believed that Schwab's reel matched the "mystical" quality he wanted for his movie. He'd been impressed with Schwab's confidence as well — and it didn't hurt that he could hire Schwab at the Directors' Guild Association minimum. If Warner agreed to the deal, the producer thought Schwab would be "perfect" for "The Riverkeeper."

The next test preview for "Bonfire" was set for the Cineplex Odeon multiplex in Marina Del Rey on October 10. The editors had trimmed twenty-four minutes out of the picture. De Palma and Pankow had spent a great deal of time trying to make the justice speech more palatable. They'd eliminated the part of the justice speech that elaborated on what "decency is not," and left in the part that explained what "decency is." So Freeman no longer said,

> And decency is not a deal. Or an angle, or a contract, or a hustle or a campaign or a trick or a bid for sympathy. Decency is not the beast that bays for money, power, dominion, position, votes and blood!

Now, after expounding on the meaning of justice, the Judge said, simply,

Decency is what your mother taught you! Decency is in your bones! Do I make myself clear! Now go home. Go home now. Be decent.

The editor David Ray and his assistant, Cara Silverman, had been working on the film up until the last minute to make the changes in time for the preview. On October 9, the day before the preview, they were booked on a 10:30 A.M. MGM Grand flight from New York to Los Angeles, and were bringing the final five re-edited reels with them. They'd be staying in Los Angeles until the mix was completed.

The 10:30 flight was delayed, again and again. When it hadn't taken off by 2:00 P.M., Ray decided they'd better make other arrangements. They switched to a Pan American flight leaving at 4:00 P.M. With some relief they checked their luggage and the bags containing the film reels. The bags were plastered with identifying labels, including the editing room telephone number. When Silverman and Ray arrived at LAX, the Los Angeles airport, at 7:00 P.M., they collected their luggage from the baggage carousel, and four of the film bags. They waited and waited until it became clear that the fifth bag, containing reels 3AB and 4AB, wasn't there.

Pan Am officials assured them that the bag would arrive on the next flight from New York. They went to their hotel, dropped off their bags, and returned to LAX. But the fifth bag hadn't shown up.

The editors were starting to panic. There were no more flights that evening, and the screening was the next day. They found an airline supervisor, who determined the bag's whereabouts on the computer file of lost luggage. It was still in New York. The supervisor assured them that the bag would arrive the next morning on flight 801. The next morning Silverman watched all the luggage from flight 801 make its way onto the baggage carousel. The film bag wasn't there.

The next Pan Am flight wasn't scheduled to land until 4:00 P.M., just three and a half hours before the screening was scheduled to start. Silverman went to the Cineplex Odeon to make sure everything was set up for the screening. The editors had enlisted the help of Warner Bros., and pressure was exerted on Pan Am to come up with the missing bag.

The 4:00 P.M. flight arrived — but the bag didn't. Silverman got a call from the studio not long after that, telling her that Bill Young, the head of production, was going to pick her up at her hotel and drive her to LAX to meet Pan Am's 6:50 P.M. flight. All the editors were booked into Le Rêve, a modest hotel in West Hollywood, a comfortable forty-minute drive from the airport. She and Young were to pick up the film and drive directly to Marina Del Rey, a twenty-minute drive up the freeway.

By 6:40 Young hadn't yet arrived at Silverman's hotel. She didn't know what to do. Meanwhile, Warner Bros. had sent a print of "Reversal of Fortune," which was scheduled to open later that month, over to the Cineplex Odeon to entertain the audience, just in case the missing reel failed to arrive.

At 6:45 Young pulled up in front of Le Rêve. Silverman was waiting outside. Young hotfooted it to the airport and was in front of the Pan Am entrance at LAX by 7:15. Someone from Warner had phoned ahead: a Pan Am employee was waiting by the curb to hand off the reel the instant Young and Silverman showed up. They ran into the Cineplex Odeon at 7:30 and gave the reel to the projectionist. The screening began at 7:45, only fifteen minutes late.

This audience was the most enthusiastic preview audience yet. But as De Palma started to sift through the responses after it was all over, he could see the scores weren't going to change. He randomly picked out comments from the 378 questionnaires.

"The story was a little shallow," wrote a male, between the ages of twenty-one and twenty-four, who had read Tom Wolfe's book and who found the movie "about as good" as he had expected. "It was difficult to really sympathize with Sherman. Maybe that's intended. It was a little silly at times and that just didn't seem right for a movie dealing with a serious issue."

He rated the movie "good," and indicated that he was "not sure" whether he would recommend the picture to his friends. He checked off several words and phrases the research company offered to describe the picture: "Entertaining," "Sexy," "Funny in spots," "Too choppy," "Thought-provoking," "Held my interest," "Has interesting characters."

De Palma scanned a few more. "I didn't like the fancy camera techniques / Some of the directing was too different," concluded a female between the ages of thirty-five and thirty-nine, who also rated the picture "good."

"I liked the comic touches," said a "very good," a female between the ages of twenty-five and twenty-nine. But, she added, "sometimes it was too cartoony. The end was over the top cartoony. The courtroom scenes with the crowd yelling was too much. It got irritating."

Those who gave the film a "poor" rating tended to be succinct. "Bad bad bad," said a forty- to forty-nine-year-old male who hadn't read the book. Scenes he liked most? "None." Scenes he liked least? "Whole film." He concluded: "Very boring. Insipid, poor script, shallow characters."

De Palma had seen enough. Nobody walked out. People laughed. But unless the analysis of the questionnaires was radically different from what he'd expected, they'd be screening the film again. The executives had told him that if the numbers didn't change, they'd try another test. They'd show the film simultaneously in two theaters. In one theater they'd keep the justice speech and eliminate the sword fight. In the other they'd include half the justice speech and the entire sword fight.

The next morning Warner Bros.' own head of research distributed his analysis of the cards to Canton, Fisher, Daly, Semel, Cristofer, and De Palma.

The news wasn't good. Only 55 percent of the audience judged the movie to be "excellent" or "very good." Worse, only 34 percent said they would "definitely recommend" the picture.

He ticked off the most frequently mentioned criticisms: The sword scene. Racism. The Annie Lamb scene in the hospital. The funeral scene. The "exaggerated visual style" and "cartoonlike" portrayal of characters. The "fuzzy moral" at the end of the movie.

He reported what the audience liked: Morgan Freeman. The scene in the Bronx. Walking the dog. Playing tape in the courtroom. The Xerox scene (though this was criticized as well).

The next night, October 12, "The Bonfire of the Vanities" was screened for two audiences simultaneously. One audience saw the film with the sword fight and without the decency speech. The audience in that theater cheered when Sherman hit the assistant district attorney with the sword, but didn't clap at the end of the movie. In the other theater, which showed the film with the speech and without the sword fight, the audience clapped at the end. They cheered the decency speech. Warner Bros. decided to move ahead with the second version.

So the sword fight was eliminated. No one would see the scene that had prolonged the search for the courtroom and added five torturous nights to the shooting schedule and close to $2 million to the budget — the scene they'd shot in slow motion which the editors had then laboriously transformed into real time. No one would see De Palma's operatic metaphor for Sherman McCoy's triumph over the opportunists who had used him.

Now, with the Henry Lamb coda gone as well, De Palma was worried that the ending would be too abrupt. Sherman McCoy would be exonerated, the judge would deliver the decency speech, and the film would return to Fallow at the awards banquet, going back to the beginning.

When De Palma and Tom Wolfe had met for dinner in the spring, much of their conversation had been about structure, about endings. The author didn't have any answers for the director. Wolfe confessed to De Palma that he wasn't entirely satisfied with the ending he'd given to his book. He knew that Sherman would eventually have to face charges, but he also felt that anything that followed the courtroom finale — which temporarily exonerated the bond salesman — would be anticlimactic. The writer solved this dilemma with an epilogue in the form of a newspaper article that summarized what happened to the characters after the courtroom scene. Wolfe thought he'd written an amusing parody of the way the *New York Times* might have written such an article, but he later believed it had been a mistake. He thought the light tone of the article undermined the end of his saga, which had gotten to be quite serious. The article was *clever*, if he did say so himself, but he wasn't certain that cleverness was what was needed at the end of a book.

Wolfe hadn't thought much more about the movie's ending after that dinner, until Lucy Fisher started calling him and talking to him about the "justice speech" and the "decency speech." He'd practically forgotten about it. He'd written the judge's sermon to the mob for *Rolling Stone*, in the initial serialized version of *Bonfire*, and then eliminated it for the book.

He had cut the speech out because he thought it was implausible, too much the noble figure stepping out on the balcony and haranguing the multitude. Michael Cristofer had taken the words for the speech almost directly from *Rolling Stone*, without realizing that Tom Wolfe thought the speech was a mistake, a hazard of writing a first draft of a novel in public.

Wolfe, who rarely found much fault with anything he'd written, didn't think there was anything *wrong* with the decency speech as a kind of message; he just didn't think a judge would ever deliver a speech like that. It was the plausibility factor that bothered him. There was also something awfully pat about the ending, he felt. But, as he thought about it from time to time, he could understand why the movie people were drawn to that speech, that theatrical gesture. Maybe, he mused, there should be a theatrical gesture in a movie.

Though all of De Palma's artistic training had taken place in the theater and in movies, he too found endings to be nearly impossible. It wasn't all that different from life. Beginnings were thrilling, the opening up of all kinds of possibilities. But endings, endings implied some kind of resolution, an epiphany or a summing up — and such moments seemed elusive to him, and false. He could rarely see how to sum up a story without trivializing it. The idea of the Magic Hour made so much more sense, an acknowledgment that it was difficult to pinpoint the exact moment when day ended and night began, that endings and beginnings were linked in some mutable, magical way.

He understood audiences wanted catharsis, some way to synthesize everything they had just seen, especially in a complicated movie like "Bonfire." He understood that one reason people went to the theater and movies was for the chance to experience the kind of satisfying endings they rarely found in life. Yet he felt that simply bringing the movie back around to the beginning, to Fallow stumbling forward to receive his award, gave Sherman McCoy short shrift. He'd wanted the sword fight to emphasize that this was Sherman's story, and that he had in some way benefited from all the misery he'd just been through. And he'd wanted the Henry Lamb coda simply to make a small ironic point, that the person who had really set the entire machine in motion — the hit-and-run victim — had been forgotten entirely by the time it was over.

But the audience rejected all that. Now the movie would cut abruptly from the speech back to Fallow. De Palma kept telling himself he believed in that speech, in its message that decency was "in your bones." It certainly was a summing up. He just wasn't certain it summed up this movie.

Chapter 16

JUNKETEERS

Bonfire" had been sequestered from the world for four months, ever since the production had moved to Los Angeles from New York back in June. Except for a few carefully planted items heralding the film's Christmas release, the press had ignored the picture while it was being edited and screened for preview audiences. For most of September and October Rob Friedman and his group were able to control the release of information.

Interest in the film had been enormous. The Warner Bros. publicity people found willing takers for the photograph that would become the movie's signature — the shot of Tom Hanks and Bruce Willis wearing suits, and Melanie Griffith in her spangly evening gown. De Palma found the publicity still unbelievably dull and uninspired, but Friedman stood by his belief that stars sell — and they did, to the newspaper and magazine editors putting together their fall previews.

It didn't matter how innocuous the articles were. *Harper's Bazaar* chose, for example, to quote Griffith earnestly saying, "In my next life I'd like to go to school and become a doctor or a philosopher. A doctor to help people and a philosopher to help them figure it out." It was coverage. Every article mentioned "Bonfire," and that was all that mattered.

Rob Friedman was pleased with the work his people were doing. But on October 26, all that work, all those puff pieces, were put in jeopardy. Liz Smith, the syndicated columnist, reported that people who had seen "Bonfire" in previews were saying it was either "brilliant" or "weird," and that "purists who appreciated the novel will be in an uproar of dismay." Smith concluded her item by reporting a rumor that Steven Spielberg had been called in to re-edit the film.

Two days later the gossip got nastier. The *Los Angeles Times* followed up in its "Calendar" section:

> "The Bonfire of the Vanities" is getting a chilly reception at test screenings, sources tell us. The cold shoulder has generated at least one local TV report that the film won't make its scheduled Christmastime release — which Warner Bros. flatly denies.
>
> "It will absolutely be at theaters on Dec. 21," says Rob Friedman, Warner's president of worldwide advertising and publicity. He stresses that the controversial film is a work-in-progress. "Any screenings you may be reporting on do not necessarily reflect the final cut of the movie."

Less than two months before the film's release, Friedman sat in his office and wondered whether "Bonfire" was in danger of getting broadsided for its budget, which was climbing toward $50 million. In 1990 the top-grossing movies so far were "Ghost," which cost $24 million, "Pretty Woman," with a $23 million price tag, and "Teenage Mutant Ninja Turtles," a bargain at $10 million.

"The media are in a current trend of talking about big-budget movies on the negative side, not the positive side," said the Warner Bros. marketing man, who was feeling a little defensive. "We don't like big-budget movies, okay? We'd like to make small-budget movies and still get the bang for the buck. But when the media are now talking about the movies, it's very rare that they talk about them in positive aspects unless it's a small little movie that's been discovered. A big movie tends to be viewed as an ogre just because it cost a lot."

Friedman warmed to his subject. "This is the way the media is looking at big movies this day. 'Okay. Show me! Prove to me you're going to be as good as you say. Show me! Prove it!' 'Bonfire,' because of its profile and its cast, is going to be looked at by the media that way. And the industry is like that too. When you get into the real movie environment, okay, it's dog eat dog, okay? If *your* movie succeeds, then mine's going to fail. The problem with many people in the industry is they believe they can only succeed on somebody else's failure."

Friedman and his advertising group had just completed the promotional trailer for "Bonfire." Willis narrated the trailer, which skipped across scenes featuring the stars. There were quick glimpses of two men in their thirties wearing business suits, and a blonde woman stripping down to her black lace underwear. Without the soundtrack, this trailer could easily give the impression that "Bonfire of the Vanities" was a French sex farce. The only clue that it might be something else was a brief glimpse of Tom Hanks looking at a headline that said HIT AND RUN and another of Morgan Freeman in judge's robes.

"This is a movie that if you boil it down to one paragraph it's pretty hard to do," said Friedman, explaining why none of the film's strong ethnic characterizations appeared in the trailer. "Out of context, you don't know what Reverend Bacon or the black crowds are. People will go: 'What is that?'

"From an advertising point of view, it buys us nothing to talk about the controversy. What is the controversy?" he said. "Let's remember how small the readership of this book is on a national scale. Unless you're a real aficionado of the book, what is the controversy? Is it the controversy about the eighties? Is the controversy about the racial issues? Is the controversy about the way you portray the Bronx? Who's going to pick? As far as we're concerned, the movie is a movie, not a controversy," said Friedman. "It will be. But the movie will be the controversy. The campaign should not be. The publicity will have to deal with controversy in whatever form it takes. Whether it's the Bronx borough, or racial issues, or what we're doing to the yuppies of the world. Or how we changed the book, versus not. It will all come out."

Warner Bros. hadn't been having a good year. None of its big pictures had "opened." Martin Scorsese's "GoodFellas" was the one bright spot; the movie had gotten great reviews and might have Oscar possibilities. But it wasn't exactly a huge hit, though it was doing better than they'd expected, financially.

Indeed, "GoodFellas" had now become the beacon of hope for "Bonfire." "GoodFellas" had scored poorly in test screenings. As Friedman put it, "On an *A* to *F* scale it got at best a *C*-minus in the preview process." Reviews saved it. "They weren't good, they weren't great," said Friedman. "They were brilliant. So, critically, 'GoodFellas' was an *A* movie, and that's what put it over."

Everything now hinged on the press's reaction to the movie. Friedman's staff was gearing up for the press junket a month away. As part of the publicity campaigns for their biggest films the studios routinely gathered journalists from all over the country and arranged for them to interview the stars and director. Warner Bros. put on twelve to fourteen junkets each year. Except in the cases of the few newspapers and television stations whose conflict-of-interest policies forbade it, the studios paid for the journalists' trips (the junkets were usually held in New York or Los Angeles, and sometimes in more exotic places, like Las Vegas or Hawaii) and their hotel rooms. Costly as the junkets seemed, they were actually a cheap way to generate publicity.

De Palma winced when he saw the "Bonfire" poster going up all over town. There were Griffith, Hanks, and Willis, their names, and a bit of copy:

> Take one Wall Street tycoon,
> his Fifth Avenue mistress,
> a reporter hungry for fame,
> and make a wrong turn in The Bronx . . .
> then sit back and
> watch the sparks fly.

But the poster was the least of his problems. He couldn't dismiss the printed gossip. It confirmed what he already knew: the "community" looked at him as a man out of control. Paramount had officially passed on him for "Ghost in the Darkness" and was hiring a relative unknown, the British actor and director Kenneth Branagh, who had made his directing debut the previous year with a film version of *Henry V.*

De Palma was out of sync with the *Variety* headlines. Big budgets were out, and right now he was a very big budget director.

The enormity of the budget only increased his feelings of apprehension as the release date drew closer. One fear seemed to trigger another, and soon he found himself recapitulating every bad experience he'd had in his life. He thought about the years before his marriage, how he had set aside his personal life in order to advance his career. He simply wouldn't tolerate an emotional life that interfered with his work. Yet it wasn't until "Casualties" that he'd felt he'd exposed his own vulnerability, and he still felt the audience's rejection as vividly as he had when the movie opened fourteen months earlier.

He wasn't sure he was prepared to face hostility again, but he was becoming more and more certain that he would. He could only imagine how Hollywood would react to the Jewish stereotypes in "Bonfire," unmoderated by the presence of good Jews now that Kovitsky was black. "Wait till they hear F. Murray saying, 'I'm a Hymie racist,' " he laughed. "That's enough to put them into a coma." The bravado barely masked his concern. "This community loathed 'Scarface' because the characters were so much like them," he said. "Manipulative, loathsome . . ."

On November 5 Dave Grusin, wearing a casual blue shirt and black slacks, stood in front of an orchestra of sixty one musicians wearing headphones over their ears. They were listening to the "click track," a metronomic beat put onto a film soundtrack so the musicians and their conductor can time the music to synchronize exactly with the film.

Grusin had been conducting and recording the score for "Bonfire of the Vanities" for two days; it would take a week to complete. At the same time the sound editors were putting together the final mix so the film would be ready for several important screenings: November 12, for another preview audience; November 15, for the Motion Picture Association of America's ratings board; December 1 and 2, for the press junket.

Grusin brought his own music editor, Else Blangsted, who sat at a table slightly behind Grusin checking a timer. Blangsted, a tiny, gray-haired woman wearing a sweat suit and a girlish air of mischievousness, was seventy years old and had been an editor for forty years. She'd worked frequently with Grusin since they'd met on "Divorce American Style" twenty-three years earlier and had become friends. Blangsted, credited as "editorial music consultant," had started the "cue breakdown" a month earlier — figuring out, to the nearest one-third of a second, the length of the musical interjections and marking exactly where they fit in the film. When Grusin sat down to write the music, he followed Blangsted's detailed outline.

The musicians had gathered in the Evergreen Studios at the MTM Studios just off Ventura Boulevard. These free-lancers were brought together by a music contractor, in this case a tall, brisk, red-haired woman who had been in the business for twenty-two years. "Dave tells me what he needs — what type of score it is: legit, jazz, rock. I put together the musicians," she said. "We have a pool of eight hundred to one thousand musicians in L.A. Chamber groups, the Philharmonic, and various community orchestras. Most of them make their living doing film and television."

Before stopping in the control room to introduce herself to De Palma, the contractor confided that Grusin was her favorite composer to work for — and she worked for twenty-two of them. "He's thought-out, tasteful," she said. "A pro."

De Palma watched the musicians from the control room, which was separated from the recording studio by a large pane of glass. The director sat on a comfortable couch and listened to the music piped into the room, occasionally glancing up at the video monitor from the book he was reading: *A Criminal History of Mankind*, by Colin Wilson. Fred Caruso had flown back to L.A. for the final mix. He dropped by to listen to the music, his favorite part of the entire process, and so did Monica Goldstein. They knew from previous De Palma films that the recording sessions were comparatively festive occasions. There was something thrilling about watching this big orchestra at work, to feel a link with the orchestras of the past that had played some of the century's best music, written for film.

As Grusin raised his baton, a video monitor played a scene from "Bonfire" next to his conductor's podium. Grusin's instructions to the musicians were piped into the room. His pleasant voice floated through the speakers, offering mild, encouraging banter to his orchestra of thirty-eight strings, nine woodwinds, nine brass players, and five in the percussion section. None of the musicians had seen the music before that morning; Grusin had composed it the day before.

During a break Blangsted walked into the control room and

dropped onto the couch as lightly as a kitten. "I'm barely alive," she said, with a deep sigh in the direction of Grusin's agent, who had stopped by. "This one was a terrible crunch because we did 'Havana' before. He can write two films, but I can't dub two films. I'm retired. I just work for Dave. I love him. I love the films, but I don't love that other bullshit. That Hollywood stuff."

There was an air of mystery about Blangsted, who lived in Switzerland and spoke with a slight German accent. She had a tart tongue and a smile as open as a child's. "You can read about me in *The New Yorker*," she said when asked about her background. In 1988 Susan Sheehan wrote a profile of Blangsted, about her Hollywood experience and her complex life as a Jewish refugee and unwed mother who thought her daughter died at birth. The two were reunited forty-seven years later, in 1984.

Blangsted was talking, with great sympathy, about the previews. "Trying to guess what the people choose is a science no one has discovered. So if they cover the film up with a lot of music and it makes a lot of money, *voilà*!"

She nodded toward the window, at Grusin. "He's writing. I'm putting marks on the film at night."

The agent said admiringly, "He's not neurotic. He wrote the score for 'Milagro Beanfield War.' The only acknowledgment that film got was an Oscar for the music. Did he get any acknowledgment from Redford? Anything? Nothing! Did it bother him? No!"

De Palma left the room with Grusin to discuss when to reinsert the jaunty theme music that introduced Willis.

Blangsted watched him leave, then said quietly, "I saw Brian at one of the previews. He was white. Stricken. You could sense they didn't like the ending." She crossed one thin leg over the other. "It's a joke. Everyone who comes for a screening brings their own lives. How are you going to get at their lives? We scored the sword scene to make Sherman a Wagnerian Master of the Universe. If you don't get participation with that scene — a sense of 'Yeah! Wow!' — you're in trouble." There had been no "Yeah! Wow!" and the sword scene was gone, and Grusin's tribute to Wagner would go unrecorded.

While Grusin was scoring the music, the editors Bill Pankow and David Ray were trying to complete simultaneously the final phases of editing, which normally would have occurred in sequence. The previews had preceded the final mix; now, as the music was being recorded, the other elements of sound were being synchronized in preparation for the negative cutting. That was the final step, when the negative would be edited to match the final workprint. To protect the original negative, a "dupe" print would be made, the source for the nearly 1,400 prints that would be shipped to theaters across the country. This frantic rush to completion had become commonplace in the business. Yet Ray and Pankow weren't as harried as the editors had been on "Beverly Hills Cop II." They had put together the final mix and previewed the film while it was still being shot.

Pankow traveled between the Evergreen Studios and the Todd-AO sound studio in Hollywood, where the sound mixers were timing all the sounds to match the action. On November 5 he met with Andy Nelson, a thin British man with shaggy hair and a mustache, who was the lead rerecording mixer. His job was to bring together all the soundtracks onto a single master track. Nelson and the other mixers sat behind a vast computer panel the knobs and dials of which controlled each of the 150 soundtracks they were working on that day. The Todd-AO mixing rooms were equipped for Dolby sound and were guaranteed to meet the standards set by the Dolby company — which routinely sent inspectors to check the sound level of the speakers.

"We're the last creative process before the film is released," said Nelson, who had moved to Los Angeles from London a year earlier because there was no room for advancement in England. He'd worked in television, and on features for Stanley Kubrick and Ken Russell. "When a film comes to us everyone is exhausted. It's the final stage. All these people who have been working on this for a year or two just collapse. Their nervous energy has come to fruition and we're just getting started so we tend to see these insane people." He glanced over at Pankow, who was speaking calmly enough on the telephone.

Because they were the final stop, the mixers were constantly working under deadline pressure. "We're very unlike cameramen and editors, who are on these things a long time and then disappear for six months," said Nelson. "We have these frantic bursts where everything has to come together and then we move on to the next one. We have no leeway on this film, for example. We have to fit all parts together and make the deadline. Then, the next group walks in, and it's the same thing all over."

Nelson's first concern was to make sure the dialogue was clean and audible. The more creative part, in his mind, followed, with the final mix, balancing the dialogue, the original sound, the looping, the music, and the sound effects. He had to size up the director quickly, to sense what tone he wanted.

"You've got to dive straight in. Every director is so different," he said. "Some want to sit through every frame of the film. Some are very nervous. You have to read them very quickly. De Palma was very confident with his editorial staff and they would keep a tight rein on us. He comes in and approves. He's very tolerant and very aware of the technicalities of what's going on, which many are not.

"He won't fiddle around endlessly. Some people can't let it go. Sometimes they're sad it's slipping away and can't let it go. Others are uncertain and think constant fiddling will improve it.

"The buzz on this one scares me because the prepublicity can be detrimental," he said, turning a knob. "In England, when a piece of work is completed, it's released. I've been surprised here at how much influence the previewing process has. Can you imagine an artist taking a painting out and asking people if they like it and then redoing it? Me, being from England, I find it very sad, this generic filmmaking."

Nelson paused to examine the screen, where a giant eagle jutting out from a building was staring ominously across Manhattan.

That eagle was Schwab's opening shot. Clearly it was going to be in the movie, though the second unit director hadn't heard yet whether De Palma thought the gargoyle shot surpassed the Concorde — and whether he'd collect on his double-or-nothing bet. Even as the sound was being mixed for the shot, which had been filmed almost three weeks earlier, Schwab was back in New York helping R/Greenberg Associates finish the special effects.

Filming the gargoyle had required a different kind of precision than the Concorde shot — and it produced a different kind of exhilaration. Greenberg brought in a computerized motion-control camera from California. Schwab worked with the technical crew to anticipate every possible light and weather condition, and to determine the camera speed. To figure out all the possibilities with the lights, the film crew literally had to change the pattern of New York City's night skyline. And to the crew's surprise, they met with cooperation at every turn. The intransigence of toughened New York City building superintendents and the urban bureaucracy simply fell away for the movie people. Wiseman convinced half a dozen building managers to light their skyscrapers ahead of schedule for the two days of tests the crew shot from 4:00 A.M. to 9:00 P.M. When Schwab saw that the Chanin Building's burned-out lightbulbs were ruining the shot, Wiseman bought replacements and had them installed immediately. The city was at their command. Its officials even agreed to illuminate the Brooklyn and Manhattan bridges early for those two days.

The weather was less cooperative. The afternoon clouds they'd captured on film were perfect: dramatic, brooding. But Schwab wasn't happy with the sunrise and sunset they'd caught in seventeen hours of filming on October 12. He asked Caruso for permission to film again on Monday, in hopes of capturing a better sunrise and sunset. By then, the production executives at Warner Bros. were watching every minute. They approved half a day. So on Monday Schwab and the crew went back up to the sixty-first floor and began to film. Not long before the scheduled wrap, Schwab decided they should try for another sunset and asked Caruso if they could go into overtime.

Caruso checked with the new production supervisor, Ron Smith's replacement, Penelope Foster. She said no, the $10,000 extra cost was unacceptable. Caruso called De Palma, who asked to speak to Schwab. Schwab called from the Chrysler Building and explained why he wanted to stay. He told De Palma the crew was leaving in fifteen minutes unless Warner Bros. approved the overtime. De Palma got in touch with Fisher, who gave the go-ahead. A few minutes later, Penelope Foster, the production supervisor, called De Palma to apologize.

Once again, Schwab had gotten lucky. Sunset in New York that Monday evening had been suitably orange. He'd returned to Los Angeles and had been preparing to fly to Thailand to celebrate his birthday with Lek when De Palma asked him to go back to New York. The special effects house was supposed to create the illusion that the lights of New York began streaking across the sky to form the title "The Bonfire of the Vanities." But the special effects were taking too long, and R/Greenberg Associates was notoriously slow. De Palma wanted Schwab on site to keep the pressure on.

Schwab canceled his trip. It didn't occur to him to refuse, even though he was officially off the picture and no longer getting paid — and even though he hadn't seen Lek for almost three months. But he couldn't say no to De Palma, not after all De Palma had done for him. Besides, he was flattered by the compliment implicit in the request, another measure of De Palma's faith in him.

He had never felt so confident and so appreciated. That feeling only emphasized his shock and anger at the cover story about "Bonfire" in the November issue of *American Cinematographer*. He couldn't believe the words in front of him as he read the magazine's cheery description of the Concorde shot. "Good luck or good timing?" asked the article rhetorically about the shot it described as "gorgeous." It was timing, the writer concluded, and then went on to describe at some length the calculations that Vilmos Zsigmond had made to get this difficult shot to work. "Zsigmond just had to determine what date a Concorde was scheduled to be in the right place at the right time," said *American Cinematographer*.

Zsigmond just had to determine! Schwab was livid. *Zsigmond! Zsigmond* had been in *Los Angeles* on a sound stage when they were doing the shot. But, he told himself, nothing could — or should — annoy him now. Everyone stole credit. He had far more important matters to think about. Missy Malkin had put together the papers for his development deal with Norm Twain so they could be signed before November 4, Schwab's thirty-third birthday. He would fulfill the Thai fortuneteller's promise — that thirty-two would be his year — just under the wire.

As part of the final piecing together of the film, Monica Goldstein submitted the credits for the title and the "crawl," the names that appeared at the end of the movie. The list did not contain the name of F. Murray Abraham. The actor had never wavered from his position that if his name wasn't given the same prominence as that of Morgan Freeman — before the title appeared on-screen at the beginning — he didn't want to be mentioned at all.

Goldstein, who had gotten married in September, had gone ahead and simply listed herself as associate producer on the list of credits, which De Palma had to approve. To her relief, and amazement, he didn't say a word. He simply signed off on her list. After that she didn't mind doing the minor chores he'd ask her to do. She felt he'd acknowledged that she was more than an assistant.

Fred Caruso felt a small twinge as he glanced over the credits. He would never complain about De Palma's refusal to make him producer as well as coproducer. He would have liked to have the credit for the leverage it would give him. But now, as he sat in on the editing and scoring sessions, he was thinking more about the money that had been spent for scenes that were no longer in the movie. "Did we think the sword scene was great, all we paid for that location? And was Morgan Freeman worth all that money and now it's cut down to nothing? Maybe Judge Roberts would have been the best choice," he said. "But once that screenplay was agreed on, that was the picture we agreed to make. Once that ball is rolling downhill, you just want to pick it up at the bottom."

On Wednesday, November 14, on the front page of the *Los Angeles Times* "Calendar" section, the reporter Elaine Dutka analyzed the box office prospects for Christmas under the headline HOLLYWOOD HOLIDAY DERBY. She noted that the schedule was more jammed than usual, with the release of twenty-one studio films. Using a racetrack metaphor, Dutka "handicapped" the films by category: "Morning-Line Favorites," "Contenders," "Dark Horses," "Longshots," "Fast Out of the Gate," and "On the Outside." She put "Bonfire" in the "Longshots" category.

She said research screenings hadn't gone well and that an "eye-witness" had called the film a "cartoon." She quoted an anonymous producer who said, "Everyone is asking if Brian can find a way to mutilate a woman in it . . . Melanie Griffith, watch out."

De Palma tried to dismiss Dutka's piece as a cheap shot. "It always makes good copy to say I'm the guy who mutilates women," he said. But he couldn't really shrug it off. He was angry. "I wonder if Saint Francis of Assisi had problems like this," he said petulantly. "Did they write about him, 'He used to fuck everything that walked'?"

De Palma couldn't believe what was happening. The nasty press was confirming his feeling that somehow this big, respectable film was turning out to be a nightmare. The last screening hadn't done anything to make things seem worse, or to bolster his hopes. The audience watched the movie without the sword fight and with only part of the justice speech, and nothing had changed. The audience was engaged, nobody walked out. Nobody laughed hysterically either. The scores still didn't change. The numbers hadn't changed substantially from the first screening in San Diego. "Bonfire" continued to score worse than "Casualties of War." All that had resulted from the previews was a shorter film, De Palma felt, not a better one.

The trailers had gone out to theaters the weekend of November 10, and now there was little to do but wait. There were odds and ends to tend to. Pankow had some ideas on how to trim a little more out of the justice speech. Canton had called to discuss one of the lines delivered by Richard Belzer, the comedian playing the producer who wants to buy Sherman's story. Canton, who had taken complete responsibility for the final phases of "Bonfire" since Lucy Fisher delivered a baby girl in October, urged De Palma to reword the offer Belzer's character makes to Sherman: "I'll suck your cock." The line had already been changed to "I'll suck your socks" for the television version of the movie.

De Palma periodically convinced himself the movie didn't matter anymore. Despite the misery and anxiety he was feeling, there was a bright spot in his life. He was in love with a woman named Gale Anne Hurd. He'd seen Hurd every day since they'd met two weeks earlier. Thinking about her made him happy and helped distract him from the movie.

Hurd was one of the few women who had become a successful Hollywood producer. Her most prominent credits were the science fiction films "The Terminator" and "Aliens," which were directed by her former husband, James Cameron. She had called De Palma on Thursday, November 1, to pitch him a movie, and he asked her if she'd like to discuss it over dinner. They went out that Saturday night, and again on Sunday, to the première of "Dances With Wolves." On Monday morning De Palma broke up with Beth Broderick. Not long after that he called his mother in Sarasota and told her he'd met the perfect woman. She was thirty-five, smart — Stanford, Phi Beta Kappa — attractive, successful, divorced — twice — and she wanted to get married and have a family.

De Palma's professional life was not all gloomy either. A British documentary crew had spent a day with him as part of a BBC series on filmmakers and other artists. He'd been invited to Madrid in April for a retrospective on his work and to head the jury at the Avoriaz Fantasy Film Festival; he was looking forward to spending January in the French Alps, where the festival took place. He'd also heard from Vilmos Zsigmond, who'd called him for advice. The cameraman was directing his first film, an Israeli-Hungarian production, starring Liv Ullman and Michael York. They were about to start shooting in Israel.

De Palma too was thinking about what to do next. For months he'd been toying with an idea for a suspense movie set on a playground, even though he knew returning to that genre was dangerous for him. It could be regarded as a step backward. But he'd begun making movies because he wanted to transform the pictures in his head into art, and the suspense form best suited that kind of visual storytelling.

People didn't understand how one decided what movie to make. Even De Palma didn't understand it entirely. "Making movies is not some very organic development," he said. "You're at a certain time in your life with twenty thousand reasons to make that decision. At a different time you wouldn't make that same decision. It's where you are in your career, in your life. With 'Bonfire' I read the book and loved it and wanted to try to adapt a book into a movie. I had made a particularly sorrowful movie before, and I wanted to make something that was kind of cynical and sarcastic and not as emotional.

"There's a whole swirl of emotions that go into the decision. A lot of times you make movies because you don't want to think about what's happening with the movie you just made. You don't want to think about the reviews out there or about how you're going to survive the pummeling that you're getting. That's how I made the decision to make 'Bonfire.' It may not have been the right decision, but it still feels to me like it was the right decision."

He couldn't do much else now but wait for December 21. Despite everything — the previews, Elaine Dutka — he had confidence the movie would open. "It's not going to bomb," he said. "The question is only, how big is it going to be?"

De Palma wasn't permitted to wait in peace. In the November 26, 1990, issue of *New York* magazine the screenwriter William Goldman took his turn at "handicapping the holiday movies," by means of quoting anonymous people he introduced simply as "Hollywood Powers." Goldman put "Bonfire" in the category of "Oscar Hopefuls," just below his analysis of Woody Allen's "Alice" and Penny Marshall's "Awakenings":

> *The Bonfire of the Vanities* (Warner Bros). "The absolute stinker of the season." "Every decision they could have made they made wrong." "I hear they're trying to turn it into a comedy now, which is an okay idea, I guess, except I also hear nobody's laughing." "Here's the deal. It cost over 60 and it's testing badly, but people are going to go. At least at the start. Too much hype to ignore. This is not *Ishtar* by any means. What's sad is it's a waste of money and time and talent and material."

In the category "Final Thoughts," Goldman, a bold self-promoter, devoted the greatest space and kindest words for "Misery," the Christmas movie for which he'd written the screenplay.

De Palma was feeling battered. "What makes this movie the one everyone wants to see fail?" he asked. "It seems as though it's a fait accompli. I'd like to be in Katmandu for the opening of this one. I've never seen them" — "them" now referring to the press and the Hollywood establishment, not the Warner Bros. executives — "so gleeful for the fall. Not since 'Scarface.' They hated 'Scarface.' They couldn't wait for it to tank." There was scant solace in the friendly one-liner Jeannie Williams offered in her *USA Today* column: "Melanie Griffith is drawing raves among early screeners of *The Bonfire of the Vanities.*"

It had become obvious to De Palma that he hadn't succeeded in separating himself from his past, from his Bad Boy image. As he'd grown older, he liked to think that he and his films had matured.

He was no longer eager to do public battle. He'd hoped that after "The Untouchables" and "Casualties of War" he'd be seen as someone to be taken seriously, who wasn't just a skilled provocateur.

A great many people had long memories, he'd discovered when "Casualties" was released. He'd expected some people to be put off by the film's darkness and emotional brutality. He didn't expect his antiwar drama to be treated as *a horror picture,* or worse, some kind of *pornography.* He remembered his shock at seeing a demonic photo of himself on the cover of the *Village Voice* with the tag line "Brian De Palma's Latest Outrage." Inside, Frances Fitz-Gerald, Pulitzer Prize–winning author of *Fire in the Lake,* called "Casualties" a "sado-porn flick . . . banally offensive."

After that, he thought nothing could surprise him, and it didn't, really. "I'm a very easy target," he said. "They can always say, 'Look who they got to direct it.' "

Shortly before 9:00 A.M. on Saturday, December 1, De Palma entered the subdued, elegant lobby of Le Bel Age Hotel, just across the street from Tower Records and from Spago, the best-known celebrity restaurant in Los Angeles. A woman greeted him as he walked in and told him to go to suite 411. He was met there by a thin blonde woman wearing a smart suit who told him her name was Doris Owens and that she was his "handler."

Owens had flown in from Cincinnati, Ohio, to help Warner Bros. with the press junket for "The Bonfire of the Vanities." She was one of forty field representatives around the country who helped the movie studios with local public relations. Owens worked Dayton, Cincinnati, Columbus, Indianapolis, and Louisville for nine studios. She monitored trailers for the studios, dealt with the press in her territory, and was dispatched to junkets when extra help was needed. She'd done the "Dances With Wolves" junket for Orion Pictures in Washington, D.C., the week before, and had gone back home to Cincinnati for a few days before Warner Bros. brought her to Los Angeles for "Bonfire."

"Bonfire" had gotten the biggest response to any Warner junket in history: fifty-one television reporters and seventy-two print reporters had shown up to interview the director and the stars. This was an enormous event for Warner's marketing department. It would take fourteen people to orchestrate the interviews — and to make sure that the hospitality suite was well stocked with fresh fruit and croissants and Brie, and that the stars and De Palma and the junketeers were made as comfortable as possible, under the circumstances.

These were the circumstances: Saturday was reserved for television interviews. De Palma, Tom Hanks, and Bruce Willis each sat in a room all day where two cameras had been set up. One camera faced the interviewer, and one faced the interviewee. New interviewers were escorted into the room every eight minutes; as they left, they were handed two videocassette copies of the interview, all paid for by Warner Bros. The process was roughly the equivalent of being trapped in a corner at a cocktail party and forced to answer the same six questions, again and again — fifty-one times — by the kind of person who always seems to be looking slightly over your shoulder to see if someone more interesting has arrived. Melanie Griffith conducted her interviews by satellite from London, where she was filming a movie called "Shining Through." Her part of the interview was recorded off the video monitor while a cameraman filmed the person looking at the TV screen asking questions.

Warner Bros. gave each junketeer a white shopping bag embossed with THE BONFIRE OF THE VANITIES in red letters, containing the electronic press kit and the tapes of his or her interview. It was all very businesslike. One gray-haired junketeer was heard complaining in the hallway that it wasn't as much fun as it used to be. He told a friend that when he started the junket circuit in 1981 there were only about twenty-five junkets to choose from each year. Now there were forty, and they were much less lavish and much more crowded because of the proliferation of cable television networks. "We used to get eight to ten minutes; now we barely get six by the time they push us through," he said. "You get in your basic questions and then you have to leave."

De Palma had just shaken hands with Doris Owens, his handler, and surveyed his suite. There was a pot of cappuccino waiting for him and a large plate of fancy fruit: mangoes, raspberries, bananas, and strawberries. Just after the director set down his nylon briefcase, Rob Friedman walked in wearing jeans and a cardigan sweater.

After a brief hello, the Warner Bros. chief marketing man picked a raspberry from De Palma's fruit plate and said, "The reaction to the movie was subdued." Warner Bros. had bused the junketeers to Westwood to see "Bonfire" the previous evening. "The book readers are confused. The non–book readers like it."

He studied the fruit plate before choosing another raspberry. "You're going to have the toughest day tomorrow with the print people. Just smile and say this is your movie, not Tom's book. This is not the Bible. Jesus didn't die on the cross here."

De Palma nodded. Friedman continued in his matter-of-fact tone. "We knew this was where we were going to be." He shrugged and moved toward the door. "I just saw Tom." This time the Tom he was referring to was Hanks, who was ensconced in a suite on the fifth floor. "I'm going to Bruce."

De Palma had worn his green khaki safari jacket, olive pants, and sneakers for his television interview. Monica Goldstein was waiting for him in room 209, where he would spend the day being interviewed. She was there to make sure that Owens made sure his requirements were being met: cappuccino, mineral water, ashtray.

At 10:00 A.M. Steve Kmetko, of "CBS This Morning," walked into the room with his producer. Kmetko was blond and had perfect small features, and spoke in a voice that was deep yet empty of emotion. He shook De Palma's hand and said, "I just want you to know one of the producer's all-time favorite movies is 'Carrie.' "

De Palma smiled weakly. Kmetko sat very straight in his chair and gave a brief instruction to the cameraman focused on him. Staring earnestly at De Palma, he asked the director the questions that would be repeated over and over, all day long: "How true is the movie to the spirit of the book?" "Do you think it will spark controversy?" "Why did you cast Tom Hanks?" "Why did you make the judge black?" "What about the problems in the Bronx?" "What about the opening Steadicam shot?"

De Palma was relaxed and polished. The interview was efficient, impersonal. The production assistant sitting next to the camera operator waved his finger to tell Kmetko he had one minute left. Eight minutes after he arrived, he left, and was replaced by a man with a square face and a deep voice much like Kmetko's.

De Palma comfortably rolled out his answers to the questions. Why Tom Hanks? "I wanted an actor who could play comedy and drama . . . It's like the search for Scarlett O'Hara . . ."

What inspired the opening Steadicam shot? "I remember I saw Truman Capote going into an awards ceremony drunk once . . . Orson Welles always walked around carrying a book, and when I asked him why, he said he carried it because he was bored with people asking about the first shot in 'Touch of Evil.' "

As the second man left, he indicated for the first time that he'd met De Palma before, and probably would again. "I shall see you again next time." Then, he added, "I believe I was number twenty-six on those tapes."

De Palma laughed. He thought he'd recognized that man. To alleviate the boredom on the "Casualties" junket, he'd brought his own video camera. At the end of each interview he turned the camera on and started to ask the *interviewer* questions.

Pat Stoner from the Public Broadcasting Service was ushered in next, wearing a black shirt, a closely trimmed beard, and a studied attitude. "Remember," he said to De Palma before the taping began, "it's PBS, so be boring." When De Palma didn't respond, he tried again. "Now remember," he said with deliberate wryness, "whatever you do, don't be interesting."

When the camera rolled, Stoner eased into the standard opening question about the difficulty of adapting a book for film. "Please, tell me . . . is this a little scary?" His voice was low, confiding. "Help me . . . you decided not to play the dark side . . ."

As he was leaving, the PBS man said, "Melanie was shot very well. She looked gorgeous."

One after another the reporters filed in. Very few said anything about the movie before the cameras rolled, though almost every one gave very specific instructions to the cameramen about how they wanted to be shot.

The interviewers began to blur together. De Palma didn't bother to listen to their names, much less register them. The television people seemed to feel that they were entitled to immediate intimacy with the people they were interviewing. Some were apologetic, some were condescending, but almost all of them assumed they were on a first-name basis. Tom! Brian! Bruce! Melanie! They were unnerving, the way they sat in their chairs without moving. They didn't blink or move their heads or nod. They barely seemed to breathe.

A woman with a mass of brown hair and a purple dress came in as De Palma was having a cup of cappuccino. She chirped her greeting: "I'd heard that you drank a lot of cappuccino, and sure enough, you're a big cappuccino person." Later, during her interview, she asked about "the nude scenes."

"Nude scenes?" The director didn't hide his irritation. "There are no nude scenes."

The interviewer with the brown hair and purple dress plowed ahead. "Were there times when you were afraid of filming in Brooklyn?" she asked. Without correcting her, De Palma gave his stock answer, all the while thinking, Why do TV people have such large heads?

At some point during the morning De Palma realized he was going to have to do something to keep himself awake. He needed to shake things up. The first time someone asked him about Spike Lee's criticisms of "Bonfire" he was measured. "He was making pronouncements based on no information," he said to the middle-aged woman with the scarf around her neck, the seventh interviewer that morning. To the ninth interviewer he said that Lee was like a character from *Bonfire*, using the media to increase his own value at the expense of others. To the twelfth interviewer he said, "If Spike Lee would concentrate on making better movies instead of pontificating . . ."

A hand-scrawled sign had been taped to the bedroom door of the hospitality suite. CONTROL ROOM, it said. Inside a technician was watching Hanks, De Palma, and Willis and the people interviewing them on six tiny video monitors.

Rob Friedman periodically dropped by to look at the monitors. "I'm looking for when people need pep talks, when they need to get their energy level up. It's work, this. It's acting."

He turned up the volume on the Willis monitor. The actor was wearing coveralls like the ones car mechanics wear and talking about his favorite subject, the press. "Some person from one of these so-called newspapers sharpens her number-two pencil and writes down these quotes that I never said and my wife never said, and then I see it next to the check-out counter at the grocery store."

Friedman extinguished Willis's sound and turned up De Palma's. "Spike Lee sort of epitomizes *Bonfire of the Vanities*," he was saying. "Talking about something he knows nothing about to get himself on the airwaves . . ."

Friedman then turned to Hanks, wearing his black shirt buttoned to the neck and a black blazer. "Yes, in a way this is the challenge of my acting career," Hanks was saying. "It's not overtly comic, and there is a lot of attention focused on it. We have made the movie version of *Bonfire of the Vanities*, and it's going to be held to a particular light."

Friedman turned down the sound and shook his head. "People have no idea about the journalistic world out there," he said. "Especially between the coasts."

In room 208 Griffith was chattering away by satellite from London. "The book is the book. The movie is the movie," she said, looking out from a television in the general direction of the interviewer from MTV, who was watching Griffith on the screen. "It would be like trying to film all of *Gone With the Wind*. It's impossible."

Griffith cheerily explained the decision to change the British Fallow to an American. "A scumbag is a scumbag," she said with a giggle.

Then Griffith gave a perky sales pitch. " 'Bonfire of the Vanities' is a great Christmas present," she said. "You go see it, and you'll definitely have something to talk about."

By 12:50 De Palma had done twenty interviews and was murmuring by rote: "Presiding over accidents . . . catching lightning in a bottle . . . Orson Welles."

He was so tired he could only nod when the woman with the long legs and long blonde hair and short skirt told him, "I hated the book and loved the movie." He came to life briefly when she asked him what he thought happened after death. "I don't know," he said. Then he laughed. "One hopes there'll be pearly gates and angels singing."

He invoked "Citizen Kane" a few more times, and signed a

photograph for a man from Montreal, who said, "Thank you for making a film that gives us something to think about, and the people of Montreal send their best wishes and luck."

After lunch De Palma spoke to twenty-six more television reporters. He signed the sketch a well-spoken man from Kansas City drew of him, and posed for a snapshot. He met a plump woman from Seattle who told him she wanted to ask a question no one else had, and then proceeded to ask questions De Palma had heard twenty-five times that day. Finally, she came up with an original. "Where did you get your socks?" she asked.

De Palma laughed for the second time that afternoon. He stretched his leg so he could see his socks, brown argyle. "Where did I get my socks," he said, taking more time to answer that question than any other. After a lengthy pause, he said, "At the Beverly Center."

Pleased with her success, the reporter pressed on. "How do you feel about how the film turned out?"

De Palma looked perplexed, then angry. "That's a strange question," he snapped. "I just spent a year and a half making this movie. Of course I like it."

The woman from Seattle reddened. As she left, she apologized.

The next day the print reporters got their chance to meet De Palma and Hanks. Willis declined because he believed print reporters distorted his words. He was replaced by Kim Cattrall, the actress playing Judy McCoy.

The print reporters were given an hour with each interview subject, but they had to share their time with other reporters; they were shuttled from one room to the next in groups of ten or twelve. The questions were more varied, and more pointed. De Palma sat on a couch and addressed the reporters gathered in a circle like a professor leading a seminar.

A large man with a red face said, "I didn't understand that speech. I was with you up until then. I feel it was hyperbole."

De Palma threw up his hands. "Now you're making directorial calls. *You* direct a movie."

Someone asked why he was so often accused of being derivative of Hitchcock.

"That's because when you're writing a story about Brian De Palma, that's the spin. I could make Disney pictures from now on, and they'd still be talking about the shower scene I'd stolen from 'Psycho,' " the director said.

Someone asked how he thought Tom Wolfe was going to like the movie. "I would be surprised if he thought this was the greatest movie in the world," De Palma said. "I would like him to like the movie, but it will be hard for him to see his work changed to fit some new form."

Then, spontaneously, De Palma started talking about the Concorde shot. He'd seen Zsigmond's grab for credit in *American Cinematographer* and had decided to set the record straight. "I told my second unit director, Eric Schwab, I'd never have an airplane landing in my movie unless it was spectacular," he said. "And it was," he said. "Spectacular."

The reporters nodded, though many of them looked puzzled, as though they were wondering, A plane landing?

The actors, predictably, were asked more questions about their personal lives than about the movie. Tom Hanks genially responded to the reporters' questions with articulate precision. Asked whether he considered himself to be a Master of the Universe like Sherman McCoy, Hanks said, "I've had the luxury of getting cold-cocked in the face every two and a half years. That forces me to consider my place in the universe."

No, he said, to someone else, he hadn't met Tom Wolfe. "I had this nightmare that I had highballs with Tom Wolfe, and he looked at me and said, 'Hmmm, Tom, I didn't much care for 'Punchline.' "

He responded to every question after grave consideration, as though it were very important. One reporter asked, "How do you like the way you look?"

"It's a bitter disappointment," he said, with his unflappably even humor. "I have this squeaky voice, this nose that won't go away, and I don't act anything like Spencer Tracy."

Kim Cattrall was having a difficult time. She knew she was a replacement for Willis, and it was obvious that the reporters she was facing didn't have much to ask her. After she told them how she researched the part of Judy by going to lunch with society ladies, and that De Palma was "a very nice man," not a misogynist at all, there was an uncomfortable silence in the room. Cattrall looked pretty and vulnerable in a black dress with gold buttons.

"Do you have a husband or a family?" someone asked politely.

"No," she said sadly. "I wish I did. I don't . . . I have a dog."

There was another silence. Then someone asked her what it was like to work with Griffith. "It's hard to be an actress in Hollywood," Cattrall said. "There's no community. I liked Melanie, but we never sat down and talked. I'm lonely . . ."

She told the reporters that she'd decided to refuse roles in movies like "Porky's" and had been waiting a year for a good part when "Bonfire" came along. "I feel very validated doing this," she said.

Warner Bros. diligently sent Tom Wolfe copies of all the publicity material on the movie — reams of it. He wasn't certain how much good all of it did. He vividly remembered the release of the movie version of "The Right Stuff" back in 1983. John Glenn was stumping the country trying to win the Democratic nomination for the 1984 presidential elections. The movie about the astronauts was given almost as much advance press as the senator's campaign.

Wolfe, an old friend of "Right Stuff" producers Irwin Winkler and Robert Chartoff, had worked hard on behalf of that movie. "I'll never forget being on a 'Nightline' show with Irwin," he said. "The subject of the show was 'Movies and Propaganda' and on the show was Costa Gavras, the most totally propagandistic director ever to breathe the air. And also whatsisname, Gene Hackman, who was in that movie 'Salvador,' no, the Costa Gavras film, whatever it was called.

"Irwin and I are all busily fielding all these questions about John Glenn, and the possible influence of the movie on the campaign, and, boy, we think we're burning up the TV airwaves. Then they turn to Costa Gavras, who had just made a movie about the Israelis slaughtering the Arabs, and they turned to him and posed the question about politics and propaganda."

Wolfe paused and assumed an accent meant to approximate the Greek filmmaker's. " 'Oh, I don't really know about such things, I just do entertainment. I just think of a story first. It may have a political setting, but it's the story that counts.' "

Wolfe chuckled as he thought about Costa Gavras. "Entertainment. He kept using that word, *entertainment*, with his foreign accent, and if he said it once, he said it forty times in a paragraph. I said to myself, 'What a lightweight.' "

Wolfe got Costa Gavras's strategy only later, when "The Right Stuff" bombed and so did John Glenn's presidential campaign. Then Wolfe understood that Costa Gavras knew exactly what he was doing. "He didn't want to turn anybody off his films by saying they're going to get a history lesson when they go to the theater. Irwin and I were busy ramming home the point, 'This is a history lesson, this is a history lesson. If you want to understand John Glenn, you better see this.' Of course it turned out no one cared about John Glenn."

In the case of "Bonfire," he'd decided not to agonize about it — and to keep his distance. He believed what he kept saying, that even a bad movie was good for a book. Not as good, perhaps, as a great movie would be, but good. Indeed, Wolfe and his publishers did capitalize on the movie's multimillion-dollar media campaign. In the autumn of 1990 Farrar Straus Giroux released a new hardcover edition of *The Bonfire of the Vanities* that differed from the original only by the addition of a "manifesto" by Wolfe on the state of contemporary fiction. Bantam reissued the paperback with the photograph of Hanks, Griffith, and Willis on the cover, right under the phrase "Now a major motion picture from Warner Bros."

This re-emergence of *Bonfire* in book form encouraged Wolfe to embark on his own little junket. He posed for photographer Helmut Newton in Condé Nast's *Traveler* magazine and talked at length to Lisa Grunwald for her *Esquire* cover story, "The Master of Vanities." There he was on "Good Morning America," introduced by clips from De Palma's "Bonfire." Joan Lunden smiled encouragingly as the pale man in the white suit repeated, in short form, his spiels on Émile Zola and Sinclair Lewis and real estate. Wolfe, settling comfortably into television patter, jokingly recalled being described as "the thinking man's redneck." At the conclusion of the five-minute, forty-seven-second segment he gave a big smile. "Good, Joan," he said. "Glad to be here."

* * *

After the press junket, there was little to do but wait, to make note of the little flags in the wind without assigning too much significance to any of them. The Warner Bros. executives and the filmmakers kept reminding themselves that nothing was predictable. The handicappers could all be wrong.

After all, none of the holiday handicappers had predicted the longest shot of all. "Home Alone," a modestly budgeted kids' movie with no stars, had become a huge hit already. Three weeks after its November 16 release, "Home Alone" — which had cost $18.2 million to make — had already taken in $70.3 million at the box office, and everyone expected it to breeze past $100 million. "Home Alone"'s progress was noted with special interest at Warner Bros. The picture had started out as a Warner Bros. release; three weeks before production was to begin, however, the studio had canceled the movie.

On December 3 *Variety* reported that "Bonfire" might not be ready in time for the major film critics associations to consider it for their annual awards — awards that were regarded as precursors to the Academy Award nominations. Rob Friedman told *Variety* that the movie would be finished in time for critics to see it, "as long as they go to the screenings we invite them to."

It began to seem as though everyone were making bets on how "Bonfire" would do: signs and countersigns began appearing in the most unlikely places. In a December 2 newspaper advertisement for Caroline's at the Seaport, a New York comedy club, comedian Richard Belzer was promoted as "featured in the *hit* film 'Bonfire of the Vanities.' "

When the ad ran a week later, Belzer was described as "featured in the *new* film 'Bonfire of the Vanities.' "

Chapter 17

"YOU'VE GOT TO BE A GENIUS
TO MAKE A MOVIE THIS BAD"

It was common practice for Hollywood studios to hold a special preview just for "the community" shortly before a movie opened. These "industry screenings" were frequently followed by a party and had the appearance of a gala. A giant searchlight outside the theater sent flashes into the sky, and paparazzi would wait outside in hopes of spotting a major celebrity, or a minor one. How well the evening would pay off for the paparazzi depended on the buzz preceding a picture — the early word-of-mouth. If the word was good, there would be plenty of high-level studio executives, major dealmakers, and stars to choose from. However, when the buzz was bad, the "industry" was suddenly populated by secretaries, junior agents, and minor actors — people who'd been handed invitations by their bosses, and people who were happy to be invited anywhere at all.

Warner Bros. screened "The Bonfire of the Vanities" for the industry at the Mann's Westwood Theater on December 19, two days before the movie's opening day. There was a spotlight, and there were paparazzi, who were rewarded with glimpses of Tom Hanks and his friend, the actor Steve Martin. Otherwise, they had to content themselves with Joel Silver, who was producing "Hudson Hawk," Willis's next film, and with Daniel Stern, the actor best known in recent years as the unseen adult narrator on "The Wonder Years," the television show about a young boy growing up in the suburbs in the sixties. Bruce Willis, Melanie Griffith, and Morgan Freeman were somewhere else. So was Steven Spielberg. So was Peter Guber, who at one time had said this was one movie première he wouldn't think of missing. Not even De Palma was there. He decided to wait until the party to make his obligatory appearance.

The audience that night responded enthusiastically to the movie — more enthusiastically than any of the preview audiences. The warm feelings continued at the party afterward. Warner Bros. had rented out Eureka, yet another of Spago founder Wolfgang Puck's stylishly minimalist restaurants. The crowd happily drank and ate and jostled one another in the vast space packed with people. Hanks and the Warner Bros. executives isolated themselves in one corner of the room with their friends and with De Palma's friends — Art Linson, Marty Bauer, Jared Martin, and Bart De Palma, who had flown to L.A. for the opening of his brother's movie. Just before 11:00 P.M., about half an hour after the party started, De Palma arrived with Gale Anne Hurd and her brother and sister-in-law.

It appeared to be a happy occasion, full of congratulations and smiles and friendly chatter that was difficult to decipher through the din. De Palma mingled with the executives, and spent some time talking to Lucy Fisher, whom he hadn't seen since she'd given birth.

Bauer spent much of the evening at a table with Art Linson, tasting the ample assortment of hors d'oeuvres. He was animated. The audience response was the best he'd ever seen to a movie, or at least to this movie. All kinds of people — some familiar, some not — came up to him after the screening and said, "I liked the movie." As the evening wore on, Bauer thought, Maybe they're not going to execute us. Maybe there's a light at the end of the tunnel. We've been sitting in that chair and somebody's called the governor. The phone is ringing. Maybe we'll get a reprieve.

De Palma's smile suggested that he was thinking the same thing. He was charming, chatting with executives as if they were all old friends who hadn't seen each other for a while. He glanced across the hordes of people laughing, talking, eating, and drinking. But in fact he wasn't thinking what Bauer was thinking at all. As he looked at all the friendly faces, he thought, They can afford to be friendly. I'm out of the competition.

* * *

Two days before the party it had hit De Palma for the first time: *he might have directed a disaster*. It wasn't a good sign that the *New York Times*'s preview piece the day before, on Sunday, didn't run on the front page of the "Arts & Leisure" section but way back on page 42. But that still left open the possibility that the picture would be considered controversial, that it would probably get mixed reviews. He'd always expected that.

On Monday, however, when he read the trades — the industry papers whose reviews measured a film both artistically and by its box office promise — he couldn't avoid the possibility. "The Bonfire of the Vanities" *could be a disaster!* That thought — *disaster* — began to sink in faster than the words he was reading.

The daily *Variety* review began:

NEW YORK — Brian De Palma's take on Tom Wolfe's "The Bonfire of the Vanities" is a misfire of a thousand inanities. A strained social farce in which the gap between intent and achievement is yawningly apparent, ultralavish production has the money, cast and bestseller name value to attract a crowd initially, but downbeat reviews and word-of-mouth will surely put a damper on b.o. [box office] prospects of Warner Bros.' $45 million-plus project.

De Palma had read enough of that one. He turned to the *Hollywood Reporter*:

Brian De Palma douses Tom Wolfe's "The Bonfire of the Vanities" with enough incendiary cinematic devices to keep 50 toxic dumps in perpetual fiery rage. While De Palma has stoked a broad and billowing comedy — one which coughs up a lot of belly laughs — it's one that will leave fans of Wolfe's scathing social satire choking and heaving with disapproval. "Bonfire" will be quickly extinguished at the box office.

Numbly he turned next to the news magazines, the first word from the popular press. Richard Schickel in *Time* panned the picture, but acknowledged that De Palma "succeeded in the . . . difficult task of finding a cinematic equivalent for [Wolfe's] singular style. Using unconventional angles, lenses and light, he accomplishes on the screen what Wolfe achieved on the page through deliciously exaggerated dialogue and deadpan parody." But Schickel concluded that the film "has no moral or dramatic weight" and lambasted the judge's speech. "It is a dreadful ending," he wrote, "which manages to travesty all the tough-minded things Wolfe tried to say, and everything a movie unafraid of its own subject matter should have said."

Worst of all was David Ansen's review in *Newsweek*, which dismissed the movie in two long, scornful paragraphs. He called Cristofer's script "mind-boggling," a "let's-spell-everything-out-in-capital-letters screenplay." Ansen too attacked the judge's speech, especially his invocation to "remember what your grandmother taught you." The line gave Ansen *his* ending: "My grandmother told me to beware bad movies."

That week began to seem increasingly surreal. On Tuesday a federal judge ruled that New Jersey chief justice Robert Wilentz was wrong not to allow "Bonfire" to film the sword fight scene in the Essex County Courthouse. Wilentz's objection to the scene, the federal judge said, violated the First Amendment. So, the week that "Bonfire" opened, the filmmakers received permission to film a scene that was no longer in the movie.

The next morning, the day of the preview party, ABC film critic Joel Siegel gave his review — punctuated by clips of the movie supplied by Warner Bros. — on "Good Morning America."

After summarizing Wolfe's book, Siegel began his killing critique of the movie:

> Well, they're calling it "Bombfire" in Hollywood, and they're being optimistic. . . .
> Let's say you were making "Bonfire." Wouldn't you pick Bruce Willis to play an emaciated alcoholic Englishman? And who would you get to direct? Brian De Palma, a great director of horror, suspense, and violence. Screenplay? The writer won a Pulitzer for a play about the terminally ill. These men are talented. You've got to be a genius to make a movie this bad. . . . This is not just a bad movie, this is a failure of epic proportions — " 'Ishtar' of the Vanities." One to remember, but not to see.

On Thursday, December 20, the day before the movie he'd been working on for almost two years was released, Brian De Palma left town. Gale Anne Hurd invited him, his brother Bart, and his friend Jared Martin to the house she owned in Snowmass, Colorado, about twenty miles outside Aspen. De Palma couldn't see a single reason to stay in Los Angeles. He intended to remain out of reach until after the holidays.

On Friday, December 21, the first day of winter and the day "The Bonfire of the Vanities" opened on 1,373 screens, an unprecedented chill fell across the West. Just north of Los Angeles, in Santa Barbara County, it snowed for the first time since 1942.

Indeed it was fiercely cold throughout the country, one of the many factors the studios were watching, on this major movie-going pre-Christmas weekend. Cold weather wouldn't keep audiences away from a movie they really wanted to see. But movies that were marginal would probably suffer.

In the case of "The Bonfire of the Vanities," it became apparent that Friday morning, December 21, that the weather wouldn't make any difference at all. The reviews in the major papers were unanimously dreadful. The picture was declared "gross, unfunny" by the *New York Times*; "a disastrous misjudgment" by the *Los Angeles Times*; "a very ugly piece of work" by the *Chicago Tribune*. Not a detail was left unchallenged by someone, somewhere. Vincent Canby of the *New York Times* concluded a paragraph on the film's "technical flaws" with this observation: "Miss Griffith's body appears to be so perfect as to look surgically reconstructed."

Still, there was hope at the studio that the movie would do reasonably well the opening weekend. Some people would be drawn by the stars, others by curiosity. No one was expecting the movie to gross the $10 million or more that would signify the makings of a hit. But it was possible that the picture might sell $6 or $7 million in tickets, enough for modest respectability.

No one even tried to call De Palma Saturday morning. There didn't seem to be any point. By Monday it was confirmed. The picture was indeed a disaster. In its opening weekend, "Bonfire" took in $3.1 million at the box office, less than a third of what was required for it to be a hit. By comparison, "Kindergarten Cop," which also opened the twenty-first, grossed $8 million — and that was considered a disappointment for Universal.

The holidays were always quiet at the studios as executives dispersed to Hawaii and Aspen. But at Warner Bros. the quiet felt ominous, not at all peaceful the way the Christmas interlude usually did. The scent of death was in the air — and it was an embarrassing death at that. The general denunciation of "Bonfire" left everyone associated with it feeling as though the family's most prominent son had died in compromising circumstances — and his shameful passing had made the headlines of every newspaper in the country. Nearly everyone at the studio was associated with the movie in one way or another. For all the company's size and diversification, almost every employee at Warner Bros. depended on the success of four or five of the studio's two dozen theatrical releases every year. Almost every job — from that of the shipping clerks to the videocassette salespeople to the corporate officers — depended on the movies that served as the base product for everything else. A big hit like "Batman" reverberated throughout the studio, making everyone swagger a bit. A failure like "Bonfire" made everyone feel a little ashamed — and then angry, as they wondered what the hell their senior development people were thinking about to make a movie like that.

Outside it became fashionable to attack "Bonfire" and to speculate whose head would roll for this awful thing, this movie that had become a metaphor for everything that was wasteful and rotten in modern moviemaking. Just as Tom Wolfe's book had become *the* book to love for exploring the folly of excess, De Palma's film had become *the* film to hate because of its excess.

"Bonfire" wasn't the only movie to fail that Christmas. Almost every big star vehicle proved to be a disappointment. Clint Eastwood didn't bring audiences to "The Rookie," nor did Sean Connery and Michelle Pfeiffer to "The Russia House," nor did Robert Redford to "Havana." Indeed, in box office terms, "Havana" was a bigger disaster than "Bonfire." Yet only "Bonfire" attracted ongoing scrutiny — and vitriol.

William Goldman, the screenwriter-columnist, eked yet another article — his third — for *New York* magazine out of the Christmas movie season. The categories this time were "Home Alone" (the unexpected success of which put it in a category by itself), "Hits," "Disappointments," "Flops," and "Disasters." "Bonfire" shared the last category with "Almost an Angel" and "Havana." Goldman wrote, "I've never heard the kind of hatred that *Bonfire* evoked." Then he quoted his usual anonymous sources:

"The stench will last for years." "I'd heard about it so I didn't go to see the movie as much as view the corpse." "There was only one good thing about it. Guber and Peters are famous for shacking up with movies that their names are on but that they had zero to do with, like *Rain Man*. It was fun watching them distance themselves from *Bonfire*."

In fact, after his brief appearance on the set that final day of shooting, Peter Guber had disappeared entirely from "Bonfire"'s orbit. Two weeks after the picture opened, the producer, who once had been thrilled to talk about his influence on "Bonfire," did everything he could to demarcate his precise moment of departure.

"It's been a year and a half since we left the studio, my partner Jon Peters and I, long before the final draft was done. It would be inappropriate for us to comment on another studio's film. I am now chairman and CEO of another studio. If I were a producer somewhere else, maybe then I could. But I'm not going to be put in that place to comment on the film of another studio that isn't my picture. Whatever the picture is, it is."

Guber took a breath and then elaborated on his "no comment."

"It would be unprofessional for me or my partner to comment. We wouldn't engage in that conversation. It's very simple. The answer is this. Neither Jon nor I produced the movie. We didn't market the movie. We weren't there for the final draft of the script. Yes, our name is on the movie, but we didn't get any money for the movie or anything like that. Our name is also going to be on 'Batman II' and 'Chico Mendes,' and we don't have anything to do with those pictures either. Our professional ethics wouldn't allow for us to talk about it."

Warner Bros. had screened the movie for Tom Wolfe shortly before it opened. The writer brought almost one hundred people with him to the Warner Bros. screening room in the company's Rockefeller Plaza headquarters, including his wife; Ed Hayes (the attorney on whom Sherman McCoy's lawyer, Killian, was modeled); his agent, Lynn Nesbit; and Burton Roberts and his wife. Afterward this small group convened at '21' for dinner.

Judge Roberts was blunt, as usual. "The movie stunk," he said. Then he reconsidered. "It didn't stink. I don't think it was as bad as people made it out to be. My wife didn't think it was that bad. Didn't think it was great. It was okay."

He thought Morgan Freeman was all right but shallow, and as he'd watched him he knew the movie would have been better if he'd been in it. He was certain, in fact. A week before the movie opened Warner Bros. finally sent him a copy of his audition tape, and Roberts had to admit it: he was very good. "In fact," he said, "I thought I was better before I followed *his* directions, De Palma. It was more Kovitsky the way I did it."

He sighed. "Who knows what trouble it might have caused me? The judiciary might have been up in arms, me acting in a movie." He laughed. "Well, there'll be other movies."

Tom Wolfe cringed over the movie, just as he'd cringed the first time he saw "The Right Stuff." He saw "Bonfire" two more times after that, hoping he might like it better. He didn't.

He never violated his rule of public silence on the subject of "Bonfire of the Vanities." He hinted that he didn't care for it much, but the worst thing he said was that "the great thing about selling a book to the movies is that nobody blames the author." Wolfe realized that in some way he was a collaborator in this venture, and that he was better off being polite about it all. He also recognized the fact that his books now had a bad track record in Hollywood and it was a good idea to be polite.

In private he confessed that he was dismayed by the picture, that he really disliked the writing in it. "My feeling is that Hollywood rules are always wrong," he said. "Everybody in Hollywood hates to think about writing. It's so uncompromisable in a sense. There's no easy way to improve it. It's so fundamental. You can't make it better with a better deal."

He sympathized with De Palma's dilemma and couldn't see any way to condense the book himself. He had liked the director's idea to use "Dr. Strangelove" as his model for "Bonfire of the Vanities." But Wolfe felt De Palma didn't pull it off. "Dr. Strangelove," he felt, was a bitter farce, with the emphasis on bitter. The director, Stanley Kubrick, had only one message and it was antiwar. In every scene Kubrick set the business of war against the idiocy of the people making the war.

Wolfe couldn't really understand what kind of farce De Palma wanted "Bonfire" to be. "It wasn't a bitter farce and it wasn't a bedroom farce and it wasn't a sweet farce or an agreeable movie," he said. "As far as I can tell they didn't take on a point of view and cleave to it. I'd be pretty hard put to tell you what the point of view is."

And though he understood that few people would believe it, Wolfe (the man who made up phrases like "Heh-hegggggggggggggg-gggggghhhhhhhhhhhhhhhh!") thought the film was too exaggerated. "It was as if Brian De Palma said, 'Well, I've got to do something extraordinary to pull this off in two hours, so I'm going to try all kinds of things. I'm going to try this "Dr. Strangelove" approach. I'm going to try the most extreme camera angles I've ever used.' "

Wolfe sighed. "If you're going to exaggerate, it has to be done just so, as in 'Dr. Strangelove.' The slightest false note can boomerang. I hesitate to find a great deal of fault with what was done because it was a tough problem to do this thing in two hours. De Palma took a chance. It really didn't pan out."

One of the most difficult aspects of making movies was the un natural cycle of life it imposed on the people who made them. For a few months they were thrown together into a glittery, rickety union, intimately linked by their diverse but overlapping ambitions and dreams. For that brief period their destinies were in the hands of one person, the director. By the time a picture was released, most of them would move on to other dreams, other directors. That was true in the case of "Bonfire," as it was for every film. By the time the thing they'd created together was born — and had died — in full view of the world, everyone had dispersed.

Although in another situation the natural inclination of a group of people might have been to turn to their leader for solace, or to vent their anger, in this case most of them didn't even think of getting in touch with De Palma. It wasn't in the nature of the business, and even if it were, it wasn't in the nature of the relationships he developed with those who worked with him. A few people called: Tom Hanks, Michael Cristofer, Lucy Fisher, Rob Friedman, Fred Caruso, Eric Schwab. They found his answering machine. For some time after the movie was released, De Palma continued to lie low.

So the cast and crew had to come to terms with "Bonfire" by themselves. Fred Caruso never stopped defending De Palma and the movie.

"Whose fault was it, not that I'm saying there was anything to blame — I was more than pleased and proud of the picture," he said. "Tom Hanks was hired before Brian De Palma. Was De Palma going to say, 'No, I'm not going to direct Tom Hanks'? Besides, I thought Tom Hanks was brilliant. You can't fault Brian for having Tom Hanks in that movie."

"Melanie Griffith wasn't a bad choice," he said in his methodical way. "The studio wanted Bruce Willis, not Michael Caine or Daniel Day Lewis or one of those Englishmen. Is Brian going to say, 'No, I don't want Bruce Willis, one of the greatest stars of our time'? And Warner Bros did hire Michael Cristofer, who, by the way, I think did a terrific job."

Caruso continued his diplomatic postmortem. "Brian wanted Walter Matthau. The studio didn't want to pay $1 million, and we hired Alan Arkin and built a set for $120,000, and they started worrying about black backlash so we go with Morgan Freeman. So maybe if we didn't have Bruce Willis and Morgan Freeman, we could have saved $7 or $8 million — or maybe $10 million. So then we'd have a $40 million picture, and maybe the audience would have forgiven Tom Hanks because we'd have had an Englishman and a Jew."

By January Caruso was negotiating a deal with director Roland Joffe's production company, to produce two pictures back to back. Most of the fall he'd been relaxing, spending time with his first grandchild, who was born in October. He wasn't expecting to be rehired by Warner Bros. anytime soon, but he felt confident that he'd get work somewhere.

The editor David Ray was still in shock from the entire experience a few weeks after the movie opened. He had gotten his first inkling that something terrible was about to happen the night they screened the film for the journalists on the press junket. Afterward he'd heard a woman say, "Well, that was one big zero."

" 'One big zero'!" Ray said. "I was so upset."

" 'One big zero'!" he repeated sadly. "Even if you didn't like the film, it wasn't one big zero. You couldn't just write it off like that."

"It's very depressing to me," he said, sitting in the spacious apartment off Central Park West he'd bought just as "Bonfire" started filming. "We tried to make a film about society and where it's going. I don't think 'Bonfire' the film attempted that to the extent the novel did, but it was an interesting film and very badly treated.

"The attitude of a lot of reviewers was that we were assholes for making this film." The thin man in the tortoise-shell glasses sat up and shook his head. "But that's exactly what we weren't. We were adventurous. I'm not saying the film wasn't flawed. It was flawed. But we weren't assholes."

Eric Schwab had been stunned by the reaction to "Bonfire." After reading the reviews on the opening day, he'd spent the afternoon in Century City, the show business hub near Beverly Hills where the picture was playing on two screens at the multiplex. Both theaters were nearly full all afternoon. He kept wandering back and forth between the two, listening to the audiences laughing. Their laughter lifted his spirits. *The audiences seemed to like it. They were laughing! They were paying attention!* Maybe, he thought, maybe the movie would be a hit after all. He had become so enthusiastic by late afternoon he decided to check out the crowd that evening at Mann's Chinese Theater in Hollywood. When he arrived at the theater at 7:15 and saw no line in front of the box office, he realized his fantasy that the movie would overcome all the bad press was just that — a fantasy. The 7:30 P.M. show on opening night was less than one-third full. Every joke seemed hollow as it reverberated through the massive theater, and only a handful of people laughed.

It was difficult for him to sort out the various emotions the film's reception stirred in him. He couldn't help but be pleased when his title shot was singled out for praise in both *The New Yorker* and the *Los Angeles Times*. Sheila Benson's attack on the film had begun,

> Brian De Palma opens his calamitous version of Tom Wolfe's dense novel "The Bonfire of the Vanities" . . . with a glittering dusk-through-dawn shot of Manhattan from the point of view of a Chrysler Building gargoyle.

And Schwab couldn't help but be angry, shortly afterward, when *Premiere* magazine, in a brief profile of Robert Greenberg, gave him — Greenberg — full credit for the shot.

He felt enormous sympathy and empathy for De Palma, almost personally wounded by the venomous attacks on his mentor. He worried too about how the film's failure — its *disastrous* failure — was going to affect his own career, and then felt guilty for being so selfish when he knew the public scorn De Palma had to endure.

Schwab had returned to Los Angeles after the title shot was completed in November, and he began working with screenwriter Michael Schiffer on the rewrite of "The Riverkeeper," the film about the Hudson River environmentalist John Cronin. For the "development deal," Schwab was paid $15,000: half (less agent commission) up front, and the rest when the script was submitted. Though he didn't have it in writing from the producers, it was understood that, if Warner Bros. accepted the script, Schwab would direct.

Would Warner Bros. be eager to sign on De Palma's protégé now? When he was first being considered for "The Riverkeeper," he'd heard that Lucy Fisher's response to his name had been "That little *pisher*." Schwab didn't know if she'd actually said it, but what if she had. Did she mean "little *pisher*" — Yiddish for someone who's inexperienced — affectionately, or was she mad at him for insisting on going into overtime for the opening shot? And that was before, when Warner Bros. still had hopes that "Bonfire" would be a success.

He'd already noticed a change in attitude from "The Riverkeeper"'s producers. Before, all his ideas were enriched by his association with "Bonfire," Warner's prize project. Now, every time they didn't like a scene they would say, "You're doing to this exactly what Brian De Palma did to 'The Bonfire of the Vanities.' "

As Schwab worked on the script for "The Riverkeeper" with Schiffer, his agent, aware of the precariousness of development deals, encouraged him to keep meeting with other producers. One of the scripts he read was an updated version of a 1950s Swiss film, about a serial killer of children. The producers had offered the movie to De Palma, who wasn't interested. Though they'd been looking for a big-name director, they were willing to meet with the student of the one-time Master of the Macabre. Schwab left the meeting feeling confident that he'd impressed them but unsure that he'd overcome their reservations about working with a first-time director. He spent the next week in limbo, wondering whether his first film would present him to the world as an ecologist or a baby-killer. By then he didn't care; he just wanted a film to direct.

Warner Bros. passed on "The Riverkeeper"; the producer was told politely the story was too much like another film the studio already had in production about the Brazilian labor organizer and environmentalist Chico Mendes, who was assassinated by his opponents. Schwab's disappointment was softened by the fact that he'd had a second meeting with the suspense picture producers the morning the "Riverkeeper" was rejected. A week later, after a third meeting with one of the producers and the scriptwriter, Schwab was hired to direct.

He knew this deal could fall through, just as the other one had. But he had attained his goal of independence. Now he was a player, on his own. As he looked at the uncertain, exciting road ahead of him, Schwab felt a pang for the days when he knew exactly what he had to do — to please De Palma. Once or twice when he'd needed cash he'd gone to the drawer where he kept the two one-hundred-dollar bills De Palma had given him to pay off his bet, the double-or-nothing bet that the opening shot would be better than that of the Concorde. Schwab ended up making a trip to the bank instead; those one-hundred-dollar bills were worth far more to him than their printed value.

He couldn't help thinking about "Bonfire" and — if they had really gone so terribly wrong — where they had gone wrong. He remembered a conversation he'd had with De Palma just before they began shooting "The Untouchables." De Palma had said to him, "I just want to make a good genre picture, Eric. This is a Western. Good guys. Bad guys. We're not doing a big thing here."

Schwab had talked to his former location scout, Bruce Frye, a few times after "Bonfire" opened, and listened to his bitter outpouring. Frye hadn't recovered from all the work he'd had to do and the sense of failure he'd felt when his locations had been rejected over and over again. He was infuriated by the movie. He couldn't believe he'd had to work so hard for *that*. Frye repeated what he'd said throughout the making of the film: "This is not a monument we're building." Had Frye pinpointed the problem with "Bonfire"? Had they tried to make a monument, not a movie?

After "Bonfire" came and went, Marty Bauer was ready to move on to the next thing. His agency was in the middle of merging with another agency, and he wasn't all that worried about De Palma's directing prospects.

"I don't think it's hurt Brian in the community," said Bauer, sitting in the office he was planning to vacate in a few months for the luxurious space Drexel Burnham Lambert was leaving behind in Beverly Hills. "I think it hurt Brian in his head. But he'll get over it."

"You know," he said, "Brian does certain things that get people nuts. I don't know what it is. It would be a real interesting psychological study. If this movie was a failure, it was an interesting failure. *If* it was a failure. But it wasn't a catastrophe of staggering proportions. The actors were interesting. You were never bored in it. I could see not liking it. I can understand it. It's frenetic, it's a hyperkinetic view of the world. But what bothered me was the unconscious, subconscious thing that happens to people with some of Brian's movies. 'Scarface' was somewhat similar. 'Scarface' was a movie that some of my colleagues at William Morris — I was still at William Morris then — wouldn't go to the party afterward. These are guys who tried to sign Adolf Hitler's son. These guys tried to sign Adolf Hitler's son and they were outraged by 'Scarface.' "

He laughed. "And interestingly enough, as time has gone by, 'Scarface' is now considered a good movie. It wasn't then. It was reviled. *Reviled*. Now they think it's a great movie. They watch it over and over on their videocassettes. Up in their trillion-dollar homes they're all watching it and loving every second of it. When it came out they hated it."

Bauer admitted he'd been worried about "Bonfire" for a long time — even before he saw it. He'd gotten a hint of the problems they'd be having in August, when he was a guest at a wedding in Scarsdale, a wealthy suburb of New York. The bride's father was a Yale professor who'd seated the agent at a table with four Yale colleagues. When they heard Bauer was in the movie business, they asked him what films he was working on. When he mentioned "Bonfire of the Vanities" the response was vehement.

"They went crazy!" he said. "They were outraged that Tom Hanks had been cast as Sherman McCoy. *Outraged.* These four professors from Yale went *crazy.*"

"But wait," he said. "That's not all. There was a gentleman, an old friend of mine, who's a real die-hard Jew. And he was *outraged* by the fact that the Jewish judge was now black. 'How could you do that?' he asked me. 'That character had to be Jewish.' And the Wasps from Yale felt the Tom Hanks character had to be Bill Hurt. That's what they believed it had to be. And the other one had to be Alan Arkin. Everyone was wedded to their own view of this book."

Bauer glanced at his watch and paused. "A book which, by the way, I never to this day have been able to finish. I mean, it's mildly amusing for the first 250 pages and then it kind of peters out. It's really not *Moby-Dick.*"

An assistant knocked on the door and said, "She's ready."

Bauer tugged on his red sweater and excused himself. The manicurist had just finished doing the nails of his partner, Peter Benedek, and now was ready for his.

Steven Spielberg called De Palma several times in January but couldn't get through. De Palma didn't return phone calls, he didn't attend the dinner party and private screening of "Lawrence of Arabia" Spielberg had arranged for a few friends. Spielberg wasn't hurt; he'd seen De Palma retreat into his cave before.

Spielberg was surprised at what a nonevent "Bonfire" had turned out to be. "The movie turned out to be so unpopular that people didn't lambast the movie. They wrote it off. I was surprised it didn't even open," he said. "It took so much bashing it couldn't open. I was surprised there was no controversy. That it was brushed off and people went on to the next thing."

Spielberg didn't expect there to be a public backlash against De Palma by Warner Bros. "Look, every executive at Warner Bros. was in on every decision Brian made. If they objected, they could have objected. They were on the lot. They saw the dailies. Half that movie was filmed on the lot. It wasn't shot in Armenia or Pakistan.

They were there. They *liked* the film when they saw it."

No, Spielberg said, he wasn't all that worried about his friend. "Brian's a survivor," he said. "It'll only hurt him until his next big hit. The worst thing that could happen out of all this would be if Brian directed 'Home Alone 2' or safe little Disney comedies. If that happened to Brian I'd know his spirit was broken. The time he signs on with John Hughes to make 'Home Alone 2' will be the time to do the postmortem on Brian De Palma because he'll be dead."

Over the Christmas holiday De Palma had taken a skiing lesson and pulled ligaments in his knee. As he limped around it occurred to him that history was repeating itself. After "Casualties" bombed he'd sprained his ankle. But this time was different. On Christmas Day, less than two months after they had met, De Palma asked Gale Anne Hurd to marry him, and she accepted. De Palma was ready for drastic change. He called Goldstein and told her to pack up his New York office and told the editors to lease out his editing rooms. He and Hurd were planning to buy a house outside San Francisco, near Palo Alto and Stanford University, to remove themselves from both Los Angeles and New York, though they would keep residences in both cities.

De Palma rarely left his house that winter, venturing out only to go to the Farmer's Market for cappuccino, or to meet Marty Bauer or Jared Martin for lunch. He returned his calls from Hanks, Cristofer, Fisher, and Schwab, and eventually talked to Spielberg, but ignored the rest. There weren't many other calls. "The community" was silent. But one prominent Hollywood person felt the urge to talk to De Palma after he saw "Bonfire" — and De Palma took his call. Warren Beatty phoned to offer his congratulations. He knew what De Palma was going through: three years earlier he'd presided over "Ishtar," the film that had been chosen as the target for universal scorn that year.

De Palma canceled his plans to accept the invitation to head the jury at the Avoriaz Fantasy Film Festival in the French Alps; he was replaced by Michael Cimino, director of "Heaven's Gate." He also told the people in Madrid planning a retrospective of his work in April that he didn't think he could attend.

He'd tried to ignore the reviews, but he couldn't. There had been some kind words, here and there. But what did it matter if the *Houston Chronicle* called the film "smart, cynical and sophisticated"? He was looking for some confirmation from someone he respected. *The New Yorker* hadn't yet weighed in with its review; he still hoped that Pauline Kael would vindicate him, that she would see what he had tried to do.

Kael's review, which ran in the January 14, 1991, issue, began, "Brian De Palma walked right off a cliff when he made his version of the Tom Wolfe novel . . ." The analysis that followed didn't dismiss the picture. Kael (who said she "disliked" the novel) admired the "splendiferous view" of Schwab's opening shot and acknowledged the precision of De Palma's directing, but then concluded, "You feel a kind of fanaticism in his directing: he's planned everything — it's an exercise in wrong-headed style."

De Palma felt completely lost. In the past he'd felt that he learned something from reviews. They made him think about whether the drill in "Body Double" had been excessive, for example. But he didn't know what to make of this kind of criticism — Kael saying the opening Steadicam shot wasn't really funny because it was "too precise." The other reviews were variations on one theme, and he stated that theme, " 'How could you trivialize this masterwork?' They act as though I've done the *National Lampoon* version of *Hamlet*."

He spent the days reading and working out the script for the thriller he'd been thinking about for months. It was the story of a man whose father had conducted psychological experiments on him as a boy, hoping to create the perfect child. The father's experiments continued, and now the son was helping him by kidnapping children to be subjects, killing a few mothers and nannies along the way. De Palma saw the pitfalls in actually directing this film, but it was a pleasurable diversion.

He still felt that his decision to make "Bonfire" had been the right one. "You always have to make an assessment of where you are," he said, "and then you wind up somewhere else. I get less and less joy out of making movies. The process you go through. You've got to find that joy again or you're going to stop making them.

"A lot of what takes the joy out of it are the tremendous

economic pressures. There's so much on the line. The bigger the film, the more you come into conflict with the studio. There are more battles."

As he worked out the details for his thriller — figuring out the killer's psychological make-up, imagining how to stage the murders — De Palma felt some of that old joy. "I wanted to make movies because I had strong visual ideas, and I wanted to make movies based on those visual ideas," he said. "That's how I started making movies and that's where I'm going to try to return to." But he knew it was going to be difficult. He knew how quickly a career could be undone. Whatever happened next, he knew "Bonfire" had been a turning point for him. He didn't know where he was going, but he knew he would never again feel the same about himself or his place in the business.

De Palma never quite understood why people hated "Bonfire" so much. He didn't understand why people behaved as though he'd sat in a room trying to make the worst movie imaginable when in fact he'd thought he was making a good movie. "While I was making 'Bonfire,' I saw what was there and it worked. I figured, It worked for me, it'll work for everybody else," he said. "But I think there was an alienation factor. I think after a while they thought, Why do I have to watch all this stuff. I'll just close my eyes and listen to what they have to say."

And then he started to cackle. "I guess this taught me one thing. I have a strange sense of humor," he said. "I guess most people don't share it."

On January 16, 1991, the day the United States went to war against Iraq, a poster showing the faces and names of actors Chevy Chase, Dan Aykroyd, John Candy, and Demi Moore appeared on a giant billboard display over Sunset Boulevard. They were stars of a new Warner Bros. movie called "Nothing but Trouble." Drivers making their way up Sunset who glanced up at the billboard would find it hard to distinguish this poster from the one that had been there a day earlier. That one had three faces and three names; this one had four. Otherwise they were almost identical.

Warner Bros. had hastily removed the "Bonfire" poster less than four weeks after the movie had opened; a few weeks later the movie would also disappear from theaters. By comparison, Scorsese's

"GoodFellas," which had opened in October, was still playing.

On February 5 the *Los Angeles Times* reported that a national poll of newspaper, magazine, and TV film critics conducted by *American Film* magazine had voted "GoodFellas" best picture of the year. "The Bonfire of the Vanities" won the most votes as worst film of the year.

On February 10 the *Los Angeles Times* reported that "The Godfather, Part III" had taken in a "disappointing" $61 million; that Universal had stopped reporting grosses on "Havana" after forty-seven days, when the movie had taken in $9.1 million; that "The Russia House" had taken in $21.4 million at forty-seven days; and that "Bonfire" had taken in $15.4 million at forty-five days.

On February 13 the Academy Award nominations were announced. "Bonfire" wasn't nominated for anything.

"Bonfire" lived on the gossip columns for some time after the movie disappeared from theaters as the professional gloaters made sport out of predicting who would take the fall. Liz Smith put her money on Mark Canton, declaring that an "impeccable" source had told her Canton would be leaving Warner Bros. for Columbia Pictures, to work for Peter Guber and Jon Peters. *Spy* magazine concluded that Lucy Fisher would be "the fall guy — er, girl." But Warner Bros. didn't rush to pin the blame on anyone. By spring, no one at the studio had taken the fall.

Warner Bros. rushed the videocassette release of "The Bonfire of the Vanities," which appeared in video stores in April 1991, and it quickly became one of the most popular new rentals. By then Tom Hanks had fired his agent, and Bruce Willis had been hired by Warner Bros. to star in "The Last Boy Scout," an action thriller whose script had cost the studio $1.75 million. Time-Warner released shareholder reports disclosing that Steven Ross, the company's chairman, received a total compensation of $78.11 million in 1990, making him the highest-paid executive in the United States that year. Pauline Kael retired as the film critic of *The New Yorker*, and David Lean, the director Brian De Palma admired so much, died at the age of eighty-three. Gale Anne Hurd and Brian De Palma made plans to marry in July.

* * *

The failure of "Bonfire of the Vanities," which came to symbolize the failure of every big-budget disappointment, inspired some collective breast-beating among the Hollywood elite. Jeffrey Katzenberg, chairman of Walt Disney Studios, issued a twenty-eight-page memorandum calling for "a major self-reexamination." Katzenberg warned his executives, in this internal document that was eventually printed in its entirety in *Variety,* that

> if we remain on our present course, there will be the certainty of calamitous failure, as we will inevitably come to produce our own "Havana" or "Two Jakes" or "Air America" or "Another 48 Hours" or "Bonfire of the Vanities" and then have to dig ourselves out from under the rubble.

Even Warner Bros. chairman Robert Daly, a taciturn man who avoided publicity, felt obliged to give an interview to *Variety* on the subject of economizing. The interview appeared on the front page, under the headline DALY KEEPING FATTY DEALS OUT OF WB DIET. Daly told *Variety,* "Sometimes it's hard to resist the temptation to put a name actor there. Sometimes you want to hedge your bet, but that can be like buying more insurance than you really need."

Many people made a mental note of the date when they read these exhortations. They figured this was the beginning of yet another five-year cycle, the wisdom that would prevail until there was a year when all the hits were big-budget films. Until then, everyone would talk earnestly about scaling back, cost cutting, "downsizing." Everyone agreed that it was time to stop the escalation of budgets that were threatening to ruin the business. The studios assigned executives specifically to the task of eliminating the frills — below the line, of course, since no one really expected stars and directors and screenwriters to lower their asking prices. They went through the motions, fully prepared, they said, to resist the temptation that had brought them to this humbling state of affairs. But the next time the devil's candy came along — that impossible, expensive, possibly monumental thing — who among them would say no?

AUTHOR'S NOTE

A few years after I began writing about film for *The Wall Street Journal* as a critic and reporter in 1983, I began thinking about following the making of a big Hollywood film from beginning to end — something that no outsider had done, to my knowledge, since John Huston invited Lillian Ross to observe the making of "The Red Badge of Courage" almost forty years before. I tried the idea on a couple of directors who were interested but couldn't follow through for various reasons. In the summer of 1989, however, Brian De Palma agreed to let me observe the entire process as he went about turning *The Bonfire of the Vanities* into a movie. He didn't ask for any editorial control.

De Palma made it clear to the "Bonfire" crew and actors that I was writing a book with his permission. Beyond that it was up to me to solicit interviews and up to individuals to agree or refuse as they wished. Though the executives at Warner Bros. initially were not pleased with the arrangement I'd made with De Palma, they eventually offered me their perspective, for which I am grateful.

I was present at auditions, location scouts, strategy sessions, research excursions, on most of the film sets in New York and Los Angeles, and at the various stages of postproduction. The vast majority of the dialogue and scenes in this book record what I saw and heard. I constantly supplemented those direct observations with interviews. So when I presume to say what someone was thinking at a given moment, I am reporting what that person later told me he or she was thinking. The interviews also allowed me to reconstruct meetings and incidents I didn't witness.

My general observations about the industry come from years of covering it and reading about it. When I use specific information from newspapers or magazines I credit them in the text. Ira Konigsberg's *The Complete Film Dictionary* was an invaluable technical reference.

Though I am a movie critic, my intent with this book always was not to judge "Bonfire" but to try to understand how decisions were made and what it took to carry them out. I hoped to illuminate the filmmaking process, and what it meant to the people who were part of it. To the extent that I have succeeded, I owe much thanks to a great many people.

First, my deepest appreciation goes to John Sterling, my editor at Houghton Mifflin, for his clear-headedness, his imagination, and his indefatigable zeal.

I thank my agent Kathy Robbins, the fiercest champion any writer could hope for.

I am forever grateful to Raymond Sokolov, editor of *The Wall Street Journal* "Leisure and Arts" page, who thought it would be amusing to take a banking reporter and turn her into a film critic.

For his resourceful and exhaustive research assistance I thank Len Van De Graaff.

I thank Janet Silver of Houghton Mifflin for her astute critical judgments, and Irene Williams for her enthusiastic salesmanship.

I credit my parents for teaching me to seek adventure, in movies and in life, and for paying my sister Suzy a dime to teach me to read. I thank Suzy for taking her obligation seriously and luring me into the world of books at an early age.

There is no way to adequately compensate a spouse for enduring the writing of a book. The best I can do publicly is to thank my husband Bill Abrams for his wise counsel, his encouragement, and his steadfastness.

From among the many others who have helped me, I would like to single out a few people whose sustenance and advice have been invaluable: Marsha Berkowitz, David Blum, Trish Hall, Noelle Hannon, Wayne Kabak, Barry Kramer, Sara Krulwich, and Russlyn Ransome.

Obviously I am indebted to the dozens of people working on

"Bonfire" who took the time to tell me about their craft as well as their lives. I also appreciate the significant help I received from Peter Guber, Tom Wolfe, Judge Burton Roberts, Monica Goldstein, Marty Bauer, Steven Spielberg, Rob Friedman, and the De Palma family.

I am especially grateful to Eric Schwab, who took me in tow at a critical moment in his life, and who forced me to overcome my acrophobia.

Finally, this book simply could not have been written without the generosity and the courage of Brian De Palma, who opened the door, without condition, and then never flinched.

INDEX